SEEKING ZION

THE LITTMAN LIBRARY OF
JEWISH CIVILIZATION

Dedicated to the memory of
LOUIS THOMAS SIDNEY LITTMAN
who founded the Littman Library for the love of God
and as an act of charity in memory of his father
JOSEPH AARON LITTMAN
and to the memory of
ROBERT JOSEPH LITTMAN
who continued what his father Louis had begun

יהא זכרם ברוך

'*Get wisdom, get understanding:*
Forsake her not and she shall preserve thee'
PROV. 4: 5

The Littman Library of Jewish Civilization is a registered UK charity
Registered charity no. 1000784

SEEKING ZION

◆

*Modernity and
Messianic Activism in the Writings of
Tsevi Hirsch Kalischer*

◆

JODY MYERS

London
The Littman Library of Jewish Civilization
in association with Liverpool University Press

The Littman Library of Jewish Civilization
Registered office: 4th floor, 7–10 Chandos Street, London W1G 9DQ

in association with Liverpool University Press
4 Cambridge Street, Liverpool L69 7ZU, UK
www.liverpooluniversitypress.co.uk/littman

Managing Editor: Connie Webber

Distributed in North America by
Oxford University Press Inc., 198 Madison Avenue,
New York, NY 10016, USA

First published in hardback 2003
First published in paperback 2012

Catalogue records for this book are available from the
British Library and the Library of Congress
ISBN 978-1-906764-26-5

Publishing co-ordinator: Janet Moth
Copy-editing: Bonnie Blackburn
Proof-reading: Lindsey Taylor-Guthartz
Index: Meg Davis

Printed and bound in Great Britain by
CPI Group (UK) Ltd., Croydon, CR0 4YY

Preface

IN DOZENS of Jewish households dotting the West Bank landscape, religious parents tuck their children into bed with the following story:

Long, long ago, in a faraway land in the heart of the Exile, the great rabbi Tsevi Kalischer, a distinguished scholar and teacher, dreamt of a home such as ours in the hills of Judah. God's spirit burned within him and he saw clearly the Torah's commandment that every Jew should move to the Holy Land and work to possess it as his own. The lovers of Exile ridiculed and denounced Rabbi Kalischer, but he persisted in his teachings and did many great deeds to hasten the redemption of Israel. . . . On his deathbed he knew in his heart that the Messianic Era had begun. And we, today, know how right he was, for all around us we see clear evidence that God's promises are being fulfilled. Soon the signs will be so manifest that no one, not even fools, will be able to deny that the redemption has come. (oral communication, courtesy of Mark R. Levy)

Unfortunately, daily realities in the isolated settlements contrast harshly with traditional messianic dreams. Settlers routinely carry arms, pass through numerous military checkpoints as they drive to work and home again, and must cope with the legacy of death and grief that currently accompanies Jewish residence in predominantly Arab lands. Religious Zionists such as these are increasingly disheartened by the possibility of relinquishing Israeli sovereignty over territory they believe is theirs by divine command, and by the reality of violence that such possession entails. Telling stories about courageous forerunners like Kalischer boosts morale and inspires the next generation to stay the course.

Outside these circles, however, Kalischer's name is not as well known. The later proponents of Religious Zionism, men who absorbed, adapted, and expanded his teachings, are more familiar. Tsevi Hirsch Kalischer lived from 1795 to 1874, and while he was not the only one in his day to advocate the rebuilding of a Jewish polity in Palestine, he was one of the first impeccably Orthodox rabbis to argue that the Torah itself sanctioned such activist efforts. His writings contain a substantial collection of approving references to messianic activism scattered throughout talmudic and medieval rabbinic literature. He also presented his own, novel interpretations of biblical and post-biblical texts promoting human initiatives to hasten redemption. In addition, he designed his rhetoric to win wide support, constructing appealing metaphors and coining slogans that evoked nostalgia and inspired activism. He promoted the agricultural development of Palestine with arguments that appealed to religious Jews as well as to the newly emancipated Jews of western Europe who, grateful for their own fortune, wished to assist the impoverished Jews in Muslim lands. Later religious advocates of Jewish nationalism did not always quote Kalischer, and many ignored his non-violent principles, but they borrowed and benefited considerably from his work. Examining the writings of such a pioneer is valuable for its own sake; additionally, it sheds light on those who carried on his legacy and modified it to suit the needs of their own day.

Studying Kalischer's life and writings is a particularly useful way to investigate religious modernization. Modernity placed serious obstacles in the way of religious authority, custom, and faith. Modernizing states were centralizing their administrative organs towards more efficient, direct, and egalitarian manners of governing, diminishing the power of religious leaders. A new economic mindset appeared that encouraged saving and investment of surpluses, long-range planning, and delay of gratification for the purposes of improving earthly life. This economic outlook undermined the religious assumption that the most important dimension of existence is that which transcends the material world. The intellectual change characterizing modernity was the widespread adoption of the belief that rational explanations are the most accurate apprehension of reality. The systematic and virtually unlimited pursuit of rational knowledge, and the application of science to the practical sphere, rapidly advanced knowledge and changed the face of society. Religious leaders at the advent of modernity began to realize that mandating religious obedience was no longer effective; they had to find new ways to promote piety in the face of the prevailing permissiveness and scepticism, or they had to articulate a convincing rationale to construct a theocratic system within the modern state. Kalischer lived at the time when modernizing pressures were on the rise. Traditional values still dominated his community during his childhood and dictated his formal education, but with adulthood it became increasingly evident that old-world values were waning. Raised to take the reins of rabbinic leadership, he attempted to construct a respectable faith and a communal framework within which religion could thrive. His location and personal situation gave him a unique perspective. He lived in east-central Europe, where political leaders vacillated between adopting the new ways of the West and affirming the older patterns of east European society. The slowness of actual change where Kalischer lived, and his own position on the margins, allowed him a singularly tempered and creative approach to the new challenges.

Reading Kalischer provides an example of how other, more outwardly positive and affirming, phenomena were incorporated into modern religious ideologies. During the nineteenth century, people witnessed the rise of individual Jews to great power, the granting of equal rights to Jews qua Jews, and the desire of some European rulers to strengthen the Jewish community in Palestine. These were unprecedented reversals of centuries-old policies. The new reality contradicted the Jewish and Christian religious understanding of Jews as a people suffering from God's punishment of oppression in exile. Kalischer reconciled the contradictions with an explanation that would, in a slightly augmented form, be shared by Protestant millenarians: these modern events were signals that God wanted Christian rulers and Jewish individuals to take the opportunity to gain control of the Land of Israel, make it bloom, and achieve the golden age foretold in the Bible. Kalischer's interpretation of current events allowed him to press for an end to such religious behaviours as messianic passivity and the denigration of agricultural labour, which he felt were no longer appropriate. A religious activism not dependent on supernatural intervention would not only appear more plausible and attractive to modernists, it would also appeal to people's emerging sense of control. Kalischer's religiosity can serve as a model for the type of religion the sociologist Charles Liebman calls 'expansionist'. Expansionism affirms modernity by reinterpreting it through the prism of tradition and bringing under the rubric of religion all aspects of life, especially those previously regarded as profane. It is through expansionism that religious people utilize aspects of modernity to reinforce their messages and build new bases of power.

Finally, an exploration of Kalischer's writings reveals the limitations of and creative possibilities within scriptural, law-bound religions. When revelation is understood as an event that occurred ages ago, as it is in Judaism, novel teachings are inherently suspect. Those who suggest new explanations must find them embedded within older language, while still treating previous teachings and earlier authorities with respect. The task, as Kalischer defined it, was particularly daunting. He aimed for a reasoned analysis of Scripture and Jewish law, because he sought a religious faith that met the demands of orthodoxy and could pass the test of reason. One result of his concern was his repudiation of miracles and supernaturalism in history. His rationalist position led directly to an ideology urging Jews to return to their original form of worship—sacrificial worship— and to their own land. Kalischer's explication of this messianic activism was a masterful and clever reconciliation of contradictory viewpoints within Jewish literature. He argued that his was the best and most faithful understanding of the ancients' teachings, although—and this he could not admit, even to himself—it constituted a rebellion against the rabbinic tradition and centuries of Jewish accommodation to the conditions of exile.

This book has two objectives: first, to present and critically analyse the principles of Kalischer's messianic ideology in the context of Jewish intellectual history; and second, to illustrate the way that he presented his ideas to appeal to certain types of modern Jews. It should not be regarded as an intellectual biography; rather, I am presenting how and why a particular religious ideology emerged and was promoted by this particular man at this particular time. In Chapter 1 I explain the function of the messianic idea for late eighteenth- and early nineteenth-century European Jews, particularly the way that messianic language was an encoded discourse defining the place of Jews in a changing society. Chapter 2 delineates the context that shaped Kalischer's own perspective on these issues, while Chapter 3 describes the earliest (1836) presentation of his messianic ideology. In Chapter 4 I discuss Kalischer's proposal to re-establish sacrificial worship, the religious problems this presented, his ambitious attempt to transform Jewish life, and the rabbinic resistance that it met. Chapter 5 examines Kalischer's essays and exegesis from the 1840s and later in which he tackled the problem of religion and reason, but through which he provided a philosophical basis for active messianism. Chapter 6 describes the political, economic, and personal changes that prompted the rabbi to seek a wider public role and reshape his agenda. Chapter 7 examines the mature version of Kalischer's messianic ideology that appeared in 1862 and beyond. This includes his system of decoding political events for their underlying messianic meaning, as well as the strategies he developed to promote his proposal to people who would not be attracted to messianic or even religious concerns. The book ends with a Conclusion that briefly surveys the growth of active messianism in the twentieth century, ending with the contemporary Zionists in the West Bank territories and Jerusalem and the more moderate religious perspective elsewhere.

JODY MYERS

Acknowledgements

I WISH to express my gratitude to the many people who have taught me and assisted me in the years in which I prepared this work.

I consider it a great honour to have had two stellar teachers while a graduate student at the University of California, Los Angeles. The late Amos Funkenstein instructed me in the intricacies of classical Jewish texts and fostered my interest in Jewish thought. Arnold Band, whose tutelage extends to this day, introduced me to the rich literary world of modern Hebrew literature. I am also fortunate to have close at hand generous colleagues and fellow devotees of nineteenth-century European history, David Ellenson, Steven Zipperstein, and Steven M. Lowenstein. They have unstintingly offered their expertise, critical insight, and friendship. To decipher complex halakhic arguments I could always turn to Chaim Seidler-Feller and Michael Rosen. Zenon Hubert Nowak graciously shared his original research in the Toruń Archives. David Sorkin, Elisabeth Kesten, and Helaine Ettinger helped and advised me through the first major revisions.

I have benefited from the resourceful librarians at the Cincinnati and Los Angeles branches of the Hebrew Union College–Jewish Institute of Religion, UCLA, the Jewish Theological Seminary, the University of Judaism, the Jewish National and University Library in Jerusalem, and the Central Zionist Archives. Special thanks are owed to Shimeon Brisman, as well as David Hirsch, Yaffa Weisman, Rick Burke, Haim Gottschalk, Sharon Muller, and Fred Bogin for tracking down obscure books, journals, and newspapers.

My research and writing was supported by stipends from the Koret Jewish Studies Publications Program, the National Endowment for the Humanities, the Memorial Foundation for Jewish Culture, and the California State University, Northridge Foundation. My colleagues in the Religious Studies Department and Jewish Studies Program at California State University, Northridge, particularly Patrick Nichelson and student assistants Lindsay Gifford and Stephanie Jackson, provided direct help and cheered me on. Jorge Garcia, dean of the College of Humanities during the revision of the manuscript, unfailingly offered encouragement and assistance.

It is unusual for a historian writing about the nineteenth century to enjoy the attention of her research subject's living relatives. I thank Clemens Kalischer, Mark R. Levy, Neil Comins, and Stephen T. Falk, who have followed my research with a warm eagerness and optimism they undoubtedly inherited from their ancestor.

I am pleased to have the Littman Library as publisher for this book. I especially appreciate Connie Webber, managing editor of the Littman Library, for her guidance and supervision of all the stages of the book's preparation; Ludo Craddock for handling the technical and business aspects of publication; Bonnie Blackburn and Lindsey Taylor-Guthartz for their copy-editing; Meg Davis for the index; and Janet Moth for coordinating the final stages of production.

I am grateful for the support of family and friends. My parents, Eleanor Ann and Michael Myers, who did not live to see the completion of this book, have served as my models: my mother for her indomitable spirit and love of learning, and my father for his intellectual curiosity. Other family and friends whose interest in my writing has sustained me include Walter and Frances Ackerman, Jane Myers, Kathryn and Cornelis deBoer, Paulo Cohen-Myers, Amy Sabrina, David and Rachel Biale, Jane Litman, and Jon Drucker.

Finally, I owe thanks to my husband, David Ackerman, for his patience and support over the long haul. Without his encouragement, advice, and gentle prodding, this work would not have reached publication. To him and to our children, Adina, Benjamin, and Aaron, I dedicate this book.

Contents

Note on Transliteration and Sources

Transliteration

The transliteration of Hebrew in this book reflects consideration of the type of book it is, in terms of its content, purpose, and readership. The system adopted therefore reflects a broad approach to transcription, rather than the narrower approaches found in the *Encyclopaedia Judaica* or other systems developed for text-based or linguistic studies. The aim has been to reflect the pronunciation prescribed for modern Hebrew, rather than the spelling or Hebrew word structure, and to do so using conventions that are generally familiar to the English-speaking Jewish reader.

In accordance with this approach, no attempt is made to indicate the distinctions between *alef* and *ayin*, *tet* and *taf*, *kaf* and *kuf*, *sin* and *samekh*, since these are not relevant to pronunciation; likewise, the *dagesh* is not indicated except where it affects pronunciation. Following the principle of using conventions familiar to the majority of readers, however, transcriptions that are well established have been retained even when they are not fully consistent with the transliteration system adopted. On similar grounds, the *tsadi* is rendered by 'tz' in such familiar Anglicized words as barmitzvah. Likewise, the distinction between *het* and *khaf* has been retained, using *ḥ* for the former and *kh* for the latter; the associated forms are generally familiar to readers, even if the distinction is not actually borne out in pronunciation, and for the same reason the final *heh* is indicated too. As in Hebrew, no capital letters are used, except that an initial capital has been retained in transliterating titles of published works (for example, *Shulḥan arukh*).

Since no distinction is made between *alef* and *ayin*, they are indicated by an apostrophe only in intervocalic positions where a failure to do so could lead an English-speaking reader to pronounce the vowel-cluster as a diphthong—as, for example, in *ha'ir*—or otherwise mispronounce the word.

The *sheva na* is indicated by an *e*—*perikat ol*, *reshut*—except, again, when established convention dictates otherwise, for example, in the Anglicized names of such organizations as B'nai B'rith.

The *yod* is represented by *i* when it occurs as a vowel (*bereshit*), by *y* when it occurs as a consonant (*yesodot*), and by *yi* when it occurs as both (*yisra'el*).

Names have generally been left in their familiar forms, even when this is inconsistent with the overall system.

Sources

In the footnotes the titles of works published in Hebrew are given in English translation to enable readers without Hebrew to gain an idea of their content; those wanting to track down such titles for further research will find the original Hebrew title given in the bibliography. The only exception to this is rabbinic and other primary works, whose titles are given in transliterated Hebrew throughout, since these titles are familiar and used throughout the literature; in addition they are often difficult to translate (though an English translation is given where possible).

A large number of the writings of Tsevi Hirsch Kalischer have been collected in *The Zionist Writings of Rabbi Tsevi Kalischer* (Haketavim hatsiyoni'im shel harav tsevi kalisher: bitosofet mavo, he'arot ubiurim), edited with an introduction and notes by Israel Klausner (Jerusalem, 1947), referred to throughout the notes as *Zionist Writings*. This volume includes Klausner's critical edition of *Derishat tsiyon*, his transcription of selected personal letters in the Central Zionist Archives, reprints of newspaper articles, and an introduction and notes. All references to *Derishat tsiyon* are to this edition. *Zionist Writings* is published entirely in Hebrew; all translations are the author's own. Where Kalischer's original letter gives only the Jewish month and year the standard Western equivalent date has been added in brackets.

ONE

The Messianic Idea in Late Eighteenth- and Early Nineteenth-Century Europe 1782–1819

JUDAISM cultivates in its followers a longing for the messianic age, without providing explicit details about just what this entails. This state of affairs has inspired Jews over the ages to proffer their opinions, producing a rich and variegated array of messianic scenarios—largely in the form of isolated pieces of biblical exegesis—for future generations to adopt or reject as they see fit. Jewish leaders seem to have fostered this state of confusion, for they have been unable to agree upon a definition of the messianic idea, and they have often bristled at those who have bothered to articulate an explicit formulation of it. Any effort to construct a uniform doctrine breeds controversy, for it involves a selection of visions of the messianic age and the processes necessary to bring it about, as well as a rejection of other visions and processes. Structurally, there was no way of achieving consensus. Like many other tenets of Jewish belief that were never clarified once and for all, the messianic concept again and again generated friction between proponents of differing views. This book focuses on a crucial modern shift in this struggle.

Late eighteenth- and early nineteenth-century Europe was the site of disputations because of the modernizing processes unfolding there. Three important changes in European society generated tension within Jewry and portended major shifts in the political and legal status of Jews. Intellectually, the primary development was the increasingly widespread belief that it was possible to seek a rational explanation of all phenomena, and that such rational explanations were the most accurate apprehensions of reality. The primary political change was the centralization of the state's administrative organs towards a more efficient and direct manner of governing and towards an equalization of subjects. Also significant was the growth of an economic mindset that encouraged saving, investment, long-range planning, and delay of gratification in order to improve earthly life. Each one of these pressures, separately and combined, portended changes in the status of Jews, and each influenced interpreters of the messianic concept. For example, Jews stimulated by the new rationalism suggested that the messianic hope should be envisaged in more naturalistic terms that incorporated the new economic ideologies. Further, when Jewish emancipation became an item on the agenda of centralizing states, both Jews and Christians were likely to comment on whether the Jews' messianic dream of returning to the Land of Israel indicated a lack of loyalty to or identity with their host nation. Jews who were inclined towards religious conservatism adopted a defensive posture, claiming that the messianic hope actually reinforced Jewish devotion and obedience to the state. Writing for external as well as internal consumption, they highlighted sacred texts that stressed the importance of Jewish political quiescence. In contrast, Jews more inclined to end Jewish social separateness reformulated the doctrine in a more universalistic manner. Both conservatives and liberals tailored their interpretations in response to the modernizing pressures of the era. Their distinctive outlooks on messianism remained, however, as emblems of the larger, underlying issue that was at stake: establishing the most meaningful mode of religious behaviour that could survive under the new conditions. Debates on the messianic concept functioned, in part, as disputes about modernization.

The battle over modernization, I am asserting, was fought in the language of messianism. A person who took a position on a relatively obscure doctrinal matter, say, whether one must believe in the future appearance of a personal messiah, was staking a position in the prevailing debate on the role of reason in religion. While at first glance the dispute might appear to be about abstract issues, its contenders knew and often declared the effect their victory would have on Jewish life: a change in the status quo would lead to a major reform of the liturgy, holiday observances, and Jewish education. One goal of this book is to decode the arguments and clarify the stakes on each side.

The intensified conflict over Jewish messianism began at the advent of modernization, immediately before Kalischer's birth. On the conservative side were men who attacked the liberals in explicit terms and in the veiled but highly charged symbols of the messianic hope. The most important of these contenders were Kalischer's teachers. The purpose of this chapter is to describe and analyse the groundwork they laid, upon which he built his innovative approach.

THE FOUNDATIONS OF MESSIANIC THOUGHT

There are many ways one can categorize and analyse Jewish messianic doctrines. For the purposes of this study, it is most helpful to delineate different viewpoints according to three key issues. The first is the historical outlook—specifically, whether the exile of the Jews from their land could be terminated by human action. The second issue is the means to be used in ending the exile. The third issue is the vision of the post-exile era. Using these distinguishing marks as a guide, two general approaches can be isolated within Jewish literature: realistic and passive messianism. These are ideal types that should be envisaged as points along a spectrum. One or the other dominated Jewish religious consciousness at a given time, but each left its mark in literary sources and could be drawn upon as needed.[1]

During the first two millennia of Jewish history, the realistic approach prevailed. In its historical outlook it leans towards a rational perspective: God controls history, but this control is subtle and often in conformity with natural laws. Human deeds, not miracles or mysterious forces, shape history and change the course of events. The Jews' landless condition, or exile, would end through an *interactive* dynamic of divine and human deeds. Perhaps divine messengers would appear to herald the possession of the land, or people designated as messiahs would play significant roles as facilitators. The most important figures, however, would be people acting decisively by conquering the land, by settling there peacefully under the land's 'foreign' rulers, or by negotiating for a restoration of Jewish sovereignty. It is understood that these human efforts would be successful only if they pleased God or if God were the guiding hand behind them. The aim of all these efforts—the vision of the post-exile era—is the establishment of a Jewish commonwealth that includes, minimally, a Temple in Jerusalem (with its sacrificial cult), a sovereign king from the Davidic dynasty, a theocratic state, and the descendants of all twelve Israelite tribes united within it. More expansive visions include one or more of the following: a preliminary battle between nations or between good and evil forces, world peace, a new role of religious supremacy for Zion, the end of strife between animals and humankind, and the revival of the dead. The new age unfolds gradually and naturally, at least in its initial stages.[2]

[1] There are a number of anthologies and surveys of messianic literature, among them Gershom Scholem, *The Messianic Idea in Judaism and Other Essays on Jewish Spirituality* (New York, 1971); R. J. Z. Werblowsky, 'Messianism in Jewish History', in H. H. Ben Sasson and S. Ettinger (eds.), *Jewish Society through the Ages* (New York, 1969), 30–45; Joseph Klausner, *The Messianic Idea in Israel* (New York, 1955); Abba Hillel Silver, *A History of Messianic Speculation in Israel* (New York, 1927); Tsevi Baras (ed.), *Messianism and Eschatology* (Heb.) (Jerusalem, 1984). The term 'realistic messianism' was coined by Amos Funkenstein, 'Maimonides: Political Theory and Realistic Messianism', in his *Perceptions of Jewish History* (Berkeley and Los Angeles, 1993), 133.

[2] Not until the post-biblical era did Jews designate the final era 'messianic'. For a more thorough treatment of the different types of messianic ideologies, see Jody Myers, 'The Messianic Idea and Jewish Ideologies', *Studies in Contemporary Jewry*, 7 (1991), 3–13. It is important to

Realistic messianism tends towards political activism. It is obviously useful in inspiring the Jewish people to conquer the Land of Israel or expand its population, and thus it can be found in abundance in biblical prophecies and narratives. Later, when Jews relied on scriptural interpretation as the means to determine God's will, they pointed to the plain meaning of biblical passages or events in order to legitimate their efforts to wrest control of their land from foreigners or to move there from afar. Of course, realistic messianism did not always erupt into political activism. This more rationalistic ideology often articulated a vision of the final goal with naturalistic, less supernatural events. These had the effect of encouraging messianic activism, for they rendered the messianic age more attainable; conversely for some, however, they made the messianic age less attractive. The dictum of the rabbinic sage Samuel, 'The sole difference between this era and the messianic days is [delivery from] servitude to the nations', was repeatedly cited by Jewish authorities hoping to subdue the passions of messianic enthusiasts and undermine the purported divine agency of charismatic figures. In other words, the realistic approach to the Jewish situation may harbour an attitude of moderation and pessimism that discourages Jewish political activism.[3] The activist outlook emerged, however, when there was a relatively strong—or (as in Kalischer's day) potentially improvable—Jewish political position in the Middle East. When Jews regarded

emphasize that this pragmatic and realistic approach pre-dates the modern period. Active messianism is as deeply rooted in the Jewish messianic tradition as is passive messianism, and it is incorrect to argue otherwise. For instance, it is not accurate to claim that the medieval messianists insisted on a miraculous redemption while the modern Zionists posited a self-achieved one. This was Jacob Katz's position in his classic article on Kalischer, 'Tsevi Hirsch Kalischer', in Leo Jung (ed.), *Guardians of our Heritage* (New York, 1958), 209–27. In his later writings Katz modified this position by maintaining that pre-modern active messianism allowed only 'spiritual' or 'ritualistic' devices for hastening the End, in contrast to the modern messianists, who pursued practical means such as the agricultural renewal of the Land of Israel; see Jacob Katz, 'Israel and the Messiah', *Commentary*, 73 (Jan. 1982), 34–41 at 35.

[3] Samuel's comment can be found in BT *San.* 91*b*, 99*a*; *Shab.* 63*a*, 151*b*; and *Ber.* 34*b*. Another example of the moderating effort is in the statement attributed to Hillel in *San.* 99*a*: 'The Jews should expect no Messiah, for they have already consumed him [that is, he has already appeared] in the days of Hezekiah.' Aviezer Ravitzky, *Messianism, Zionism, and Jewish Religious Radicalism*, trans. Michael Swirsky and Jonathan Chipman (Chicago and London, 1996), 21, argues the opposite point: 'it is precisely the moderate image of redemption that, seizing upon a suitable personality or circumstance, is most likely to provoke a tempest of messianic fervor'. Ravitzky shows (pp. 6, 17–19) that opponents of Religious Zionism seized upon the moderate image of redemption, or a redemption that unfolded in stages (the initial stages being increased Jewish immigration to Palestine), as inflammatory. I agree that this is generally the case, but there are times when even moderate visions of the messianic age—for example, 'delivery from servitude to the nations'—seemed (and were) entirely out of reach of Jewish activism, and made the risks involved less attractive.

themselves as occupying a position of strength, they found it quite plausible that they would be able to maintain a quasi-independent or sovereign hold over the promised land. It is not necessarily the objective reality of the Jewish situation that is crucial for triggering messianic activism; an optimistic outlook seems to be essential. Those who were determined to interpret events in a positive light could construe even dire occurrences as 'the birthpangs of the messiah' and use them to promote greater activism.

In contrast, passive messianism starts with a historical attitude in which God's controlling power is paramount and there is little room for human influence. According to this outlook, Jews determine their fate in so far as they follow or disobey God's commandments: obedience is necessary for Jewish possession of the Land of Israel, but God determines whether Jews merit their land, and only God can change history's course. The Jews' ability to remedy the situation is relatively limited; opinions range from the belief that sovereignty over the Land of Israel is wholly independent of human behaviour (for example, as part of an irreversible, predetermined plan) to the conviction that fulfilling the covenant through ritual acts or moral behaviour could influence God to end the exile.[4] In any event, passive messianists agree that demonstrative or independent actions—for example, rebelling against foreign domination or returning to Zion en masse—are illegitimate.

Those who espouse this more passive approach envisage the post-exile era in terms much like those of the activists. They, too, anticipate a rebuilt Temple, Davidic king, theocratic state, and so on. Because they regard the process as supernatural and out of human hands, however, they emphasize the extraordinary miracles that will occur. Their emphasis on human powerlessness tends to lead towards apocalyptic scenarios involving radical and sudden changes.[5]

During the second century CE the tide began to swing towards passive

---

[4] A discussion of the tannaitic debate on the power of repentance versus predestined redemption can be found in Ephraim E. Urbach, *The Sages: Their Concepts and Beliefs* (Cambridge, Mass., 1987), 668–84. BT *San.* 97*b* is the classic rabbinic expression of the belief that, because the predestined dates for the redemption have passed, the only valid human activity to hasten the end of the exile is repentance: 'R. Eliezer said: If Israel repent, they will be redeemed. R. Joshua said to him, If they do not repent, will they not be redeemed?! But the Holy One, blessed be He, will set up a king over them, whose decrees shall be as cruel as Haman's, whereby Israel shall engage in repentance, and He will thus bring them back to the right path.'

[5] On passivity and powerlessness, see Yonina Talmon, 'Pursuit of the Millennium: The Relation between Religious and Social Change', *Archives européennes de sociologie*, 3/1 (1962), 125–48 at 136. Also, Ravitzky, *Messianism, Zionism, and Jewish Religious Radicalism*, 21, observes that 'In a seemingly paradoxical way . . . it is the miraculous, supernatural, utopian vision of redemption that, in many cases, succeeds in blocking the way, preserving and defending the status quo.' There are those who imagine the sudden arrival of a partial redemption followed by a

messianism. Jews repeatedly rebelled against Roman rule, but Jewish leaders were rarely united on the question of whether God approved of these battles. Political zealots and moderates alike mustered supportive precedents to strengthen their case. With each failed revolt, the passive outlook gathered more force. In the Bar Kokhba revolt of 132 CE, notable rabbis were prominent among those who championed the upstart Jewish regime and regarded its leader as God's messiah. However, after the Romans crushed the revolt and devastated the countryside, succeeding leaders represented rabbinic support of Bar Kokhba as minimal and eccentric.[6] When the centre of Jewish power shifted from Palestine to Babylonia in the fourth century, and especially after the Muslim conquest in the seventh century, it appears that most Jews came to believe that only miracles could re-establish their kingdom in the Land of Israel.[7] Although there were multiple meanings assigned to the Roman-era national tragedies, the widespread use of the term *galut*, exile, for the post-70 CE era discloses the understanding of the Jewish national condition as one of divine punishment rather than a consequence of natural phenomena reversible through political action. Political activism per se was not frowned upon, as it was considered wise and even praiseworthy to be politically active in order to better the condition of Jewish life. Political activism had to stop short, however, of taking steps to hasten the arrival of the messianic age.[8]

more gradual completion of all its stages. For a variety of rabbinic statements on this subject, see Raphael Patai, *The Messiah Texts* (Detroit, 1979), 54–64.

[6] In a later and less activist era, the actual widespread support of the Bar Kokhba revolt was reduced to Rabbi Akiva's lone belief in Bar Kokhba's messiahship. See Gedalia Alon, 'The Attitude of the Pharisees to Roman Rule and the House of Herod', in *Jews, Judaism, and the Classical World*, trans. Israel Abrahams (Jerusalem, 1977), 18–47 at 45–6. Aharon Oppenheimer, 'The Messianism of Bar Kokhba', in Baras (ed.), *Messianism and Eschatology*, 153–6, reviews the statements attributed to Rabbi Akiva, showing that those originating closest to the time of the Bar Kokhba revolt clearly indicate that Akiva harboured only moderate and realistic goals for the 'messianic movement', in contrast to the extravagant objectives later attributed to him. This echoes the viewpoint of Urbach, *The Sages*, 672–6.

[7] This transition in Jewish thinking has been described by numerous historians. I am relying here on the summary by Haim Hillel Ben-Sasson in the *EJ*, s.v. 'Galut'.

[8] Jacob Katz, 'Orthodoxy in Historical Perspective', *Studies in Contemporary Jewry*, 2 (1986), 3–17 at 9, explains and describes the deep-rooted mentality of pre-modern Jewry as follows: 'Ever since its loss of political independence, Jewry had lost faith in its capacity to extricate itself from exile. A basic change could be expected only through an act of miraculous, divine redemption. In the interim, it was taken for granted that the Jews would remain dependent upon the present holders of political power. Action taken to alleviate problems besetting the communities was limited to intervention with these authorities, and were by their very nature of an ad hoc character, with but short-range intentions.' Here Katz identifies the short-range nature of Jewish planning with passivity; true activism is understood as any effort to end the exilic condition of Jewish life.

The rabbinic Judaism that eventually became the norm and held sway until the late eighteenth century had passive messianism as one of its central tenets. Its classic expression was a talmudic teaching based on the thrice-uttered oath from the Song of Songs, 'I adjure you, O daughters of Jerusalem, not to stir, neither to awaken love, until it pleases.' The talmudic discussion of this oath was structured as a debate between a Palestinian and a Babylonian rabbi. Both rabbis agreed that the oath taught the divine limitations on human messianic activism. The Babylonian (seemingly an advocate for Diaspora Jewry) insisted that the oath prohibited individual emigration to Palestine. The Palestinian maintained that the oath merely prohibited conquest of and en masse emigration to the Land of Israel, rebellion against the gentile nations, and *excessively* hastening the end of the exile. Despite the erudite responses of the Palestinian rabbi, rabbinic disapproval of active messianism was—and still is—expressed by decrying the violation of this triple oath.[9]

The textual interpretations that the rabbis recorded, the rituals they developed, and the prayers that they composed increasingly reflected a conciliatory attitude towards foreign political power and passive acceptance of the Jews' exiled condition. Even unlearned Jewish men and women would be familiar with the supplications in the daily Amidah prayer that asked God to restore Jerusalem 'and dwell in it as thou hast promised; rebuild it soon, in our days, as an everlasting structure, and speedily establish in it the throne of David'.[10] On Jewish festivals, which incorporated a heightened hope for the rebuilding of the Temple, the additional (Musaf) prayer elaborated as follows:

Because of our sins we were exiled from our country and banished far from our land. We cannot go up as pilgrims to worship thee, to perform our duties in thy chosen House, the great and holy Temple which was called by thy name, on account of the hand that was let loose on thy sanctuary. May it be thy will, Lord our God and God of our fathers, merciful King, in thy abundant love again to have mercy on us and on thy sanctuary; rebuild it speedily and magnify its glory. Our Father, our King, speedily reveal thy glorious majesty to us; shine forth and be exalted over us in the sight of all the living. Unite our scattered people from among the nations; gather our dispersed from the far ends of the earth. Bring us to Zion thy city with ringing song, to Jerusalem thy sanctuary with everlasting joy. There we will prepare in thy honor our obligatory offerings . . .[11]

---

[9] Song of Songs 2: 7, 3: 5, 8: 4; BT *Ket.* 110b–111a. Ravitzky shows that in Jewish religious literature, the power of the three oaths grew in importance as the Zionist movement grew in strength: 'The direct confrontation with Zionism greatly contributed to sharpening this traditional passive posture and raising it to consciousness, bringing it from the margins to the center, at times transforming it from a mere folk image into a well-defined concept.' See his *Messianism, Zionism, and Jewish Religious Radicalism*, 22–6, and appendix ('The Impact of the Three Oaths in Jewish History'), 211–34.

[10] *Daily Prayer Book: Ha-Siddur Ha-Shalem*, trans. and annotated with an introduction by Philip Birnbaum (New York, 1977), 90.   [11] Ibid. 614–16.

God is the actor and the Jews are merely supplicants. They are entirely at God's mercy, and the most they can do is plead for attention through their prayers. Passive messianism dominated because it was congruent with the medieval environment. Christian and Muslim powers guarded against a reconstitution of Jewish sovereignty in the Holy Land, the rebuilding of the Temple, and any formal enhancement of Jewish political power there. They dealt harshly with Jewish messianic movements and rebellions. The Jews' accommodation to their loss was a pragmatic response to their political situation, ensuring both survival and an abiding fatalism.

Passive messianism could not fully overcome the authentic religious tensions of Jewish life in exile; indeed, it was a reminder of these tensions. Passive messianism explained God's apparent abandonment of the Jews, yet it maintained the hope that he would be responsive to Jewish pleas for reconciliation and renewal. It encouraged obedience to post-Temple institutions and authorities, yet preserved the belief that in the messianic days God would restore the royal dynasty and the Temple cult. It encouraged the Jews to defend their political interests and better their conditions of life in the Diaspora, their long-term home, yet taught that the exile was an unnatural condition. These tensions were epitomized in the Diaspora Jews' relationship to the Land of Israel. They endowed it with cathartic powers and maintained the Jewish community there as a holy congregation outside the normal framework of life, yet they regarded it as their natural, national home. Thus, when the conditions that typically reinforced messianic passivity weakened—for example, when a new, untried, regime gained control over Palestine, holding out promise that limitations on Jewish religious activity in Jerusalem might not be enforced—messianic activity was likely to occur.[12]

The residual discomfort with this messianic ideology is reflected in ambivalent rabbinic attitudes towards non-Jewish rulers. In the apocalyptic messianic scenarios of the passive messianists, the rulers' participation in the coming of the messianic age was an entirely unwitting one: if the Jews were good, God would send a messiah and the non-Jews would suffer humiliation and punishment before submitting to Jewish dominance; if the Jews were undeserving, however, God would first send a cruel (foreign) king to torment them until they repented, and then the non-Jews would suffer humiliation and punishment.[13] In fact, the Jews' political status was entirely dependent on the benevolence of non-Jewish rulers. In medieval Europe, the Crown promised

---

[12] The Persian conquest of Palestine in the 7th c., the Crusader conquest in the 12th c., and the Ottoman seizure of Palestine in the 16th c. spawned messianic activism.

[13] This summary of the redemptive process is based on the version by Sa'adiah ben Joseph (882–942), *Seder ha'emunot vehade'ot*, ch. 8. It is one of the most inclusive formulations and is culled from talmudic, midrashic, and other sources.

protection to the Jews in exchange for their sizeable financial contributions to the royal treasury. Medieval rulers governed by granting jurisdiction to corporate units beneath themselves, and Jews were one of a number of entities that enjoyed communal autonomy. When kings and princes no longer found the Jews' presence advantageous, they expelled them or taxed them excessively. Still, Jews managed to describe their dependence in terms flattering to themselves. One fifteenth-century rabbi explained that Jews' legal status as *servi camerae* (literally: serfs of the chamber) meant that they were 'the special possession of kings and lords, and not slaves to the rest of the people'.[14] Jews' unique link to the Crown paralleled their unique link to God. Rabbis, as interpreters of God's will, prided themselves on being the guardians of this relationship.

THE FIRST CONFLICTS

During the medieval era there had been consonance between the political-religious environment and Jewish messianic beliefs. That harmony was disrupted in the late eighteenth century in western and central Europe. The absolutist rulers began to develop a more efficient and direct mode of ruling and managing their subjects. Prompted by revolution, military action, or peaceful internal reform, they sought to dismantle the autonomous governing units that had held together their medieval states; specifically, they moved towards eliminating corporate distinctions, emancipating serfs, cancelling the limitations imposed on religious and ethnic minorities, and replacing the system of inequitable tax obligations with a single, uniform system. Theoretically, all subjects would be placed on an equal footing with one another and with regard to the Crown. Support grew for the notion that economic restrictions and disadvantages stemming from religious identity hampered economic growth and were unjust. Reformers criticized the extensive political authority and the coercive powers of religious bodies, arguing that religious institutions should become subject to state regulation. In some countries, the middle and lower classes claimed governing rights. While the enactment of these principles across central and western Europe was by no means uniform, over the course of the nineteenth century their eventual institution produced an equalization of political privileges and obligations among all segments of society.

These political principles would significantly alter the relationship between the Jews and the state. As early as 1750, Frederick II of Prussia implemented a

[14] Isaac Abravanel, as quoted in Eli Lederhendler, *The Road to Modern Jewish Politics: Political Tradition and Political Reconstruction in the Jewish Community of Tsarist Russia* (New York, 1989), 18.

new policy towards the Jews that offered greater individual freedoms while regulating and limiting Jewish communal institutions. The autonomy and religious authority of Jewish governing councils were curtailed, rabbinic juris-diction was limited to marriage and family matters or reduced to a mere per-suasive voice, and excommunication was no longer allowed as a means of coercion. Individual Jews had greater freedom to chart their own religious paths and, if they chose, to disregard the will of Jewish communal leaders. A similar, but less far-reaching, reform was announced by Joseph II, the emperor of Austria. In 1782 he issued a series of decrees granting new rights to the major non-Catholic denominations of Austria, contingent upon their compliance with the requirements of the absolutist state. One of these decrees, later called the Edict of Tolerance because of the theme of tolerance that appeared to infuse it, was directed to the Jews of Vienna and Lower Austria. It nullified restrictions on movement and residence, allowed the exercise of more professions and enabled more economic opportunities, expanded educational options for children, and struck down certain prohibitions stemming from religious hostility. However, since the edict was an effort to integrate the Aus-trian Jews into Austrian society, as such it limited Jewish communal auton-omy. For example, it cancelled the legal and economic power of the Jewish communal bodies and prohibited the use of Hebrew and Yiddish in various documents.[15]

While the edict's attenuation of Jewish communal privileges was certainly regarded by most Austrian Jews with dismay, its benevolent tone and liberat-ing rulings provoked great joy among many. Rabbi Naphtali Herz Wessely (1725–1805), living in Prussia, outside the reach of the edict, declared that Joseph II's decree marked a new era for all European Jews. Wessely was part of the enlightened circle surrounding Moses Mendelssohn, whose support for expanding the boundaries of Jewish education was well known. Wessely was relatively conservative among the maskilim, and his books on Jewish thought and literature earned him the respect of his more traditional colleagues. Much to their surprise, Wessely responded to the Edict of Tolerance with a radical proposal for Jewish educational reform. In an essay entitled *Divrei shalom ve'emet* (Words of Peace and Truth), he argued that the tolerant and accepting epoch that was unfolding necessitated a curricular reform that would econom-ically and socially equip the Jews for a new reality. His outline of a new cur-

---

[15] Abridged versions of the 1750 Prussian charter and the Edict of Tolerance can be found in Paul Mendes-Flohr and Jehuda Reinharz (eds.), *The Jew in the Modern World: A Documentary History*, 2nd edn. (New York and Oxford, 1995), 22–7, 36–40. Most of the provisions of the Edict of Tolerance were so radical that they could not be implemented, and following Joseph II's death in 1790, his successors reverted to the older, more restrictive policies; see Haim Hillel Ben-Sasson (ed.), *A History of the Jewish People* (Cambridge, Mass., 1976), 756.

riculum for Jewish primary schooling proposed that the first stage of instruction should retain its current focus on Talmud study, but that thereafter the boys who showed no talent for Talmud should receive occupational training. He suggested that the Jewish community should give greater value to a boy's manners, ethical behaviour, and secular knowledge in relation to his religious learning and ritual observance. According to Wessely, God mandated *torat ha'adam*, the teachings of humanity, before *torat hashem*, the teachings of God's Torah, and proper fulfilment of the latter was dependent upon knowledge of the former. He justified these priorities, which amounted to an overturning of the age-old norm, by reference to religious principles, supported by a variety of biblical and talmudic texts. This was a strategy commonly used in promoting change, but Wessely's quotation of ancient rabbinic hyperbole— most notably, 'As for a scholar who lacks sense, a carcass is better than he'— inflamed many rabbinic leaders and convinced them that he was attacking the rabbinate.[16] They were further alarmed when Wessely's proposal found a small but receptive audience and sparked a movement to establish Jewish schools incorporating secular studies and the founding of literary journals dedicated to broadening Jewish cultural knowledge.

The geographic scope of the rabbinic opposition was quite wide, and assuming prominent roles were two rabbis personally connected with the Kalischer family. The most influential opponent was Ezekiel Landau of Prague, Austria's leading rabbi, and a member of the Kalischer family.[17] Landau praised the emperor and the Edict of Tolerance, but condemned Wessely: '*He* is worse than an animal carcass, and in the end his corpse will lie like dung upon the field.'[18] Most significant, however, is that Landau introduced the language of messianism into the discussion. He wrote several pieces censuring Wessely and addressing the edict, but his most thoughtful contribution to the polemic was his sermon delivered on the sabbath before Passover. The holiday of Passover is naturally associated with redemption, and Landau built upon this theme to argue that the promise and comfort of messianic redemption was incompatible with modern reforms.

According to Landau, Wessely had failed to see God's hand behind the

[16] The passage is from *Leviticus Rabbah* 1: 15. In subsequent publications Wessely appears to have retracted his radical suggestions. Moshe Pelli, *The Age of Haskalah: Studies in Hebrew Literature of the Enlightenment in Germany* (Leiden, 1979), 127–30; Mordechai Eliav, *Jewish Education in Germany During the Haskalah and Emancipation* (Heb.) (Jerusalem, 1961), 39–51.

[17] Landau's exact connection is unknown. Tsevi Kalischer noted the family connection, without details, in a letter to David Tevele Efrati; see the reprint of this letter in Isaac Arigur [Gur-Aryeh], 'Rabbi Tsevi Hirsch Kalischer', *Hator*, 37 (June 1927). Landau's comment may be found in the English translation of his sermon in Marc Saperstein, *Jewish Preaching, 1200–1800: An Anthology* (New Haven, 1989), 365.   [18] Ibid. 365.

benevolent decree of the emperor, and thus he erroneously concluded that reason, and not faith, was the watchword of the new era. Landau found no rational reason for the change in policy, and he could scarcely imagine that history proceeded without divine guidance. 'It was God who impelled the exalted government to think well of His people', Landau asserted, and the question is why God was so disposed towards the Jews, considering their many faults. He answered his own question by referring to the teaching that God's providence over the Jews is sustained by the merit of pious ancestors, as well as by sacrificial offerings:

Now we might well ask, why through the merit of the sacrifices? After all, there is study of Torah and performance of commandments [which gain us merit], which apply to us everywhere [but sacrificial worship is restricted to Jerusalem and has ceased during this exilic period]. I would say in response that of all the commandments of the Torah, nothing is as remote from human reason as the sacrifices. . . . there is no rational explanation of the sacrifices at all. They are based entirely on faith: God said, and it was; He commanded, and it was established, though the reason be hidden from us. In this there is a warning that we should not delve too deeply into investigating matters pertaining to faith. All such inquiries, whether emanating from our own people or any other, are nothing but futility when applied to that which human reason cannot comprehend. The basis of all is faith, not reason or philosophical inquiry.[19]

Landau's point is that God is good to the Jews because they are firmly committed to their faith, and this specifically means faith in the efficacy of sacrificial worship. The sacrifices symbolize the Jewish duty to observe the Torah, despite the pull of logic or the temptation to adopt an easier life.

Landau also invoked messianic themes by reminding the Jews that their faithful Torah observance would ultimately be rewarded:

This Sabbath, called 'the Great Sabbath', is a reminder of the Sabbath of creation, and a reminder of the redemption to come, which will truly be a Great Sabbath, a day that is entirely Sabbath and rest, if we too will sanctify ourselves through Torah and commandments. It can happen today, if we would but hearken to his voice. May we soon be worthy of the full redemption, when we shall eat of the sacrifices and the Passover offerings, and a redeemer will have come to Zion.[20]

The sacrifices transmit two symbolic meanings: they refer to faith in and observance of the Torah as a whole, and they refer to the future reward for that observance. He warned Jews to beware of errant individuals who try to seduce them from the Torah with the lure of temporary, ephemeral happiness. In short, the edict's promise of freedom and acceptance by non-Jews was nothing

[19] Saperstein, *Jewish Preaching*, 367. The use of the sacrificial motif was inspired, at least in part, by the upcoming holiday. For rabbis such as Landau, the key symbol of Passover was the sacrificial offering even though, in the time of the exile in which he lived, it was a purely theoretical matter.   [20] Ibid. 373.

in comparison with the real redemption. Envisaging the eternal, sacred joy of the messianic age would enable God-fearing Jews to stay on the proper path. This argument, with its dependence on messianic images to concretize its message, would become central to the polemic against religious reform.

Rabbi David Tevele of Lissa in Poland (Leszno) also took a prominent role in the opposition. Lissa had been an important centre of Talmud study and one of the capital cities of the Jews in the Great Poland region since the early seventeenth century. Members of the Kalischer family had moved there from the city of Kalisch (Kalisz) at the beginning of the eighteenth century. Kalischer men had begun serving as judges and trustees of Lissa's Jewish community by 1709, and they were no doubt still prominent during the Wessely episode. Although Lissa's glory had faded as a result of the various catastrophes that afflicted Poland in the eighteenth century, its leaders regarded themselves as zealous guardians of Torah learning. Tevele had once issued a blanket approbation for Wessely's future writings, and he was horrified that his own name and the entire rabbinate of Lissa came to be associated with and to legitimize such a negative critique of the Jewish educational system.[21] He and others sent letters of protest to the trustees of the Berlin Jewish community, Wessely's immediate superiors.

Tevele did not incorporate explicitly messianic themes into his polemic, but within his letters one can already discern the concerns that would consistently appear in conservatives' presentation of the messianic idea. Further, he moulded a rhetorical style that was employed by traditionalists for years to come. Its first component was the use of metaphors of battle. Rabbinic opponents of excessive adaptation described themselves as fighters in God's war, defenders of the Torah, repairers of the breaches in the walls of the holy city, and so on. Their 'weapons' in this battle were legal precedents. Customary models of halakhic argumentation used in responsa literature were adapted to this adversarial situation.[22] The rabbis marshalled proof texts from Scripture, commentaries, and codes; noted the saintly reputations of their brilliant authors; reminded the reader of the ancient provenance of the traditions; and declared themselves victorious, passing sentence on the perpetrator. To do less was shameful. In one of Landau's condemnations of Wessely, he wrote that the chief rabbi of Berlin had abdicated his soldierly role in the face of resistance

[21] Louis Lewin, *Geschichte der Juden in Lissa* (Pinne, 1907), 195, notes that the whole rabbinate in Lissa, not just Tevele, gave Wessely an approbation for his first book, *Yein levanon*.

[22] This is a genre of rabbinic literature in the form of questions and answers to matters of Jewish law. For a description of the form and structure of the responsum see David Ellenson, 'Jewish Legal Interpretation: Literary, Scriptural, Social, and Ethical Perspectives', in his *Tradition in Transition: Orthodoxy, Halakhah, and the Boundaries of Modern Jewish Identity* (Lanham, Md., 1989), 9–32.

from the non-rabbinic leaders of the community. Rather than fulfilling his role
as defender of the faith, the chief rabbi had allowed himself to be swayed by
the enemy. This incident helped shape Berlin's reputation, among traditional
Jews, as the Jewish community where the walls of Torah were weakly defended.[23] The third recurring feature in these polemics was the delineation of the
problem at hand as the critic himself. According to Tevele, Wessely was guilty
of denigrating Torah study and trying to imitate Christians. Tevele demanded
that all right-minded rabbis should condemn his behaviour and put him in
line. He noted with satisfaction that the Jews of Vilna had burned Wessely's
book in the streets, after they had first hung it from an iron chain in the synagogue courtyard.[24]

Central also to the third polemical task, assigning blame to the challenger,
was an appeal to patriotism. Wessely had himself introduced this motif when
he suggested that modern political life required educational reform. In response to Wessely—and because he was correct in his assessment that Jews
were entering an era in which their political loyalty would be scrutinized—the
conservative camp was constrained to parade its patriotism. Within a few
years, both the conservatives and the liberals would demonstrate their loyalty
through reference to the messianic concept in Judaism. At this early date, however, neither side adopted that strategy. Instead, the rabbis insisted that traditional Judaism and its supporting structure were indispensable to the smooth
functioning of the state, and Wessely, the troublemaker, had distorted the
emperor's intent by implying otherwise. Both Landau and Tevele insisted that
Joseph II wanted only to add a minimal dose of practical education to the existing curriculum, and had no desire to modify Jewish religious culture or diminish the number of school hours devoted to Talmud study; indeed, Tevele
asserted, the emperor wanted to strengthen religious culture, not to scorn or
weaken it. In support of his interpretation, he noted that the lord of Lissa had
imposed a tax on dowries to sustain the religious schools for the city's poor
Jewish children. Tevele assumed that what was true for a minor nobleman in
Poland was true for an emperor, and among their shared convictions was the
belief that every ruler should 'strengthen the fortress of religion'.[25] Of course,

[23] This specific comment is from a letter by Ezekiel Landau of Prague, who wrote after it
became known that the leaders of Berlin had rebuked the Jews of Lissa and Posen for criticizing
their rabbis' behaviour; see Simcha Assaf, *Sources for the History of Jewish Education* (Heb.), 4
vols. (Tel Aviv, 1954), i. 263. For a social history of the transformation of the Berlin Jews during
this period, see Steven M. Lowenstein, *The Berlin Jewish Community: Enlightenment, Family and
Crisis, 1770–1830* (New York and Oxford, 1994).

[24] Tevele's sermon is available in a German translation in Lewin, *Geschichte der Juden in
Lissa*, 195–8, and in English in Mendes-Flohr and Reinharz, *The Jew in the Modern World*, 74–6.

[25] According to Tevele (from Mendes-Flohr and Reinharz, *The Jew in the Modern World*, 75),

Joseph II was an enlightened despot with a quite different approach to religious institutions and very dissimilar to Polish rulers, who did not all conform to Tevele's idealized portrait. The Austrian despot respected only those political conventions that he found to be in accordance with reason and the needs of the state, and he regarded rabbinic power as an infringement of the prerogatives of the Crown. This misreading of the emperor's intent shows the extent to which traditionalists failed to acknowledge the changing political reality. It is unclear whether Tevele realized that the absolutist rulers of Austria and Prussia were not of the same breed as the Polish nobility, who barely waged battle as their lands were whittled away by their neighbouring states. The rabbi from Lissa, however, paid no attention to the distinctive concerns of different political entities, assuming that all non-Jewish rulers were essentially the same. Similarly, all the rabbinic actors in this controversy assumed that Jews, too, despite their different countries of residence, constituted one body; Wessely himself made this assumption. Thus, the rabbis did not fault the Berlin Jew for taking as his starting point a decree of the Austrian emperor; nor did they find it inappropriate that the Berlin Jew should be scolded by Polish, Austrian, and Russian rabbis.

In this component of the polemic, the rabbis' statements reveal their deep attachment to the medieval conception of Christian–Jewish political relations. They understood Wessely to be belittling the very basis of rabbinic authority and driving a wedge between rabbinic and lay leaders.[26] By championing the medieval link between religion and state, they were buttressing their claim to leadership. That this polemical literature was written entirely in Hebrew and Aramaic underlines the extent to which, from their perspective, this battle was about internal control of the Jewish community.

The responses of both Tevele and Landau highlight the fundamentally conservative nature of rabbinic thinking. They could not embrace modern

'The Emperor has commanded all his subjects the following: Every child shall be taught to speak and write the German language so that he will know the language of the land. Everyone shall [also] remain true to the rites and principles of his faith; no part of his faith shall be made alien to him. . . . But this impostor, Wessely, perverts and distorts the counsel of His Majesty, the Emperor, claiming that he commanded that Jewish children shall no longer attend schools [of the traditional curriculum]. . . . This is a prevarication. Far be it for any intelligent man to think this of the righteous and sincere lover of mankind and leader of nations, his most pious Majesty the Emperor. In the abundance of his righteousness he actually wishes to strengthen the fortress of religion, each man according to his faith.'

[26] I would argue that Wessely, who was himself a rabbi, was trying to preserve rabbinic control over the new form the Jewish community would be taking. Were the *rabbis*—rather than less knowledgeable lay people—to establish the extent to which Jewish integration was to be reflected in the curriculum, they were less likely to be cut out of the decision-making procedure (as they were, later, in many places).

political ideas: these called for the weakening of their religious authority. And even when the traditional rabbis acceded, albeit minimally, to the pressures for change, they could not openly admit it. The Lissa and Posen rabbis, in fact, had already made concessions in the matter of integrating Jews into Christian society by allowing *ḥeder* instructors to teach some German—a practice not allowed in *ḥeders* to the east and south. In their response to Wessely's proposal, Tevele and Landau moved even further. For the first time they publicly voiced explicit support for secular studies and for teaching Jewish children a grammatical knowledge of German. The rabbis, of course, would never acknowledge that they had made a concession, for such an admission might legitimize other, more radical, modifications to traditional practices. As defenders of the walls of Judaism, they could not concede that they had permitted fissures to appear. Ironically, however, because they had committed themselves to the position that the king was acting in their best interest, they were party to the very modernization that they were trying to resist.

Because of the Lissa rabbi's leadership in the Wessely controversy, and because moving to Berlin increasingly became the aim of many poor and ambitious Jews of the Posen region, Lissa's Jews took this incident to heart. Wessely's 'betrayal', Tevele's justifiable anger, Landau's passionate sermon, and the 'heretical' response of the Berlin trustees passed into local lore. Lissa's communal leaders feared the consequences of pious Polish Jews becoming contaminated by the profligate Berliners, and they worried that ideas emanating from Berlin would penetrate their own community.[27] Rabbinic teachers armed their students with the polemical tradition of rhetorical militancy, the appeal to sacred precedents, and the identification of the problem as the critic; their influence is evident in the writings of the next generation of leaders, particularly Kalischer's teachers Jacob Lorbeerbaum and Akiva Eger. The Kalischer family, which boasted of its kinship link to Ezekiel Landau of Prague and was part of the Lissa rabbinical elite, certainly included this episode in its inherited family wisdom.

[27] Lewin, *Geschichte der Juden in Lissa*, devoted nine pages (192–200) to this incident in his history of the Jews of Lissa, including excerpts from Tevele's sermon. To what extent the common Jews of Lissa accepted their rabbi's assumptions cannot be ascertained. However, widespread fear of the dangerous ideas of Berlin destroying the pristine piety of Posen (and other towns) was already present a few years earlier, according to the testimony of Solomon Maimon, who lived there for about two years, beginning in about 1779. See *Solomon Maimon: An Autobiography*, trans. Moses Hadas (New York, 1967), 56–62, which gives a detailed report of the Posen Jews' naive piety and concern for sheltering themselves from his rational approach to religion. For a slightly later account, see the testimony to this effect in the memoirs of Jacob Adam, a young man from the Posen region who arrived in Berlin in 1803, cited in Lowenstein, *The Berlin Jewish Community*, 65.

TRANSITIONS

Controversy over the messianic idea lessened but did not entirely disappear over the next few decades. The messianic symbols would be evoked in the context of a struggle within the Jewish community over the extent of accommodation to a new political framework, and these internal struggles temporarily subsided. In Austria, emancipation and meaningful political reform came to a halt in 1790 with the death of Joseph II and was not revived for decades. Jewish civic emancipation was out of the question for the vast majority of European Jews who lived in Russia, as it was for the Jews of Italy after the defeat of Napoleon. France had emancipated all its Jews by 1791, but because of the revolutionary nature of the change, Jews had little say in the matter. When Napoleon brought these issues to the fore in 1806–8, he gave Jewish leaders no choice but to accede to his decision to end Jewish autonomy and place all religious functionaries under the supervision of the state. Virtually all French Jewish leaders essentially agreed to promote cultural integration and assimilation. Great Britain's Jews enjoyed a great measure of legal equality by the early nineteenth century. In Prussia and the other German states, there was a different dynamic. Emancipation was mandated by Napoleon in his conquest of Germany, and Prussia decreed citizenship for its Jews in 1812, but these measures were largely reversed on the defeat of the French emperor. Thereafter emancipation occurred slowly, at a rate which differed from region to region; it was typically only a partial emancipation, and was generally contingent on the individual or group proving a sufficient degree of acculturation.[28]

Under these difficult circumstances in the German states, where Jews eagerly awaited the removal of the disadvantages of inequality, messianic concepts were a subject of some debate within the Jewish community. In France during the public discussions of Jewish emancipation during the revolutionary period, three elements of the messianic doctrine were deemed incompatible with the principles of equality and integration: the dream of a Jewish return to Zion, the notion that redemption was a good which fell primarily or only to Jews, and the teaching that Jews constituted a separate nation.[29] In the German states, where Jewish civic emancipation was publicly contested for

[28] Pierre Birnbaum and Ira Katznelson (eds.), *Paths of Emancipation: Jews, States, and Citizenship* (Princeton, 1995). Reinhard Rürup, 'The Tortuous and Thorny Path to Legal Equality: "Jew Laws" and Emancipatory Legislation in Germany from the Late Eighteenth Century', *Leo Baeck Institute Yearbook*, 31 (1986), 3–33 at 5. On French Jewry, see Paula E. Hyman, *The Emancipation of the Jews of Alsace: Acculturation and Tradition in the Nineteenth Century* (New Haven and London, 1991).

[29] Gil Graff, *Separation of Church and State: Dina de-Malkhuta Dina in Jewish Law, 1750–1848* (University, Ala., 1985), esp. chs. 2–4.

decades, and where emancipation was conferred as a quid pro quo for reform of Judaism and Jewish behaviour, Jews' messianic doctrines were held up as an impediment.[30] Non-Jewish opponents of emancipation would seize upon them as proof that Jews could never be loyal citizens. Jewish liberals were sensitive to these charges, and they also believed that traditional messianic beliefs retarded acculturation of the Jews. They would object to expressions of a national messianic deliverance and suggest alternatives in their place. Jewish leaders of a more conservative bent would feel constrained to defend older teachings, although they, too, would redefine them in less objectionable terms. Other aspects of messianic thought, while not liabilities politically, were also likely to provoke some discomfort among enlightened Jews. The hope for the restoration of the sacrificial cult, the faith in the coming of a messiah, and the belief that the messianic age would be heralded by miracles generally did not meet the standards of reason they had accepted for themselves.

Initial attempts to reinterpret messianic ideas appeared in Germany in the first decade of the nineteenth century. The journal *Sulamith*, first appearing in 1806 as the voice of enlightened German Jews, published a number of editorial pieces over the next five years proposing that the messianic concept be understood in more naturalistic terms. One editorial from 1806 suggested that the correct apprehension of redemption was that it was simply an era in which Jews were not oppressed by non-Jews. The novelty of this statement was not its naturalistic understanding of the messianic age, but the author's belief that the tolerance of his own era fitted the messianic criteria.[31] By 1811, in the midst of the Napoleonic conquest, *Sulamith* authors began explicitly to equate the Jewish messianic hope with the civic emancipation of the Jews and the general liberation of humanity. The editorials were an attempt to find an authentically Jewish messianic concept that was devoid of miraculous elements and in conformity with reason. While the authors did not address the expectation that the messianic era would include the Jews' return to Zion, they took pains to emphasize the universal scope of the redemption. Finally,

[30] See Johann David Michaelis's rejoinder to Christian Wilhelm von Dohm, excerpted in Mendes-Flohr and Reinharz, *The Jew in the Modern World*, 43. In response, Moses Mendelssohn emphasized that the oaths prohibited messianic activism; see ibid. 48. Mendelssohn's claim that the Talmud forbids Jews 'even to think of a return by force' was repeated by the French defender of civic emancipation, Abbé Gregoire; see the excerpt from his 1789 'An Essay on the Physical, Moral and Political Reformation of the Jews', ibid. 51.

[31] The editorial cited the statement of the sage Samuel and its endorsement by the medieval philosopher Moses Maimonides, 'The sole difference between this era and the messianic days is [delivery from] servitude to the nations.' Samuel's statement was quoted by Maimonides in *Mishneh torah*, 'Laws of Kings', 12. The editorial, from *Sulamith*, 1/4 (1806), 341–2, is discussed in Baruch Mevorach, 'Messianism as a Factor in the First Reform Controversies (1810–1820)' (Heb.), *Zion*, 34 (1969), 189–219 at 191–2.

their naturalistic conception of the redemptive process allowed them to interpret current events as divine. In this case, they were encouraging an enthusiastic and active Jewish response to the removal of discriminatory laws. In sum,
while they regarded the conventional understanding of the messianic hope as
problematic, they found meaning and inspiration in the concept and were
unwilling to abandon it entirely.

While enthusiasm for emancipation in Germany was widespread, here and
there could be heard the voices of disgruntled rabbis who were well aware that
the benefits of integration came at a high cost to Jewish society. Even without
full emancipation, rabbinic authority and communal control had been curtailed. The guardians of tradition had to find new strategies to entice Jews voluntarily to choose social and religious distinctiveness. Over the centuries
Jewish preachers typically complained that Jews were forgetting that their dispersion, *galut*, was a divine punishment; they scolded Jews for being too com-
placent in their exile instead of humbly beseeching God to send the messiah to
return them to Jerusalem. However, the concept of *galut* as physical punishment was less plausible during an era when the conditions of Jewish life were
improving or seemed on the verge of amelioration. Here is how Rabbi Tsevi
Hirsch Horovitz of Frankfurt redefined *galut* in 1807 for his contemporaries:

Look, my friends, we have much cause to lament the *galut* which has become ever more
destructive in our days. For in bygone generations there was only a *galut* of the body,
while the *galut* of the soul was not so heavy as concerns the study of Torah and the practice of religious laws and customs. But nowadays things have become reversed: the *galut*
of the body has diminished a little on account of some new liberties, but because of this
the *galut* of the soul has increased.[32]

For this German Jew, *galut* could not be measured solely in terms of physical
and political oppression. It was more useful to understand the term as a psy-
chological condition. No matter how materially comfortable the Jews were,
they were in exile as long as they had difficulty studying Torah and fulfilling
God's laws—even if this difficulty was self-imposed.

MESSIANISM AND CONFLICT OVER
LITURGICAL REFORM

New interpretations of the messianic idea remained largely theoretical. Reform of the liturgy and the curriculum of communal Jewish schools did not
occur or was so minimal that it attracted little attention. Both the liturgy and

---

[32] Mordechai Breuer, 'Emancipation and the Rabbis', *Niv hamidrashiyah*, 13 (1978–9), 26–51,
surveys traditionalist rabbis' pronouncements on the process of civic emancipation. Rabbi Horovitz's comment is cited on p. 29.

the curriculum were controlled by Jewish communal boards, and the vast majority of them were not ready to institute reforms. Enlightened parents with the means could (and usually did) educate their children privately in a manner according to their liking. However, the communal nature of Jewish prayer meant that they were more dependent on others for satisfaction in worship. Private prayer services were often the only setting in which the liturgy could be altered. In Germany, where reform of the synagogue service was first broached, government officials were not eager to permit private services in the interest of maintaining religious uniformity and preventing the growth of radicalism. Consequently, most instances of liturgical reform were short-lived and hesitant.

One notable example was the effort towards liturgical reform made by David Friedländer of Berlin. Inspired by the 1812 Prussian Edict of Emancipation, Friedländer urged Jews to omit from the liturgy elements that marked them as foreigners in their lands of residence. He assumed that modern Jews no longer desired to return to Jerusalem, to rebuild the Jerusalem Temple, or to re-establish the sacrificial service there. He recommended that these matters should be excised from the liturgy.[33] Friedländer was denounced by many, and even those who sympathized with his views did not feel they could simply dispense with the concept of Zion. Abraham Muhr, one of his colleagues, published a response that both supported and softened Friedländer's proposal. Muhr suggested that the hope for the future restoration of Jerusalem and its centrality could be understood as symbolic of God as sovereign over and fully accepted by all humanity. Rather than omit the traditional liturgical language, he advocated that it should simply be reinterpreted allegorically.[34] The organizers of a modernized prayer service established in a private home in Berlin in 1815 also had to satisfy the diverse concerns of the attendees. Their modified liturgy dealt with the matrix of messianic elements in an inconsistent, somewhat contradictory manner. They retained the prayers referring to Zion and the sacrificial service, while omitting or altering the hope for the future ingathering of Jews.[35] These compromises did not much impress the king of Prussia. Immediately upon learning of the existence of this private prayer service, Frederick William III prohibited it.

Systematic liturgical modernization began in the second decade of the nineteenth century in a region outside the Prussian emperor's control. In the atmosphere of political and religious conservatism that swept Germany after

---

[33] Michael A. Meyer, *Response to Modernity: A History of the Reform Movement in Judaism* (Oxford and New York, 1988), 44–5.

[34] Mevorach, 'Messianism in the First Reform Controversies', 195.

[35] Meyer, *Response to Modernity*, 51.

1815, a small segment of Hamburg's highly acculturated Jews wanted to create a rite of worship that would express both their attachment to Judaism and their identity as cultured Germans. Because Hamburg was a free city, its Jews were unhampered by the conservative authority of the Prussian monarch. The city's ruling body, the Hamburg Senate, permitted the establishment of the 'New Israelite Temple Association in Hamburg' in 1817. The leaders of this group revised the prayer book and sabbath and festival synagogue service in accordance with modern principles, and they opened their temple to the public the next year. The 1818 publication of two works defending the reformed liturgy of the outlawed private synagogue in Berlin enhanced the epoch-making aura surrounding the temple.[36]

The traditionalist Jews of Hamburg jumped at the challenge. They did not recognize this reform as an affirmation of religious feeling or as legitimate in any way. The conservative judges of the Hamburg Jewish community court tried and failed to disband the temple and censor its prayer book. They appealed to the leading rabbinical authorities in Europe to join in their denunciation of the reformers to the Hamburg Senate. Twenty-two denunciations, signed by forty rabbis, were collected and published in the volume *Eleh divrei haberit* (These are the Words of the Covenant) in 1819. The most avid respondents were from Poland and Hungary. Jacob Lorbeerbaum, Akiva Eger, and Moses Sofer figured prominently among the rabbinic opponents.[37] The first two men had already been central to Tsevi Hirsch Kalischer's education, while Sofer would later play an important role in Kalischer's effort to win rabbinic approval of the restoration of the sacrificial cult.

What is important about the Hamburg temple debate for this study is that here messianic ideas became extensively woven into the debate on modernization. Ezekiel Landau had first injected messianism into the anti-modernization polemic in 1782. Now both sides, the reformers and the traditionalists, made it their explicit focus and pivotal to their separate agendas. They both regarded the messianic idea as the foundation of Jewish separateness. For the reformers, this was its failing; for the traditionalists, it was its virtue.

There were three types of modification enacted by the leaders of the New

[36] Eliezer Liebermann published two works dealing with the legal, halakhic basis for the modifications in the Berlin synagogue, entitled *Nogah hatsedek* and *Or nogah* (Dessau, 1818).

[37] The New Israelite Temple Association produced not only a prayer book, but also pamphlets written in defence of both the Hamburg temple and the 1815 attempt at liturgical reform in Berlin. This treatment of the Hamburg temple incident relies upon the narrative and sources contained in Meyer, *Response to Modernity*, 53–61; Jakob J. Petuchowski, *Prayerbook Reform in Europe: The Liturgy of European Liberal and Reform Judaism* (New York, 1968), 49–54 and *passim*; and W. Gunther Plaut, *The Rise of Reform Judaism: A Sourcebook of its European Origins* (New York, 1963), 27–38.

Israelite Temple Association, and each one had some connection with messianic concepts.[38] The first was in those prayers found to be offensive or irrational. These often included expressions of Jewish particularism. Prayers addressing the messianic promise involving a separate Jewish fate—for example, prayers for the return of the Jewish people to Zion or the restoration of Davidic kingship—were targeted for modification, for these concepts exemplified the Judaism of the past. To the reformers the hope of a separate Jewish future in the Land of Israel was an outdated and unappealing fantasy no longer suitable in the present era, when emancipation promised to make Jews full members of European society. Other messianic concepts found lacking were the notion of a personal messiah and the desire for the restoration of the sacrificial cult—these were considered irrational and unappealing. But the liturgists could not simply excise or modify all these symbols, nor did they want to. They retained references to God's love of Zion and prayers for God's return to Zion; these could be reinterpreted in a manner acceptable to modern sensibilities, presumably, such as that suggested in 1812 by Abraham Muhr. They omitted the explicit request for the return of the Jerusalem Temple and its sacrificial cult, but they substituted a petition that recognized the primacy of sacrificial offerings.[39] They omitted the petitions for the appearance of a personal messiah and the Jews' return to Zion, and they substituted (and preserved the existing) references to an era of peace and freedom for all, a universal messianic age.[40]

The second goal of the Hamburg liturgists was to make the service more meaningful by modifying the language of Jewish prayer. The traditional prayer book and service consisted of Hebrew and Aramaic prayers, texts for study, and meditations. The members of the New Israelite Temple Association admitted that they no longer understood the ancient languages nor considered them sacred. They spoke German and wanted to pray in German. Thus, they omitted many passages from the liturgy and included in their prayer book

[38] Because the new prayer book did not contain an explanation of the modifications, the logic and motivation behind them must be discerned through textual analysis and the sympathetic statements published by supporters in the following year.

[39] For example, the festival prayer for the return of the sacrificial cult was modified as follows: 'May it be Your will, O lord our God and God of our fathers, to receive in mercy and favor the expression of our lips in place of the obligatory sacrifices' (quoted in Meyer, *Response to Modernity*, 56). See Petuchowski, *Prayerbook Reform in Europe*, 50–3. I have not been able to locate any pre-1840s published philosophical or aesthetic objections to sacrificial worship.

[40] Mevorach shows throughout his study 'Messianism in the First Reform Controversies' that the concept of the personal messiah was problematic to reformers because, first, it appeared irrational, and second, it was closely linked to Jewish particularism rather than the universalistic ideals they preferred. He also observes that the problem with the concept of a personal messiah engaged the reformers more than the prayers for the return of sacrifices.

German translations to be used alongside or in place of the Hebrew. Advocating greater use of the vernacular also reflected these Jews' aspirations for social integration. They understood the ethos of modern nationalism and were seeking a way to demonstrate their patriotism. They were willing to risk the possibility that in their assertion of their identity as German Jews, they would disrupt the unity between other Jews and themselves.

Finally, the Hamburg reformers sought to improve the aesthetics of Jewish prayer. This, too, would make a statement about Jewish identity. Jewish prayer services were typically somewhat raucous, as they were lengthy and highly participatory, and social as well as religious in nature. To the more cosmopolitan, acculturated Jews of Hamburg, improved aesthetics meant moving towards German Catholic and Protestant styles of worship: they incorporated into the service organ music and a choir and insisted on a high level of decorum and a more passive congregation. The Hamburg reformers were not uncomfortable with the notion of learning from Christians. They admired the music and aesthetics of the Christian liturgical tradition, and felt no need to maintain this particular distinction. Thus, both in form and substance, the new service was an expression of greater Jewish integration into European society.[41]

The members of the New Israelite Temple Association, in addition to creating a meaningful service for themselves, were also conducting a campaign on two fronts. Internally, they were developing a means of moving Jews faithful to tradition away from traditional behaviours and beliefs that hindered integration and emancipation. They believed that the ideological underpinnings of Jewish separatism, of the Judaism of the past, were embedded in traditional messianism. They sought to transfer messianic hopes from the Land of Israel to Europe and the world as a whole, where new forms of worship would be a permanent substitute for the sacrificial cult in Jerusalem.[42] Externally, the reformers were addressing the wider society. Cognizant of the reaction against

---

[41] David Ellenson, 'A Disputed Precedent: The Prague Organ in Nineteenth-Century Central European Legal Literature and Polemics', *Leo Baeck Institute Yearbook*, 40 (1995), 251–64, examines the halakhic literature on the organ. Organ music in synagogues was not unknown in Europe—some 17th-c. Italian synagogues had organ music, for example, and one Prague synagogue. There was considerable rabbinic discomfort with the organ, on the grounds that playing the organ violated the rabbinic prohibitions against work on the sabbath and holidays; that the exilic mourning for the destruction of the Second Temple requires a general prohibition against music; that it is an imitation of Christian customs. Ellenson demonstrates, however, that the debate on the use of the organ became less a matter of halakhic problems and more a means for European Reform and Orthodox denominations to establish boundaries between themselves. This is clearly what is occurring in this incident.

[42] Meyer, *Response to Modernity*, 59. They did not hesitate to refer to traditional messianic doctrines, however, if they proved helpful. For example, Eliezer Liebermann, in his book defending the Berlin worship service, cited the Song of Song oaths for evidence that Jews had no

Jewish emancipation that set in after 1815, they were defending themselves against the charge that they were resident foreigners, unpatriotic and unattached to the body politic. Their reformed service was a declaration that Jewish separatism and inequality were neither sanctioned by Judaism nor held dear by Jews. Jewish existence, as they defined it, would not threaten the unity of Germany. Their view of Judaism, which to them was inevitably the Judaism of the modern world, was compatible with the ideals of the wider European society.

Traditional Jewish leaders, in their collective written response, were conducting a parallel but contradictory effort. They, too, were mounting a campaign on two fronts. They wrote in Hebrew and Aramaic and so were addressing people like themselves, those who were already convinced that the innovations were illegitimate as well as those who might be sympathetic. But the traditionalists also knew that their responses in *Eleh divrei haberit* would be made available for scrutiny by the Hamburg Senate, which was deliberating on whether to close the temple.[43] Not only did they have to show that the reformers were violating sacred norms, they had to defend the older practices against the charge of being unpatriotic.

The traditionalists defended the status quo with the polemical pattern established earlier. They adopted the rhetoric of war and described themselves as zealous guardians of God's will. Because the Hamburg temple prayer book did not include a rationale for the changes, rabbinic opponents focused on the authors of the recently published defence of the 1815 Berlin reform effort, rabbis Eliezer Liebermann and Aaron Chorin.[44] They saw themselves in a contest between competing rabbinical authorities. The bulk of their statements was a refutation of Liebermann's and Chorin's halakhic reasoning, a display of proof texts, and a declaration of their superior rabbinic authority. Consistent with the third element of the polemic, the conservatives located the source of the controversy in the behaviour of a few troublemakers, since they saw nothing in the status quo that mandated change.

The most significant development in this part of the polemic was the tradi-

intention of rebelling against the nations in which they lived, for such behaviour had long been prohibited; see *Or nogah*, 24.

[43] Mevorach, 'Messianism in the First Reform Controversies', 206.

[44] The traditionalists were not always aware of the reasoning behind a particular religious reform. The non-halakhic literature explaining the reasoning was written primarily in German, which made it accessible to non-Jews and secularized Jews but inaccessible to most traditional rabbis. In these early stages of religious modernization, advocates of change still tended to support their reforms on the basis of halakhah. Only later would they regard halakhic support as unnecessary, on the basis that Jewish legal literature (especially the Talmud and codes) was not, in itself, necessarily authoritative for their time.

tionalists' discussion of messianism. In the first confrontation between conservatives and innovators in 1782 over Wessely's proposal for educational reform, Ezekiel Landau had referred to messianism as the foundation of Judaism. Now, hearing messianism under attack for being incompatible with Jewish existence in modern Europe, the traditionalists elaborated on the messianic idea as the very basis of Jewish existence in Europe. They maintained that the messianic hope promoted obedience and loyalty in Jewish subjects. It was necessary for the smooth functioning of the Jewish community and a boon to non-Jews as well. The contributors to *Eleh divrei haberit* who asserted this most adamantly and explicitly were Jacob Lorbeerbaum, Akiva Eger, and Moses Sofer.

Akiva Eger (1761–1837) made special note to point out that Jews were required to regard their separate, national hopes from a position of political quietism. He reaffirmed the ideology of messianic passivity by emphasizing that the redemption was in God's hands alone. Jewish passivity was reinforced by the religious obligation to pray for the strength of secular governments. He wrote:

We are required to pray for the rebuilding of Jerusalem, even though we dwell quietly among the nations of the world, and entreat God to incline the hearts of the kings towards us favourably. We are likewise commanded to express gratitude to the kings and pray for the welfare of the Crown. Although we anticipate and pray for the rebuilding of Jerusalem, it is not because we aspire to earthly pleasures, but rather to worship God in purity through sacrificial worship at God's Temple.[45]

That is, traditional messianic beliefs do not encourage separatism and rebelliousness, but generate patriotism and subservience to the king. Messianic hopes were primarily spiritual, not political, according to Eger, and this was evidenced by the ultimate goal of the redemption, the renewal of sacrificial worship. How could such politically quiescent spirituality be problematic?

It is important to note that Eger's explicit affirmation of messianic passivity was actually in agreement with the reformers. The innovators embraced messianic passivity in the sense that they consistently described the return to Zion in abstract, symbolic terms that precluded taking concrete steps to end the exile. Messianic passivity served their goals of achieving full integration in the wider society.[46] One could argue that those Jews who identified the contemporary era of emancipation as messianic, and called for Jews to respond actively to the new demands of citizenship, were engaging in a modern variant

---

[45] *Eleh divrei haberit* (Altona, 1819), 28, letter 10.

[46] For example, Eliezer Liebermann referred approvingly to the talmudic passages proscribing messianic activism, pointing out that Jews should not actively 'force the end' through excessive prayer. See Mevorach, 'Messianism in the First Reform Controversies', 203.

of messianic activism. However, they had so significantly altered the content of the messianic hope as to make this label untenable.

While both sides professed a commitment to political quietism, the reformers' rejection of Jewish separatism made them appear more patriotic and put the conservatives on the defensive. Jacob Lorbeerbaum (1760–1832) used even stronger terms than Eger in expressing what he claimed was the essentially patriotic core of Jewish messianism:

Just as we believe with total faith that the Creator, may he be blessed, is the ruler of the world, so we believe *that the king and the government is God's chosen, to rule on his behalf and alongside him*. When we pray in all our prayers for the rebuilding of the Temple, we are anticipating the time when we can fulfil God's explicit commandment, achieve supernal wisdom, receive God's presence at the Temple on the festival days as is commanded—and this hope is also for those who live in far-off lands, that we may all be gathered together and offer sacrifices. Therefore, when we pray, in all our prayers, *for the welfare of the government and its continued sustenance*, this prayer too is also of the essence of our faith and the basis for the continuation of our religion and fulfilment of commandments. The underlying principle is that *there is nothing in our prayers against the welfare of the government, God forbid: its benefit is necessary for our benefit*.[47]

Here, then, Lorbeerbaum links the prayers for the rebuilding of Jerusalem to the prayers for the welfare of the government; both are of central importance in Jewish faith, he insists, because both are commandments from God. The same Jews who pray fervently for the former are also praying fervently for the latter. Lorbeerbaum evokes, as well, the king's divinely given right to rule. Jews understand that their subjugation to secular kings is of God's doing, and for their ultimate benefit. A more extreme formulation of this Jewish subservience was made by Moses Sofer (1762–1839), who described present-day Jews as prisoners of war; their status derived from their defeat in the Roman–Jewish war of 66–70 CE and the destruction of the Second Temple that put them into exile.[48] All three rabbis argued that the messianic hope was not for future Jewish dominance over non-Jews or fulfilment of material desires, but for an era of enhanced spirituality. Again, the return of sacrificial worship was at the pinnacle of Jewish religious expression and the ultimate goal of Jewish history. Lorbeerbaum neglected to point out the secondary and essentially negative portrayal of non-Jews in messianic literature. This would have been too impolitic.[49]

[47] *Eleh divrei haberit*, 80, letter 19. The emphasis is in the original.
[48] See ibid. 9, letter 3.
[49] Consequently, no one mentions these notions, discussed at the beginning of the chapter. Moses Sofer, for example, emphasizes only that God will repay the non-Jewish kings for their good; see *Eleh divrei haberit*, 9, letter 3.

Denigration of secular rule, in addition, went counter to the rabbis' goal of buttressing their own authority, which was tied to the state. In the earlier conflict with Wessely, Tevele and Landau harked back to the alliance between the religious authorities and the Crown. Then it was a radical notion to claim that the individual must have intellectual freedom and should not be coerced in the name of religion. For conservative rabbis, it was still a radical idea. Lorbeerbaum linked freethinking to anarchy in order to discredit it as a political philosophy. The notion that a person should be guided by his individual reason, he believed, reflected an arrogance found also in the ancient philosophers. Governments had always rejected this claim, he wrote approvingly: 'Kings and governments, may their majesty be enhanced, in every land have been zealous in ensuring that every person *is shackled in the chains of his religion, and that there not be factions within it* because everyone does what his heart desires. The preservation of the state depends on this unity . . .'.[50] Here it is evident that Lorbeerbaum could think of governing only in authoritarian terms. He contemplated religious tolerance only for corporate groups and not for individuals. By his definition, a good king is paternalistic and protective of the authority of religious institutions. Religious reformers, therefore, are political rebels; only religious conservatives can be true patriots.[51]

The discussion of sacrificial offerings in this polemic developed considerably from Landau's use of it in 1782. For Landau, the sacrifices were the symbol of and the reward for faith. Although the reformers had not yet articulated their distaste for the sacrifices, they clearly regarded prayer, presented with beautiful music and with formal decorum, as the most elevated form of worship. This pushed the traditionalists to go a step further: opposing the restoration of the sacrifices was tantamount to opposing God's authority. Lorbeerbaum tied this to his criticism of the Hamburg temple's organ. He pointed out that the halakhic reasoning used to justify the use of an organ rested on the erroneous assumption that the joy of prayer is like the joy of a wedding. According to Lorbeerbaum, 'the essence of our prayer and petition is the expiation of sin . . . and how can we approach the king of the world with musical instruments and joy when we know that we are sinners?' Fortunately for the Jews, God provided sacrificial rituals that could remove sin. 'During the time when the Temple stood', he wrote, 'no person ever lay down to sleep in Jerusalem in a state of sin.' But after the destruction of the ancient Temple,

---

[50] Ibid. 80, letter 19. Emphasis is in the original.

[51] This is an early indicator of the meeting of minds that often occurs in the modern period between Orthodox Jews and Christian (and Muslim) religious conservatives. Both would put great weight on traditional concepts—for the Jews, the notion of *galut*, and for Christians, the notion of divine punishment of Jews for rejecting Christ—as a basis for continuing Jewish separatism.

there was no way that one could really be certain of forgiveness. Prayer was an inadequate substitute for the sacrifices. Moses Sofer agreed with this point, noting that not even the rabbinically authored prayers were a complete substitute for the Temple cult.[52]

Thus there was no reason for joy during verbal worship. Joy was not appropriate if one was a sinner, and one could only achieve the assurance of being freed from sin after performing the sacrifices. A joyous worshipper during the period of the exile was an arrogant worshipper. To Lorbeerbaum, the organ music of the Hamburg temple was a denial that one was in a state of exile. Rejecting this—indeed, rejecting any aspect of the messianic concept—was a rejection of divine authority.[53]

Another notable feature of the rabbinic responses was the assertion that the messianic redemption was essentially a universalistic concept. Moses Sofer argued that non-Jews were well aware of Jewish messianic concepts and had never before vexed the Jews about their particularism. Eger took pains to point out that the messianic era had never been envisaged as a narrow, parochial affair, but was a cosmic event that benefited all humanity. This was obviously a response to the reformers' charge that the messianic idea was offensive and fostered Jewish separatism. This open avowal of universalism by the conservatives marks a new stage in Jewish messianic thought. It was an accommodation, albeit minimal, to the pressures of the time.[54]

Yet Lorbeerbaum and Eger, like the other traditional rabbis who responded

---

[52] *Eleh divrei haberit*, 29, letter 19. The similarity between this and certain Christian ideas is certainly no accident, but I seriously doubt that it can be attributed to Christian influence. The attack on the sacrifices impels Lorbeerbaum and the others to counter-attack with a pre-rabbinic priestly ideology (that Christianity adopted and that the rabbis, for the most part, supplanted with an ideology stressing the acceptability of deeds and prayer). More on this in Ch. 4. Moses Sofer's argument appeared in *Eleh divrei haberit*, 10, letter 3. He noted that the composers of the weekday prayer must have known from God himself that there cannot be any arbitrary substitutes for the sacrificial cult. If substitutes could so easily be found, why have a Temple and a sacrificial cult in the first place? It follows, he argued, that nothing can be a complete substitute for the Temple cult, although the weekday prayer comes close.

[53] For the purposes of public debate, these men argued that only the restoration of the Temple cult during the messianic age would bring a feeling of spiritual completion. We shall see later that at least Eger may have, in private, questioned the desirability of resuming sacrificial worship in their own day.

[54] This is one of the major points demonstrated by Mevorach, 'Messianism in the First Reform Controversies', 204–18. Sofer's comment is in *Eleh divrei haberit*, 9, letter 3. It was certainly disingenuous, as there were celebrated cases in the medieval era when the Jews were challenged by their Christian hosts to defend certain phrases in their prayers (calling for God's revenge on the nations of the world, for example). The difference between then and the 19th-c. challenge is that the latter arose from within. Eger's comment appears in *Eleh divrei haberit*, 28, letter 10. Lorbeerbaum made no reference to the universal nature of the messianic reward.

to the challenge, did not have a problem admitting that the Jews were a distinct nation. According to them, Jews were one holy body, though dispersed through an act of God; everyone else constituted another body, the non-Jews. To them this was a simple fact, and they were quite proud of their distinctive status. They did not understand, because they did not grasp the principles of modern nationalism, that this would make Jewish emancipation unthinkable to many Europeans. This naivety is evident in Akiva Eger's letter: 'We are disgraced among the nations, for every nation speaks in its own language and loves its language, but should we abandon our holy language? They [the reformers] are teaching their children French, Latin, and the like, and neglecting the holy tongue, aha! Is this the wisdom and discernment they want to show to the nations?'[55] According to Eger, the non-Jews had respect for Jews only when they embraced their separate culture and language. They, like he, would regard Jewish assimilation as an act of self-abasement. Eger's sincerity must be questioned here; it is hard to imagine that he was ignorant of the long-standing desire of many Europeans that the Jews should abandon their distinctive ways.

It cannot be established whether the traditionalist rabbis were simply unaware of the new political climate, or whether they chose to misunderstand it in order to preserve the status quo. It must be kept in mind that the rabbis of Lissa and Posen lived in a fairly closed environment within the kingdom of Prussia, where the monarch's distrust of private prayer services was well known. Since it is in the nature of political institutions to resist change, or to change very slowly (and this was certainly the case in central Europe), evidence of the state's protective attitude towards religious tradition abounded. Traditionalist rabbis paraded this evidence in their polemics as proof of the veracity of their world view.[56] Men like Lorbeerbaum and Eger needed to deny that political life was being transformed and that the old alliance between the state and the rabbinate was disappearing. They had not yet determined how to lead the Jewish community without the aid of the state's coercive powers.

Notwithstanding the clash of opinions between reformers and traditionalists, both sides manifested a new awareness of the shifting relationship between the Jews and European society. The desire to avoid offence to non-Jews or to avoid jeopardizing Jews' chances for civic emancipation meant that all parties strengthened the universalistic features of the messianic promise. Liberal as well as conservative Jews pointed out that when Jews prayed for redemption they meant the bestowal of God's beneficence upon all humanity.

[55] *Eleh divrei haberit*, 28, letter 10.

[56] Moses Sofer of Hungary was exemplary in developing this tactic. See Jacob Katz, 'Towards a Biography of the Hatam Sofer', in Frances Malino and David Sorkin (eds.), *Profiles in Diversity; Jews in a Changing Europe, 1750–1870* (Detroit, 1997), 223–66 at 259.

This same concern not to offend inclined some Jews to excise from the liturgy all references to the centrality of Zion or the return to Zion. Most liberals did not require that level of ideological purity; they were content to interpret this concept symbolically, in a manner that divested it of all political meaning. Those on the conservative side of the spectrum divested the Zion concept of its political force by highlighting the religious taboo against messianic activism. Messianic passivity was, for them, a guarantor of Jews' loyalty to their foreign hosts. Finally, as reason was held in greater esteem and became manifest in the desire for more rational religious belief, enlightened Jews rejected the concept of a personal messiah and the hope for future miracles. Also arguing from reason, traditionalists insisted that the state's smooth functioning required devotion to the conservative religious values implicit in the messianic idea.

By the end of 1819 the lines had been drawn in the battle over modernization as its issues were articulated in the messianic concepts of the liturgy. Outside the realm of debate, the Jewish communal realm, the advocates of change had a lasting impact. Hamburg's Senate did not repeal its earlier decision to allow the Temple Association members to meet, pray, and teach; however, they were not permitted to call their place of worship a temple or synagogue, nor their spiritual leaders and preachers by any title but 'teachers'. The Hamburg community received permission to hire a community rabbi who would replace the elderly rabbinic judges and institute a modernized synagogue ritual, albeit one that was in accordance with Jewish law.[57] Elsewhere in Germany, the cause of liturgical reform was stymied by government officials fearful of the growth of sectarianism within the Jewish community. The process of modernization proceeded apace, of course: Jews throughout Germany increasingly adopted the language and dress of the wider society and expanded the scope of their children's education. Nevertheless, the vast majority of Jews continued to be steeped in pre-modern religious values and comfortable with a passive messianic hope that promised miracles.

[57] Meyer, *Response to Modernity*, 57–8.

TWO

Raising a Rabbi in the
Posen District, 1795–1823

ALTHOUGH Tsevi Hirsch Kalischer finished his schooling under Jacob
Lorbeerbaum and Akiva Eger shortly before the Hamburg temple controversy, he must have learnt first-hand from his teachers about the recent ritual
innovations and proposals for educational reform. One of the chief rhetorical
weapons in the rabbinic opposition was an appeal to messianic beliefs. Even
though messianic concepts were under suspicion for their political implications and found wanting on the basis of reason, the foremost rabbinic leaders
of the time touted them as the sustenance of the Jewish people and the symbol
and reward of faith. Given this context, it is not surprising that Kalischer was
deeply intrigued by messianism.

Yet Kalischer would surpass his teachers in messianic enthusiasm, in his
avid eagerness for the spiritual glory promised in the ancient visions of the
messianic age, and in his deep conviction that the days of redemption were at
hand. This optimistic certitude was not bequeathed to him by Lorbeerbaum
and Eger. They disdained the contemporary taste for rationalism and were
stymied by the new political relationship between the Jews and the state. Eger
would later attempt to dampen his student's messianic ardour. As we shall see
in this chapter, both teachers suffered from the impoverishment of their communities and lamented the dwindling enthusiasm for Torah study. Kalischer's
response to the new developments of the era, however, was quite positive. He
would notice the increasing opportunities for Jewish power and interpret them
as God-given vehicles enabling the Jews to initiate redemption. He greeted the
hunger for reason as a tool to be used in the strengthening of religious belief.
From where did this optimism spring? It seems clear from his writings that he
was graced with a hopeful disposition, and his religious faith was of the sort
that casts a warm light on all events. In addition, his environment and elements
of his family culture contributed to his positive outlook. He was raised within
the protective cocoon of a rabbinic family that imbued him with a deep respect
for a broad range of Jewish learning. His particular revision of the messianic
concept was indebted to the values of the yeshiva world and its mode of study,
especially its deep respect for the sacrificial commandments and the need to

resolve tensions between conflicting opinions. Sheltered in the backwaters of Prussia, Kalischer was removed from the dynamic urban centres of European Jewry where belief in the messianic restoration had dissipated under the impact of acculturation and an unbounded rationalism. This chapter will examine the contours of Kalischer's life and education that help explain his singular approach to messianism.

POLISH JEWISH SOCIETY AT KALISCHER'S BIRTH

Tsevi Hirsch Kalischer was born in 1795 on the fourth day of the Hebrew month of Nisan, or 24 March, in Lissa, Poland. Until just shortly before his birth, Lissa had been part of the Polish Commonwealth. It was situated in the district of Great Poland, a plain bounded by the Oder and Vistula rivers and bisected by the River Warta. Its even terrain was sprinkled with lakes, meadows, and forest tracts. Well suited to growing grain, Great Poland's flatness and network of waterways made it an important link in central European trade. Grain, manufactured goods, and natural resources were transported between Germany and Russia along its east–west routes, and goods flowed north and south along the Vistula to and from its main port city, Danzig.

The features that made Great Poland so favourable for trade served less peaceful ends as well. The powerful states to the east, west, north, and south regarded the western Polish plain as an ideal arena for invasions and warfare. After every conflict, the victors invited foreigners to settle in the cities and on the land and help them recover from the devastation. This repeating cycle produced a chaotic political history and a multi-ethnic, polyglot population; according to one estimate, less than two-fifths of the population of the Polish Commonwealth was Polish.[1] Political authority was held by the Polish Catholic landowning gentry, the *szlachta*, which elected representatives to regional and central diets, chose a king, and supplied the bishops and high officials for the Catholic Church. The bulk of the population consisted of peasant farmers of mainly Polish but also German, Russian, and other stock. The majority of the peasants were enserfed to the landlords and bound to the soil. The burgher class—a diverse group in terms of national identity—was excluded from the central diet and struggled with the magnates for political supremacy. Some of the towns were owned and controlled by the nobility, and some owed allegiance only to the king. Great Poland, because of its geography,

---

[1] Gershon David Hundert, 'Some Basic Characteristics of the Jewish Experience in Poland', *Polin*, 1 (1980), 28–34 at 31.

included more cities and was less dominated by the serf-estate system than the rest of Poland.[2]

Jews and Germans were the most numerous of the foreign minorities in Great Poland. Jews fleeing expulsion from Germany had been welcomed there as early as the thirteenth century by the Polish king. They were granted generous residential rights, occupational freedom, and exemption from serfdom and slavery. Still, they remained distinct in religion, language, and social relations. Although their vernacular, Yiddish, was a fusion of German dialects and Hebrew, it was distinctive from the regional languages and written in Hebrew script. Only those Jewish merchants and communal leaders who had extensive economic and political dealings with Poles and Germans would have been fluent in these languages; rabbis, artisans, and others whose economic activities were restricted to the Jewish community very likely had some knowledge of the non-Jewish vernacular, but they would have been comfortable only with the regional Yiddish.

The Germans constituted a less socially isolated foreign class, with fewer privileges than the Jews. Over the centuries, German immigrants had drifted over to Great Poland from the west or were invited to establish farming colonies of their own. Initially, they tended to become polonized within a few generations; after the Reformation, however, the sizeable influx of Protestant Germans remained linguistically and socially distinct from Polish Catholics. Each group—Poles, Germans, and Jews—regarded itself, and was regarded by contemporaries, as a separate nationality. Their relations were characterized by a great deal of suspicion and hostility that occasionally erupted in violent clashes. Nevertheless, they viewed their interspersion as a part of the natural order of life, unfortunate though it might be.[3]

The Jews had many reasons to be content in Poland. They enjoyed tremendous freedom relative to the rest of the population; only the nobility was more privileged. Indeed, according to an old Polish proverb, the Polish Commonwealth was 'heaven for the nobles, purgatory for the townsfolk, hell for the peasants, and paradise for the Jews'.[4] Their almost unlimited internal autonomy enabled the Jews to nurture a level of Torah scholarship acknowledged as the highest in the world. Yet the extent of Jewish communal power could not

[2] An author of a textbook on the history of Poland suggests that one of the factors contributing to Poland's 'cultural ossification' in the late 17th and 18th cc. was that 'the urban element remained culturally unassimilated': E. Rostworowski, 'The Commonwealth of the Gentry', in Alexander Gieysztor et al. (eds.), *History of Poland* (Warsaw, 1979), 257.

[3] By the mid-18th c. the Jews comprised 5 per cent of the population, and the Germans were at least three times that number. This rough estimate is based on the data in William W. Hagen, *Germans, Poles, and Jews: The Nationality Conflict in the Prussian East 1772–1914* (Chicago, 1980), 7–30.   [4] Quoted ibid. 13 from an old Latin proverb still current in mid-19th-c. Posen.

obscure their status as a nation in exile. The Jews used to explain that Poland got its name from the Hebrew phrase *poh lin*, meaning 'Here, stay overnight'.[5] In other words, their stay in Poland was temporary, lasting only until the messiah came and brought them to the Promised Land. In the meantime, because God had punished them for their many sins, they were destined to be subjugated by others.

Of course, the Jews exerted themselves to make the best of a bad situation. They guarded and sustained their separateness through a system of local Jewish governance. A small number of men drawn from the wealthier, better-connected, or educated families were elected as *parnasim* (trustees) by eligible voters from each Jewish community. Within the *kahal* and its satellite communities on the outskirts, the *parnasim* ensured that the basic educational, religious, and social welfare needs of Jewish life were met. They, and the rabbis they engaged to serve the community, wielded considerable authority over the whole range of Jewish life, with the right to offer guidance, supervise behaviour, and inflict punishment on those who deviated from community norms.[6] All formal education—both elementary school and the yeshiva, the institute of higher rabbinic learning—was supervised by the *parnasim* or their appointees. The *parnasim* also represented the Jewish community to the Polish officials, negotiated with them over the Jewish contribution to the poll tax, and apportioned and collected these monies themselves. Local Jewish expenditures were paid for by taxes on kosher slaughtering, dowries, the ritual bath, and property transactions. The judiciary powers of the local Jewish courts were nearly absolute; Jews were prevented from resorting to secular courts by the threat of excommunication. The individual's religious, economic, and social life was, to a large extent, subordinated to the community's interests. Myriad details of daily life were circumscribed by Jewish law, and custom dictated many other matters outside its scope.

During the course of the sixteenth century, local Jewish communities in Poland organized a regional and then a national Jewish governing apparatus. In this structure, local community councils sent representatives to a Jewish provincial council, which both represented the Jews to the regional Polish authorities and served as the regional voice to local community leaders and to Jews elsewhere in Poland. Seated above all local and provincial bodies was the

---

[5] Bernard D. Weinryb, *The Jews of Poland: A Social and Economic History of the Jewish Community in Poland from 1100–1800* (Philadelphia, 1972), 19.

[6] Rabbis did not necessarily serve the community as salaried employees of the *kahal*. They could earn their livelihood from other means. In the well-educated communities of 17th-c. Poland there were many men with rabbinic certification, some who served as *parnasim* or in the various paid or unpaid positions in the *kahal*. This status in relation to the Kalischer family will be discussed below.

Council of the Lands, the controlling body for the Jewish provinces of Poland. This body represented the Jews to the Crown and other central institutions, administered the collection of the Jewish tax throughout Poland, issued regulations governing all Polish Jews, and was a forum for individual and communal grievances. While the Council of the Lands was not as powerful as its detractors claimed, it was an obvious expression of the separate Jewish agenda in Poland. The first province consolidated for the territorial Jewish government was Great Poland. Its regional council met, over the years, in the three principal Jewish communities of the region, Posen, Kalisch, and then Lissa.[7]

It was within this governing system that Kalischer's ancestors achieved social, political, and intellectual primacy. Like most rabbinic families, the Kalischer dynasty cemented its communal dominance through marriage ties and scholarly associations. The family recalled with pride its paternal connection with the late sixteenth-century luminaries Judah Loew of Prague (known as Maharal) and his in-law Mordecai Jaffe, the author of *Halevush*, a commentary on the *Shulḥan arukh*. Both men served Posen as chief rabbis. Succeeding generations of the Jaffe family produced eminent Talmud scholars who attained influential posts in the region. Kalisch, however, was the town associated with Kalischer's direct forebears and from which they took their name. The first Kalischer to reach Lissa was a Rabbi Judah Leib, who became a *parnas* immediately upon his arrival in 1709.[8] Although members of the family remained in Kalisch and maintained branches in Prague and Berlin, from the eighteenth century on it was within the Lissa Jewish community that the Kalischer clan became most influential.[9]

Despite its prominence, the Kalischer family shared the precarious existence of the Jews of Great Poland. While the Jews were invited into the region to serve as moneylenders, minters, and financiers for the Crown, they soon branched out into commerce and crafts, eventually dominating the grain trade and the textile industry. Despite their reputation for economic resourcefulness

[7] On the establishment and development of Polish Jewish government, see Ben-Sasson, *A History of the Jewish People*, 669–87.

[8] The name Judah Leib was apparently handed down through his family for generations, to the great confusion of genealogists. The Rabbi Judah Leib who arrived in Lissa in 1709 was not identical with but probably related to Judah Aryeh Leib of Kalisch, also known as Leib Kalisch, who died in Kalisch that year. Tsevi Hirsch's uncle Judah Leib seems to have been the third generation after the first Lissan Kalischer, and Tsevi Hirsch named one of his sons after him.

[9] Tsevi Hirsch's uncle Judah Leib recounted some of the family genealogy in the introduction to his book *Hayad haḥazakah* (Breslau, 1820), and Tsevi Hirsch recollected his family ties in a letter to Rabbi David Tevele Efrati, reprinted in Arigur, 'Rabbi Tsevi Hirsch Kalischer'. These are summarized in Abraham Isaac Bromberg, *Rabbi Tsevi Hirsch Kalischer* (Heb.) (Jerusalem, 1960), 9–13. On Jaffe, see *EJ*, s.v. 'Jaffe, Mordecai ben Abraham', author E.K.

and commercial energy, they were generally impoverished.[10] Their rickety wooden dwellings, crowded together in the towns, were periodically devoured by fires, and whole sections of the town would have to be rebuilt. Anti-Jewish riots, the endemic warfare, and other catastrophes threatened their lives and livelihoods. The Cossack rebellion and pogroms (1648–54) wreaked havoc, both through direct violence and because of the economic burden of caring for refugees from the east. Posen and Kalisch were devastated by the Northern War (1700–21). Lissa, which had escaped the war, became the new home of many of their residents, and it is perhaps for this reason that the Kalischer family moved there.

These various disasters took their toll on the political functioning of the Polish Commonwealth. While the surrounding rulers became increasingly absolutist, Poland's *szlachta* took a different course. The gentry, determined to retain its privileges and prevent the centralization of authority, weakened the power of both the central government and the representational diets. The central government lost its power to local magnates, upon whom authority over the Jews devolved as well. The Polish Commonwealth disintegrated into virtual civil war. Only in 1764, when Poland was threatened by the expansionist designs of its neighbours, did its leaders institute some governmental reform. The revived central Polish Diet was inspired by the liberal strain in Enlightenment political thought. It aimed to centralize and democratize the government, and among its many decrees was the abolition of the regional and national Jewish councils.[11] These reforms came too late. Poland was unable to defend itself from the imperialistic designs of its well-organized neighbours and in 1772, 1793, and 1795 was divided between Russia, Prussia, and Austria.

When Prussia acquired the western and north-western parts of Poland through the partitions, it appeared as though major changes would soon be under way. Eighteenth-century Prussia offered startling contrasts to the Polish Commonwealth. Prussia's emperors were autocratic crown princes of a powerful and well-organized entity. Society was highly stratified, with each social group owing distinct obligations to the Crown and permitted to possess only

[10] According to anecdotal evidence, their industriousness distinguished them from the Poles and Germans. See Hagen, *Germans, Poles, and Jews*, 9; Norman Davies, *God's Playground: A History of Poland*, 2 vols. (New York, 1982), i. 287–91; and Gershon Hundert, 'The Implications of Jewish Economic Activities for Christian–Jewish Relations in the Polish Commonwealth', in Chimen Abramsky, Maciej Jachimczyk, and Antony Polonsky (eds.), *The Jews in Poland* (Oxford, 1986), 55–63 at 59–60.

[11] The higher Jewish governing bodies continued to impose some authority for years to come, but Jewish autonomy on the local level remained intact. Ben-Sasson, *History of the Jewish People*, 765. The parallel and interconnected breakdown of Jewish communal authority and Polish provincial rule is colourfully described in Isaac Lewin, 'A Desecration of Yom Kippur in Pre-Partition Poland', in id., *The Jewish Community in Poland* (New York, 1985), 141–6.

that property deemed suitable to its status. The state attempted to regulate economic forces towards greater productivity and the needs of the state. Government administrators and bureaucrats were inculcated with the belief that duty to the king was the highest human virtue. This absolutist system and political ideology ran counter to the Polish system; even during the Poles' last-ditch efforts at internal reform, they still upheld quasi-democratic principles that granted individuals and social groups relative freedom from central control.

In further contrast to Poland, Prussian society was ethnically homogeneous. Its only significant 'alien' class was a small Jewish population that lived in thinly populated Jewish enclaves. Prussian Jews faced the long-standing hostility of Germany's Protestant culture and lived under strict regulations imposed by the Crown and burghers. Jewish governance barely extended beyond the local level, although a large measure of religious autonomy in internal Jewish affairs was the norm.[12] In contrast with Poland's economically diversified and highly autonomous Jewish population, Prussian Jewry was a highly regimented economic elite dispersed throughout the kingdom.[13]

The absorption of Poland presented Prussia with a dilemma in regard to its newly acquired Poles and Jews. The state was far more concerned with the Poles, whose dissatisfaction with Prussian rule might erupt into violent rebellion. Prussian officials made no secret of their distrust of and disdain for the Poles. This had nothing to do with nationalism; Prussian rulers wanted subjects who were industrious, submissive, and orderly. Junker society valued these characteristics above all others, and prided itself for instilling and maintaining them in its members. They doubted that the Poles were capable of meeting these standards. The stubborn independence of the Polish *szlachta*, its lack of a strong military tradition and commitment to state service, and the cultural dominance of the Polish Catholic Church dismayed Prussian statesmen. Above all, they feared the democratic reform spirit that had surfaced within the ranks of the gentry during the last days of the Polish Commonwealth.[14]

---

[12] Early in the 17th c. an attempt was made to establish a centralized system of Jewish governance after the Polish model, but it was severely suppressed by the state as an act of high treason. See Ben-Sasson, *History of the Jewish People*, 689–90.

[13] The 1750 General Jewish Regulations had established two classes of Jews: the more privileged category comprised rich Jews with highly developed financial connections and the talents necessary for the state's mercantilistic and military ventures. They were heavily taxed, excluded from many occupations, given limited credence in courts of law, and could generally pass on their status to only one of their children. All other Jews fitted into the second, 'unprotected' category: they were allowed into the country as servants or employees of the first group, but had fewer rights and could be expelled at any time. See Rurup, 'The Tortuous and Thorny Path', 5.

[14] See Hagen, *Germans, Poles, and Jews*, 34–44, for ample documentation of these attitudes. Frederick the Great's lack of love for things German was notorious and he believed that French

Polish nationalism was not a vital force in local politics. In the territory taken by Prussia in 1772, which the Prussians named West Prussia, the non-Jewish population was split equally between Germans and Poles. When Prussia's Polish gentry responded with passive and indirect resistance to the partition of 1772, the government replaced insufficiently submissive Poles in government service with Germans, set a higher taxation rate for Polish land-lords, sold bankrupt Polish estates to Prussians, and the like. Administrative, police, military, and judicial systems were established similar to those in the rest of Prussia. These policies gradually lessened the Polish character of the area. A noticeable number of Polish noble families, particularly those who were proud of their national heritage, leased or sold their estates in West Prussia and moved elsewhere. The Poles who remained were conservative and timorous. The area seized in the second partition, which was named South Prussia and included the city of Lissa, was far more Polish. The second partition provoked a rebellion of the Polish gentry. Yet the revolt never reached the Prussian-held territories; the centre of the Polish resistance movement was in Russian and Austrian Poland. The three empires responded to the insurrection by dividing the remaining part of Poland between them.[15]

The formulation of a policy towards Prussia's new Jewish subjects was hin-dered by the regime's anxiety over its Poles. The vast majority of western Poland's Jewish subjects were poor pedlars, artisans, and petty merchants, and therefore undesirable from the perspective of Prussian policy. Officials influ-enced by the Enlightenment argued for quick emancipation and moderniz-ation of the newly acquired Jews. They reasoned that traditional restrictions and prejudice actually caused the alien character and the undesirable economic profile of so many Jews. In order to transform the Jews into useful citizens, they argued, the state should direct the Jews towards what were then con-sidered the most desirable occupations (agriculture and manufacturing), abolish Jewish legal autonomy, and draw them away from insular religious

was the language of culture. This is how Hagen describes his attitude (p. 44): 'German he accept-ed as the unavoidable medium of communication—not only, as he once said disparagingly, with his horse, but in Prussian government and public life generally. Hence the Poles would have to learn it.' Administrative preference for the German language was a purely practical matter, and so German-speaking Poles who met Prussian standards were employed in public service.

[15] The chart on p. 15 of Hagen, *Germans, Poles, and Jews*, which estimates division of popu-lation by religion in 1795, shows that in the districts included in West Prussia there were rough-ly an equivalent number of Protestants and Catholics. In the area taken in the second and third partitions, the combined figures for the Netze district and Poznań district show slightly more subjects, two-thirds of whom were Catholic. In both cases, the vast majority of Catholics were Polish and not German Catholics. Gieysztor, *History of Poland*, 325–32, describes the 1794 rebellion in detail. Warsaw and Kraków were the centres of the insurrection under Tadeusz Kościuszko. The route of the Polish rebels did not reach the cities of Posen, Lissa, or Kalisch.

traditionalism by fostering intellectual and social intercourse with Christians. If this state-directed programme were to be accompanied with an immediate grant of civic emancipation, proponents claimed, Jewish assimilation would follow.[16] However, most officials in the Prussian government rejected such a radical course of action. They feared that emancipating the Jews would antagonize the rest of the population—especially the Poles. It might also foster the growth of democracy and lead to lack of respect for political authority. These consequences were anathema to Prussian officials anywhere, but they were very concerned that in this heavily Polish region, these measures would inspire an insurrection. The initial reaction of Emperor Frederick the Great was to restrict Polish Jews from settling in the older Prussian provinces. He then attempted to weed out, through expulsion and other measures, all but a small number of the desirable type of Jew. This attempt was unsuccessful.[17] The next emperors established a more realistic long-term objective. They sought to transform the traditional structure of Jewish life: to end Jewish legal autonomy and produce an assimilated and socially integrated Jewish population with more 'productive' occupations.

In reality, however, Prussian officials left the mass of tradition-bound Polish Jews much as they were. Few new economic opportunities were made available, for Prussia's rulers were intent upon protecting the fledgling industries and markets of her older western provinces and guarding them against contact with the foreign elements in the newer eastern provinces.[18] Until the middle of the nineteenth century the regime's indecisiveness and lack of initiative prevented the implementation of a systematic Jewish policy; instead, new policies emerged piecemeal out of the bureaucracy and courts. Wide regional variations in policy abounded. For example, the Prussian Emancipation Edict of 1812, which conferred equality of legal status on all Jews who could prove their legitimacy as Prussian subjects and who adopted a European surname,

[16] Steven M. Lowenstein, 'The Rural Community and the Urbanization of German Jewry', in id., *The Mechanics of Change: Essays in the Social History of German Jewry* (Atlanta, 1992), 133–6. One of the earliest and most articulate spokesmen in Prussia was Christian Wilhelm von Dohm, *Ueber die buergerliche Verbesserung der Juden* (Berlin, 1781). A translated excerpt of this can be found in Mendes-Flohr and Reinharz, *The Jew in the Modern World*, 28–35.

[17] Hagen, *Germans, Poles, and Jews*, 46, describes Frederick the Great's failed attempt to expel most of the Jews. Local officials had difficulty executing the order, because even the very poor Jews were essential to the economy. By the time of his death in 1786 only 7,000 Jews had been expelled into the Polish lands to the south and east. Later, measures limiting residency rights and inhibiting reproduction were implemented.

[18] Heavy export tariffs were imposed on east-bound goods in order to break the new territories away from the segments of Poland held by Russia and Austria. Merchants and manufacturers from the Polish territories were not allowed to sell their cheaper goods in the older Prussian provinces to the west, lest they hurt the economy there. See ibid. 54.

was not applied to West Prussia and Posen.[19] New rulings were often compromises, and the cancellation of Jewish limitations was frequently accompanied by new restrictions on Jewish individuals and the community.[20] Furthermore, the corporate Jewish institutions were preserved with their power diminished only moderately.[21] In practice, the Prussian approach was to grant equality of legal status on an individual basis only after Jewish assimilation was explicitly demonstrated. The burden of responsibility for change rested primarily on the Jews and secondarily on government inducements for Jewish progress. This meant that Jewish civic emancipation was slow and gradual. It occurred within the context of a political conservatism that was incompatible with liberal nationalism.

Thus during the first stage of Prussian rule, between 1772 and 1806, modernizing pressures were increasing, but they were mainly in the realm of rhetoric. Jews were introduced to a new type of government that urged them to fit

[19] See Rurup, 'The Tortuous and Thorny Path', 15. In the initial discussions of 1815, 1816, and 1817, it was determined that the post-1814 accretions to West Prussia were excluded from the edict, as were some cities that had their own municipal regulations pertaining to Jews, such as Thorn; see Max Aschkewitz, *Zur Geschichte der Juden in Westpreussen* (Marburg an der Lahn, 1967), 53. Within a few years after the edict was issued, the reform spirit ebbed and it was clear that the edict would not be fully implemented even in the more 'advanced' areas of Prussia. There was also genuine confusion as to which regulations applied and which had been superseded or postponed; according to M. Brann (*Jewish Encyclopedia*, s.v. 'Germany'), between 1815 and 1847 in the eight Prussian provinces there were twenty-one territorial Jewry laws, each of which applied to a part of the Jewish population.

[20] Herbert Strauss, 'Pre-Emancipation Prussian Policies towards the Jews 1815–1847', *Leo Baeck Institute Yearbook*, 11 (1966), 107–36 at 132–5. See also the survey of Prussian Jewish legal policy by Stefi Jersch-Wenzel in Michael Brenner, Stefi Jersch-Wenzel, and Michael A. Meyer (eds.), *German-Jewish History in Modern Times*, 4 vols. (New York, 1997), ii. 24–9.

[21] The first major piece of Jewish legislation, the 1797 Jewry laws, is a case in point. The new rules reduced the power of the Jewish communal governing boards, established inducements for Jews to enter agriculture and crafts, and encouraged them to learn the vernacular and mix socially with non-Jews. Alongside these progressive measures, however, were those mandating an increase in special Jewish taxes and the continued prohibition against South Prussian Jews moving to other Prussian provinces. This legislation was largely empty of effect. Because no new industries or employment opportunities were introduced and Polish guilds did not open their ranks, Jews continued their same occupations. The governing boards continued their previous functions, and the government utilized them to collect the increased Jewish taxes. Jews did begin to settle in some previously closed cities (and illegally cross into restricted provinces) and a small number enrolled their children in German schools. However, five years after the regulations were issued, the new ruler, Frederick William III (1797–1840) demanded that they should be set aside and replaced by the older regulations since all attempts at improvement of the Jews had failed. See Rurup, 'The Tortuous and Thorny Path', 14. Artur Eisenbach, *The Emancipation of the Jews in Poland, 1780–1870*, trans. Janina Dorosz, ed. Antony Polonsky (Oxford, 1991), 116–17, argues that Jewish life underwent a radical change in this period, but he seems not to have assessed the extent to which the regulations were not instituted.

the modern mould but did little to facilitate this transformation. Economically, the region was in stagnation. The cancellation of some Jewish limitations was not accompanied by the demand that Jews should abandon their social separateness. Consequently, Prussian Polish Jews did not experience significant social and political modernization for quite some time. The Jews of Prussian Poland, unlike their co-religionists in the more dynamic urban centres further west, did not feel constrained to demonstrate their patriotism, apologize for Jewish separatism, or deny their messianic hopes. Rabbis continued to emphasize that the Jews were a people apart, fated, until the messiah came, to live under the control of Christians in foreign lands. It seemed to matter little that Prussian rulers had replaced the Poles. There was some ambivalence towards the Prussians: the Poles had given Jews more freedom than the more invasive and paternalistic Prussians, but the latter were more successful at ensuring civil tranquillity.[22] Nor was there anything in the environment to foster Jewish identity with the Poles as fellow victims of Prussian domination.[23] The fundamental self-concept of Jewish national subjugation was not altered. Few Jews paid much attention to the elusive promise of emancipation. Liberation, to them, still meant the Jewish return to Zion in the manner depicted by the prophets Isaiah and Ezekiel.

EDUCATION

Although the Prussian state already ruled Lissa when Kalischer was born, Polish Jewish culture shaped his education and upbringing. Jewish communal leaders there and in the surrounding communities obstinately resisted the half-hearted government efforts to reform their schools, and it took many years to see the Prussian imprint on Jewish education.[24]

[22] As they had done in the past, the Jews offered communal prayers and staged ceremonies welcoming and pledging allegiance to their new rulers. Lewin, *Geschichte der Juden in Lissa*, 159, describes how the Jews of Lissa had to go through new bureaucratic procedures that were at best a nuisance and at worst a humiliation. Yet Hagen, *Germans, Poles, and Jews*, 66–7, shows evidence of the Jews' increased satisfaction with the Prussians, as more fair and even-handed than the previous Polish lords.

[23] This conception appeared decades later, in the 1860s, in select circles of the Jewish bourgeoisie and assimilated Jewish youth, and should not be attributed to any time earlier. See Magdalena Opalski and Israel Bartal, *Poles and Jews: A Failed Brotherhood* (Hanover, NH and London, 1992), 15–18.

[24] Eliav, *Jewish Education in Germany*, 326, describes the Posen region as 'the bastion of Jewish piety in Germany during the first half of the nineteenth century, [and] there was no other place in Germany in which there was as stubborn and prolonged a struggle against the penetration of education informed by the spirit of Enlightenment and reform'.

The boy's early education was probably a more intensive or accelerated version of the norm. He would have been sent at the age of 5 to a *ḥeder*, which provided elementary education for boys conducted in the teacher's home. The curriculum typically consisted of learning some basic arithmetic, reading and writing Hebrew and Yiddish, mastering the prayers and synagogue service, and then studying the Torah—this meant the Pentateuch, considered God's written revelation, accompanied by the medieval commentary by Rashi. The curriculum in Lissa, somewhat unusually for the region, included some German language instruction.[25] In the later years of *ḥeder* study, the focus would turn to the study of Torah in its broader definition—rabbinic legal literature such as the Mishnah and the Talmud, which was regarded as the explication of God's oral revelation. Boys would attend *ḥeder* until the age of 13. At this point their parents sent them to work or, if they could spare their sons' labour, enrolled them in a yeshiva. A particularly bright child like Tsevi Hirsch would probably enter a yeshiva after two or three years of elementary Talmud studies.

Yeshiva learning consisted exclusively of the Talmud, talmudic commentaries, and codes of law. The yeshiva year was divided between private study and formal study under the supervision of the *rosh yeshivah* and his advanced students. Students would also sit with their principal at the synagogue and accompany him to fairs on market days, a common meeting spot for rabbis and communal leaders. A favoured student might serve as the principal's secretary when he prepared his written responses to halakhic queries. These documents, the authoritative judgements of rabbis in response to specific cases, comprise an important genre of rabbinic literature, called responsa. A single responsum consists of the question asked; the responder's presentation of a multitude of options; rebuttal of all positions but the most defensible stance; presentation of a wide array of proof texts and supporting precedents from venerated rabbinical scholars and sacred texts; and a firm conclusion. Yeshiva students would be particularly interested in seeing how their teacher applied his knowledge of Torah to the pressing and novel issues of the day.[26]

---

[25] Lewin, *Geschichte der Juden in Lissa*, 118–19, notes that only Lissa and Posen schools included German instruction in the elementary curriculum. This practice was in place even during the Polish Commonwealth, before Prussia's state-supported movement for Jewish educational reform. Posen and Lissa Jews prided themselves on their great scholarly achievements, and they may have felt that knowledge of German would serve as an enhancement and not a detraction. The level of proficiency that was commonly attained has not been established, but Lewin is of the impression that it was quite low. According to Eliav, *Jewish Education in Germany*, 138, Polish was taught in the Jewish schools as well.

[26] The formal study time was limited to a term of just over three months in late spring and summer, and then another term of just over two months in the winter. Most of these days were spent with other students preparing sections of text, perhaps with the assistance of the advanced students, after which the *rosh yeshivah* would present a lecture on the material and explain diffi-

Tsevi Hirsch's parents prepared him to become a member of the Jewish intellectual elite. His education was put in the hands of the most respected scholars in the region. He probably learned from his uncle Judah Leib, a highly respected scholar who had been for decades the head of Lissa's yeshiva and rabbinic court. He attended the yeshiva of Jacob Lorbeerbaum, a great halakhist who had arrived in 1809 to fill the vacant rabbinic seat of Lissa. In 1815 Akiva Eger moved to nearby Posen when the community engaged him as chief rabbi. He became connected with the Kalischer family through marriage when Judah Leib married one of his sons to Eger's daughter.[27] Eger was also a dear friend of Lorbeerbaum and had lived in Lissa for a time. Most important, he was considered the supreme talmudic scholar of his time. Studying with him was both a great opportunity and a privilege, and Tsevi Hirsch moved to Posen to be his student.

We have no record of the boy's experiences in the three yeshivas he attended. The only surviving correspondence with his teachers after his departure from the yeshiva is the exchange of letters with Eger from the late 1830s. It is not surprising that few details of Kalischer's personal life are available to us. In pre-modern Jewish society, the meaning of one's life was found in collective structures, myths, and experiences. Basic personal facts—for example, the date of marriage or births of children, the location of the workplace, the social landscape—were not considered essential. Personal information was preserved only if it would be useful for transmitting to children or followers a commitment to communal values such as piety, dedication to community, and scholarship.[28] Particularly important for a rabbi's legacy were details that affirmed

cult passages. My description of traditional Ashkenazi education is based primarily on Jacob Katz, *Tradition and Crisis: Jewish Society at the End of the Middle Ages*, 2nd edn., trans. B. D. Cooperman (New York, 1993), 156–69.

[27] The following illustrates both how family networks were created and what traditional rabbinic authorities considered noteworthy in a family history. Bromberg, a biographer who shares traditional rabbinic values, explains in *Rabbi Tsevi Hirsch Kalischer*, 135 n. 5, that Akiva Eger's daughter Sarah, and Judah Leib's son Abraham Moshe, who died in 1812, bore a daughter named Radish. After the groom's early death, however, Eger arranged for Sarah's second marriage to the great talmudist of Lemberg, Moses Sofer. Radish was apparently raised by her mother and Moses Sofer. She was known as a quite learned woman, and her parents married her to Rabbi Joseph Schlesinger, the founder of a book-publishing company in Vienna that later published the works of Moses Sofer.

[28] According to Alan Mintz, *Banished from their Father's Table: Loss of Faith and Hebrew Autobiography* (Bloomington, Ind., 1989), 20 and 206, only when a society accepts 'the value of individual experience in its individuality' will it preserve the personal data that is the stuff of biography. Charismatic leaders require additional documentation testifying to their individual magnetism and powers, thus justifying widespread submission to the leader's authority. Kalischer was beloved, but not a charismatic leader.

his rabbinic authority; this included the names of his teachers, where he studied, the rabbis who praised him and approved his writings, the rabbis with
whom he exchanged halakhic opinions, rabbinic positions he was offered, and
the kinship ties to rabbinic scholars. Such information describes an almost
entirely male universe. Even the family tree often excluded women, since
women were not directly occupied with rabbinic scholarship and could not
confer rabbinic prestige. (Though the daughters of great rabbis might be included since their father's authority would devolve on their spouses.) Because
Kalischer nearly always moved within traditional society, neither he nor his
colleagues penned detailed accounts of his life. What little we know has to be
deduced from their correspondence and their scholarly writings.

Kalischer's narrow and specialized education was not unusual in pre-
modern central European Jewish society, where Jewish cultural separatism
remained strong. Secular subjects were hardly included in the formal Jewish
school curriculum; they had to be learnt informally, as part of work appren-
ticeship, or from a private tutor. The lack of regard for them is indicated by
the fact that they were considered appropriate for girls, for whom Jewish tradition neither required nor encouraged Talmud study. During the time of Tsevi
Hirsch's childhood, wealthier parents who did not need their daughters'
labour might hire a tutor to teach them languages and music. But the Jews of
this region, like the Poles and Germans among whom they lived, generally
regarded their neighbours' culture with scorn. While Jews may have considered some knowledge of German useful, their rabbis forbade them to read
'foreign' literature and consequently there were few Jews fluent in the language. Tsevi Hirsch, for example, despite the German instruction he may
have received in elementary school, wrote his personal correspondence in
Yiddish or, less often, German in Hebrew characters. His German essays were
translated by others from the original Hebrew.[29] Though non-Jewish in-

---

[29] For example, Kalischer's essay 'Maimonides und sein neuern Gegner' was translated by
the editor, Isaac Marcus Jost. According to Lewin, *Geschichte der Juden in Lissa*, 119, in 1796
only two of the seven *parnasim* of Lissa knew how to write German (but by 1833 almost all 602
family heads could do so). In the front of volume vi of the English edition of Heinrich Graetz,
History of the Jews, 6 vols. (Philadelphia, 1898), 5–15, is a memoir of the author's life compiled
by Dr Philipp Bloch from Graetz's diary and writings. He testifies to the suspicion in which
German books were held in the Posen region. In one town in which Graetz's family lived,
Zerków, there were about 800 inhabitants in 1817, and only one of them could read German.
When a German letter was received in the town, all assembled around this person, who would
read the letter on the open street in public. He reported that reading German was considered so
sinful that any rabbi in the Posen district who could read it was the object of rumours. Graetz
reported that Rabbi Samwel (*sic*) Munk of Wollstein was in the habit of reading German books
and journals, but 'in the hours that are "neither day nor night"'. Graetz's 'enlightened' refusal to
participate in the family's *kapores* ceremony (in which one's sins are symbolically attributed to a

fluences are obvious in Jewish customs and literature, they were certainly not perceived by the Jews as being of outside origin.

The education of Jewish boys was designed to perpetuate religious values and behaviour, rather than to prepare for earning a livelihood. The *ḥeder* introduced boys to communal expectations and provided them with the fundamental skills necessary for participation in the religious life of the community. At the next level, the yeshiva provided Jewish society with the means to reach its ultimate goal: the rearing of scholars. In Ashkenazi Jewish society, the highest ideal for a male was to be a talmudic scholar. He might have to earn his livelihood through business or a craft, since the community could afford to support only a few non-income-producing scholars, but he was expected to make Torah study a regular habit. Women had a different role to play: since Jewish tradition neither required nor encouraged them to study Torah, none of these schools included them. The highest ideal for a woman was to marry a scholar and raise children to Torah.

To some extent a yeshiva education served a practical purpose, in that it was used for those boys who wanted to enter the communal rabbinate. But it was not designed with this in mind; indeed there was often little connection between the curriculum and the actual halakhic problems faced by rabbis. Yeshiva students divided their time between the study of theoretical law and the study of halakhah as it applied to practical problems. They were inculcated, in the process, with some feelings of the tension that existed within the life of the Jewish intellectual elite: the highly trained scholar by necessity dealt with practical halakhic problems presented by his community, but he longed for more opportunity to study theoretical law. Of course he wanted to guide the Jewish community in the ways of the Torah, but the determination of theoretical law was less fettered by the hard facts of reality—it was Torah in its purest form. The more arcane the subject, the more incisively could logic and analysis be applied to it, and the more the scholar's abstract halakhic creativity resembled God's unrestrained creative powers.

It was not unusual for scholars intent on exhibiting their halakhic dexterity and pious love of Torah 'for its own sake' to devote whole works or chapters of their books to detailed study of the sacrificial laws. The most erudite would reconstruct the ancient service as it had been, or pose halakhic problems and offer solutions for the restoration of the cult.[30] Kalischer would have been

chicken, which is then swung around the room) led to his father's threat to burn all the non-Hebrew books found in his son's possession. The German edition of Graetz's diary that is currently available excludes these anecdotes as, apparently, too unflattering to Graetz's past. I thank Steven M. Lowenstein for drawing this source to my attention.

[30] For a listing of a number of these works from the 17th to 20th cc., see Joseph B. Soloveitchik, *Halakhic Man*, trans. Lawrence Kaplan (Philadelphia, 1983), 147–8 n. 27.

exposed to this literature when he was a student. This scholarship was often described as a fulfilment of Hosea 14: 3, 'we offer the bullocks of our lips'. That is, the study of the sacrifices was to be understood as a substitute for the sacrificial ritual, the highest form of divine worship, which, because of their many sins, God denied to the Jews during the era of exile. These scholars did not necessarily pore over the sacrificial laws with the hope that they would be applied in the near future, although (as would be the case with Kalischer) some certainly had this in mind. However, scholarly preoccupation with the sacrifices did reinforce the messianic longing that was part of exilic Judaism. By focusing on laws that were in abeyance, rather than ignoring them or declaring them eternally nullified, scholars were affirming that these were also part of the Torah. They were indicating that their own historical period was a temporary aberration marked by its privations, and some day, at the time of Israel's redemption, the wholeness of the Torah would be restored. They believed that during the messianic age the ideal image of reality found in their intricate halakhic reconstructions would become manifest in the empirical world.[31] Studying the sacrificial commandments, the consummate Torah 'for its own sake', was thus a foretaste of the messianic era and would hasten the arrival of those glorious days.

The exclusive focus on talmudic education was not easy to maintain. The prolonged and gender-stratified instruction depended on the largesse of relatives and the community at large. Yeshiva education did not have a term limitation; with the consent of the principal of the yeshiva, students could remain for many years. When the yeshiva was not in one's own town, as when Tsevi Hirsch studied with Eger in Posen, living expenses were greater. The usual arrangement was that individual families in the host community provided food and lodging for the students. Each community established charitable societies whose task was to raise funds to help pay these expenses and the costs of maintaining the educational institutions. These funds were often insufficient, and in those cases, staying in the yeshiva was contingent on the financial support of the student's family or the parents of his wife or betrothed. By about the age of 15, however, most boys left the yeshiva to work for their families.[32] Those students who wanted to enter rabbinic positions would stay beyond this point and learn enough to receive certification from the *rosh yeshivah*.[33]

[31] For a beautifully and powerfully written description of this mentality, see Soloveitchik, *Halakhic Man*, 23–9. Although Soloveitchik focuses on the world of his Lithuanian ancestors, he argues that this ethos applies also to the halakhic enterprise elsewhere.

[32] Eliav, *Jewish Education in Germany*, 326–7, maintains that most boys stayed at the yeshiva until the age of 13.

[33] According to Katz, *Tradition and Crisis*, 167–8, the type of certification was determined by

A gradual but noticeable change occurred in Lissa and Posen during the years Kalischer was at school, roughly 1803–18. The number of Torah scholars declined considerably, and Kalischer's teachers Jacob Lorbeerbaum and Akiva Eger, chief rabbis of Lissa and Posen, experienced strained relations with the *parnasim* of their towns. These problems, however, were not a function of religious dissent; the Jewish communities of the Posen region remained steadfast in their loyalty to traditional forms of Jewish practice. Rather, tension between the rabbinate and the community was a product of the impoverishment of the region that came with the disintegration of the Polish Commonwealth, and it was exacerbated by the transfer to Prussian rule. The Jews were less able to sustain the normally heavy expenses of rabbinic scholarship. Even elementary school tuition was too burdensome for a sizeable minority of parents, and their children remained unschooled.[34] Rabbis Lorbeerbaum and Eger were directly affected by the changing communal priorities: they needed salaries, a flow of students into their yeshivas, provisions for their disciples, maintenance of study houses, and so on. They also knew that the decline of rabbinic culture would make it harder to sustain traditional Judaism. Indeed, while the rabbis described their flock as pious Jews, they complained that their communities were growing indifferent towards Torah study. Frustrated, they did not know how to remedy the situation. They utilized their forebears' polemical tactics, but as these were designed only to quell dissent, they were of limited value.

Kalischer did not witness all these conflicts directly; he had already left his teachers' yeshivas when the more serious ones occurred. Yet even then it is certain that he kept his eyes on his teachers' battles. Not only did they concern his former homes: the yeshiva fostered crucial social bonds between men. Students made lasting friendships with each other and established connections that they would later make use of when seeking professional advice or halakhic consultation, or making wedding matches. A strong network of communication and mutual support was maintained between students during and after the yeshiva years, and between students and teachers. Kalischer first met Elijah Guttmacher at Lorbeerbaum's yeshiva, and they both then went to Eger's yeshiva, becoming lifelong friends and collaborators.[35] A personal link and often a deep sense of loyalty were made between students and the *rosh*

the extent of their knowledge, the number of years of their study, and their married status. The community often stipulated the prerequisites for certification.

[34] *Eliav, Jewish Education in Germany*, 326 n. 74, quotes a study finding that in 1816 17.3 per cent of school-age children in Posen were not attending school. We can presume that this was largely due to poverty.

[35] According to Lewin, *Geschichte der Juden in Lissa*, 208, Guttmacher was also one of Lorbeerbaum's students in Lissa.

yeshivah, even though the actual time spent with him was minimal. Gutt-macher, who was especially close to Eger, wrote to Kalischer after Eger's death, 'we are bound to our rabbi, may his memory be blessed, just as [we are bound] to a Torah scroll'.[36] Kalischer often referred to himself as Eger's student, but it appears that Jacob Lorbeerbaum was the seminal influence on his thinking.[37]

The first serious indications of strain in the dominance of rabbinic culture was the difficulty of maintaining a chief rabbi in Lissa and Posen. This post was not indispensable to a learned community, but the chief rabbi could provide a clear hierarchy of leadership, attract students, and bring prestige to the city. The Jewish community in Lissa suffered from the disorder of the eighteenth-century Polish Commonwealth, as well as the centralizing reforms instituted by the failing regime. With the suppression of the regional Jewish councils, Lissa lost the prestige and business that had accompanied its post as the Jewish capital of the province. In 1767 a fire left virtually all its Jewish families homeless. The Jewish quarter was rebuilt, but another equally destructive fire in 1790 was not so easily overcome. Many residents joined the thousands of other western Polish Jews emigrating to the east and south-east. Lissa's Jews became poorer, and the community's financial distress prevented any serious investment in the advancement of talmudic scholarship. When the communal rabbi died in 1792, the trustees decided that they lacked sufficient funds to engage a new one. Lissa did not fill its rabbinic post for seventeen years, until Jacob Lorbeerbaum was appointed in 1809. Despite the absence of a chief rabbi, the city was full of learned men at all class levels; upon Lorbeerbaum's arrival, he marvelled at the large number of Talmud scholars who lived there.[38] Tsevi Hirsch was one such young man. Already well versed in talmudic studies

---

[36] Abraham Isaac Bromberg, *Rabbi Elijah Guttmacher* (Heb.) (Jerusalem, 1969), 6.

[37] It was to Kalischer's advantage to refer to himself as Eger's rather than Lorbeerbaum's student: Eger's name carried more weight among the regional rabbinate, as his son was the rabbi of Posen after his father. Yet Kalischer had greater ideological affinity with Lorbeerbaum. Bromberg, *Rabbi Tsevi Hirsch Kalischer*, 14, supports this conclusion, based on Kalischer's very frequent references to Lorbeerbaum in his *Moznayim lamishpat* and commentary on the Mishnah.

[38] Abraham Isaac Bromberg, *Rabbi Jacob Lorbeerbaum* (Heb.) (Jerusalem, 1957), 24–5, repeats an anecdote about Lissa and Lorbeerbaum that illustrates this. It was a custom, when the newly appointed rabbi first arrived in the city, for the learned men to meet him just outside the city limits, discuss Torah and exchange *pilpul* (halakhic disputation) with him, and accompany him the rest of the way. Among the men who went out to meet Lorbeerbaum was a seller of tar, a trade considered rather low-class. When the tar seller began to exchange *pilpul* with Lorbeerbaum at a very sophisticated level, the rabbi got back into his carriage and ordered the driver to return him to his former abode. The men from Lissa asked him what was wrong. Lorbeerbaum told them that if Lissa had so many scholars that even simple tar sellers were great scholars, then there was no need for him. They reassured him that this man was exceptional among his

when Lorbeerbaum arrived, the teenager continued his studies at the chief rabbi's yeshiva.

Yet the deleterious effect of the region's poverty figured prominently in Lorbeerbaum's eventual dissatisfaction with Lissa. In 1818 he complained that the number of Talmud scholars had decreased significantly since he had arrived. He was upset that parents were no longer interested in supporting yeshiva students or marrying their daughters to Talmud scholars. According to him, this situation was the result of a failure of generosity. He claimed that Jews stopped giving to communal charities, and consequently God responded in kind and 'ceased shedding his mercy on earth'. A dearth of surplus funds, in other words, should be met by an increase in charitable donations. But the opposite behaviour caused God to decree the increase of taxes and the drying up of livelihoods. Clearly, Lorbeerbaum was not entranced by rational analysis, and he warned Lissa's Jews not to seek a solution in scepticism. The real solution, he counselled, was to return to God by giving generously again, and then God would grant better conditions for all.[39]

Apparently, the Jews of Lissa were not convinced by this logic. Lorbeerbaum, whose lack of business acumen was renowned, was arguing on the level of religious principles, while his flock was thinking in very concrete terms. He finally left in 1821. The rabbinic position in Lissa remained vacant until 1864, when the economic health of the region improved sufficiently to warrant engaging a rabbi.[40]

Posen had similar problems. When the chief rabbi died in 1806, the weak economy prevented the community from filling the post. In 1814 Akiva Eger, by then considered a great talmudist, let it be known that he wanted to leave his present position for a town of scholars that had sufficient students and support for his yeshiva. The leaders of Posen offered him the position, but a number of influential members of the community lodged a protest, and he was appointed only after a number of stipulations were made: he could accept no

peers, and Lorbeerbaum agreed to stay. Lewin, *Geschichte der Juden in Lissa*, 207, cites evidence from the communal records that more than a thousand students attended Lorbeerbaum's classes.

[39] A central principle of kabbalah is the causal influence of earthly behaviour on the Godhead. This notion was central to the messianism of Kalischer and Guttmacher, and will be discussed below. These complaints were made in his eulogies of rabbis Azriel Halevi Hurvitz, David Landau Pollak, and Abraham Tiktin from the year 1818. They can be found in Lorbeerbaum's *Naḥalat ya'akov* (Breslau, 1849), 36*b*–39*a* (and not in *Emet leya'akov*, as Bromberg, *Rabbi Jacob Lorbeerbaum*, 34, notes).

[40] The office holders of Lissa's rabbinic seat are listed in *JE*, s.v. 'Lissa', by Samuel Baeck (viii. 107–8). Other reasons for Lorbeerbaum's displeasure with Lissa are discussed below; see also Ch. 1 for his disdain for the religious policies of Germany's rulers.

more than six out-of-town yeshiva students; he could grant the highest rabbinic certification (the title *morenu*) only to married scholars; and he could not
issue public reprimands, but was restricted to swaying the community's
morals through positive references to virtuous behaviour.[41] While these conditions appear to be a rebellion against rabbinic authority, they were more likely
an expression of the region's economic distress.[42] The first stipulation, setting
a small number of yeshiva students, was meant to limit the expenditure of the
Jewish householders who customarily bore the expense of boarding yeshiva
students. The limitation of rabbinic certification to married scholars was an
attempt to correct an abuse that had crept into the rabbinic profession, since
marriage had long been a prerequisite for certification. Economic hardship,
most probably, had led to the premature certification of rabbis, for it was cost-
ly to finance the many years of yeshiva study, and the region's poverty was a
factor in the delay of marriage and the increase in bachelor yeshiva students.[43]
Economic and religious issues were intertwined, and together they present a
picture of a weakening in the rabbinic culture that had been the region's pride.
The cumulative effect of poverty had a corollary effect on religious values; that
is, when communities cannot invest in institutions that perpetuate talmudic
learning, it is not long before their appreciation for it decreases. At such times,
it was not unusual for the impractical character of Jewish education to come

[41] The reports from Eger's supporters indicate that the dissenters were sympathetic to modern values and objected to Eger because he was not. Yet this data is neither reliable nor fully
explanatory. The depth of respect for traditional values on both sides is evident from the fact
that the conflicting parties agreed upon Lorbeerbaum, who was anything but modern, as the
mediator. He helped them draw up a compromise contract that imposed the three limitations on
the new rabbi. See A. Heppner and J. Herzberg, *Aus Vergangenheit und Gegenwart der Juden und
der jüdischen Gemeinden in den Posener Ländern*, 2 vols. (Koschmin, 1909), ii. 813–16.

[42] These stipulations must be interpreted against the background of the economic situation in
the eastern territories. The region's Jews still owed payments on debts incurred during the last
years of the Polish Commonwealth, and they were hurt by the economic policies of the new
Prussian region. There was some relief from these measures during the interlude (1806–15) in
which Lissa and Posen were part of the Napoleonic Duchy of Warsaw—which may have been a
factor in the decisions to engage rabbis. It was not a healthy economy, however, and not unusual
that more circumspect members of the community were reluctant to engage a rabbi. What typically occurred during bad spells was that communities ceased appointing new communal rabbis
or opening new yeshivas, and students and teachers abandoned their studies, temporarily or per-
manently, and turned to income-producing work. On the economic problems of this period, see
Hagen, *Germans, Poles, and Jews*, 54. Only landlords benefited in this period, as grain exports
through Danzig were allowed.

[43] Lowenstein, 'Voluntary and Involuntary Limitation of Fertility in Nineteenth-Century
Bavarian Jewry', in his *Mechanics of Change*, 65–84, shows the later age of marriage across all
professions within Bavarian Jewry, and I surmise that this can be generalized to the Posen situation.

under attack, or for there to be irritation with rabbinic paternalism, as reflected in the stipulation limiting the rabbi's role in rebuking congregants.[44] Thus opposition to an ambitious chief rabbi like Eger may have been initiated by traditionally pious Jews.

There were, however, some Jews in Posen influenced by the enlightened Jews of Berlin. They were a thorn in Eger's side despite their minuscule influence over the Jews of the city. The focus of their activity was Jewish elementary education. The vast majority of Jewish elementary schools in Posen were of the traditional type, and they operated to Eger's liking. Shortly after he was engaged as chief rabbi in 1815, however, one of Wessely's more radical disciples, David Caro, established a new sort of Jewish elementary school in the town. German was the language of instruction and secular studies comprised most of the curriculum. Its goal was to prepare children for entrance to the non-Jewish secondary schools. Thus more than three decades after Wessely's education proposal, a school inspired by it finally appeared in Posen. Unlike Tevele, Eger did not mount a campaign throughout the land against the innovation. Perhaps he hesitated to fight the school because he was too new and still on shaky ground after his contract dispute. He presumably railed against it to his students, Kalischer among them. His public opposition, however, took the form of repeated and futile requests to Prussian officials to close the school because it was operating without his permission.[45]

[44] The insistence that the rabbi should not rebuke the members of the community was not entirely unprecedented, as Ismar Schorsch seems to imply in his 'Emancipation and the Crisis of Religious Authority: The Emergence of the Modern Rabbinate', in Werner E. Mosse, Arnold Paucker, and Reinhard Rürup (eds.), *Revolution and Evolution: 1848 in Jewish History* (Tübingen, 1981), 208–9. Moses Sofer heard the same request, although it was embedded in a contract dispute, from the wealthy merchants of Pressburg in 1806, who claimed that local custom had never given the rabbi of the city licence to supervise the normal (as opposed to religious) activities of the members of the community; see Katz, 'Towards a Biography of the Hatam Sofer', 247–8. It seems entirely plausible, given the not infrequent conflicts between Polish Jewish yeshiva scholars and the communally appointed rabbis and *their* leaders, that even late medieval Polish communities had insisted upon this provision. The most obvious evidence for the economic (and not religious) basis of the contract dispute seems to be the long-standing and widespread support that Eger did receive from Posen.

[45] On the school's founder, see Robert L. Katz, 'David Caro's Analysis of the Rabbi's Role', *CCAR Journal*, 13/2 (1966), 41–6. The controversy over the school is described in Heppner and Herzberg, *Aus Vergangenheit und Gegenwart*, ii. 823, and Eliav, *Jewish Education in Germany*, 326. Eliav implies that Eger lacked sufficient support for his effort to close the school. He bases his view on a petition to the government in 1816 by two of Posen's trustees, in which they request the government to support proper education for poor Jews (the assumption was that rich Jews were not dependent on community schools for the proper education of their children).

MARRIAGE AND EARNING A LIVELIHOOD

The Kalischer family respected and perpetuated traditional intellectual and religious values with zeal, at least in the case of their son Tsevi Hirsch. He was allowed to devote himself entirely to study and to pay no attention whatsoever to acquiring business skills. When he left Eger's yeshiva in 1818 he rejoined his parents' household.[46] They had moved to Thorn (now Toruń), a town about fifty miles north-west of Lissa that was also in Prussian territory. Within a couple of years, his parents had arranged a marriage suitable for their scholarly son. They found a couple who agreed to the prospect of a son-in-law who would not earn a living for their daughter.

Kalischer's devotion to study was unusual but not without precedent. In the vast majority of cases, a man like him would accept a position as a communal rabbi. Salaried by the community, he would serve as the *posek* (halakhic authority), be a judge in the court, act as principal of a yeshiva, perhaps represent the *kahal* at meetings with government officials, or teach a special class for adult males. This work required the rabbi to devote himself to the study of practical halakhah, and it was likely to include as well some time dealing with the *parnasim*, the leaders of the *kahal*. An unsalaried scholar was freer to determine his own balance between communal service and Torah study; nevertheless, a communal position still allowed a fair amount of time for the latter. Some highly educated families in the region dealt with the tension between Torah study and earning a livelihood by having the men alternate periods of study and unpaid teaching with periods of engagement in trade. Kalischer, however, did not compromise; he wanted to be a full-time scholar, and though he accepted some communal rabbinic duties, he had no intention of earning money from them. This principled stance would, later, lead directly to his promotion of Jewish agricultural communes in Palestine.

Rabbi Kalischer's refusal to take a salary was based, in part, on the ancient rabbinic warning against making the Torah 'a spade for digging'. This was an ideological stance that was motivated by a fear of exploiting the Torah for personal gain or a desire to avoid corrupting halakhic authorities facing communal pressures. It was a principle honoured more in the breach than the observance and not mandated by Jewish law, since such a restriction would soon lead to the end of scholarship for all but the independently wealthy.

---

[46] Kalischer's commentary on the Mishnah is dated '1818 Thorn'. Bromberg, *Rabbi Tsevi Hirsch Kalischer*, 14, suggests that he spent the week studying in Posen and commuted to Thorn to spend the sabbath with his wife. This opinion, which has been widely repeated, must be modified in the light of the archival data presented below. (At any rate, the 50-mile trip between Thorn and Posen was not that easily accomplished.)

Remuneration had always been widely accepted, and although one could find halakhic opinions stating that earning from the Torah was sinful, the practice of awarding salaries was firmly established and supported by the rabbinate. Indeed, by the late Middle Ages in Poland and Lithuania, the chief *posekim* effectively overturned the earlier ideal by insisting that refusal to accept payment was behaviour that 'shamed' the Torah.[47] Nevertheless, fulfilling rabbinic duties without pay was still regarded by many rabbis, and especially by the lay population—which was more inclined to resent rabbinic privilege—as a mark of great piety.

Family tradition, as well, taught Tsevi Hirsch that not earning income from Torah knowledge was a principle to be cherished. His uncle Judah Leib had never taken a salary from the Lissa *kahal* during his fifty years of service. He relied for sustenance on the labour of his first and then his second wife—dependence on one's wife and family was not considered a violation of the purist stance—and he acknowledged their generosity and piety in the introduction to his magnum opus, *Hayad haḥazakah*.[48] Kalischer's teachers also preached the virtues of financial independence from the community. Jacob Lorbeerbaum tried desperately, and unsuccessfully, to avoid paid communal service. He married several times, but none of his wives could adequately support the family. Early on, Lorbeerbaum took up trade in order to avoid accepting pay from the community. However, the discrepancy between standard business practices and rabbinic monetary laws greatly disturbed him. He quickly failed as a businessman and had to resort to taking a communal post. Lorbeerbaum's fame as a scholar grew and enabled him to move to a more prestigious position, but he was not happy about being in the public eye; he published his magnum opus, *Ḥavat da'at*, anonymously. When his authorship of this highly respected work became known, he was offered and accepted the rabbinic seat of Lissa. This, too, eventually soured for him and he left Lissa. He left his next post, too, after quarrelling with the communal leaders. Although there were varied reports of the reasons for his departures, it is clear that he chafed at the need to answer to the *parnasim*.[49] Kalischer did not

---

[47] The rabbinic warning appears in Mishnah *Avot* 4: 5. For a historical discussion of its application, see Yeshayahu Leibovitz, *Discussions on* Pirkei avot *and Maimonides* (Heb.) (Tel Aviv, 1979), 18 ff., esp. 33, where he describes the pro-payment opinions of *Magen avraham* and Shabetai ben Me'ir Hakohen.

[48] Bromberg, *Rabbi Tsevi Hirsch Kalischer*, 12–13, quotes at length from this introduction.

[49] Rumours include the disapproval in Lissa of his multiple divorces, and the overabundance of 'heretics' in the city who made his life miserable. Bromberg, *Rabbi Jacob Lorbeerbaum*, 48–52, quotes and reviews a number of contemporary testimonies and concludes that Lorbeerbaum left in 1821 simply because he was tired of the opposition he faced from the more liberal wing of Lissa's community. This conclusion seems historically problematic and lacks appreciation of

observe Lorbeerbaum's departure from Lissa first-hand, as he had already moved to Thorn, but there is no doubt that he knew of Lorbeerbaum's disdain for the institution of the salaried rabbi.

Akiva Eger shared this ideal as well, and he, too, had difficulty finding satisfactory financial support. As a young man, his prodigious knowledge of Talmud made him an attractive marriage prospect. He was matched to the daughter of a wealthy scholar in Lissa who supported the entire family for more than a decade while Eger studied and taught. When the Lissa fire of 1790 put an end to his father-in-law's beneficence, Eger had to accept a rabbinic position elsewhere. It was no secret, however, that he was repelled by the practice of earning money from Torah and aspired to be independent of communal support. This was not his fate, and in 1815 he accepted a position in Posen, where he served with a great measure of dissatisfaction until his death in 1837.[50] Certainly both Lorbeerbaum's and Eger's displeasure stemmed from the changing conditions of Jewish communal life, but these problems merely strengthened their idealistic stance towards Torah study. These teachers, like Kalischer's uncle Judah Leib, bequeathed to Kalischer the belief that a scholar who earned money from his learning, even in the most pious of communities, was sullying the Torah.

By the time Tsevi Hirsch became an adult, it was quite unusual in Polish Prussia for a scholar to find a woman and her parents who would help her husband uphold such a lofty, or old-fashioned, ideal for more than a few years. (Had it been more common, a renowned rabbi like Lorbeerbaum would have found such a match when he remarried.) This situation explains why Tsevi Hirsch, who had a sterling reputation as a brilliant scholar from a good family, did not marry into another rabbinic dynasty and move to a well-endowed Jewish community.

Kalischer's wife Gittel, about whom we are woefully ignorant, was from a family in Nishava (Nieszawa), a town on the River Vistula south of Thorn. That her parents agreed to such a son-in-law indicates that they were distinguished for both their piety and their prosperity. The couple married in 1820, when Gittel was 18 and Tsevi Hirsch 25, and they alternated living with both sets of parents for the next three years. However, the couple could not depend on their parents to support their family. They moved back to Thorn and Gittel

Lorbeerbaum's idiosyncrasies. It is significant that he moved to Kalisch, a more insular, less demanding Jewish community than Lissa, and he left there eight years later, after quarrelling with the town's *parnasim*; see *EJ* s.v. 'Lorbeerbaum, Jacob ben Jacob Moses of Lissa', author E.K.

[50] 'Eger, Akiva ben Moses Guens', *EJ* vi. 469, author A.P./ED. His experience in Posen will be discussed below.

entered business. The family was poor for quite some time, and no wonder: Tsevi Hirsch did not earn a living, and Gittel gave birth to fourteen children in twenty-seven years.[51] She was certainly a rare find: it was hard enough for a woman to support her husband and family during difficult economic times, but it required real mettle to do so when other able-bodied husbands generally earned a livelihood, and when lucrative positions were available to her husband. This is how Tsevi Hirsch described her in the introduction to his major work, *Moznayim lamishpat*, in 1855:

I bless the Lord, may he be praised, who gave me counsel, and who also gave me a help-meet, my wife the righteous mistress Gittel, may she live a long life, who never grieved me by saying, 'Go out and enter trade, so we may acquire fortunes and riches'. She never spoke thus to me, but she exerted herself in the business of buying and selling, and the work of her hands allowed me to be free from everyday burdens in order to busy myself with Torah.[52]

A pious Jew like Gittel would have considered it a tremendous spiritual attainment to be credited with her husband's Torah scholarship.

The size and character of Thorn probably dissuaded many aspiring rabbis from settling there. Unlike Lissa and Posen, Thorn was a relatively new and weak Jewish community. It was just across the northern border of the province of Great Poland. Thorn was an extremely old city which for centuries had

[51] I am most grateful to Zenon Hubert Nowak, who shared with me this data from his research in the Toruń archives (Archiwum Panstwowe w Toruniu). Based on the belief that yeshiva boys were routinely married at the age prescribed in the Mishnah to the even younger daughters of wealthy parents, Bromberg assumed that Kalischer married at the age of 18 and that he moved to Thorn in order to marry the daughter of a local wealthy family. However, the archival documents, as well as Kalischer's reference to the betrothal of his daughter in 1872 (when she was in her mid- to late twenties), support Steven M. Lowenstein's argument that a later marriage age was far more common, and teenage marriages were merely a stereotype; see his *Mechanics of Change*, 65–84. Furthermore, Kalischer's later marriage supports my description above of the waning Torah culture in the region, a situation that had the effect of making it difficult for dedicated scholars like Kalischer to find partners.

Gittel's age at marriage was stated in one of the petitions in the Thorn archives, where she is referred to by her German name Jette (from Henriette) Cohn, the daughter of Jacob Cohn, making her only seven years her husband's junior. This contradicts the testimony of Tsevi Hirsch's friend Fabianus Mieses, who wrote in Kalischer's death announcement that Gittel was nine years his junior (*Hamagid*, 41 (1874), 364). A general carelessness towards birth dates prevailed in traditional Jewish culture, especially with regard to women (Kalischer's Hebrew birth date was preserved by his family). According to the Jewish community's records in the Thorn archives, Gittel bore fourteen children, at least two of whom died in infancy; her first was born in 1821 when she was 19, and her last was born in 1853 when she was 46.

[52] From the introduction to vol. i of *Moznayim lamishpat* (Krotoszyn and Königsberg, 1855). There is another acknowledgement in the introduction to vol. i of *Emunah yesharah* (Krotoszyn, 1843). In making this type of public acknowledgement of his wife, Kalischer was following the precedent set by his uncle Judah Leib.

guarded its legal privilege *de non tolerandis Judaeis*, despite the occasional presence of Jews during the seventeenth and eighteenth centuries. When Prussia
claimed Thorn as part of the 1793 partition, the new regime allowed a limited,
very cautious, official toleration of Jews in the city; indeed, an unskilled man
like Tsevi Hirsch had some difficulty obtaining permission to live there.[53] At
the end of the second decade of the nineteenth century, the Jewish community numbered just under 300, out of a total population of about 7,000.[54]
Thorn could not, like Lissa and Posen, boast of yeshivas and Torah learning.
The Jews did not have a synagogue building; they prayed together in a series
of rented facilities until a synagogue was built in 1847. At least two other
rabbis lived in the town. One, Samuel Heilman Leyser, may have been the
Kalischer family's original link to Thorn, as he had moved there from Lissa in
the late eighteenth century. He clearly shared the Kalischer family's rabbinic
ethic, for he served as Thorn's official communal rabbi without pay. Shortly
after Kalischer's arrival, the community elder appointed another rabbi. This
led to a conflict with the Kalischer family that had to be resolved by the town
Magistrat. Nevertheless, over the years Tsevi Hirsch described Thorn as a
community faithful to the Torah.[55] The modest features of the city probably
did not bother him. By all accounts, he was a person who enjoyed spending

[53] According to the petitions found in the archives by Zenon Nowak (see n. 51), the couple
lived with the Kalischer parents in Thorn for the first year of their marriage. During the next
two years, during which their first child was born, the couple lived in Nieszawa with Gittel's
parents. At the beginning of 1823, Kalischer petitioned the Thorn city council to allow him to
return with his wife and child and establish an independent household there. He reassured the
council that allowing him into the city would not create any competition for the existing merchants there, since he had never learnt any marketable skill (and he promised that he would not
enter trade), but he merely wanted to continue studying in order to become a rabbi. This petition apparently failed to persuade the town leaders to grant entry permits, for within two weeks
Kalischer wrote to them that the couple had received a 'not inconsiderable fortune', including a
small amount of cash from his father. This ploy succeeded, for their second child was born in
Thorn that year.

[54] Zenon Hubert Nowak, 'Zur Geschichte der Thorner Juden in der ersten Hälfte des 19.
Jahrhunderts', *Leo Baeck Institute Bulletin*, 87 (1990), 19–28 at 20, gives the following population
data: in 1815, there were 257 Jews out of a total of 6,730 inhabitants; in 1816, 262 Jews out of a
total of 6,911; in 1825, 311 Jews out of a total of 9,619 (a reduction in percentage). Jacob
Goldberg, 'Toruń', in *EJ*, states that there were 248 Jews in 1823.

[55] I. Rosenberg, 'Thorn', in *JE*. The other rabbi in Thorn, Herman Simon, is not mentioned
in the above article, which was written by the officiating rabbi of Thorn. According to Nowak,
'Zur Geschichte der Thorner Juden', 22, Herman Simon was appointed rabbi by 'the community elder' in 1825. It is unclear whether he received an income. Objecting to Simon, 'the
Kalischer family' organized a separate prayer service in their home which drew about twenty
members away from the primary community synagogue service and thus decreased the community income. The *Magistrat* intervened and forbade holding private services. The town records

the entire day and much of the night alone immersed in learning. He did not need to be surrounded by students, at centre stage in the *kahal*, or within easy reach of many rabbinic peers.

It is also probable that Thorn suited Kalischer because he felt it would be the type of community that would respect his judgement. He believed that it was his responsibility as a rabbi to guide and keep Jews within the bounds of the Torah. As a member of a rabbinic family loyal to older ways, Kalischer had imbibed an enduring sense of communal duty. He even had occasion, years later, to lecture his own teacher on this account. Eger once expressed the desire to spend the end of his days in the Holy Land. There, supported by the *halukah* (the fund maintained by the Jews of the Diaspora for the support of scholars), he could devote himself to study freed of the burdens of communal leadership. Tsevi Hirsch urged him to stay, 'for when he would leave our land, the generation would resort to wild and wanton ways'.[56] Jews' obedience to the Torah depended on their rabbis, he firmly believed. He would describe rabbis as guards along God's holy path, vigilant shepherds who kept the wayward flock on the straight road and out of danger. Thus it would be selfish and sinful to avoid public service. Perhaps Kalischer's experience in Posen convinced him that he could not or would not want to handle a large community. At any rate, in Thorn he took on rabbinic responsibilities alongside the other rabbis: he made halakhic rulings, assisted at weddings, led a study group, and (outside the usual rabbinic role) performed ritual circumcisions. He consistently and resolutely refused all payments and gratuities. For years he sat in his study, immersed in sacred texts, taking occasional breaks to direct the pious Jews of Thorn in the ways of the Torah. Thorn's Jews responded well to his guardianship, and he consistently rejected offers to relocate elsewhere.[57]

As a young man, Tsevi Hirsch Kalischer had benefited from some of the greatest opportunities offered by Polish Jewish society. His parents had pro-

do not explain the basis for the Kalischer family's objection to Simon. For Kalischer's positive account of the Jewish community in Thorn, see below, Chs. 5 and 7.

[56] Kalischer confided this in his letter to Zevulun Leib Brit, published in *Halevanon*, 9/3 (1872), repr. in *Zionist Writings*, 370–4 at 371. This incident occurred when Kalischer had already left Posen, for he explained that he and a number of Eger's other students together confronted the scholar, and he still had a copy of the letter that they wrote.

[57] Kalischer acted as a *mohel* (ritual circumciser) as late as ten days before his death at the age of 79, according to his son's testimony to A. M. Luncz, 'The Biography of the Great Rabbi, Seeker of Zion, Tsevi Hirsch Kalischer' (Heb.), *Luah erets yisra'el* (Jerusalem, 1897), 126–46 at 145. Kalischer himself made numerous references to his refusal to accept payments of any kind. One example is in his letter to Zevulun Leib Brit mentioned in the previous footnote. Bromberg, *Rabbi Tsevi Hirsch Kalischer*, 15, states (without documentation) that Kalischer received numerous offers of rabbinical positions throughout Germany as his scholarly reputation grew, even as a student.

vided him with an extended Jewish education at the feet of the finest scholars in central Europe. His wife and her family had agreed to assume all the world-ly burdens of family and livelihood so that he might continue his scholarship undisturbed. His community respected his guidance. Kalischer had, thus far, succeeded in exemplifying the traditional values and way of life affirmed by his family and teachers. He remained firmly devoted to them his entire life. Even when he charted a new route to redemption, he believed he had merely discovered the pristine path from the days of old.

THREE

The Letter to Rothschild
1836

V ERY little is known of Tsevi Hirsch Kalischer's life in Thorn from the time of his arrival until the first manifestation, almost twenty years later, of his religious activism. We can presume that Gittel sustained their growing family while the rabbi enjoyed relative repose, studying and working on his manuscripts on Jewish law. Years later Kalischer would refer back to the 1830s as the time when he began to recognize 'the holy path'. Any number of factors might have drawn him out of his insular world of abstract Torah study into the realm of politics. Although there are no records of how he came to his epiphany, an early testimony of his religious awakening has survived. One would expect this to be in a letter to a friend or teacher. To such intimates he wrote later, however, after revealing his startling insights to a total stranger, the Frankfurt banker Amschel Mayer Rothschild.[1] Written just before his fortieth birthday in the late summer of 1836, Kalischer's letter to Rothschild marks the beginning of his dedication to hastening the arrival of the messianic age. The letter represents his initial rethinking of the whole notion of the messiah and, given his new understanding of it, his attempt to act upon his theory. It contains all of the elements and much of the text of what he later published, in 1862, as *Derishat tsiyon* (Seeking Zion). An analysis of the letter and the context in which it was written will show the enduring contours of Kalischer's messianic theory as well as provide clues to the forces that propelled him into action.

---

[1] Amschel Meyer Rothschild, who lived from 1773 to 1855, should not be confused with his father, also of Frankfurt, Meyer Amschel Rothschild (1743–1812), the founder of the Rothschild banking house. The original letter to Rothschild has not been preserved; Kalischer's record of his letter was first published in its entirety in *The Zionist Writings of Rabbi Tsevi Kalischer* (Heb.), ed. Israel Klausner (Jerusalem, 1947), 1–14. It is dated 12 Elul 5596 (25 Aug. 1836). Israel Klausner surmises, in his 'Rabbi Zvi Hirsch Kalischer's Derishat Zion', *In the Dispersion*, 5–6 (Spring 1966), 281–9 at 286, and in his introduction to *Zionist Writings* (introductory section, 35–6), that Kalischer wrote to Montefiore as well as to Rothschild in 1836. However, there is no evidence for this.

THE MESSIANIC THEORY

Kalischer's letter to Rothschild is a rich and complex weave of poetry, exegesis, halakhic argumentation, and pragmatic reasoning. It was written entirely in Hebrew and Aramaic, and Kalischer kept a copy for his own record. It was not a personal, intimate confession; there was no personal information in it beyond the rabbi's expressions of awe towards Rothschild, the urgency he felt in beseeching the banker to take action, his signature, and his identity as a student of Akiva Eger.[2] Much of the letter's structure and tone resemble a learned treatise. Its principle theme is God's role in history, particularly God's dependence upon a prominent figure such as Rothschild to serve as the instrument of his will.

Messages of such import require drama and ceremony, and since it was customary to address famous people with expressions of high praise, Kalischer began his letter with an elaborate poem laden with messianic references:

> Glorified, you see him:
> A noble and lord in Israel.
> Many nations pay him tribute —
> For his purse is ample.
> Men of understanding seek to learn
> Why his cloak is red.
> His helping holy shield
> . . . [indecipherable]
> Surely he is from the stock of Jesse,
> A sprout from Judah bearing fruit.
> The shield of his banner reddens,
> His breastplate is righteousness
> And a helmet of salvation lies upon his head.[3]

Contemporary Jews would easily recognize the references to the Rothschild coat of arms as well as the messianic identity attributed to the banker. This was not mere flattery: Kalischer was firmly convinced that the banker was a potential messiah. After the initial poem and a summary of his request in poetic form, he explained to Rothschild that the unprecedented scope of his power attested to God's design:

[2] Kalischer signed his name with all the customary forms and honorifics: 'The insignificant Ts. Hirsch Kalischer, student of the great, famous, and pious *gaon*, rabbi of all countries, our teacher and rabbi Akiva Eger, head of the rabbinic court of the holy community of Posen.' He followed it with his address in German, 'Hirsch Kalischer in Thorn in Preussen' (*Zionist Writings*, 14).

[3] *Zionist Writings*, 1. The poem is an acrostic, spelling out 'Sir Asher Anshel Red Shield, Peace to him'. Amschel Mayer was the German form of his name.

His name is great among all the nations, and all the kings of the earth bow before him, and all the princes and wise men praise him to Heaven. . . . Search back to the beginning of creation, has there ever been one like this? For it is a house so high and mighty and extensive throughout all corners of the earth, that everyone must rise before it. The princes and nobility of the world bow before him and request his wealth, even those from distant islands, and he fulfils their requests . . .[4]

Kalischer was awestruck by the international reach of the house of Rothschild, and he shared the popular perception that Rothschild dictated policy to world rulers. The political power of this wealthy Jew was, to Kalischer, an entirely novel phenomenon. He could not situate it within the political and economic context of his era, or any earlier one. This was the first indicator that God was responsible for Rothschild's ascendancy.

The second indicator was Rothschild's character. His reputed religious convictions greatly impressed Kalischer. Addressing Rothschild in the third person, he wrote: 'He considers all the wealth and the authority over nations to be nothing in comparison with the love of God, showing righteousness, and walking modestly before his creator.'[5] Kalischer regarded these personality traits as evidence of a religious attitude of humility before God. He believed God guided all things, and that he must have had a special purpose in mind when he gave so much power to one man of this type. To Kalischer, this was a sign that God had designated Rothschild as the messiah: 'For God, praised be his name, loves him greatly, and this is nothing less than [a fulfilment of the prophecy] "a sprout from Judah shall bear fruit" [Isa. 11: 1].'[6] He also assumed that the banker was sufficiently learned in biblical and rabbinic literature to grasp complex halakhic argumentation, for he included in the letter an extensive, detailed analysis of the legal requirements for resuming sacrificial worship. He clearly felt that Rothschild would not accept his proposal unless it were in accordance with Jewish law. He must have reasoned that, even if the halakhic research was too complex for Rothschild, it would still earn the banker's respect.

---

[4] Ibid. 2. Kalischer gives the impression that the Frankfurt Rothschild was the sole head of the banking house. This was the case at the founding of the enterprise, but by 1836 there were five sons who controlled the bank's interests, one of whom was living in Frankfurt. See Fritz Backhaus, 'The Last of the Court Jews: Mayer Amschel Rothschild and his Sons', in Vivian B. Mann, Richard I. Cohen, and Fritz Backhaus (eds.), *From Court Jews to the Rothschilds* (Munich, 1996), 79–95. Howard M. Sachar, *The Course of Modern Jewish History*, 2nd edn. (New York, 1990), 130–44, argues for the accuracy of the popular perception of the Rothschilds' control over European rulers and their foreign-policy decisions.

[5] *Zionist Writings*, 2. Testimony to Rothschild's pious demeanour can be found in Egon Caesar Corti, *The Reign of the House of Rothschild, 1830–1871* (New York, 1928), 292.

[6] *Zionist Writings*, 2.

Not far into the body of his letter, Kalischer proclaims the foundational principle of his unorthodox outlook:

The redemption of Israel and the righteous messiah! [*sic*] whom we constantly await—do not imagine that God, blessed be his name, will suddenly descend from on high and say to his people 'Go forth', or that he will send his messiah without warning from heaven to blow the great shofar and gather the scattered of Israel and surround [Jerusalem] with a wall of fire, as he promised through his servants the prophets. Not so . . . [indecipherable] certainly all the promises of the prophets will be fulfilled in the end of days as the redemption is completed, but we will not go swiftly or hastily in one day. The redemption of Israel will come gradually, salvation will slowly flower, until finally Israel will wax strong and flourish, and all signs and promises of the holy prophets will come to pass. All this I will clarify for you, with God's help, through proof texts from the prophets . . . and reason.[7]

Here Kalischer describes a redemption that unfolds in a gradual process, not like the sudden event imagined by most pious Jews. He imagines the redemption's beginning as a quiet affair, similar to the organic process of a flower blossoming. Only in its later stage would miracles and wonders appear. His conception does not require a suspension of reason or any change in the natural order of things. These traits, he implies, strengthen the veracity of his interpretation.

Kalischer continues with a messianic scenario that is orderly, with each event unfolding in turn. The sequence is as follows: God prompts gentile kings to permit Jews to move to Palestine, the Jewish population of Palestine and Jerusalem swells, the Jews rebuild the altar in Jerusalem and resume sacrificial worship, and then God is roused to respond with more manifest signs of redemption: wars, the appearance of the messiah, eternal happiness. According to Kalischer's scenario, the redemptive process is actually a two-stage phenomenon:

Redemption will begin through natural causes, through human actions, and through the will of the kings to bring together a few of the scattered of Israel to the Holy Land . . . like Cyrus did, and so too in the future redemption will occur when God stirs the gentile kings to send out the Jews. . . . When a larger number of the remnants of Israel accumulate in the Holy Land and Jerusalem, and they repair the destroyed altar and offer a sacrifice as a savoury smell to God, then the Lord will be pleased to send the light of his countenance to descend upon his people. . . . For certainly when we appeal to God

---

[7] *Zionist Writings*, 3. Note the oratorical mode of writing, especially in the staccato phrases at the opening. This paragraph was modified very slightly when it was included in *Derishat tsiyon* (*Zionist Writings*, 38). The *Derishat tsiyon* version is perhaps one of the best-known passages from Kalischer's writings, as it is included in the selection of his writings in Arthur Hertzberg's *The Zionist Idea: A Historical Analysis and Reader* (New York, 1960), 111. My translation differs slightly from Hertzberg's.

through a sacrifice, we become cleansed of all our sins, and God will once again be merciful to us and bring the complete redemption and eternal happiness. At that time the wars over the Land of Israel will occur, the wars of Gog and Magog mentioned in the Book of Ezekiel, and then God's messiah and all his holy minions and God will rejoice in his creation and alone rule over all humanity.[8]

The first stage of redemption—the events leading up to and including the sacrificial offering—is fully in accordance with natural law and comports with the way of the world. It echoes the return to Zion that occurred at the end of the biblical era. Just as God had orchestrated the end of the first exile by inspiring the Persian King Cyrus to assist the Jews, he would today wish world rulers to encourage the flow of Jews to Palestine. Their decrees would enable a small number of Jews actually to settle the land. The returning Jews would farm the land, Kalischer implies later in the letter when he notes that 'the land will be joyous in its cities and the desert will turn into a fruitful field'.[9] In the letter itself, however, Kalischer pays scant attention to the agricultural revitalization of the land. Instead, he focuses on the importance of following the ancient Judaeans' example of rebuilding Jerusalem and re-establishing sacrificial worship. He emphasizes that the offering of sacrifices is the goal and the climax of this first, natural phase of redemption. It would trigger the second, supernatural phase, and only then would all the prophesied miracles and wonders occur and the messiah arrive.[10]

According to Kalischer's schema, the entire process is a chain reaction, a dynamic of human initiative and divine response, in which sacrificial offerings play a crucial role. The sacrifices are central because they expiate the Jews' sins and allow them to stand in purity before God, and God would then listen to their prayers for redemption. His understanding of the sacrifices bears a considerable resemblance to that which appears in Lorbeerbaum's letters in *Eleh divrei haberit*. For Kalischer as for Lorbeerbaum, sacrificial worship is a powerful, theurgical ritual that profoundly influences God and has an extraordinary effect on the human condition. Verbal prayer is a poor substitute. In contrast to his elders, however, Kalischer foresees the actual offering of sacrifices in his own time. Rather than sit helplessly and hope for God to reintroduce the sacrificial system, Kalischer believes that he and others should reinstate the ancient cult themselves—such, he believed, was God's will. Also in marked contrast to his teachers, his discussion of the sacrifices in the

---

[8] *Zionist Writings*, 4.   [9] Ibid. 14.

[10] Ibid. 3–4. Historians intent on showing that Kalischer was a proto-Zionist, like Israel Klausner, have overlooked the relative unimportance of agriculture in his early writings. In the letter to Rothschild, there are only two references to the blossoming of the land (Ezek. 38: 12, p. 4, and Isa. 27: 6, p. 5). Kalischer also interpreted Isa. 27 ('in days to come, Jacob shall strike root / Israel shall sprout and blossom') as a metaphor of a naturalistic redemption.

Rothschild letter is not at all abstract. The sacrificial offerings do not function as symbols of anything else: they are not metaphors for faith or tradition or a future hope, nor do they serve a polemical purpose. The rabbi does not write of them as a pious enactment of Hosea's view of prayer as offering 'the bullocks of our lips'. The sacrifices are the real, tangible portions of animals and grains that burn upon a stone altar in Jerusalem and produce a plume of smoke that will drastically change the future of the world. Kalischer manages to retain the concept of the sacrifices' inviolate sanctity within the framework of a rational perspective that shapes the rest of his messianic ideology. Indeed, he tackles the logistics of restoring sacrificial worship with a pragmatism that stupefied his teachers and most rabbis for generations to come.

Kalischer was not the first to argue that the Jews had actively to initiate their redemption, but his letter is the first explicit literary expression of Jewish messianic activism in modern Europe. He was advocating a position at odds with the dominant view shared by virtually all rabbis of his era. Furthermore, he was not simply propounding a theory; he was urging a powerful man to take concrete action. The letter to Rothschild bristles with his intensity and fierce sense of duty. He admitted as much, revealing that the strength of his conviction overcame his embarrassment that the banker might regard him 'as, God forbid, a joker or a crazy man requesting a matter beyond all measure'. He confessed

my heart supports and guides me, saying, All your body and possessions and might are worth nothing to me when compared to the one out of a million possibilities for the redemption of Israel. For you should easily devote your life and wealth to this, and you should be ashamed to be ridiculed when faced with even a remote possibility of acting on behalf of this great thing, the aim of all life.[11]

To Kalischer the world would be as it was meant to be at the final stage of redemption, and this could occur only with human assistance. It was his mission—it was the mission of *all* Jews, he told Rothschild—to help bring it about. Even if their effort was not successful, he wrote, 'the seeking and blessing brings great merit. . . . And anyone who does any activity wholeheartedly has attained the merit of seeking Zion and the Temple. Whether the activity succeeds or not it will be considered in his favour . . . and the opposite is true: if a possibility comes to mind and I am silent, then my sin is too great to bear.'[12] In other words, he was writing to Rothschild in response to a specific

[11] *Zionist Writings*, 2.

[12] Ibid. 2–3. Significantly, the expression for the heaviness of his sin is the language that Cain uses (Gen. 4: 13) in reference to the punishment for his murder of his brother Abel. Kalischer sums up the religious commandment with the Hebrew phrase *derishat tsiyon ushekhinat uzo*, which literally translates as 'the seeking of Zion and his mighty abode'. The phrase *shekhinat uzo*

religious obligation mandating an active effort towards the messianic restoration of Zion and the Temple. This was the commandment of *derishat tsiyon*, seeking Zion. Because Rothschild was pivotal to seeking Zion, but unaware of his role, Kalischer was fulfilling his own religious obligation of *derishat tsiyon* (and, presumably, his rabbinic duty) by instructing Rothschild personally. Yet his religious passion, intertwined as it was with messianic enthusiasm, did not quite fit the rabbinic role; typically, rabbis would denounce such messianic enthusiasm as foolish or as a threat to social stability. In early nineteenth-century Europe, rabbis across the denominational spectrum agreed that it was a grave sin to act upon the dream of returning to Zion. Kalischer was charting a singular path for himself among his contemporaries.

The messiah is relatively unimportant in Kalischer's vision. In some parts of the letter, he depicts him as a figure who appears quite late in the redemptive process, after most of the work has been completed by everybody else. In these examples, the messiah would enact the biblical miracles that were beyond the normal abilities of the Jews, such as commanding the wars of the Land of Israel and rebuilding the Temple.[13] In one passage in the letter, however, Kalischer explains that the term messiah refers to 'a righteous man who arises and rules over the Jews and subjects them, in his land, to the laws of the Torah, and restores sacrificial worship to Jerusalem'.[14] This definition has the messiah appearing in the early stage of redemption and enacting the deeds that would arouse God to action. Nevertheless, both definitions constituted a disagreement with the prevailing conception among the Jews of the supernatural and all-essential messiah.

The rabbi was not breaking new ground by de-emphasizing the figure of the messiah, but in this case, too, his position was unique. There were ample biblical and post-biblical texts that depicted the messiah as an ordinary man of power. 'Messiah' was the designation given to the Persian king who allowed the exiled Judaeans to return to their homeland, and various Israelite kings also merited the title.[15] There were the talmudic sages and medieval philosophers who maintained that the messiah was a mere mortal, and kabbalistic sources that described his coming as the culmination of a long process of Jewry's spiritual purification, but the common view was that of a supernatural

appears in Jewish prayers, usually in reference to God's heavenly dwelling, as a mythic parallel of the earthly place where God's name dwells, the Temple. Here, however, it is apparent that Kalischer is referring to the earthly dwelling.

[13] *Zionist Writings*, 6–7. He refers at times to 'a prophet' and at times to 'the messiah', but it is likely that he did not regard these as identical; nevertheless, both indicate more direct supernatural influence. [14] Ibid. 12.

[15] Isa. 45: 1; 1 Sam. 2: 10, 24: 6, and many other references to the king as God's anointed (*mashiaḥ*).

figure who directed key events. Indeed, there was a long-standing kabbalistic tradition that the messiah would arrive in the year 5600, which corresponded to 1839/40 in the Christian calendar; it is noteworthy that Kalischer did not bother to cite this teaching to his advantage. Consistent with the principles of realistic messianism, he adopted a naturalistic approach to the figure of the messiah. Convinced that history advances by human initiative and God's guiding hand, proponents of realistic messianism would place the messiah within human bounds and redemption within reach. They could call their own era 'the Messianic Age' or 'the first flowering of the redemption' if certain indicators pointing to the potential or actual growth of the Jewish presence in the Holy Land were evident. Ironically, a more rational approach to messianism would allow the term to be applied more casually, as he was doing in his letter to Rothschild. Kalischer's bold use of the title for Rothschild was not repeated in *Derishat tsiyon*, where he referred to Rothschild and other influential Jewish men as noble men close to royal power—not messiahs, but signifying that the era of redemption was at hand.[16] Kalischer's naturalism and optimism placed him in the same league as other nineteenth-century Jews who described their era of liberation as a fulfilment of the messianic promise. Yet his fundamental dissatisfaction with a Jewish future in the Diaspora (or, in religious terms, living in the limited realm of *galut*) prevented him from dispensing with the separatist nationalistic tasks assigned to the Jewish messiah. He would react with horror when, in the next decade, Jews committed to a thoroughgoing rationalistic Judaism rejected the concept of a personal messiah altogether.

What Kalischer did in the Rothschild letter was to advance active messianism by presenting it as a coherent theory, buttressing it with supportive texts from Jewish literary sources, and outlining an explicit plan of action. Perhaps one reason he was more successful in this endeavour than his medieval forerunners was because he lived in an era in which redemptive activity was more plausible, in which Jews had greater opportunities to act upon their convictions and desires in the larger, political sphere. Although he too would eventually be criticized by rabbinic peers as foolish and dangerous, the privacy of his appeal to Rothschild enabled him to articulate his ideas without the pressure of rabbinic censure.

The cleverness of Kalischer's theory lies in the way it allowed him to affirm Jewish tradition even while transforming it. At first glance he seems to be rejecting two fundamental elements of Judaism, the sudden arrival and super-

---

[16] See the first edition of *Derishat tsiyon*. In *Zionist Writings*, 148, Kalischer mentions Moses Montefiore, Isaac Adolphe Crémieux, and Achille Fould; the second edition of *Derishat tsiyon* omits Fould.

natural character of the redemption. The reader soon realizes, however, that these elements were retained in the second stage of redemption when God would abruptly enact the miracles foretold in the Bible.[17] Kalischer thus respected and incorporated within his theory the contemporary desire for a more rational religion, while retaining the non-rational elements that many Jews still embraced. His theory was at a middle point between the two ends of the continuum. A similar mid-point position characterized his stance on activism. He rejected the option of sitting and waiting for the messiah to come, yet he upheld the non-violent and conservative ethic of passive messianism, for he did not advocate conquest or anything illegal. His approach also rendered pointless the old Jewish sport of messianic calculation (which most rabbis—except for those who indulged in it—tended to regard with exasperation) because a gradual redemption contingent upon the free-will decisions of many actors could not be predetermined or predicted. Kalischer's two-stage theory thus included the disparate elements transmitted from the past—naturalistic and supernaturalist, sudden and gradual, anticipated and suppressed—without appearing too extreme. It was an impressive display of his intellectual acuity to include in one coherent vision the entire range of events found in speculative literature.

It was precisely this inclusiveness that enabled the rabbi to convince himself that his understanding of the redemptive process was the correct one. Kalischer's particular revision of the messianic concept was indebted to the values of the yeshiva world and its mode of study. Resonating through both were a deep respect for the commandments pertaining to sacrifice, a determination to link narrative traditions and legal argumentation, and the impulse to resolve tensions between conflicting traditions. Within talmudic literature there is the tendency to differentiate carefully between viewpoints and to sharpen the distinctions between opinions; there is also the desire to show that all perspectives are, on some level, consistent with each other. The first principle multiplies disagreements, while the second seeks to deny them.[18] Both principles were valid, and both were essential in exhibiting one's intellectual acumen. The second principle, however, would be the one to engage if a practical solution was sought. At a time when rabbinic scholars were not encouraging messianic activity, they did not mind the multiplicity of conflicting speculations; the confused data enabled them to throw up their hands and con-

---

[17] Sometimes keeping these elements in their proper place was difficult; this is evident in the poetic opening of the letter, where Kalischer identified the bloody war shield of God's messiah with the red shield of the Rothschild family, even though he anticipated a peaceful messianic role for the banker.

[18] Robert Goldenberg, 'Talmud', in Barry Holtz (ed.), *Back to the Sources: Reading the Classic Jewish Texts* (New York, 1984), 150.

clude that the matter had best be ignored.[19] Kalischer sought to engage his peers in messianic activity, and so he sought consensus. Through his particular sequencing and explanations, he—at least theoretically—resolved the difficulties between the realistic and passive messianists, and between the rationalists and supernaturalists.

Although Kalischer was convinced that his interpretation was true to the Torah, he *had* significantly altered the prevailing viewpoint. He made the miracles quite irrelevant by placing them later and making them contingent on human activism. His activist stance was a radical departure from the norm and would, if enacted, drastically redirect the focus of Jewish communal life. He was engaged in a not uncommon mode of religious transformation. By developing a particular strand within the range of traditional ideas, and expressing himself in a religious idiom, he restructured religious belief to fit current needs while maintaining the impression that his was the oldest and most authentic version of revelation. He, like many creative religious thinkers, seems not to have been the least bit conscious of this adaptive process—had he been, he could not have felt that he was being faithful to the ancient and timeless truths of the Torah.

The net effect of Kalischer's revisions was a messianic ideology that was more modern than the prevailing one: it was more humanistic, and it comported more closely with a purely rational approach to history. History would change not because of a wonder-working messiah, but because of prominent Jewish figures, non-Jewish rulers, and countless other individuals who acted sometimes independently, sometimes co-operatively. Human initiative, not divine intervention, was the paramount influence on history. Reason could support the idea that a small number of Jews, aided by powerful allies operating in their own self-interest, would migrate to Palestine and reinstate a modest version of ancient ceremonies. Kalischer, however, did not articulate a totally naturalistic vision of reality; his was a dynamic of human and divine interaction. He catered to his rationalistic inclinations without denying his desire for and belief in a God who personally intervenes in history. Thus he was certain that divine intervention had no part at the beginning of the redemptive process, but neither could he imagine history devoid of divine influence. This type of intervention was so subtle and so accorded with the natural flow of history that many would not perceive that God was even involved. Kalischer believed he was guided by a true understanding of God's ways and so could grasp the significance of these men's achievements; he

---

[19] Funkenstein, 'Maimonides', in *Perceptions of Jewish History*, 133, argues that this was the main intent in ending the list of calculations of the end of days with the curse, 'Let the spirit of those who calculate the end expire' (the reference is to BT *San* 97*b*).

thought he was seeing miracles of a non-supernatural kind. He also knew that without the appropriate human response, the potential of these everyday miracles to hasten redemption might fade. Hence it was crucial to contact Rothschild, teach him the real reason for his prominence, and inspire him to play his proper messianic role.

KALISCHER'S PROPOSAL

Only at the end of the letter does Kalischer make a specific request of Rothschild. He opened his letter with the poetic praise and the messianic scenario described above. Because the contemporary revival of sacrificial worship was deemed to play a critical role in the redemptive process, he then engaged in a lengthy discussion of how the sacrificial cult could be restored in accordance with Jewish law (this is discussed in the next chapter). Following that, after a little flattery, he presented his plan:

perhaps God has great success in store for you. And at this time in particular, when the Land of Israel is not ruled by a powerful ruler as it was in the previous years under the Roman ruler and the government of the great Ishmaelite [Muslim] ruler (the Turkish sultan). This is not the case now, when the land is governed by the Pasha. Perhaps it would be acceptable to him if my lord, friend of the Most High, would shower him with a great fortune and buy him another country in exchange for the land presently insignificant in size but vast in quality. . . . But if that ruler does not want to sell him the entire land, then maybe he would sell Jerusalem and its surroundings. . . . (And if perchance that ruler does not want to sell the city of Jerusalem, at the very least buy from him the site of the [destroyed] Temple and a plot of land next to it, and with the condition that liberties and permission should be given to Jews to do there as they wish, to gather there from all lands without any obstacles, high taxes, or oppression from the ruler of the country, in order that we may offer sacrifices to the Lord our God. But the first way brings more honour and is worthier.)[20]

Kalischer is referring here to Mehemmed Ali, the ruler of Egypt since 1805 and vassal of the Turkish sultan. In 1832 Mehemmed Ali wrested control of the Sinai desert, Palestine, Lebanon, and portions of Syria from Ottoman hegemony. He then instituted reforms that significantly improved administration and law enforcement in Egypt and the provinces. The Jews of Palestine, especially those in Jerusalem, benefited considerably from the consequent reduction in violence and bribery, and they broadcast their relief by hailing Mehemmed Ali's conquest as the beginning of a better era. This situation may have sparked Kalischer's belief that he was living at a time ripe with messianic possibilities. He felt that the ruling regime in Palestine was more inclined to give up land than it had been at any time in the previous two thousand years.

[20] *Zionist Writings*, 13.

Kalischer was correlating the conjunction of two novel occurrences: the rise of a pious, wealthy Jew to international power and the conquest of the Holy Land by a ruler in need of assistance. Apparently, he was aware of the tenuousness of the Pasha's rule, particularly his need for European support to maintain his claim and satisfy his ambition to expand further. Mehemmed Ali's need for both money and European approval could be obtained by the sale of Palestine, Kalischer thought. Were Rothschild to buy the Land of Israel, the Jews could carry out the deed that would bring redemption. For, as Kalischer had already explained at great length in his letter, the savoury smell of the sacrificial offerings would awaken God's mercy, and God would then deliver the miracles and eternal happiness of the End of Days. The rabbi seemed unaware that the Temple Mount was a holy Muslim site covered with mosques and other structures that would probably not be surrendered to non-Muslims without a struggle. He was also oblivious to the depth of the Muslims' political, historical, and religious ties to the land. He obviously believed that possession of the land was a problem that money could solve, and he envisaged a peaceful financial deal between two gentlemen.

When we consider Kalischer's political plan in context, it is far less fantastic and outrageous than it may at first sound. Widespread ignorance of Palestine and its Muslim rulers and inhabitants was the norm for Europeans. Kalischer's knowledge of the country was probably typical of the well-read European adult. Communication and transportation links to the Near East were still quite primitive in the 1830s. The telegraph was just being developed; not until 1855 did it connect Europe to Constantinople, and the connection to Palestine began in 1864. Before that, the quickest link was through a three-week steamboat connection, and before 1840 the schedule was erratic and the trip dangerous.[21] Out-of-date and often inaccurate reports of life in Palestine were published in the daily newspapers in the large cities of Europe and in the monthly Jewish press in Germany.[22] Jews also received information through personal letters and from emissaries sent to raise funds for the Yishuv, as the Jewish community in Palestine was known. None of these sources provided a very realistic or detailed account of Near Eastern society. However, Kalischer was familiar with them, and so he probably knew more about the political situation than most Jews.

Kalischer's suggestion that Rothschild should buy Palestine from the Pasha was not unusual. Since Napoleon's military expedition to Egypt and Palestine,

---

[21] Arnold Blumberg, *Zion Before Zionism 1838–1880* (Syracuse, NY, 1985), 6, 46.

[22] There was no Jewish weekly until the German language *Allgemeine Zeitung des Judenthums* began publication in Leipzig in 1837 (appearing initially three times weekly). The first Hebrew newspaper appeared in 1856 (*Hamagid*). *Halevanon* was the first Hebrew publication from Palestine, appearing in 1863. Yiddish weeklies first began sustained publication in the 1880s.

similar proposals involving acquisition had been publicly advanced. Europeans were interested in establishing a foothold in the Near East. Some of these proposals were motivated by religious concerns; for example, it had long been a staple of English Protestant thought that the restoration of the Jews to Zion was a prerequisite for the Second Coming. Since the turn of the century, Protestant millenarians advocating that European rulers should consider acquiring Palestine for the Jews had been gaining political power.[23] Kalischer makes no reference to them in his letter to Rothschild (he did so in his later writings), but he obviously was aware of proposals voiced by Europeans motivated by more purely imperialist designs. Whatever the motivation, over the next ten years the suggestion that Palestine should somehow be turned over to the Jews (who would, of course, serve as the agency of the European powers) was heard increasingly and with greater elaboration in the European press. As late as 1860, the private secretary of Napoleon III of France found such a plan worthy of publication.[24] Kalischer's proposal of 1836 was an indication of his knowledge of foreign affairs and not his benightedness.

Kalischer sought to win Rothschild's agreement by appealing to him on a number of grounds. He thought that the desire for redemption and all that it entailed would be enticing for any pious Jew, including Rothschild. But the banker would also be interested in the profitability of the venture:

Considering this matter rationally, this investment would not be a total loss, but would bear fruit and increase. The leading Jews from all over the world will gather together and make [the Land of Israel] a settled land, full of many Jews. For without a doubt there will be many rich, pious Jews from all over who will travel there for an honoured burial

---

[23] Christian concern for the 'Restoration of the Jews', as it was commonly phrased at the time, had been gaining considerable support in Protestant countries since the Reformation; see David S. Katz, *Philo-Semitism and the Readmission of the Jews to England 1603–1655* (Oxford, 1982); Franz Kobler, *The Vision Was There: A History of the British Movement for the Restoration of the Jews to Palestine* (London, 1956); Mayir Verete, 'The Restoration of the Jews in English Protestant Thought 1790–1840', *Middle Eastern Studies*, 8/1 (1972), 3–50. On the political influence of Christian millennialists in British politics, see Jonathan Frankel, *The Damascus Affair: 'Ritual Murder', Politics, and the Jews in 1840* (Cambridge, 1997), 284–310.

[24] See Walter Laqueur, *A History of Zionism* (New York, 1976), 42–6, for a brief survey of these proposals and the religious, political, social, and military considerations motivating them. The French proposal by Ernst Laharanne so impressed the highly educated and sophisticated Moses Hess that he quoted it at length in an appendix to his *Rome and Jerusalem* (1862), including the following comment: 'What European power would today oppose the plan that the Jews, united through a Congress, should buy back their ancient fatherland? Who would object if the Jews flung a handful of gold to decrepit old Turkey and said to her: "Give me back my home and use this money to consolidate the other parts of your tottering Empire?"' This quotation is from the translation in Hertzberg, *The Zionist Idea*, 134. Hertzberg remarks that except for Hess, no one seems to have taken Laharanne's book seriously at the time, but he does not support this claim.

in holy soil, under a Jewish government, and also to merit their part of the savoury smell of the sacrifice, accepted by God on the altar. And just as a flock increases under a person's guidance, without a doubt his wealth will quadruple—as will his righteousness without measure.[25]

Here Kalischer is making a case for a sound business investment, one that pays attention to a businessman's livelihood. At the very least, Rothschild would reap huge profits from the growing Jewish settlement.

What is perhaps most intriguing about this argument is its connection to Jewish sovereignty. In the above passage Kalischer assumes that the purchased land would be 'under a Jewish government' and at the same time Rothschild's private enterprise. This would occur, he explains, at the instigation of the world rulers: 'Eternal happiness will be his, because the good of all Israel depends on him, and all the kings of the earth will grant him majestic kingship, for they will rejoice in his greatness.'[26] Rothschild's ascension to royalty in this manner would be a natural and peaceful progression of events. This passage indicates some seriousness in identifying Rothschild as the messiah. This scenario fits his description of the messiah as 'a righteous man who arises and rules over the Jews and subjects them, in his land, to the laws of the Torah, and restores sacrificial worship to Jerusalem'.[27] Yet establishing Jewish sovereignty was not Kalischer's goal, or even a major concern—it appears as a passing remark designed to strengthen the proposal's appeal. He did not seek a Jewish state for its own sake or, as Zionists would later argue, for the normalization of Jewish status. For him, the establishment of a Jewish kingdom was but one of many steps in the journey to full redemption.

It does not seem to matter to the rabbi which reasons would stir Rothschild to purchase Palestine, so long as he carried out the task. Believing in a natural redemptive process means that one makes a virtue of necessity; that is, the redemption in its first stage might very well unfold though natural events, such as a business transaction or one man's desire for power. Kalischer assumed that the banker would be more inspired by the higher values of love for the Jewish people and concern for his soul. He imagined Rothschild as a divine agent much like the biblical Queen Esther. According to the story, providence was the guiding hand behind Esther's appointment as queen to ensure that the Jewish people had a powerful ally in their time of need. Kalischer began and ended his letter to Rothschild with the words addressed to Queen Esther when she was reluctant to use her influence: 'Who knows whether you have not achieved royalty for such a time as this?'[28] Rothschild

---

[25] *Zionist Writings*, 13.

[26] Ibid. It is hard to reconcile this argument with Kalischer's impression that Rothschild was shy and humble.   [27] Ibid. 12.   [28] Esther 4: 14, quoted in *Zionist Writings*, 2 and 13.

should understand that he was powerful only because of God's subtle intervention in history through the seemingly natural course of events. He must act responsibly and follow God's commandment to seek Zion and the Temple. For, as Kalischer pointed out, 'is there anything in the world as great as this?'[29]

Nowhere in the letter did Kalischer entertain the possibility that Rothschild, or the Jewish people as a whole, had any reservations about the messianic belief. He was convinced that Rothschild's investment would be profitable precisely because rich, pious Jews throughout the world would move to Palestine for a number of reasons, including their eagerness to participate in sacrificial worship. But others, too, would go. Polish Jews would be especially receptive to Rothschild's initiative, Kalischer felt, because of their poverty:

For when Israel hears that 'Ephraim is shaken', they will immediately repent and return to God, and especially in the lands of Poland, where they are now impoverished [when once] God's lamp shone over their head [Job 29: 3]. They will repent when he appears, and purify their hearts towards their Lord and cry to God to bring salvation through his righteous anointed one, my lord Rothschild![30]

Kalischer's description of the Polish Jews centres on their economic difficulties, for their plight is likened to that of Job, a righteous man who, in the passage quoted, fell from wealth to a state of poverty.[31] Polish Jews' memory of previous economic health and present poverty would make them especially receptive to the promise of messianic deliverance. Kalischer has actually put a positive slant on his fellow Jews' poverty, and he may have imagined (although he did not say it) that this, too, was part of the divine plan. It is important to note that in this letter he did not explicitly suggest that the Jews would move to Palestine to farm the land and earn a decent livelihood. Decades later he would promote agricultural settlement in Palestine as a means of economic betterment, but in 1836 he thought only of the allure of the restored sacrifices and other messianic events.[32]

Nowhere in the letter did Kalischer imagine that Jews' modern sensibilities would render them averse to the restoration of sacrifices; indeed, he seemed oblivious to any such sensibilities. He thought that the very piety and trad-

[29] Ibid. 13. This comment actually precedes the specific request to Rothschild to buy land.

[30] Ibid. 14. For Kalischer, 'Poland' was a meaningful territorial designation even though it had ceased to exist as political unit in 1795 (or 1815 if one considers the Duchy of Warsaw).

[31] Job 29 compares Job's present poverty with his former state of materialistic glory when he was a pious rich man. The Hebrew term is *bematsor*, literally, in straits.

[32] The quoted reference to the Polish Jews is the only place in the entire letter where the economic state of the Jewish masses is mentioned.

itional nature of the banker and Jewish society presented him with two serious challenges. The first was Jewish passivity that derived from the—to him—mistaken old teaching that the Jews should wait for the messiah to bring the messianic age. He responded to this challenge by presenting his alternative interpretations of biblical and rabbinic texts, as we have seen above. The second challenge he identified as the—again, to him—mistaken impression that Jewish law raised insurmountable difficulties in regard to the restoration of sacrificial worship. Both of these concerns illustrate how deeply immersed the rabbi was in the world of pre-modern rabbinic literature; he believed that Jews' attachment to pre-modern values, and not their acceptance of modern attitudes or political realities, was the greatest obstacle to his plan's success.

THE PRUSSIAN TERRITORIES DURING THE 1820S AND 1830S

Kalischer's assessment of the traditional piety of Jews was probably accurate. In 1836 the Jews in the region where he was raised, which the Prussians had recently renamed the Posen District, and the adjacent territory he lived in as an adult, called West Prussia, were still overwhelmingly traditional in their behaviour.[33] They observed the sabbath, ate kosher food, respected rabbinic authority, and followed Jewish customs. Synagogue liturgy, life-cycle ceremonies, and home rituals contained many references to the messianic hope: the ingathering of Jews in Zion, the restoration of sacrificial worship at the rebuilt Temple, the rule of a Davidic king, and so on. Men and women recited these prayers every day.[34]

[33] The names for the region of Kalischer's birth changed frequently. The Prussians initially called it South Prussia. In 1807 Napoleon included it in the Duchy of Warsaw, and after 1815 the Prussians reclaimed it and called it the Duchy of Posen. After the 1830 Polish rebellion, Prussian officials renamed it simply the Posen District. Some bibliographic sources prefer to use the Polish name Poznań in place of Posen.

[34] It is unclear, of course, to what extent they understood what they were reciting. Religious reformers frequently claimed that the mass of Jews simply recited the prayers by rote, with no understanding. Steven M. Lowenstein, 'The 1840s and the Creation of the German-Jewish Religious Reform Movement', in id., *The Mechanics of Change*, 85–6, delineates four different responses to the pressures for increased Jewish integration: rejecting pressures and living in accordance with the letter of Jewish law, violating the norms while continuing to believe in their validity, rejecting the traditional system and separating from it socially, and creating a new Jewish religious system more in accordance with modern culture which also incorporated some older beliefs and laws. The Jews of this region in the 1830s were engaging in the first two responses. Women tended to hold on to traditions longer than men. Even in the imperial period, women were uttering traditional prayers and expressing their commitment to older ideals; see Marion A. Kaplan, *The Making of the Jewish Middle Class: Women, Family, and Identity in*

There was no indication that the Jews of the eastern territories, except for the rabbinical elite, were even aware of the debates on the prayer book that had so shaken their leaders. The liturgical reform efforts of the first few decades of the century had engaged only a very small circle of Jews in scattered cities in western and central Europe. None of the three reformed prayer books that had been published in Germany (all between 1816 and 1819) was widely distributed; they had been printed in small quantities for use in a few synagogues or school settings, and strong rabbinic opposition minimized their influence. In the eastern territories there was no first-hand experience with the movement for synagogue reform.[35] Even in western Europe during the 1820s and 1830s there was very little debate on the messianic idea in general or the sacrificial prayers in particular. Although some German Jewish philosophical writings included a critique of traditional messianic concepts, these works were not influential at the time. Public discussion on these matters did not occur until the 1840s, during and after rabbinic conferences convened to address religious reform.[36]

Imperial Germany (New York and Oxford, 1991), 64–9. Anecdotal evidence of the region's traditionalism is abundant in Heinrich Graetz's memoir, *Tagebuch und Briefe*, ed. Reuven Michael, Schriftenreihe wissenschaftlicher Abhandlungen des Leo Baeck Instituts 34 (Tübingen, 1977); see also the memoir of Hermann Makower in Monika Richarz (ed.), *Jewish Life in Germany: Memoirs from Three Centuries*, trans. Stella P. Rosenfeld and Sidney Rosenfeld (Bloomington, Ind., 1991).

[35] According to Meyer, *Response to Modernity*, 59, during the Hamburg temple controversy Nahman Berlin of Lissa published a Hebrew tract severely denouncing the reformers. He suggested burning Liebermann's work and insisted that because the innovators were rebelling against constituted political authority as well as against religious authority it would not be difficult to get government help to stop them. The traditional climate in the city of Posen is testified to by David Caro, who wrote in 1820 in support of the Berlin and Hamburg reformers, but published his work pseudonymously; see Meyer, *Response to Modernity*, 60 n. 183. Kalischer's lack of experience with the Reform movement is discussed in Ch. 5.

[36] In Salomon Steinheim's first volume of *The Revelation According to the Doctrine of the Synagogue*, which was published in German in 1835, the messianic hope is dismissed as a fantasy of the foolish masses that Jewish leaders, cognizant of the danger to those who tried to make it reality, deliberately projected into the distant future; Steinheim's very negative statements about sacrificial worship were published in the second volume, which appeared in 1856. See Joshua O. Haberman, *Philosopher of Revelation: The Life and Thought of S. L. Steinheim* (Philadelphia, 1990), 80–1. Steinheim's book was not widely read, even among liberal Jews. Among traditionalist circles, the only indication of discomfort with the sacrifices was the interpretation by Samson Raphael Hirsch, rabbi of the Duchy of Oldenburg; see David Ellenson, 'Sacrifice and Atonement in the Literature of German-Jewish Orthodoxy: Defense of a Discarded Institution', in id., *Between Tradition and Culture: The Dialectic of Modern Jewish Religion and Identity* (Atlanta, Ga., 1994), 28–35. Ellenson shows that in Hirsch's *Neunzehn Briefe über Judenthum* (Altona, 1836), *Choreb, oder Versuche ueber Jissroels Pflichten in der Zerstreuung* (Altona, 1837), and in his later works, he omitted any mention of the sacrifices' theurgic powers, and explained that the impor-

Furthermore, there were many indications that the traditional substance of Jewish religious life would continue unabated. The Prussian government had taken a strong stand against the growth of a reformed Judaism. Despite the Prussian regime's dissatisfaction with its 'backward' Jews, it had, with minor exceptions, acted to preserve the status quo within the synagogue. This stance was hardened shortly after the Hamburg temple controversy. Alarmed by the controversy over private reformed prayer services, and wary of the breakdown of social barriers between Christians and Jews that these services encouraged, Emperor Frederick William III signed a decree in 1823 prohibiting prayer services held in private homes. Only prayer services held in the community synagogue were allowed, and these were to be conducted 'without the slightest innovation in language, ceremonies, prayers or hymns, wholly according to the established custom'.[37] This decree was enforced by Prussian officials for the next twenty years with the help of conservative Jews who would notify officials of irregularities they had witnessed. The state's protective stance towards this very visible aspect of traditional culture reinforced in the minds of conservative Jewish leaders such as Rabbi Kalischer the old Polish Jewish conviction that the Crown wanted to preserve traditional Judaism.

Nor did the Prussian state exercise much interference in the insular, tradition-bound Jewish school system. In the Posen district, all but the one Jewish elementary school established by David Caro followed the *heder* model.[38] Prussian officials issued a ruling in 1825 closing all elementary schools not devoted to secular studies. Under the impression that the officials were objecting to the Talmud as the centre of the curriculum, Akiva Eger engaged

tance of the sacrifices lay purely in their pedagogical symbolism; he refused to understand them literally, although he anticipated their restoration in the messianic age. Nevertheless, his position was regarded as a defence of the cult, as were his later writings. Because Hirsch's book was written in German and first published in 1836, it was not readily available to Jews in the eastern provinces. I find no basis for the assertion made by Yosef Salmon, 'The Rise of Jewish Nationalism on the Border of Eastern and Western Europe: Z. H. Kalischer, David Gordon, Peretz Smolenskin', in Isadore Twersky (ed.), *Danzig, between East and West: Aspects of Modern Jewish History* (Cambridge, Mass., 1985), 126, that '[Kalischer's] appeal to Rothschild may also be seen as a reaction to Hirsch's universal spiritualism in the *Neunzehn Briefe*, which lessens the importance of the Land of Israel within the totality of Jewish history'. Kalischer probably did not know of Hirsch's book for some time, if at all (he never mentioned it), nor would he have regarded Hirsch's apologetic as critical of traditional Judaism. Indeed, Kalischer sought Hirsch's support in the 1860s for his proposal for agricultural settlement in Palestine; see below, Ch. 7.

[37] The 1823 decree, which also prohibited private synagogues even if their prayers did not deviate from tradition, is quoted in Meyer, *Response to Modernity*, 52. Only in the 1840s did the more liberal forces in the administration succeed in getting the decree cancelled. For the application of this decree in Thorn, see Ch. 2 n. 55.

[38] The controversy around this is described at greater length in Ch. 2.

Solomon Plessner, a Jewish preacher who had mastered elegant German, to write a treatise addressed to the government in defence of the Talmud. The volume included quotations from Christian scholars throughout the ages testifying to the Talmud's worthiness. When the state rescinded its decree, largely because alternative schools did not exist, Eger's faith in the state's benevolence was restored. He concluded that officials had never wanted to prohibit talmudic learning, but merely to add some secular studies to the curriculum, and he endorsed that position.[39] When Prussian officials began to insist upon the licensing of teachers according to standards that required evidence of proficiency in German and some secular studies, Eger organized the teachers in protest and led the appeal to the government. Unwilling to provoke hostility and recognizing the tremendous shortage of qualified teachers, government officials again backed off. Again, he concluded that the state was essentially supportive of rabbinic Judaism. Writing of the crisis to his colleague and son-in-law Moses Sofer in 1830, Eger explained, 'Truly the officials are not evil-doers, and thank God that they heed my words, but there is one troublemaker [*satan*] from our community who continues to behave wickedly.'[40] Just as the earlier generation's leaders had blamed Wessely for the pressure for change, Eger, too, focused on a single individual in Posen—most likely Wessely's protégé David Caro. Posen Jews, except for a few dissidents, sympathized with Eger's resistance to educational modernization. Yet more than a handful sought a broader education for their children in the Christian schools and through private tutors, and some of the poor were availing themselves of the free schools established by missionaries.[41] While Eger proclaimed victory, he admitted that the general attitude towards the older standards was not as enthusiastic as he would have liked. In the same letter he wrote: 'With God's

---

[39] Rabbi David Tevele concluded the same in 1782 about Emperor Joseph II's intent in reforming Jewish education in the Edict of Tolerance, in the Wessely controversy described in Ch. 1. Eger, in 1825, appeared not to be perturbed by the addition of some secular subjects in the *ḥeder* curriculum. He described the current practice in his letter to Plessner, collected in the volume of Sofer family letters edited by Shlomo Sofer, *Igerot soferim* (Vienna, 1929), 25, noting that mathematics and secular studies were already taught at the end of the day, when the students were no longer sufficiently alert to absorb Talmud.

[40] Sofer, *Igerot soferim*, 30. The data from an 1845 article in *Der Orient*, 13 (1845) surveying the establishment of Jewish public schools in the Posen district indicates that the school reforms were quite recent, and that traditionalist opposition was still effective in preventing the establishment of public schools. The schools in the city of Posen, even in 1845, were among those scorned for their 'backwardness'.

[41] According to Eliav, *Jewish Education in Germany*, 327, most of the communal leaders supported the aspirations of the enlightened Jews and agreed with the government's position on licensing. Eliav states (p. 328) that in 1831 12% of Posen's schoolchildren attended Christian schools (the majority of these were missionary schools), and in 1832 the number jumped to 16.5

help, virtually all the Jews here are God-fearers, but there is no fire in their hearts and they do not take action, so I alone remain to fight God's war.'[42]

Although the Jews of West Prussia, where Kalischer lived, were also anxious to preserve the Jewish content of elementary education, neither they nor their leaders resisted change as vigorously as the Jews of Posen. West Prussian Jews—religious leaders, too—regarded the state's desire for educational reform as a pragmatic matter, and not a religious one. They understood from the beginning that the government and Jewish education activists wanted to establish public co-educational Jewish elementary schools offering both religious and secular studies. Their goal of making German the language of instruction did not alarm the West Prussian Jews, since proficiency in the German language had been increasing noticeably among them anyway. Yet educational reform proceeded so slowly in Kalischer's immediate environment that it had virtually no effect on the formal teaching of Judaism in the schools. Very few examples of this new type of school materialized in West Prussia. As in Posen, there were not many teachers equipped to teach the proposed dual curriculum and no school to train such teachers. Liberal activists who had prepared catechisms and manuals of Jewish religious instruction promoting a more liberal version of Judaism found that their material was not widely used.[43] What is notable about West Prussian Jews is that they were more obedient with regard to the compulsory education laws than Jews in the Posen district. They were far more likely to enrol their children in the traditional Jewish schools or in Christian schools—the latter option exercised by a sizeable minority of Jewish parents, who were confident that their children would not be influenced by the proselytizing aims of some of the schools.[44] Children in Christian schools had

per cent. Attendance at these schools, however, seems to have been motivated solely by the free tuition and was accompanied by fierce resistance to the Christian message of the teachers; see Christopher Clark, 'Protestant Missions to the Jews of Prussia', *Leo Baeck Institute Yearbook*, 28 (1993), 33–50 at 41. According to Heppner and Herzberg, *Aus Vergangeneheit und Gegenwart*, ii. 823–4, the *ḥeder* remained the prevailing mode of elementary education in Posen until well after Eger's death in 1837.

[42] Sofer, *Igerot soferim*, 30. Anecdotal evidence seems to indicate that rabbinic scholars increasingly sought positions in the Austrian empire and Russian Poland, where they were likelier to receive the respect of the Jewish community for their talmudic expertise; see the case of Jacob Lorbeerbaum in Bromberg, *Rabbi Jacob Lorbeerbaum*, 48–52.

[43] Eliav, *Jewish Education in Germany*, 137, describes the model of these schools. He is able to document, in his review of West Prussian schools on pp. 332–3, perhaps one school in West Prussia that followed this model. Only in the 1840s and 1850s did the Jewish public schools become increasingly available. Even then, educational modernization did not occur swiftly; and even in the best of situations, elementary school reform would have visible impact only years later when the children reached adulthood.

[44] Eliav, *Jewish Education in Germany*, 333, cites the findings of M. Laubert, 'Zur Entwicklung des jüdischen Schulwesens in der Provinz Posen', *Zeitscrift für die Geschichte der Juden in*

to be given any formal Jewish education by private tutors hired by their parents. In all cases, instructors in Judaism continued to be hired from the pool of impoverished traditional Jews from Russian Poland who steadily flowed (often illegally) into the region.[45] As late as 1848, according to a German Jewish paper, Jewish communities with as many as 250 school-age children could not afford a full-time Jewish teacher and had to settle for one who supplemented his income by working on the side as a butcher, cantor, tax collector, or grave digger.[46] This harsh reality constantly undercut the very moderate reforming sentiments of the Jewish educational activists and the Prussian government and reinforced the power of Jewish tradition in West Prussia.

Prussian economic policies for the eastern territories also retarded Jewish acceptance of modern norms and ideas. The economic policies designed by the Prussian state at the end of the eighteenth century to isolate the Polish eastern territories from the older Prussian provinces were still in force. The Polish rebellion (in Russian Poland) of 1830 lent new energy to the state's fear of Polish independence. Prussian rulers sought to win the loyalty of the peasant masses and drive a wedge between them and the gentry, whom Prussian officials regarded as potential revolutionary leaders. The state therefore exhibited more concern for and paid more attention to the emancipation of the (mainly Polish) serfs and their economic well-being than the welfare of the urban classes, including the Jews.

Thus Jewish poverty remained, and indeed worsened in the 1820s. The Prussian government took steps to transform the region into a granary of food and a source of raw materials for the other Prussian provinces. This had the effect of weakening the region's urban centres while strengthening its agrarian character and pushing it towards capitalistic agriculture. In 1823 the Prussian regime emancipated the serfs in a way that financially benefited the gentry, allowing the growth of large farms and creating a pool of hired labourers.[47] Government assistance was lacking, however, for the local industries. Because

Deutschland, 315, that in 1829 fully 35% of school-age children in the Posen district went without schooling, and the figure dropped to 25.8% in 1832. He has no data on this for West Prussia, but the problem does not appear to be as severe. Jewish enrolment in Christian schools was much higher in West Prussia, especially after 1840; compare the data on pp. 329 and 333. The missionary efforts towards the Jews in some Christian schools were, according to the data, a miserable failure; see Clark, 'Missionary Politics', 40.

[45] Aschkewitz, *Zur Geschichte der Juden in Westpreussen*, 32, 33, 43–5, discusses the numerous problems caused by the flow of poor Jews into the region from Russian Poland.

[46] From *Der Orient*, 14 (1848), 343, as quoted in Eliav, *Jewish Education in Germany*, 333. Similar reports are found in Aschkewitz, *Zur Geschichte der Juden in Westpreussen*, 120, 125, 126.

[47] Piotr S. Wandycz, *The Lands of Partitioned Poland, 1795–1918* (Seattle and London, 1974), 68–9.

of the loss of the British market in the 1820s, the Russian government's fostering of handicrafts and industry reduced the need for imported goods, and the competition for markets from the western provinces, the local textile industries, and small manufacturing suffered, and the few attempts to establish new concerns failed. By 1825 the economy of West Prussia and the Posen region became predominantly agrarian. The poorest element of the population had become landless, and those who could not find work as hired labourers or in the struggling local industries roamed the countryside or emigrated.[48] The vast majority of Jews lived in small towns and worked in trade and handicrafts, the segment of the economy harmed by the new policies. By law Jews were prohibited from purchasing farm land, but because few were interested in working in agriculture, they did not regard this prohibition as a handicap. A steady number of small-town Jews either left for larger towns or for settlements of equal size elsewhere in the provinces, or were pauperized. Jews in the larger towns and cities, who were still excluded from the guilds, invested their efforts in the dwindling trade possibilities and urban services. Many, including the Kalischer family, supported themselves from petty trade: peddling, hawking, second-hand sales, pawnbroking, retail sales, and small-scale agricultural trades. The Jewish economy was depressed, and did not seem to hold promise of improvement.[49]

Jewish poverty was an obstacle to civic emancipation and the cultural modernization that typically accompanied it. There was a deep-seated resistance on the part of local and provincial officials, matched by opposition on the state level, to naturalizing any but prosperous German-speaking Jews. A strong inhibiting factor was the fact that naturalization included freedom of movement within Prussia, and there was a widespread desire to contain the 'Polish

---

[48] Julian Bartyś, 'Grand Duchy of Poznań under Prussian Rule: Changes in the Economic Position of the Jewish Population, 1815–1848', *Leo Baeck Institute Yearbook*, 17 (1972), 191–204 at 191; Wandycz, *The Lands of Partitioned Poland*, 71; Aschkewitz, *Zur Geschichte der Juden in Westpreussen*, 69–78. Stefan Kieniewicz, 'Poland under Foreign Rule, 1795–1918', in Gieysztor *et al.*, *History of Poland*, 369, describes how the enterprising landlords in the Kingdom of Poland, under Russian sovereignty, attracted the experienced textile workers to settle and work under favourable conditions, thus further weakening the Prussian territories' share of the market.

[49] Widespread immigration to the United States did not begin until the middle of the century. For more detailed data on the economic status of the region, see Aschkewitz, *Zur Geschichte der Juden in Westpreussen*, 69–98; Bartyś, 'Grand Duchy of Poznań under Prussian Rule'; Steven Lowenstein, 'The Rural Community and the Urbanization of German Jewry', in id., *Mechanics of Change*, and the sources cited there; the stagnation of the Posen region is evident in the survey of occupational change by Stefi Jersch-Wenzel in Brenner, Jersch-Wenzel, and Meyer (eds.), *German-Jewish History in Modern Times*, ii. 69–89. The impoverishment of the Jews, which Kalischer noted in his letter to Rothschild, improved only in the 1860s with the industrialization of the region.

Jews' in the eastern provinces. The first emancipation edict that affected the Jews of the eastern provinces was the 1833 Jewry law. It stipulated that Jews who knew German and owned a factory, house, or a considerable fortune could become naturalized (though even this did not include full political and civil rights). All others were merely 'tolerated' and were limited with regard to their occupations, residence rights, the age at which they could marry, and freedom of movement to other provinces. A significant majority of Jews, including Kalischer, could not meet these preconditions.[50] While this policy was designed as an inducement to Jewish assimilation, it also had the opposite effect: Jews were not motivated to acquire the skills necessary for the exercise of citizen rights, nor did they feel pressured to adopt the outward appearance of their non-Jewish neighbours. Observers lamented the fact that the Jews in West Prussia and Posen still appeared 'totally Jewish' in their dress, manners, morality, and customs. Only in the 1840s did the visible transformation of the Jews—and only the rich Jews—first become noticeable.[51]

It is clear, then, that Kalischer did not develop his messianic scheme as an antidote to assimilation or as a response to upwardly mobile Jews supportive of the Reform movement. These phenomena were not evident in his world in 1836.[52] There were still too many forces militating against the creation of a

[50] The majority of the Jews remained without civic rights, and could neither buy real estate under their name nor settle freely in Thorn. Their precarious legal position, which improved only in 1846, is described by Nowak in 'Zur Geschichte der Thorner Juden'. I am indebted to Professor Nowak for sharing his research in the Toruń Archives documenting Kalischer's difficulty in gaining permission to enter the town in 1823; see above, Ch. 2 n. 53. Weinryb, 'East European Jewry', 352, notes that in the city of Posen in 1834, only 535 out of the Jewish population of 6,000 qualified for naturalization. Eisenbach, *Emancipation of the Jews in Poland*, surveys the process of Jewish emancipation and the political and social issues surrounding it in Prussian, Russian, and Austrian Poland.

[51] Aschkewitz, *Zur Geschichte der Juden in Westpreussen*, 99–100, argues that the visible change of Jews from their Polish (meaning traditional Polish Jewish dress) to German appearance occurred only at mid-century. The rich Jews began to transform themselves in the early 1840s; the poor followed. This transformation stimulated Kalischer's activism, as discussed below in Ch. 6. See also Alan Levenson, 'The Posen Factor', *Shofar*, 17 (Fall 1998), 72–80, who points out that 'Posen represents neither the German nor Austro-Hungarian model of Jewish acculturation, but something in between the two.'

[52] I am taking issue with Yosef Salmon's thesis in 'The Rise of Jewish Nationalism', 124, that 'The intellectual milieu in which Kalischer grew up and was active was largely determined by the confrontation with the Reform movement.' Salmon argues that, even as early as 1836, Kalischer's promotion of sacrifice renewal and 'Jewish nationalism' was his counter-attack to the Reform movement. This claim is echoed by Ehud Luz, *Parallels Meet: Religion and Nationalism in the Early Zionist Movement, 1882–1904*, trans. L. J. Schramm (Philadelphia, 1988), 25; and appears in the work of Jay Ticker, 'The Centrality of Sacrifice as an Answer to Reform in the Thought of Zvi Hirsch Kalischer', *Working Papers in Yiddish and East European Jewish Studies (Max Weinreich Center)*, 15 (New York, 1975), 1–26.

discernible class of modern, assimilated Jews. Jewish civic emancipation, a process that could have hastened cultural modernization, was neither a factor in his environment nor in his consciousness. He did not even recognize that he lived in a new era of freedom. Decades later he would claim that God was responsible for Jewish emancipation, but in 1836 he thought that only distant events involving Mehemmed Ali and Rothschild suggested divine intervention.[53] Kalischer developed his messianic proposal precisely because he thought it would work. He thought that Jews would accept it at its face value. He assumed, reasonably, that pious Jews, especially those among the impoverished Jews of former Poland, accepted in their hearts the prayers they were uttering for the renewal of sacrificial worship, the return to the Holy Land, and the onset of the redemption.

THE PRUSSIAN POLITICAL ETHOS

Kalischer's messianic vision expanded key religious concepts in a manner that indicated his debt to Prussian political values. There was an affinity between his Jewish values and the core elements of the Prussian political ethos: submissiveness, orderliness, and industriousness. Rabbinic leaders had always stressed the centrality of submissiveness in the life of a Jew, and Kalischer did this as well. Beyond that, however, his realistic messianism evoked the paternalistic style of royal authority and addressed the social concerns voiced by spokesmen for the Prussian Crown.

We have already seen that an attitude of respect for the state was part of the heritage of rabbinic leadership in Poland and throughout the Diaspora. Jewish leaders in Poland were particularly beholden to the Crown for upholding the extensive system of Jewish communal autonomy. An obedient posture towards the state also derived from the religious conviction that the king acted as God's steward in preventing anarchy. Lorbeerbaum and Eger certainly accepted all this, adding patriotic rhetoric to fit the needs of the moment.

The assent of these rabbis to the king's authority, however, must not obscure the fact that a pivotal change was occurring in the relationship between Jewish and civil authorities. Under the Polish Commonwealth, communal leaders had been given free rein within the Jewish community: they exercised juridical power, and neither the curriculum of Jewish schools nor the

[53] Not until the 1860s did Kalischer write about Jewish civic emancipation as a sign of the messianic era. He attributed Rothschild's power to a divine selection that had no connection with any contextual political changes. I find no basis for the claim by Jacob Katz, 'Tsevi Hirsch Kalischer', 224, that 'the Providential explanation of Emancipation' is expounded in the letter to Rothschild.

content of the synagogue service had been subject to interference from the government. It was therefore not surprising that Jewish leaders touted this alliance as indispensable to the smooth functioning of both the Jewish community and the state. The Prussian rulers, however, felt entitled to determine many aspects of communal Jewish life: the curriculum of elementary education, synagogue liturgy, and so on. Communal leaders could value this form of government only if its direction and goals matched theirs; otherwise, government paternalism would be problematic.

During the early stage of Prussian rule, the bureaucracy's intervention was limited by its inexperience and a shortage of funds, and Prussian officials discouraged rapid modernization. Government meddling was not the norm, and the few instances that occurred were highly supportive of the conservative agenda of most Jewish communal leaders.[54] Yet these leaders must have had some awareness that politics had changed, for by the 1820s they needed government interference to quell religious rebelliousness in their midst. Traditionalists concluded that the best hope of perpetuating Jewish norms in an era of growing liberalism was to seek the assistance of an illiberal state. This greater dependence upon external authority marked a subtle but momentous change from the earlier Polish Jewish conception of the alliance between the Crown and the rabbinate.

Kalischer incorporated within his messianic theory the new style of royal authority. Lorbeerbaum and Eger had connected the king to the redemption only indirectly when they explained that the king's enforcement of Jews' observance of the Torah would enable the Jews to merit redemption. Kalischer, however, explicitly and directly linked the kings to the arrival of the messianic era: 'Redemption will begin . . . through the will of the kings to bring together a few of the scattered of Israel to the Holy Land.'[55] Without the concerted actions and willing co-operation of the world rulers, redemption would not take place. The kings' intervention was essential. God operated through earthly figures who reflected divine authority.

One could argue that this logistical dependence on the kings grew out of the naturalism of Kalischer's messianic theory; it required him to take a pragmatic approach to the situation at hand to achieve his ends. The coming of redemption was contingent on bold human activism—but it had to be legal and peaceful. Yet there were a number of possibilities; for example, a radical or liberal

[54] Contrast this with governmental interference later in the century. Mordecai Breuer, in *Modernity within Tradition: The Social History of Orthodox Jewry in Imperial Germany*, trans. Elizabeth Petuchowski (New York, 1992), 91–147, graphically describes how the increasing and constant pressures that Jewish school directors faced from government bureaucrats contributed to the quite minimal amount of Judaica taught in Jewish public schools.   [55] *Zionist Writings*, 4.

Jew might suggest that this initiative could stem from the masses or from a duly constituted congress. Kalischer, however, did not think in democratic terms: he contemplated human activism within the controlling frame of monarchy.[56] The Jewish masses and their leaders would play a minimal role in initiating the partial ingathering of Jews, for the enterprise would be directed entirely by the highest authorities of the land. It became one of Kalischer's truly unshakeable beliefs that the state, which was responsible for maintaining the religious authority over its subjects in the pre-messianic era, was likewise God's ally in instituting the messianic reign of Torah over the Jews.[57]

Whether the Prussian concern for orderliness and industriousness influenced Kalischer's theory is a more speculative matter. The rabbi had, indeed, put some order into the abundant and contradictory pieces of Jewish messianic conjecture with his schematic and inclusive messianic theory. The redemptive process he described was a multi-stage drama with a minimum of chaos: the return to Zion would be a gradual, managed procedure that conformed with natural and political laws. And although Kalischer was hardly industrious in the sense favoured by Prussian monarchs, his activist philosophy and his zealous concern to seek Zion could be regarded as its religious equivalent. More indicative of external influence, however, was his concern for Jewish economic productivity. In his letter to Rothschild he suggested that Jewish poverty could be utilized to hasten redemption; decades later, he articulated a much stronger and more nuanced Jewish work ethic within his messianic ideology.

Kalischer was not unique among his peers in desiring a more rational religion and Jewry's greater control over its history, and in expressing enormous respect for political rulers and regimes; German Jewish religious reformers did this as well. Clearly it was part of the milieu. In contrast to Kalischer, however, the first generation of reformers devalued as narrow and parochial much that was particularly Jewish and national.[58] In explicit language they identified

[56] German Jewish religious reformers also held an exaggerated respect for the state and believed that the present era was infused with redemptive possibilities. This similarity was not coincidental; rather, the reformers' patriotic rhetoric, like Kalischer's, was shaped by the fact that their success was so dependent upon the goodwill of the state. Like Kalischer, the reformers were imbued with a sense of mission but were relatively powerless. Also like Kalischer, they regarded their era as propitious because, in addition to their conviction that conditions were promising and that they had already seen evidence of important changes, they also needed to convince themselves that they could succeed. The exaggerated patriotism of German Jews (given the state's low opinion of them) has very complex origins, and cannot be attributed solely to Jews' desire for political integration and social acceptance.

[57] In the 1870s he even expressed the conviction that the officials were desirous of supporting the authority of Jewish law over the Jews; see Kalischer to Kalonymus Ze'ev Wissotzky, 1873, in *Zionist Writings*, 426.

[58] Many did this while acting out of their concern for the well-being of Jews and Judaism; I do not mean to imply otherwise.

politically and culturally with Germany, and they were desirous of feeling part of German society and exploring and mastering German culture. Kalischer's Prussian patriotism was different, for it served Jewish ends. He had no desire to participate in European culture or to become politically or socially integrated into European lands. His messianism concerned the Jews abandoning their residences in Europe and leaving for what he considered uniquely Jewish territory. The Jews' Diaspora existence was to him a temporary sojourn, and he meant to see it end as quickly as possible. Nevertheless, his Zion-centredness should not be confused with Jewish nationalism. He did not seek a Jewish state in his letter to Rothschild; he was willing to settle for Jewish authority over the Temple Mount in order to resume sacrificial worship there. Eventually, a Davidic kingdom would be restored, but his vision of the messianic kingdom involved an effacement of normal political life.

It is doubtful that European nationalism had any significant influence on Kalischer in 1836. Nationalism, German or Polish, was not yet a major force in Prussia's politics, nor would it be for some time.[59] Prussian political culture was fuelled by the principles of an enlightened absolutism that regarded ethnic loyalties as regressive—even German nationalism was considered deficient, for it was no guarantee of loyalty to the Prussian ruler. The Prussian regime showed an obvious preference for ethnic Germans, but this was due to its pragmatic rather than ideological conviction that it was easier to make them loyal subjects. Neither was nationalism a vital force in local politics. Thorn was part of the predominantly German territory acquired by Prussia's first partition of Poland in 1772. Its Poles were not known for their nationalistic passions; on the contrary, they were notorious for the mildness of their sentiments. The Prussianization policies instituted at the time of the partitions were largely successful. In the Posen district to the south, where Kalischer was raised and educated, the Poles were only slightly more demonstrative. The Posen district was heavily Polish, and its impoverishment made it less attractive to potential German migrants. Prussia's imprint was not as noticeable, for the regime believed that instituting its Prussianization measures as thoroughly as it had in West Prussia would be unfeasible and unwise. Yet here too, after the rebellion during the time of the partition, the Polish gentry was not inclined to voice resistance. Those few who ventured to request more autonomy from the Prussians did not receive public support from their colleagues; everyone knew that the Prussians regarded Polish aspirations as impossibly

---

[59] I am arguing here against Hertzberg's claim in *The Zionist Idea*, 109, 'Nationalism was the major force of European history during the whole of Kalischer's adult life, but he was particularly aware of it because of his geographic position.' I reject the identification of Jewish messianism with Jewish nationalism; both concepts are indicative of Jewish group feeling, but their conflation erases the unique and quite contradictory elements in each.

radical. For the most part, then, Polish agitation focused on cultural issues.[60] When the Russian Poles rose up in revolt in 1830, the Prussian Poles did not rebel, although a number crossed the eastern frontier to join the rebel forces.[61] Nevertheless, the revolt so alarmed the Prussian regime that after 1830 it began to apply more aggressively the Prussianization measures already instituted in West Prussia. In response, over the next decade many Poles resigned their administrative posts, leaving the government more firmly in Prussian or accommodationist Polish hands.[62] Following a pattern set at the onset of Prussian rule, the most fervent Polish nationalists left Prussian Poland entirely.

Thus at the time Kalischer was researching and writing his letter to Rothschild, the eastern provinces were not a site of nationalistic agitation. It would have been foolish for him, given the Prussian censor, to express admiration for the Polish nationalists in his letter, but it is highly unlikely that he even entertained such notions in 1836. It appears that most Jews in the provinces of West Prussia and Posen, except those in the south-easternmost region or closely associated with the higher ranks of the Polish business class, were more sympathetic towards German than Polish authority.[63] In the Rothschild letter Kalischer assumed, as had his elders in Lissa and Posen, that there were two categories of people in the world, Jews and non-Jews. He wrote as if Jews, even Rothschild, lived in a meta-national dimension. He paid no attention to the separate national entities and the distinctive and conflicting loyalties that might have affected his plan. Only in the 1860s did he express any recognition of nationalist movements, and even then these statements were ambivalent.[64] In the meantime, either he did not notice Polish nationalism, or he was not inclined to support sentiments that ran so counter to the Prussian system upon which he depended.

Kalischer's family and teachers had nurtured in him a spiritual unease that would not allow him to be content with the truncated Jewish life of the exile. He felt the absence of the Temple particularly strongly, but he also lamented

---

[60] Se Ch. 2 above. Hagen, *Germans, Poles, and Jews*, 83–4, notes the protest against the official preference for the German language and the requirement that officials needed to master Prussian administrative law.

[61] According to Hagen, *German, Poles, and Jews*, 86, the Polish organizers of the revolt planned to limit it only to Russian Poland. Only 1,600 civilians from the Grand Duchy of Poznań and 1,400 from Prussian military service were involved, out of an adult male population of roughly 650,000.   [62] Ibid. 88–90.

[63] Ibid. 95–109. Typical of Jewish sympathizers of Polish nationalism was Herman Seligsohn, with his links to the Polish aristocracy; his memoir is excerpted in Monika Richarz (ed.), *Jüdisches Leben in Deutschland*, 2 vols. (Stuttgart, 1976), i. 150–3.

[64] Kalischer's 1860s comments about nationalism are discussed in Ch. 7.

the other privations of the exile that diminished the world's completeness. He took to heart the fundamental belief that Jewish fulfilment meant living united in the Land of Israel under the sovereignty of a Davidic king and the elders of Israel, observing all the commandments of the Torah. Immersed in the study of theoretical law, he became increasingly eager to see the Torah in its ideal form become manifest in the material world. He never tired of repeating the biblical promises that the messianic age would be one 'of eternal happiness', when 'God will rejoice in his creation and be the sole king over all humanity'. He looked forward to the complete redemption, when 'truly wondrous will be God's deeds, a new heaven and a new earth, with spirituality swallowing death itself eternally, amen'.[65]

Most pious Jews mitigated their sorrow over the *galut* by immersing themselves in daily life and by reminding themselves of the rabbinic teaching that study, prayer, and righteous deeds substituted for sacrificial rituals. Those who could not be distracted by these considerations and who dared actively to hasten redemption were usually restrained by rabbinic leaders who warned that such activism was a sin that actually prolonged the exile. Kalischer, who was not preoccupied with earning a living, had ample time to lament the Jewish condition. One advantage of his withdrawn and scholarly life was that the day-to-day problems that occupied others did not distract him from religious speculation. While he was stimulated by the political and social developments, his vantage point enabled him to keep in focus the larger messianic picture. He did not accept the rabbinic assurances that substitute rituals were adequate, nor was he impressed by the teachings of messianic quietism. Inculcated with the responsibility 'to fight for the holy', he had mastered enough Torah to articulate confidently that such responsibility entailed initiating redemption. On the eve of his fortieth year, he had attained the rabbinic dream: he studied Torah day and night, free from everyday concerns, and had the satisfaction of guiding a dutiful flock. Perhaps that is why he was so acutely aware of the distance between the present and the messianic age, and why he finally decided to act. He sought a wholeness that was missing even in the God-fearing communities of former Poland. His messianic ideology was a complex weave of the different threads that made up his life there.

The activist role that Kalischer shaped for himself was more positive than that of his teachers. He incorporated elements of modernity into his thinking and reinterpreted them through the prism of tradition, and in so doing he expanded the scope of the Torah. By shaping messianic concepts to conform more with reason, he appealed to contemporary tastes and acknowledged their legitimacy. He articulated a naturalistic religious ideology that incorporated

[65] *Zionist Writings*, 4 and 5.

elements of the modern political scene. He described the increasing opportunities for Jewish power and well-being as God-given vehicles enabling the Jews to bring about their own redemption, and thereby defined new responsibilities for Jews under the rubric of religion.

FOUR

Sacrifice and Redemption
1836–1837

H AD members of the rabbinic profession been aware of Kalischer's letter to
Rothschild and his subsequent halakhic correspondence with his teacher
Akiva Eger, they would have considered them as acts of boldness. To be sure,
Kalischer's literary initiatives involved none of the physical exertion or public
rallying usually considered under the rubric of activism. Neither does it seem
that there is much room for change when a person is firmly committed to operating within the bounds of the Torah. Yet within the usual constraints of the
rabbinic world, Kalischer was actually making a very bold move. He was proposing a revolutionary change in the structure of Jewish life and throwing behind it his authority as a rabbi. Even within the confines of Jewish law there
was room to manoeuvre, because rarely in rabbinic literature is a matter ever
decided absolutely and with finality. Reviving sacrificial worship had never
been absolutely forbidden, and because it was essential to his messianic scheme
Kalischer exerted all his halakhic training and creative powers to construct a
case for it.

The letter to Rothschild contained Kalischer's technical and highly sophisticated analysis of the halakhic issues involved in resuming sacrificial worship.
Clearly the work of many months of research, the analysis would have been
comprehensible only to a person with a yeshiva education. In accordance with
the centuries-old technique of halakhic argumentation, Kalischer stated and
rebutted opposing positions, presented a wide array of proof texts and supporting legal opinions from venerated rabbinical scholars and sacred books,
and concluded that the matter was resolved favourably. Anyone who read it,
he thought, would be assured that they were free to act upon their desire and
obligation to restore the sacrificial cult.

The halakhic analysis that Kalischer included in his letter to Rothschild
and that he sent separately to Eger was, on the surface, highly obscure. It dealt
with the sanctity of Jerusalem's terrain, the laws of ritual purity, priestly
genealogy, and the like. His sacrifice responsum, however, must be seen as
operating on two levels: on the surface it was a narrow halakhic analysis of a
particular problem of Jewish ritual; on a deeper level, it was his response to

the debate on the extent to which Jews controlled their national fate—that is, the issue of realistic or passive messianism. Might it not be arrogant to reclaim political sovereignty and restore their ancient institutions—in short, bring about the messianic age themselves? On the other hand, might not God regard the Jews' passive accommodation to their present condition as lack of desire for a renewed intimacy with him? One could attempt to resolve this dilemma through exegesis, as Kalischer did in the first part of his letter to Rothschild, or through philosophical reasoning. Rabbinic scholars believed that Jewish law was the most direct expression of God's will, however, and so they preferred legal analysis to resolve the question of the propriety of activism. Were there a way to re-establish sacrificial worship according to the strict letter of God's own laws, one could conclude that God surely wanted to Jews to act. Insurmountable legal problems, on the other hand, would indicate that God wanted the exiled status of Jewish life to remain beyond human control. Thus, Kalischer's intricate halakhic deliberation was a legal judgement as well as an encoded referendum on realistic messianism. His teacher's response should also be read on both levels. Their disagreement is the first hint of the conflict over activism that would later tear apart religious Jewry.

HALAKHIC PROBLEMS AND SOLUTIONS, 1836

The first problem that Kalischer tackled was actually a combination of two questions: whether sacrificial worship required the presence of the Temple building itself, and, if not, whether the altar site was sufficiently sanctified for the ritual. He began by stating that 'it is impossible to build the Temple properly without the wealth and wisdom of King Solomon'.[1] He did not divulge if he actually had investigated the halakhic problems of rebuilding the Temple itself. Having given up the possibility of rebuilding it, however, he delved immediately into the extant legal sources testifying that certain sacrifices were and could be offered on a simple altar at the Temple site.[2] His approach was pragmatic and determinedly realistic. The halakhic problem, then, was not whether sacrifices could be offered without the Temple building, but whether the proper site for the altar (the Temple Mount) was still holy ground. And if it was not, could it be resanctified by mere mortals? In rabbinic literature this question was answered in the negative by some and in the affirmative by

---

[1] Kalischer to Rothschild, 12 Elul 5596 (25 Aug. 1836), in *Zionist Writings*, 7. The entire letter is in *Zionist Writings*, 1–14.

[2] Ibid. 8. He analyses Mishnah *Edu.* 8 in the light of the interpretation of Moses Maimonides, *Mishneh torah*, 'Laws of the Temple', 15; and the commentary on this passage by Joseph Karo, *Kesef mishneh*. Kalischer refers the reader to, but does not discuss, the elucidation of the Mishnah in BT *Shevu.* 16a, *Zev.* 107b [erroneously cited as *Zev.* 27], and *Meg.* 10a.

others. A few dissenting rabbis argued that after the Temple's destruction the ground was no longer sanctified and therefore offering sacrifices there was forbidden. For them, the resumption of sacrificial worship required a resanctification of the Temple Mount that would occur only at the next rebuilding of the Temple during the messianic age.[3] Their stance was the quickest way to call a halt to the whole discussion of the re-establishment of sacrificial worship; it took so much out of human hands that it made any further deliberations irrelevant. This restrictive judgement, on its deeper level, was a rejection of all forms of messianic activism.

Most legal authorities over the ages, although they prescribed messianic passivity in the course of daily life, were not so hasty as to relinquish everything to divine control in their halakhic writings. They rejected the opinion that the Temple Mount's sanctity had lapsed, and they maintained that the priest Ezra's sanctification of the Mount had made it eternally fit for sacrificial worship.[4] Given the prominence and centrality of sacrificial worship in the Pentateuch, it was hard to imagine that post-biblical Jewish legal authorities would have prohibited it so quickly and absolutely. Their halakhic discussions of the renewal of sacrifice usually dealt with *how* to comply with the requirements of Jewish law at the Temple site rather than *whether* the renewal there was permissible in principle. During the first few centuries after the destruction of the Temple, when its reconstruction was considered a human possibility, rabbinic rulings were still quite permissive regarding sacrificial worship at the site. In fact, there is evidence that individuals continued to offer sacrifices on the altar site for some time after the destruction.[5] Rabbis admitted explicitly that their lenient rulings on ritual purity (*taharah*) and holiday observance were motivated by their desire to enable the quick resumption of the Temple

[3] For a review of the halakhic debate on the pre-messianic restoration of the sacrifices, see Jacob Levinger, 'The Renewal of Sacrificial Worship', in id., *From Routine to Renewal: Pointers in Contemporary Jewish Thought* (Heb.) (Jerusalem, 1973), 112–37; and J. David Bleich, 'A Review of Halakhic Literature Pertaining to the Reinstitution of the Sacrificial Order', *Tradition*, 9 (Fall 1967), 103–24.

[4] Asserting the lapsed sanctity of the Temple Mount were the 2nd-c. sage Eliezer and the 12th-c. Abraham ben David of Posquières (known as Rabad). The initial discussion of the question occurs in the Mishnah as a disagreement between Rabbis Eliezer and Joshua; see *Edu.* 8: 6. Rabad's comment is in his gloss on Maimonides' affirmative opinion in *Mishneh torah*, 'Laws of the Temple', 6: 14–15. For Rabad, both resanctification and sacrifice could occur only in the messianic age. His opinion was considered the minority viewpoint.

[5] This was the *pesaḥ* (Passover, paschal) sacrifice. The practice ceased in 135 CE when the presence of Jews in Jerusalem was banned by Hadrian. On the continuation of sacrificial worship, see Gedalia Alon, *Studies in Jewish History in the Times of the Second Temple, the Mishnah, and the Talmud*, 2 vols. (Heb.) (Tel Aviv, 1957–8), i. 164–5; Alexander Guttman, 'The End of the Jewish Sacrificial Cult', *Hebrew Union College Annual*, 38 (1967), 137–48. This was first suggested in the 18th c. by Jacob Emden, *She'elat yavets*, 2 vols. (Lemburg, 1883), i, no. 89.

service. Were it not for the Romans' emphatic refusal to permit the rebuilding of the Temple, the likelihood is that the Jews would have rebuilt it. Construction of a new Temple began during the reign of Emperor Julian in the fourth century, but the work was interrupted and had to be abandoned completely on the emperor's death.[6]

Eventually, however, the consensus shifted on the matter of rebuilding the Temple. The future reconstruction came to be regarded as bound up with the miracles and not to be attempted before the messianic age. Perhaps contributing to this more submissive attitude was the Muslim conquest of Palestine and the erection of a mosque on the Temple Mount. Eventually Jewish authorities also relegated to the messianic era the restoration of a sovereign Davidic kingdom and the convening of the Sanhedrin. Over time, any attempt to revive these pre-exilic institutions was considered by the dominant Jewish authorities as an illegitimate means of hastening redemption.[7] Actively restoring the *status quo ante*, an effort that once had been viewed favourably, was cast as an act of religious rebellion. Traditions and texts supportive of this type of religious activism were overlooked, reinterpreted, or discredited.[8] The fact that Kalischer shared the conviction that the Temple could be rebuilt only by God shows how deeply entrenched it was.

Yet because the principle of the eternal sanctity of the Temple Mount remained, the possibility that one could offer sacrifices on an altar at an otherwise devastated Temple site was kept alive. A paler, eviscerated version of the older Temple rituals was not considered a rebellion against God. For obvious reasons, Jews of priestly descent were most eager for the return of the cult, and they continued to guard and keep records of their priestly lineage for centuries. But non-priests as well, nurtured by Scripture, the liturgy, and the study of law, evinced a desire for a return to sacrificial worship, and rabbinic scholars maintained that some sacrifices could be offered at an altar on the Temple Mount.[9] Thus Kalischer had ample basis for his claim that sacrificial

[6] M. Avi-Yonah, *The Jews of Palestine: A Political History from the Bar Kokhba War to the Arab Conquest* (New York, 1976), 185–207.

[7] The consensus opinion that the Temple would not be rebuilt until the messianic age is expressed by Rashi in his commentary on BT *Suk.* 41*a* and *RH* 30*a*. The restoration of the Sanhedrin before the messianic age was addressed favourably by Maimonides in his commentary on Mishnah *San.* 1: 3, and was attempted in 16th-c. Safed. Most rabbinic authorities regarded this as an inappropriate attempt to hasten the messianic age, and Maimonides' opinion was thereafter dismissed as a private opinion of his youth that he later discarded; see Jacob Katz, 'The Ordination Controversy between Rabbi Jacob Berab and Rabbi Levi ibn Habib' (Heb.), *Zion*, 17 (1959), 28–45, repr. in *Binah*, 1 (1989), 119–41.

[8] The textual legacy of the Bar Kokhba revolt is a good example of this. See the sources cited in Ch. 1 n. 6.

[9] Avi-Yonah, *The Jews of Palestine*, 26, describes the desire to maintain the presence of priests

worship could be resumed at an altar on the Temple Mount before the coming of the Messiah.

The rabbi found a ruling on the Temple Mount's sanctity that explicitly articulated a positive attitude towards this type of messianic activism. He quoted in full a statement from the late medieval master of rabbinic law Joseph Karo (1488–1575, author of the *Shulḥan arukh*): 'I say that we have an authoritative tradition and a decisive judgement [affirming eternal sanctification]. For why would Ezra have not sanctified [the Mount for that time and] for the future, lest in the time of the destruction [of the Temple in the future] we are given permission to sacrifice [and would be prohibited by this requirement alone].'[10] Kalischer cited this passage not just because Karo here affirms the Temple Mount's sanctity; it is crucial because it shows Karo sharing two of Kalischer's postulates: first, that the reigning power might grant the Jews permission to offer sacrifices, and second, that when that occurred the Jews must actually bring sacrifices. Kalischer read this passage as encouraging the Jews to claim control over their national history. Petitioning the government for possession of or access to the Temple Mount was simply a logical and necessary response of any Jew in the post-Temple period. Kalischer regarded Karo's statement as an endorsement of realistic messianism.

The second problem Kalischer faced was more of a challenge. Because the Temple Mount was holy ground, it was off limits to Jews with a type of ritual impurity called *tumat hamet*, impurity from contact with or proximity to the dead. Those with *tumat hamet* were also not allowed to receive any hallowed food from the sacrifices or tithes. *Tumat hamet* could be removed only by sprinkling the affected persons with sin-offering water, that is, water that contains the ashes of a ritually immolated red heifer, which could only be prepared by ritually pure priests. This situation resulted in a serious circular dilemma: all Jews are assumed to have incurred *tumat hamet*, but sin-offering water to make people ritually pure was no longer available, and producing

in Palestine and to guard their genealogical purity. This was not to rule out other, less spiritual reasons for the retention of priestly status. See also J. Klausner, *The Messianic Idea in Israel*, 514. For supportive examples from rabbinic literature, see Mishnah *Ta'an.* 4: 8 and *Tam.* 7: 3; and BT *RH* 31*b* and *Ker.* 9*a*. Estori (Isaac ben Moses) Haparhi (1238–1355?), in his topography of Palestine, *Sefer kaftor vaferaḥ* (Venice, 1549), reported an anecdote current among the Jews in Jerusalem that a medieval rabbinic authority had travelled there during the era of the Crusades in order to offer sacrifices. The identity of the medieval rabbi and the specific sacrifice he intended to make is a matter of some dispute, but the anecdote was regarded as having some halakhic weight; see Levinger, *From Routine to Renewal*, 116–17.

[10] *Zionist Writings*, 8. Karo's remark is in his commentary *Kesef mishneh* on Maimonides, *Mishneh torah*, 'Laws of the Temple', 6: 14–15, and is a rejection of the opinion of Rabad, cited above. Kalischer revised the halakhic section of the letter to Rothschild and included it in *Derishat tsiyon*, 72–8. He quotes the same passage on p. 73.

more required the participation of ritually pure people.[11] This dilemma manifested a deep conviction of human deficiency: people need supernatural assistance to attain the degree of purity held by earlier generations.

Kalischer did not believe that God would have set up such a barrier to sacrificial worship. Basing his argument on the judgement of Maimonides (1135–1204), he argued that the prohibitions on *tumat hamet* were not as absolute as had been presumed. Maimonides' guarded approval of active messianism meant that he found ways around what others regarded as insurmountable obstacles. In his legal code (the *Mishneh torah*), Maimonides had asserted that ritually impure non-priestly Jews were permitted to repair and clean the holiest section of the Temple if there were no other options.[12] Based on this, Kalischer argued that ritually impure Jews might also tread upon the section of the Temple Mount where the altar had been located (a less holy section), ascertain the exact site of the previous altar, and construct a new one. At that point, some offerings could be made despite everyone's ritual impurity; specifically, the *pesaḥ* (Passover) offering—which ordinary individuals could prepare—and community sacrifices offered by priests. These could be made because, according to Maimonides, the obligation to do so supersedes the prohibitions against *tumat hamet*.[13] Thus, Kalischer's elaboration of these earlier rulings permitted, in a narrow legal sense, the reconstruction of the altar while in a state of ritual impurity; in its broader sense it was an assertion that the Jews could achieve the spiritual heights of previous generations without direct supernatural assistance.

The third problem Kalischer presented was one of finding proper priests. Priests were not essential for individual sacrifices, but community sacrifices required their administration. This was the most difficult of the three halakhic

[11] On the presumption of *tumat hamet*, see Abraham Gombiner, *Magen avraham* on *Shulḥan arukh*, 'Oraḥ ḥayim', 561–2.

[12] Isadore Twersky, *Introduction to the Code of Maimonides (Mishneh Torah)* (New Haven and London, 1980), 207, 227, argues that Maimonides' legal decisions allowed the most latitude for Jews to re-establish, before the arrival of the messiah, institutions such as the Temple and Sanhedrin. In *Derishat tsiyon*, 74, Kalischer cites Maimonides, *Mishneh torah*, 'Laws of the Temple', 6: 3, but the correct reference is 7: 23.

[13] *Zionist Writings*, 8. Kalischer included this discussion in *Derishat tsiyon*, 75. Appearing in his letter to Rothschild, but omitted from his submission to Eger, is the following enthusiastic reference to the red heifer ashes that remove *tumat hamet*: 'But we do not have the ashes of the heifer . . . not until that day when a spirit from above will awaken us and reveal to our eyes the ashes [of the red heifer] prepared by Moses or will teach us through a prophet how to prepare a new heifer, then we will be entitled also to offer individual sacrifices in holiness and purity.' Kalischer is referring here to the tradition that Moses prepared enough ashes to last until the messianic age, but hid them. A prophet who would arrive, as one of the miracles of the full redemption, would either reveal their hiding place or help prepare new ashes.

obstacles. A priest who is the product of a union between a priest and a convert or divorcee, or the offspring of an adulterous union, is considered unfit for service. Written proof of valid genealogy was considered essential to establish that one was of authentic and pure priestly status (*kohen meyuḥas*).[14] In the Mishnah (composed after the Temple service had ceased), the Sages raised the question whether someone who had no definitive proof of his status could, nevertheless, serve in the Temple. They were not of one mind. The following passage, which Kalischer would cite in full, records their dispute:

> Rabbi Joshua said, 'I have received from Rabban Yohanan ben Zakkai, who heard it from his teacher, and his teacher from his teacher, as a law from Moses on Sinai [*halakhah lemosheh misinai*] that Elijah will not come to pronounce unclean or declare clean, or who must be expelled or who must be received, but to expel such [ineligible ones] that were received by force and to reinstate those who were removed by force. . . .' Rabbi Judah said, 'Elijah will come to bring near but not to expel.' Rabbi Simeon says, 'Elijah will come to settle disputes.' The Sages teach, 'Neither to expel nor to bring near, but to bring peace between them, as it is written, "Behold I send you Elijah the prophet, who will turn the hearts of the fathers towards their sons and the hearts of the sons towards their fathers."'[15]

Here Rabbi Joshua cites a teaching that only the reappearance of Elijah the prophet would dispel all doubts. Furthermore, Elijah would purify the ranks of the priesthood of its alien elements and return to it priests who had been unfairly expelled. Disagreeing with him are the Sages and Rabbi Judah, the supreme authority within the Mishnah, who maintain that Elijah would accept all claims of priestly status; even those whose ancestors had become priests through violent means would remain in the priesthood. Thus there were two opposing positions, the first asserting that only miracles could restore real legitimacy to the priestly class, the second—and prevailing one—asserting that all who count themselves as priests are affirmed in their legitimacy at the present time.

Despite this ruling, the permissive position was challenged time and again in later rabbinic literature. Just as the future reconstruction of the Temple came to be regarded as bound up with miracles, so too was the re-establishment of the priestly class. Record-keeping of priestly genealogy ceased in the early Middle Ages, and since then all priests have been considered to be

---

[14] According to biblical and rabbinic traditions, presumed priests are not allowed to serve at the altar or in the Temple, and, according to rabbinic ordinances, they are also limited in regard to the eating of tithes. See Ezra 2: 62; Neh. 7: 64; and Mishnah *Midot* 5: 4 and *Kid.* 4: 5.

[15] Mishnah *Edu.* 8: 7, cited in *Zionist Writings*, 9 and in *Derishat tsiyon*, 74. According to the arguments mustered later by Kalischer and Eger, examination of only four prior generations of priests was required.

priests by presumption only.[16] Legal authorities tended to argue that the presumptive legitimacy of priestly status was insufficient, and that it would be well nigh impossible to find men who could prove that they were born from an unbroken line of priests who had fathered them through marriages with women of the right family background. This meant that even were the altar to be rebuilt, resuming priestly duties in regard to sacrifice was problematic.

Kalischer argued, of course, that the presumptive status of priests was sufficient for purposes of administering sacrifices. He emphasized the great halakhic authority of those who held the permissive position, such as Rabbi Judah and, later, Maimonides.[17] Everyone presumed to be a priest at the present time could be considered a priest of authentic and verifiable priestly status and could offer community sacrifices. Awaiting guidance from a prophet was simply unnecessary. Kalischer added a new twist to this debate by explaining why Elijah's future role was described as *halakhah lemosheh misinai*, a law given to Moses on Sinai directly from God but recorded only centuries later by the rabbis. He pointed out that surely Elijah, a prophet, was aware of God's message to Moses and of his own future role; thus the designation *halakhah lemosheh misinai* was mentioned for the sake of the rest of the Jewish people, specifically the rabbis. It was meant to reassure them, to give them confidence in their own authority. It signalled to them not to wait for a prophet before proceeding with the community sacrifices.[18]

From the standpoint of legal argumentation, what Kalischer was doing was finding a principle of change within tradition. He was arguing that God himself anticipated a time when conditions would change, when the normal procedures for establishing priestly purity would prove to be a hindrance to the observance of the sacrificial commandments. At such a time, a new procedure would apply, one that would enable the resumption of sacrificial worship. The law of relaxed priestly standards had been given at Sinai, he wrote, along with the rules for establishing a priestly pedigree, in order to show that the latter should not supersede the former. He really had no choice but to argue in this manner. During the lengthy period of sacrificial worship in Judaism, the ritual had developed into an elaborate pageant tied in to other institutions of ancient Jewish society. If religious authorities were to argue that the ritual had to be conducted just as it had been before the destruction of the Temple, there could be no progress and the matter would, in effect, be out of human hands. Acceptance of the principle of change was indispensable for a modern renewal

[16] Maimonides, *Mishneh torah*, 'Laws of Forbidden Intercourse', 20: 1, 2; Gombiner, *Magen avraham* on *Shulḥan arukh*, 'Oraḥ ḥayim', 457: 2.

[17] The source of this teaching is Maimonides' commentary on Mishnah *Edu*. 8: 6. Kalischer's reference can be found in *Zionist Writings*, 9–10, and *Derishat tsiyon*, 77. The moral compromise within this legal conclusion apparently had no bearing on the law.   [18] *Zionist Writings*, 9–12.

of the cult and for those who believed that the course of history was in human control. This position had its drawbacks, however. Jewish doctrine insists that the Torah is immutable, and another scholar who was more literalist might regard Kalischer's position as compromising the Torah's immutability. Indeed, religious reformers used such principles of change to justify their innovations.[19]

Kalischer was facing the halakhic dilemma with tremendous optimism. He was convinced that legal solutions must exist, because he was convinced that God gave Jews some control over the course of their history. Armed with determination, legal acumen and creativity, and the breadth of his talmudic knowledge, he removed the seemingly intractable obstacles to the renewal of sacrificial worship. Yet he retained some moderation. His solution allowed merely a truncated, imperfect sort of sacrificial service, a partial resumption of the sacrifices offered by people in a state of ritual impurity. But this sufficed. According to the two-stage messianic scenario that he imagined, all that was needed to trigger redemption was the savoury smell of a sacrifice on the altar.

SEEKING RABBINIC CONSENT TO THE RENEWAL OF SACRIFICE, 1836–1837

Rothschild did not respond to Kalischer, but the rabbi proceeded with his plan. Within the month, he copied out the halakhic section of his letter and sent it to his teacher, Akiva Eger.[20] Peer review was customary among scholars, and a helpful colleague could potentially strengthen another's case with different or additional legal arguments. Eger's approval was pivotal. Were the internationally respected scholar to agree that Kalischer had solved the outstanding halakhic problems regarding the renewal of sacrificial worship, rabbinic authorities the world over would endorse the re-establishment of the cult. Rothschild would then surely secure the Temple Mount for the Jews, and the

[19] Years later, Kalischer would take the opposite side of this debate. When Reform leaders and Rabbi Jacob Ettlinger maintained that the Torah itself signalled the eventual annulment of the sacrificial laws, Kalischer angrily accused them of denying a fundamental doctrine of Judaism. See below, Ch. 7.

[20] Kalischer's first letter to Eger is not preserved. He indicated later (in *Derishat tsiyon*, 79) that he simply sent his halakhic arguments (*pilpulim de'oraita*, literally, Torah argumentation) to his teacher. Eger informed Kalischer that he had received his letter during the holiday of Sukkot, roughly four and a half weeks after the date of the Rothschild letter (12 Elul 5596 [25 Aug. 1836]). My conjectured reading of Kalischer's first letter to Eger is based on two texts that sandwiched it: the halakhic section of the Rothschild letter and the version of this halakhic section included many years later in the first appearance of *Derishat tsiyon*, published in 1862. The differences between the two texts are minimal and insignificant.

messianic process would begin. Were Eger to reject his halakhic solution, Kalischer's cause would be well nigh impossible.

It must have given Eger great satisfaction to receive a letter from one of his prize students eager to exchange words of Torah. By this time, Eger was 75 years old, and he knew his remaining days were few.[21] For years he had been struggling to preserve traditional practices and his own authority among Posen's Jews. What could be further from the communal bickering or the destructive aspirations of Jewish upstarts than the selfless pursuit of Torah knowledge contained in a halakhic study of the sacrificial commandments? Indeed, Kalischer's exposition dealt with matters quite removed from Prussian reality: the sanctity of the ground where the Temple once stood, the ritual purity of priests exposed to contact with the dead, and the presumptive status of priestly lineage. We can only guess at how he introduced this halakhic work to Eger, and whether he added anything to it indicating that it was more than a theoretical endeavour. Judging from Eger's answers, which deal solely with halakhic issues, it appears that Kalischer sent the halakhic arguments and nothing else. For eight months Kalischer exchanged letters with Eger, and these letters (published later in *Derishat tsiyon*) contain no speculation about the propriety of hastening the arrival of the messianic age. This in itself is not unusual; Jewish halakhic literature typically discusses problems only in their most narrow, legal sense, often omitting underlying philosophical or speculative matters. After presenting each of the legal obstacles to the renewal of sacrificial worship, Kalischer offered solutions. All his comments led to the conclusion that, from the perspective of Jewish law, the offering of some sacrifices was feasible at present. Eger might have regarded the letters as the work of a scholar engaged in Torah study for its own sake and as a substitution for engaging in the actual ritual ('we offer the bullocks of our lips'). It appears, however, that he had no such illusions.

The (possibly) theoretical nature of Kalischer's arguments did not incline Eger to regard them lightly. Eger's first response was a serious and detailed disagreement. He let stand Kalischer's findings that the Temple Mount was still sanctified ground and that the ritual impurity of the common Jew was no obstacle to finding the altar site and rebuilding it. But he would not accept Kalischer's argument that the status of contemporary priests was sufficient for the resumption of sacrificial worship. Eger furnished rulings from several important authorities who denied lesser privileges to current priests. 'How, then', he asked, 'can we allow them to serve in sacrificial worship?' In addi-

---

[21] By this time, Eger had already made plans to pass on his rabbinic post to a like-minded successor, his son. Because of the kinship link to the Sofer family, biographical details are included in Sofer (ed.), *Igerot soferim*, preface. See also *EJ*, s.v. 'Eger, Akiva ben Moses Guens'.

tion, he felt it was impossible to make the clothing required for officiating priests. Even an ordinary priest, he maintained, required a girdle (*avnet*) woven of threads dyed with four special colours. One of the colours, *tekhelet*, was derived from a sea creature that was reputedly extinct, and the exact shade of the colour known as *argaman* was also in dispute. He concluded his letter with a pessimistic pronouncement: 'We are not capable of making [the priest's tunic] until God arouses his spirit to bring the true redeemer to teach us properly.'[22] In other words, the entire matter was out of human hands and would have to wait until the arrival of the messiah.

Kalischer persisted. He crafted an extensive rebuttal of Eger's position on priestly status, insisting that only the High Priest required the special clothing: community sacrifices could be offered by common priests requiring simpler clothing.[23] Eger began his response, written within a month of his first one, with a lament that his weakness and exhaustion had hampered his ability to examine Kalischer's arguments with adequate attention. Nevertheless, he was not convinced by his student's rebuttal. He argued that the obstacles could not be overcome, the consequences of violating prohibitions were quite grave, and the hope of agreement between them was minimal. He seemed content to remain at a stand-off.[24]

The younger rabbi, however, sought a favourable resolution, and wrote to his teacher a third time. He conceded a minor point, but he complained that Eger had presented conflicting descriptions of a scholar's opinion, and in so doing had increased the difficulty of the problem from one letter to the next.[25] In response, Eger informed him that he was handing the question over to his son-in-law, Moses Sofer, to whose opinion he would defer. There is no record of what Eger actually asked Sofer, whether he identified the original questioner, or how much of the previous discussion he conveyed in his query. Eger's complete report of Sofer's reply, which Kalischer received in late spring, 1837, reads as follows:

I will inform you that yesterday I received a response from my honourable and learned son-in-law, and he wrote to me these words: In regard to what my teacher and father-in-law wrote, to request permission from the rulers of Jerusalem to offer sacrifices. He [the ruler] is a very strict one, and no one who is not of the Ishmaelite creed can come near

---

[22] Kalischer reprinted Eger's first letter in *Derishat tsiyon*, 79–81. Both comments appear on p. 81. Eger acknowledges that he rejects Maimonides' rulings in *Mishneh torah*, 'Laws of the Temple Vessels', 8; however, he finds more convincing the dissenting opinion of Judah ben Samuel Rosanes (1657–1727), the author of the *Mishneh torah* commentary *Mishneh lamelekh*, and the problems raised by Rabad on the matter of *argaman*.

[23] *Derishat tsiyon*, 82–9. The letter is undated.

[24] Ibid. 89–90. Eger's letter is dated 19 Marheshvan 5597 (30 Oct. 1836).

[25] Ibid. 90–2. The letter is undated.

this site, because their house of worship is built there, and it is said that the Foundation Stone is in the middle of the dome, and no one not of their creed can come near. Two weeks ago two faithful emissaries from there were here, and a holy congregation in Jerusalem sent me a gift, a wonderful drawing of the Temple Mount, and built on it in its centre is the dome mentioned above—it is a wondrous thing to see. At any rate, if we had permission, except for what my father-in-law wrote correctly concerning the priestly clothing [dyes] of *tekhelet* and *argaman*, it would be of use only for the *pesah* sacrifices, because individual sacrifices cannot be offered due to impurity and the [other] community sacrifices must be purchased with the shekel tax of Israel, as [Jacob] Emden wrote in [his responsum] number 89.[26]

According to this report, Sofer agrees that the resumption of sacrificial worship before the appearance of the rebuilt Temple is permitted. The question is a purely theoretical one, however, because of firm Muslim opposition. Sofer fully endorses Eger's opinion that the dyes are a serious obstacle, and he adds a new problem, the lack of a shekel tax. In sum, if the political situation improved, only the *pesah* sacrifices could be resumed. The lack of any additional comment by Eger indicates his agreement with Sofer. It appears that Eger was not enthusiastic about ruling favourably on the resumption of sacrificial worship, and he was trying to cool his student's ardour for it as well.

Nevertheless, Kalischer persevered and responded once again to Eger. Because of the consultation with Sofer, there now appeared to be two obstacles preventing community sacrifices, priestly clothing and the shekel tax. Kalischer chose to address only the latter. According to the Torah, all adult Jews were required to pay annually one-half shekel—a weight of silver and gold coinage of ancient Israel—towards the upkeep of the Temple and its service.[27] Sofer had agreed with a previous authority that shekel funds must be used to acquire the materials for community sacrifices. Kalischer took issue with this. Since funds from all the tribes of Israel had never been received for the Second Temple sacrificial rituals, he wrote, he did not understand why they were necessary now; funds from just a minority would be sufficient. Following this opinion comes a revealing statement. Obtaining funds, according to Kalischer, would not be too difficult. He wrote, 'apart from those living there [in the Yishuv], many in the Diaspora will joyously send their donations in order to merit [fulfilling the] commandment of sacrificial worship'.[28] This comment exposes the real nature of Kalischer's query: he believed that resuming sacrificial worship was possible, despite Muslim opposition, and he intended to pursue it. Perhaps from the beginning, Eger had been aware of Kalischer's motives or had discerned them in the course of the correspondence. He would

---

[26] *Derishat tsiyon*, 92. The letter is undated.

[27] Exod. 30: 11–16. Variations of the original tax were in force sporadically at the end of the Second Temple period.   [28] *Derishat tsiyon*, 92.

have been alarmed by and discouraged such an effort of messianic activism. Indeed, evidence suggests that Kalischer was continuing to make overtures to Rothschild. That spring, in the midst of the correspondence, Kalischer casually mentioned that he had recently returned from a visit to Frankfurt.[29] Perhaps there, the home of Amschel Mayer Rothschild, he had sought an audience with the banker. There is no extant record of any encounter between the two, however, nor any response from the banker to Kalischer's letter.

Kalischer was discouraged by Eger's reply, however. He concluded his letter to Eger by reiterating his earlier position: 'As for the matter of the *tekhelet* and *argaman* [dyes for priestly clothing], I have already argued my case with you that they are not needed, or even if they are it would not be an obstacle, and I cannot offer anything more.'[30] He would not concede. It appears that he found little comfort in the fact that both Eger and Sofer had permitted the *pesah* sacrifice; Kalischer wanted more. It may be—he never articulated this— that the *pesah* sacrifice would have no effect on redemption. According to Kalischer's messianic theory, the savoury smell of the sacrifice on the altar was indispensable for triggering redemption. As it was described in the Torah, however, the *pesah* sacrifice was slaughtered on the altar, but not offered there; it was to be taken away and entirely consumed by the designated owners. Post-biblical sources stipulate the burning of fat and entrails on the altar, but neither there nor in Scripture is there a reference to a savoury smell, the *rei'ah niho'ah*, in connection with it, unlike the other sacrifices.[31] Kalischer had reached an impasse. Achieving widespread rabbinic approval for restoring community sacrifices was no longer possible, even if the Muslim ruler would permit it.

Eger died shortly afterwards, in October 1837, and never answered Kalischer's letter. Kalischer must have felt tremendous grief. He seems also to have been disheartened about restoring sacrificial worship, for he did not write independently to Sofer or to anyone else about it. He turned to other matters, leaving aside his sacrifice responsum for almost two decades.

Eger's opposition to the restoration of sacrificial worship was even deeper than Kalischer realized. He did not inform him that he was in fact sending him an edited version of Sofer's letter, and that the actual text of the letter was

---

[29] The comment appears in *Derishat tsiyon*, 92, in Kalischer's introduction to Eger's report: 'After all these halakhic disputations, our rabbi [Eger] did not write further to me, only that he would write of these things to his son-in-law the righteous giant of Torah, Rabbi Moses Sofer, of blessed memory, who was then the head of the rabbinic court of Pressburg.

After some time, our great rabbi Akiva Eger, of blessed memory, wrote to me on 12 Iyar 5597 [18 May 1837], as I was coming to my home from Frankfurt, and these are his pure words.'

[30] *Derishat tsiyon*, 93.

[31] Mishnah *Pes.*, chs. 5–7. Kalischer's religious interpretation of the *pesah* sacrifice is found in his commentary on the Torah and on the Haggadah; this will be analysed in Ch. 5.

far more favourable than he indicated.[32] Why had Eger been so firmly opposed to restoring sacrificial worship? One possibility is that his opposition
was rooted in personal motives, perhaps that of an aged teacher irritated by
the youthful enthusiasm of a pupil. Another possibility is that Eger's letters,
including the misleading report of Sofer's opinion, were merely an innocent
response characteristic of a weakened old man who was dying. Even if one of
these possibilities were true—and there is no way to establish any of them—it
is important to offer a third possibility that clarifies exactly what was at stake
had Kalischer been able to win rabbinic approval for the resumption of sacrificial worship.

Eger was espousing a well-established position in the millennium-old debate concerning messianic activism. He was as passionate about his stance as
Kalischer was about his. Their argument was, at its core, about the structure
and authority of post-Temple Judaism. The rabbinic leadership that eventually dominated Jewry in late antiquity was deeply ambivalent about the priestly
authority that it had supplanted when the Temple was destroyed. On the one
hand, the Sages did not stand in the way of the reconstruction of a sacrifice-
centred Judaism; the Roman and Muslim empires did. The rabbis regularly
praised sacrifice as a mode of worship that was divinely ordained, powerful,
aesthetically pleasing, and foreordained to return. They acknowledged the
legitimacy of priestly governance of Israel in the past, preserved priestly traditions, and taught respect for the institution. On the other hand, rabbinic leaders frequently drew attention to the non-priestly authorities who had jointly
ruled with or over biblical priests; they regarded their rabbinic authority as a
continuation of the biblical prophets and sages, excluding the priests from the
classic expression of the rabbinic chain of tradition in the opening statement of
the mishnaic tractate *Avot*: 'Moses received Torah from God at Sinai, transmitted it to Joshua, Joshua to the Elders, the Elders to the prophets, the
prophets to the Men of the Great Assembly.' Rabbis affirmed the sanctity of
rituals that had been developing for centuries alongside the sacrificial rites:
Torah study, verbal prayer, good deeds, and rituals that each individual was
obligated to fulfil without priestly mediation. Rabbis, not priests, defined
these behaviours, and after the Temple's destruction priests were left with
only honorific roles and had no final authority over even priestly matters.
Thus schemes and suggestions to restore Judaism to its condition during the
time of the Temple—this is essentially what Kalischer was doing—would have
been regarded as an indictment of post-Temple Judaism and the authorities
who had shaped it. Because of his age and experience, Eger was more deeply

---

[32] Kalischer's discovery of the original version did not occur until the 1850s, and this incident
will be discussed in Ch. 6.

invested than Kalischer in maintaining the prerogatives of rabbinic leadership and the form of Judaism it had shaped and sanctioned after the demise of priestly Judaism. He may have discerned his student's deep dissatisfaction, and he designed his response to keep it suppressed.

Kalischer's exchange with Eger is particularly poignant because it stifled the very sentiments that his teacher had cultivated within him. Kalischer was taking his learning to its logical end. Lorbeerbaum and Eger had planted in him the seed that was blossoming in his sacrifice responsum. These men, and Moses Sofer as well, had defended the ancient system of sacrificial worship and pronounced it superior to prayer. They had explicitly argued in the 1819 debate on the reform of the prayer book that Jews should hope continuously for the restoration of the sacrifices. Kalischer's letter to Rothschild and his correspondence with Eger were the fruit of their labours. Expecting his teachers' enthusiastic approval, he was instead rebuffed.

Kalischer did not yet realize, apparently, the polemical context of his elders' teachings. Their discussions of sacrifice had been shaped by the debate on modernization. Alarmed by the weakening of Jewish belief and the assimilationist pressures of nineteenth-century European society, they affirmed the desirability of sacrificial worship in order to remind Jews of their separate origins and unique national fate. Sacrifice became a code used by traditionalists to signal the serious gap between 'authentic Judaism' and modern European culture.[33] Because these men did not devote much attention in their scholarship to sacrificial worship, it is unclear whether they personally longed for a chance to bring offerings to a rebuilt altar; at any rate, none of them explicitly advocated taking steps to resume sacrifice. Kalischer, in contrast, held the highest hopes for the restoration of sacrificial worship as a reality in his own day. He could not, like them, balance the opposing weights of post-Temple Judaism: to hope for the messianic age and to embrace the present shape of Judaism as God's will.

The very nature of rabbinic discourse militated against a solution to the task at hand. The rabbinic elite's occupational concern with codifying and analysing Jewish law had negative consequences for the reinstatement of sacrifice-centred Judaism. The ancient sages had recorded what they remembered of the defunct rituals, including contradictory accounts and idealized constructs of the ancient service. All these legal traditions, according to rabbinic thinking, were legitimate elements of God's Torah. A scholar who wanted to make a final judgement on procedure had to integrate them all into his argument, or make a

---

[33] This rhetorical pattern is discussed at length in Ch. 1. On the polemical context of the debate on the sacrifices, see Jody Myers, 'Attitudes toward a Resumption of Sacrificial Worship in the Nineteenth Century', *Modern Judaism*, 7 (1987), 29–49.

case that conflicting opinions were irrelevant to the matter at hand. Practical considerations grew over time: the further one was from the actual Temple service, the more difficult it was to prove that the pristine conditions necessary for sacrificial worship could be recreated. Humility also hampered this quest, for the later rabbinic scholar, being that much more distant from the original revelation and from the rabbis who laid the foundation of Oral Law, was likely to be inhibited from imagining that he could reconstruct that which had stymied the previous giants of Torah. It may be that Kalischer's determination to solve the halakhic problem was overwhelmed, in the end, by such a sense of humility; after all, two elder authorities of Jewish law had ruled against him. Whatever the reason, he laid aside his pursuit of the halakhic examination of the renewal of sacrifice and turned to more productive efforts.

FIVE

Finding a Proper Faith
1837–1855

Having failed to persuade Rothschild to purchase Jerusalem, and having appealed unsuccessfully for support from pre-eminent halakhic authorities for the resumption of sacrificial worship, Kalischer refocused his energies: he sought a public role for himself as a voice of enlightened religious faith. He took up his pen to assist Jews who were struggling with modern intellectual challenges to their traditional beliefs. In 1840, three years after the death of his teacher, he wrote an article on contemporary philosophy for a Hebrew-language journal. Over the next six years, he published a book and more articles on the same subject, and these contained references to other, already completed manuscripts awaiting publication. Among these were criticisms of the newly presented innovations for religious reform. Pious Jews who felt that their religious faith was impugned by the current standards of rationality in intellectual thinking received from him a message of reassurance. Through these writings Kalischer acquired a name for himself beyond Thorn. He became known as a rabbi who could explain traditional Jewish beliefs from a multitude of perspectives, in philosophical, kabbalistic, halakhic, or in common-sense, everyday terms.

At first glance, it appears as if Kalischer had abandoned his quest to hasten the messianic redemption in favour of more immediate problems. However, a close examination of his new writings reveals a more complex picture. True, he put aside his halakhic study of the renewal of sacrifice, and he no longer wrote about redemption as an immediate possibility. In his published writings from 1837 to 1855, he never mentions the existence of his responsum on renewing sacrifice, nor does he refer to his involvement with the question. There is no evidence that, until the late 1850s, he lobbied anyone in the manner that he had Rothschild and Eger. But the outward change of focus and reticence should not be confused with a substantive change in his views. Instead, it marks his increased willingness to spread his ideas to the larger public in a more broadly appealing and subtler way. His religious apologetics, biblical exegesis, explanations of the daily and holiday liturgy, and Passover Haggadah incorporate a theology in which God no longer enacts miracles, yet guides history so that humanity increasingly recognizes his unity and authority, and welcomes—indeed, requires—Jewish assistance in advancing history towards redemption. Without bearing the inflammatory appearance of a messianic proposal, his new writings nevertheless provided an intellectual and religious foundation for realistic messianism.

REASON AND TRADITIONAL LEARNING

Addressing matters of faith from a philosophical perspective was unusual for a traditional Polish rabbi. Neither metaphysics nor natural sciences was included in the rabbinic curriculum, and early modern European rabbis who studied them felt constrained to defend themselves to their colleagues.[1] This tension continued during the Enlightenment, particularly in Polish and German lands. The Jews who sought to put the principles of the Enlightenment at the service of the Jewish community saw as their agenda the inclusion of philosophy, the sciences, and Hebrew-language study in intellectual discourse and in the Jewish educational curriculum. The more conservative of these maskilim, such as Moses Mendelssohn, employed contemporary philosophy to articulate and defend the principles of Judaism.[2] Yet their conservative goals were not widely embraced in the next generation of west and central European maskilim, most of whom were pressing for more radical reforms in Jewish society. Consequently, during Kalischer's youth, the study of philosophy and science was linked (and correctly so) to the curricular changes advocated by Mendelssohn's disciple Naphtali Herz Wessely and the attempts of more radical Jews to weaken the Jewish community's hold over the individual.

Kalischer was deeply entrenched in traditional Jewish society, and he shared its wary attitude towards the pursuit of reason. Yet he was a proud descendant of the Maharal of Prague and Mordecai Jaffe, rabbis who engaged in study of the sciences and wrote about the need to integrate some of the sciences into a broadened Jewish curriculum.[3] Tsevi Hirsch Kalischer either taught himself philosophy or studied privately under the guidance of another autodidact. It appears that he read only that which was available in Hebrew-language texts. His expertise was limited to medieval Jewish philosophers, the Greek philosophy that had been incorporated into their works, some basic ideas of European philosophers from the time of Descartes onwards, and contemporary Jewish thinkers with a conservative bent. He was particularly in-

[1] David B. Ruderman, *Jewish Thought and Scientific Discovery in Early Modern Europe* (New Haven and London, 1995), 54–99.

[2] David Sorkin, *Moses Mendelssohn and the Religious Enlightenment* (Berkeley and Los Angeles, 1996).   [3] Ruderman, *Jewish Thought and Scientific Discovery*, 76–82, 87–90.

debted to the medieval scholars Moses Maimonides and Moses Nahmanides, and of the more recent writers he had the most praise for Moses Mendelssohn and Isaac Samuel Reggio.[4] He knew enough to expound upon Judaism in rational, abstract terms and to point out where non-Jewish thinkers had erred. He was, therefore, more modern and more philosophically adept than his rabbinic colleagues, yet on a different plane than the sophisticated urban Jews who easily read German literature and counted themselves among the disciples of Kant.

Our first glimpse of Kalischer's new role is evident in 1841 when he responded to a letter in the Hebrew monthly *Tsiyon* from a man who, newly exposed to Kant's critique of religion, disparaged kabbalah and its religious assumptions. Kalischer pointed out that the man's criticism of kabbalah revealed his ignorance of its underlying meaning. He carefully rendered kabbalistic terms into more accessible language, and then restated and answered Kant's challenges from a kabbalistic perspective. He concluded that kabbalah provided a more successful response to Kant's challenges than the philosopher's own writings. 'He who seeks to use his reason should regard kabbalah as our inheritance, and then his faith will be strong in his heart and his intellect and discernment will be sharpened', he advised, and then went on to describe how the talmudic sages had responded successfully to Aristotle's challenges. In the course of the essay Kalischer mentioned that he had a manuscript in his possession that dealt with these matters at length.[5] Two years later, he managed to publish part 1 of his manuscript, which he entitled *Emunah yesharah*, that is, proper belief.

Emunah yesharah was written for young or older men—women were highly unlikely to have understood his Hebrew—of substantial education, intellectually curious about the world outside the protective walls of the Jewish community, but wishing to remain pious. He took as his task the clarification of reason's role in the pursuit of wisdom, highlighting the ways that it could affirm and sharpen faith. The path to enlightenment through reason was full

[4] In the first volume of *Emunah yesharah* (Krotoszyn, 1843), 20–2, Kalischer quotes at length a section from Isaac Reggio, *Hatorah vehafilosofiyah* (Vienna, 1827), and a number of his arguments echo (not necessarily with attribution) Reggio's from that volume. On p. 22, Kalischer writes of Mendelssohn and Reggio that their brilliant thinking was widely recognized, even by the contemporary sect of 'freethinkers'.

[5] The original letter was written by a Shelomoh Rosenthal of Pest. It was entitled 'Hakabalah vehafilosofiyah' and appeared in the Shevat 5601 (Jan.–Feb. 1841) edition of *Tsiyon*, a short-lived Hebrew monthly published by Marcus Creizenach and Isaac Marcus Jost. Kalischer's response was given the same title and appeared in two parts later that year. The quotation and the reference to his manuscript can be found in *Tsiyon* (Av 5601 [July–Aug. 1841]), 179. The discussion of talmudic literature is from *Tsiyon* (Elul 5601 [Aug.–Sept. 1841]), 190–1.

of pitfalls, he remarked, and sensible people were rightfully aware that they needed a guide so as not to be 'brought down to ruin'.[6] Particular discernment was necessary when perusing non-Jewish sources, and all the great Jewish philosophers knew this; for example, he explained elsewhere, Maimonides 'borrows much from Aristotle, particularly in the use of his forms, but he only took the kernel and threw away the shell; he accepted the good and left the bad lying'.[7] He would also provide weapons against those who, through a wrong-headed approach to reason, would destroy faith, and 'sharpen the arrows of every God-fearing hero against the lovers of evil, whose tongues shoot darkness on a perverted path into the hearts of the upright'.[8] What people have to realize, Kalischer wrote, is that wisdom is established through four 'elements': investigation, faith, examination by reason, and tradition. Arguing from the medieval concept of the four elements of nature, which he still regarded as valid, he explained that the spiritual elements relate to each other just as do the material elements: they repel each other, but when bonded together, the attraction between them is strong; when an ingredient is absent, the bond can dissolve completely and the elements return to their separate states. The object is to unify these four elements into a complementary whole. Without this unity, a person is faced with sin and the world of lies.[9] *Emunah yesharah*, therefore, was intended to introduce the innocent seeker to the joys of engaging in reasoned analysis, and to explain why and when to call the exercise to a halt.

In this enterprise, Kalischer was in one sense following the lead of German and Jewish philosophers who criticized what they believed was the previous generation's exaggerated confidence in human reason. By the 1830s, under the influence of Kant, Jewish thinkers began to reassess revelation and characterize it positively as a category of knowledge perhaps even superior to reason. Unlike Kalischer, however, they denied the basic doctrine of rabbinic Judaism that revelation had been given all at one time or in one place. They held that what one generation had regarded as revelation could be discerned by a later

---

[6] *Emunah yesharah*, i. 8.

[7] Kalischer, 'Maimonides und seine neuern Gegner', *Israelitische Annalen*, 1 (1840), 6. The image of the kernel and the shell is quite old, appearing in BT *Ḥag.* 15b and repeated over the ages by those who borrowed from foreign sources, and their defenders.

[8] *Emunah yesharah*, ii (Lyck, 1871), 56.

[9] Ibid. i. 12. In reference to the relations between the four material elements, Kalischer noted that 'this is known to natural scientists'. In the note on p. 14, he illustrated his point about the fallibility of reason with reference to Descartes. According to Kalischer, Descartes began with a position of total doubt but did not doubt himself, 'and after all his labours he too fell into accepting some nonsense that cannot be explained here'. In *Emunah yesharah*, ii. 56, he prefaced his comments on revelation with the remark that he would provide some explanations for the commandments of the Torah; but he could by no means make this an exhaustive treatment since 'there are many reasons, some of which are secret, that we will never know'.

generation as only selectively the word of God, or that what God revealed to a later generation might negate that imparted to an earlier one.[10] These positions were too radical for Kalischer. He felt that, despite their critique of pure reason, they still employed it excessively, and he disparaged them as 'freethinkers'. Kalischer saw himself as continuing the earlier, more moderate approach of maskilim such as Mendelssohn, Wessely, and Reggio.[11] He, like them, had found just the right balance of faith, reason, investigation, and tradition (the four elements of wisdom). One of the deficiencies of *Emunah yesharah*, however, is that it does not contain a systematic guide of when, say, to employ reason and when to be content with faith. The apologetic aim of Kalischer's philosophy is primary. Long-standing religious doctrines are termed 'beyond reason' if they cannot be defended by reason, and the concept of tradition can embrace virtually any concept.

It is important to point out that Kalischer felt that the temptation to follow unrestrained reason was an endemic problem, not limited to his own period. Although he occasionally referred to this problem as one that 'we see in our own day', more often than not he described it as a universal phenomenon common to all historical periods: Abraham had to respond to rationalist sceptics, as did Moses, and so on. Perhaps he was unwilling to give undue attention in his books (as opposed to his articles in the German Jewish press) to the opinions of people he regarded as religious rebels. However, there is no evidence that he thought his own period (the 1840s) was particularly irreligious. He comes across as a man without a sense of urgency, securely residing within the walls of the Torah, thoughtfully recommending ways to prevent breaches from appearing in the fortifications.[12]

Because *Emunah yesharah* focused on how to think, rather than what particular doctrine to believe, it alone cannot show how Kalischer situated the messianic idea within the 'proper faith' of a Jew. Other works are available. During this period the rabbi had already completed or was in the midst of preparing his commentary on the Torah, *Sefer haberit*, and he may have begun writing his commentary on the Passover Haggadah, *Yetsiat mitsrayim*. These works are exegetical in form, but the content is, like *Emunah yesharah*, a blend

[10] See Solomon Ludwig Steinheim, *Die Offenbarung nach dem Lehrbegriff der Synagoge* (Frankfurt, 1835) or the work by Samuel Holdheim, *Das Ceremonialgesetz im Messiasreich* (Schwerin, 1845). Kalischer read the latter and responded to it in an article discussed below.

[11] In *Emunah yesharah*, i. 22, Kalischer quotes approvingly Mendelssohn's comments about the necessity of keeping one's desire to examine everything through reason within strict limitations. Following Mendelssohn, he wrote, 'a new sect arose which can be called freethinkers [*freigeist*], and they did not believe [the warnings of] the earlier thinkers'.

[12] The absence of significant Reform influence in Kalischer's environment is discussed above, Ch. 3.

of reflections on philosophy, kabbalah, and exegesis. Together these works offer a fuller picture.

There is considerable overlap in Kalischer's philosophical and exegetical writings, and it is most profitable to examine them as a whole even though some were written later than others. There are no significant differences in the way that each depicts his messianic thinking: they all reveal the same messianic conception that is in the 1836 Rothschild letter and the 1862 *Derishat tsiyon*. In addition, his difficulties in publishing these works in a timely fashion makes it impossible to establish exactly when they were written. Publishing books often involved a laborious and time-consuming procedure. An author such as Kalischer, who lacked a patron, independent wealth, or a supportive printer, would generally travel to various towns (or hire someone to do this for him) seeking subscribers for the book.[13] At the same time, if not earlier, the author would solicit respected rabbinic leaders for approbations (*haskamot*) which, printed at the beginning of the book, testified to its acceptability and worth. In the hope of arousing the interest of potential subscribers, Kalischer published, in 1842, an excerpt from a work in progress he called *Moznayim lamishpat*, a commentary on Jewish tort law. However, there was clearly greater interest in his more reflective writings. In 1843 volume i of *Emunah yesharah* appeared and over the next year three more articles on philosophy and contemporary issues were printed in the Jewish press. *Yetsiat mitsrayim* was not published until 1864; *Emunah yesharah*, volume ii, appeared in 1871; and the multi-volume *Sefer haberit* appeared in 1873 and posthumously. All these works were likely to have been revised and augmented over the years.[14]

It is beyond the scope of this study to examine this literature in full. Three themes from these writings will be isolated here: reason and the existence of miracles, divine guidance of history, and the meaning of the sacrifices. These themes connect most directly with Kalischer's messianic perspective.

[13] Mentioning the existence of a manuscript in an article could often arouse enough public interest to attract a publisher; this tactic was successful in achieving the publication of the first volume of *Emunah yesharah*.

[14] The following is an example of some of the difficulty. According to Kalischer's comment in the *Tsiyon* article, his manuscript on philosophy and religion was ready for publication. It is unclear whether this included vol. ii, which was published only in 1871. In *Emunah yesharah*, ii. 61, he notes to the reader, 'this is similar to what I elaborated upon in my commentary on the Torah'—a commentary that was published over three successive years starting in 1874. He closed the second volume of *Emunah yesharah* on p. 188 with a reference to *Derishat tsiyon*. *Yetsiat mitsrayim*, the commentary on the Passover Haggadah, was not published until 1864. Because of the kabbalistic and very explicit discussion of the sacrifices within it, I conclude that it was a product of the late 1850s, when Kalischer's enthusiasm for the restoration of sacrifices re-emerged and he collaborated with Elijah Guttmacher. The first two volumes of *Moznayim lamishpat* were not published until 1855, and each was produced by a different publisher.

MIRACLES

One of the key issues plaguing the naive seeker, Kalischer felt, was the matter of miracles. Central to Jewish belief was the conviction that God was providential, rewarding and punishing humanity and steering nature and history along a course he saw fit. In the Bible God frequently acted through nature-transforming miracles or through bold manipulation of historical events. Kalischer imagined that this was a problem for enlightened Jews who did not know how to reconcile the biblical narrative with their new understanding of natural law.

Kalischer's response borrowed liberally from medieval writers and neglected the more recent scholars. He relied the most on the philosophy of Moses Maimonides and the exegesis of Moses Nahmanides. Using these two sources gave the impression that he was harmonizing reason and faith, for Maimonides addressed the claims of science while Nahmanides used the language of religion and kabbalah.[15] Furthermore, he was showing that the contemporary dilemmas of faith had troubled past Jews and had been resolved by them, and there was, therefore, no reason for his contemporaries to seek solutions outside the Jewish heritage. Perhaps his insularity accounts for his ignoring a challenge to faith that was relatively new, the historical-critical school of biblical scholarship. A pious Jew would have been disturbed by its assertions that the Bible was not of divine authorship, that the final text contained corruptions and had been constructed from numerous documents, and so on. Medieval exegesis and reason could be harnessed to respond to these claims, as Mendelssohn did in his commentary on the Pentateuch.[16] Kalischer, however, seems entirely unaware that historical criticism might be a major challenge for his readers. He repeated time and again that it was clear to all who exercised their reason that God had spoken the words of the Torah to Moses. Moses

[15] For Nahmanides' indebtedness to the intellectual heritage of Maimonides, see Bernard Septimus, '"Open Rebuke and Concealed Love": Nahmanides and the Andalusian Tradition', in Isadore Twersky (ed.), *Rabbi Moses Nahmanides (RAMBAN): Explorations in his Religious and Literary Virtuosity* (Cambridge, 1983), 11–34.

[16] See Sorkin, *Moses Mendelssohn and the Religious Enlightenment*, 78–87, for a discussion of Mendelssohn's response to the historical claims of Johann Gottfried Eichhorn, author of *Einleitung in das Alte Testament*, which first appeared in 1780, was published in four more editions, and was repeatedly reprinted over the next hundred years. Sorkin describes how Mendelssohn responded to Eichhorn's claims through his commentary, and quotes Mendelssohn's conviction that Eichhorn's method was a fad that involved the abandonment of human reason: 'so long as the fashion has the charm of novelty, one must allow it to take its course. In time people will lose their taste for it; and then it will be time to redirect them to the path of healthy reason.' Kalischer would certainly have agreed with this judgement. Among his points that could have been reinforced by citing the commentary of Mendelssohn is his view of miracles as

recorded these accurately, and through oral transmission the meaning of the written text and other teachings were passed on to the next generation.

Kalischer responded to the problem of miracles and reason by adapting Maimonides' arguments in *Guide of the Perplexed*. Maimonides maintains that nature is well ordered by laws, but not determined in all respects; otherwise, it would be entirely self-sufficient and require neither ruler nor creator. Within nature's rationally determined structure, there are areas that are inherently variable and contingent. Because of this element of contingency, God can intervene in history without violating natural laws. He works through the contingencies in nature, rather than abruptly changing the course of events, in order to achieve his goals. This mode of intervention is not a genuine miracle because no natural laws are violated; because it is a divine intervention, however, Maimonides calls it a 'miracle within the domain of the possible'. According to Maimonides, God resorted only rarely during Israel's early history to genuine miracles that violated natural law, and he would not do so again until the end of history.[17] Kalischer argued along the same lines. Nature operated through autonomous laws, he wrote, but was not completely determined. This was a reflection of 'God's great wisdom . . . for the world proceeds on its accustomed path, according to its natural order, but at the same time God manifests his providence over it'.[18] The element of contingency in nature allowed God to influence the course of events without violating natural laws. For example, in matters of business success, in the conduct of a nation towards its ruler, and in the rise and fall of powerful men, God unobtrusively exercises his will.[19] This, of course, is exactly what Kalischer had explained to Amschel Mayer Rothschild about his rise to power.

The concealment of God's involvement in human affairs, Kalischer explained, was necessary for moral reasons. Obedience could be evaluated accurately only if people's actions were uninhibited by a display of divine power: 'At the present time God does everything through natural means, and it is

a divine reward, belief in which does not abrogate the notion of natural law; see Sorkin, *Moses Mendelssohn and the Religious Enlightenment*, 62–3.

[17] Funkenstein, *Perceptions of Jewish History*, 142; Moses Maimonides, *Guide of the Perplexed*, trans. Shlomo Pines and Leo Strauss (Chicago, 1969), ii. 48, and id., 'The Essay on Resurrection', in *Crisis and Leadership: Epistles of Maimonides*, trans. Abraham Halkin (Philadelphia, 1985), 222–5.

[18] Tsevi Hirsch Kalischer, *Sefer haberit al hatorah*, 5 vols. (Warsaw, 1873–6), iii. 209 (on Lev. 23: 16).

[19] Ibid. 209. This point is repeated over the next few pages as well (pp. 211–14). Whereas Maimonides had called this subtle intervention 'miracles within the domain of the possible', Kalischer called them 'hidden miracles' (*nisim nistarim*), a term he borrowed from Nahmanides. One discussion of this is *Sefer haberit*, iv. 118 (on Num. 13: 13).

preferable that he does not make miracles, for if we always saw genuine miracles, we would not really have the free will to obey him.'[20] The constant appearance of genuine miracles—that is, miracles that are obvious violations of natural laws—would also inhibit human initiative, he observed. Human initiative was particularly important for moral behaviour. God acts unobtrusively, he wrote, 'so that all generations know that God will bless you in all that you do, and that we must not rely on a miracle and be silent, but we must act on our own behalf, for example to fight a war justified on religious grounds [*milḥemet mitsvah*] and to sacrifice our lives for him'.[21] Taking the initiative is an act of faith because no one can ever know with certainty whether a set of circumstances is a hidden miracle until some time after the human response is made. Then, 'any clear-minded individual will understand and see the hidden miracles of God and discern them plainly, and will not remark "it is only chance"'.[22]

Yet genuine miracles—he also called them revealed miracles, in contrast to hidden miracles—did have a legitimate place in the faith of an enlightened Jew, Kalischer believed. Genuine miracles were not a violation of reason, he argued. Reason was but one of the four sources of wisdom and spiritual truth, he taught. One must also consider faith and tradition, which testify to the existence of these miracles: rejecting faith and tradition in the name of reason is an act of folly. The type of genuine miracles performed for the Jews were acts 'above' reason, not 'against' reason. In the former, God in his omnipotence abrogates natural law, and in the latter he enacts logical impossibilities. The latter were not part of Jewish belief. Judaism did not demand belief in anything 'against reason', Kalischer asserted proudly, in contrast to some religions that insisted on the dogma that God was simultaneously three and one.[23]

Genuine miracles were rare, however, and should be considered an expression of divine favour. In this he was following the opinion of Nahmanides, who maintained that God tampered with nature in order to reward and punish. In his commentary on the Pentateuch, Nahmanides disagreed with Maimonides' unsympathetic view of genuine miracles and highlighted the frequency of miracles, even identifying seemingly natural events as miraculous.[24] Kalischer did

---

[20] Ibid.   [21] Ibid.

[22] This comment appears a number of times in *Sefer haberit*, ii. 88–9 (on Exod. 12: 2); iii. 209–14 (on Lev. 23: 16 and on S. of S. 2: 9); iv. 118, 126, 127 (on Num. 13 and 14).

[23] *Emunah yesharah*, i. 19. Kalischer does not name Christianity here. The distinction between beliefs 'against reason' and 'above reason' was probably taken from Isaac Samuel Reggio, from whose book Kalischer quotes at length on the next page. See Reggio, *Hatorah vehafilosofiyah*, 108.

[24] Amos Funkenstein, 'History and Typology: Nachmanides's Reading of the Biblical Narrative', in his *Perceptions of Jewish History*, 106. See also David Berger, 'Miracles and the Natural Order in Nahmanides', in Twersky, *Nahmanides*, 107–28.

not go this far. He described genuine miracles as an open manifestation of God's love, evidence of his willingness to break nature's laws for his people.[25] Miracles were a reward. They occurred very rarely; they were performed only for the Jewish people in the land of Israel 'when they obeyed God's will with all their heart'.[26] The sinful Israelites would not earn many miracles, he noted: only a few occurred in the period after the conquest of the promised land. Since it was not seemly to bestow such beneficence on the punished nation, genuine miracles ended when the Jews were sent into exile.[27] After this point, only hidden miracles were performed. These were not as great a sign of God's love; hence, Kalischer allowed that God performed them for all peoples of the world, though they occurred with greater frequency for the Jews.[28] But even in Israel's early history, genuine miracles had to be earned. He expressed it as follows: 'Why should he make miracles for us? This was the case during the parting of the Red Sea. . . . Our sages explained that Nahshon forged ahead into the water, and only then, owing to his faith in God, the waters parted.'[29] The miracle at the Red Sea was a reward for the initiative of Nahshon, who stepped into the sea before the waters parted, secure in his belief that God would honour his promise to save the Jews from the Egyptians. This point is crucial: God's love and assistance are aroused when Jews act decisively out of faith in him. This was a pillar of Kalischer's messianic ideology.

Kalischer's interpretation of miracles was an attempt to rescue traditional belief from the attacks of what he regarded as an amateurish rationalism. He was attempting to satisfy the desire for a rational faith while limiting reason's potential damage. He asserted that God made the world orderly, he could guide history without abrogating natural laws, and he directed human beings to operate within those laws to effect change. According to Kalischer, the rational seeker can accept the existence of genuine miracles, for he will understand that they are 'above', not 'against' reason; and even genuine miracles are governed by rational principles of reward and encouragement. His concept of miracles synthesized rationalism and non-rational faith in a way that reaped the optimum benefit from both.

These principles of enlightened belief also provide a philosophic basis to Kalischer's messianic understanding of current events. All these concepts could be (and eventually were) used to identify unprecedented historical phenomena as God's hidden miracles. They provided a vocabulary for and a religious understanding of Rothschild's acquisition of vast wealth and ascent to

---

[25] Tsevi Hirsch Kalischer, *Seder hagadah shel pesaḥ im biur yakar yetsiat mitsrayim* (Warsaw, 1864), 23–4 (hereafter *Yetsiat mitsrayim*).

[26] *Sefer haberit*, ii. 15 (on Exod. 18: 11), and also iii. 209 [p. 205 according to the Hebrew pagination] (on Lev. 23: 16).   [27] *Emunah yesharah*, ii. 93.

[28] *Sefer haberit*, iii. 209 (on Lev. 23: 16).   [29] Ibid. iv. 126 (on Num. 14: 8).

power, Turkey's dire need for funds, and Mehemmed Ali's conquest of Palestine: these were all hidden miracles, the result of God's subtle and non-miraculous intervention in history. Other historical developments could potentially be regarded as hidden miracles, too. The pious Jew—one who has a correct apprehension of God's ways, a proper faith—would recognize hidden miracles and, without waiting for genuine ones to occur, initiate or support redemptive activity. That is what Kalischer did in writing to Rothschild and in crafting the sacrifice responsa and sending them to Eger. He knew that God would regard his efforts as an expression of firm belief. What remained was for other Jews to recognize these truths.

GOD'S ROLE IN HISTORY

God had a plan for history, Kalischer knew. The hidden and revealed miracles were part of a larger scheme. God guided history towards a specific end that would finally be achieved during the messianic age: to bring the world to perfect knowledge of and service to him. This was a long-standing doctrine within Judaism, and Kalischer's assertion of it was to be expected. Yet he gave a great deal of attention to it both because of the apologetic character of his philosophical and exegetical writings and because of his agenda to promote realistic messianism.

As in Kalischer's response to the challenge of reason, in his discussion of history he did not identify individuals who were disputing a particular Jewish concept. The rabbi knew that there were sceptics who denied a purpose behind history. The notion of divinely ordained historical progress, unlike the concept of miracles, was not an unpopular concept among European intellectuals of this era, who were generally confident that humanity advanced towards higher truth or towards a greater awareness of the Absolute. Some felt they were moving rapidly towards a universal golden age and were even on the brink of it. For Kalischer, however, this was not enough. He had to persuade the pious seeker of enlightenment that the specific details of Judaism's messianic idea were reliable and deserved respect.

For his philosophy of history Kalischer relied primarily on Maimonides' reasoning in *Guide of the Perplexed*. According to Maimonides, the laws God gave to the patriarchs and Moses were designed to promote pure monotheism among the masses. Even though the Jewish religion retained some pagan practices, such as sacrificial worship, it brought the world to a correct apprehension of God. God made use of these older rituals as a concession to prevailing and widespread religious practices to ease the acceptance of the Torah; at the same time, he modified them in such a way that they were instruments for the furtherance of monotheism. The sacrificial laws were just such a ruse. They were a divine stratagem, a mode of utilizing human error in its own defeat, and thereby avoided an abrupt change in history. Another example of this was the growth of Christianity and Islam. Maimonides contended that these religions were not truly monotheistic, but they were 'of the nature of a [true] religion'. God enabled them to flourish because they would inadvertently spread monotheism throughout the world. This notion correlates with the concept of 'miracles within the domain of the possible' discussed above, the belief that God intervenes in human affairs without violating natural law. Eventually, Maimonides predicted, the expansion of divine wisdom would climax in the messianic age. He cautioned people not to expect that the advent of redemption would be heralded by miracles or the annulment of anything in the customary order of things. The messianic era would see the restoration of pre-exile institutions and world peace, so that Jews could observe and study the Torah without oppression and all the world would acknowledge God. Miracles and wonders and changes in nature were not a feature of the new age.[30]

Kalischer accepted virtually all this narrative except the negative view of sacrifice and the non-miraculous content of the messianic age. He agreed that the historical process, even leading up to redemption, was gradual, natural, and mainly non-miraculous. Even the creation of the world followed this pattern: 'The world in its entirety was created gradually even though it could have been created with one utterance and in one instant. His will could make it all, but God desired that it be enacted one after the other, flowing from the one before it, and tied together like a connected chain.'[31] God's creative energy, then, does not manifest itself as a force pitted against nature, but as a specific direction given to it. Furthermore, the world was left incomplete, he wrote, and man was enjoined to 'complete himself and strive to bring the world to completion with him'.[32] Human activy was integral to all advances.

Revelation, like creation, proceeded gradually and with human assistance. Like Maimonides, Kalischer explained that knowledge of God spread unevenly and was met with occasional setbacks that were actually part of the

---

[30] This narrative is summarized in Funkenstein, *Perceptions of Jewish History*, 150–3. These ideas are embedded within Maimonides' discussion of design in nature and the reason for the commandments in *Guide of the Perplexed*, iii, chs. 26–32; in *Treatise on the Resurrection of the Dead*, in *Epistle to the Jews of Yemen*, *Mishneh torah*, 'Laws of Kings', 11, and *Mishneh torah*, 'Laws of Idolatry', 1. In *Mishneh torah*, 'Laws of Kings', Maimonides insists that the Messiah is not required to perform miracles such as the resurrection of the dead. In *Treatise on the Resurrection of the Dead*, he says that resurrection would be enacted by God during the messianic era or after. *Epistle to the Jews of Yemen* also reviews the progress in history from the early biblical period, including the reference to Christianity and Islam.

[31] *Emunah yesharah*, ii. 19.   [32] *Sefer haberit*, i. 6 (on Gen. 1: 1).

divine plan. According to Kalischer, Adam was a true monotheist, but when his descendants equated worship of God with worship of his celestial creations they fell into idolatry.[33] The widespread acceptance of idolatry threatened to deny the minority of right-thinking people any chance to prevail. God undermined the hegemonic wrong-headedness—symbolized by the effort to build the Tower of Babel—by diversifying humanity's languages. With the subsequent growth of multiple national loyalties and religions, the minority of non-idolatrous monotheists were then able to achieve some success in turning human society again towards the right direction. Generations later, God revealed divine knowledge bit by bit to the Patriarchs, and to Moses he revealed himself in his full glory.[34] Thus God intervened in history in a non-miraculous and non-abrupt manner.

Kalischer was careful to point out the necessity of divine intervention in bringing the world to a correct perception of God. It was incorrect to think that God, through revelation, was merely accelerating the achievement of what humanity would have acquired by itself over a longer period. Here he was rejecting the notion of natural religion, a central tenet of Enlightenment thought.[35] He stressed that reason alone was never sufficient for the achievement of divine knowledge, for reason alone could lead even the wisest astray. This did not mean that the Torah was contrary to reason, Kalischer noted; indeed, the Torah was the perfect revelation, and its laws could be understood with reference to reason, unlike the revelation of other religions.[36] But even unerring reason could not produce the Torah, he insisted, for the Torah was divine and contained elements beyond reason. It would be infinitely less significant were it to be merely the product of human exertion. Yet human efforts were essential for the spread of monotheism. The Jews spread the Torah to others in a deliberate manner, Kalischer taught. For example, Abraham journeyed through the desert bringing idolaters to the correct perception of

---

[33] Ibid. ii. 163–4 (on Exod. 20: 3).

[34] *Emunah yesharah*, ii. 103, 120. Kalischer believed that the proliferation of sects in a religion was an obvious sign of its non-divine origin. This conviction helps account for his refusal to acknowledge religious reformers as a sect within Judaism, a point that is examined later in this chapter. In *Emunah yesharah*, i. 202, he proudly observed that Judaism had no sects, unlike Christianity, in which 'this one believes in the son, the other one believes in the mother'.

[35] In this he parts company with Moses Mendelssohn, who accepts the naturalistic origins of Jewish belief. See Moses Mendelssohn, *Jerusalem, or, On Religious Power and Judaism*, trans. Alan Arkush (Hanover, NH, 1983), 89–90.

[36] This point is made repeatedly in *Emunah yesharah*, ii. 67, 68, 103, 120. See also *Sefer haberit*, iii. 276 (on S. of S. 1: 3–4). It also appeared in Kalischer's 1845 review of Levi Herzfeld's sermons on the messiah (discussed below), where he labels as heresy the claim that the revelation was simply the accumulated wisdom of the Jewish people.

God.[37] The Israelites under Egyptian slavery were not passive, but were actively engaged in a struggle for the survival of religious truth. Endowed by the superior weapons of revelation, unity of belief, and divine assistance, the Jews were a model for the wise and good among the nations of the world. Many non-Israelites, he noted with obvious approval, joined the Israelites in leaving Egypt and accepting the Torah at Sinai. All others 'failed and fell behind'.[38]

One can find within Jewish exegetical literature great ambivalence on this theme: on the one hand, an emphasis on the purity of Jewish stock, on the other, pride in Jewish proselytism and the many converts drawn to the Torah. Kalischer came out strongly on the side of the latter. For centuries, external pressures and penalties had made proselytizing a dangerous act, and rabbis had discouraged active proselytism, occasionally arguing that the foreign essence of non-Jews could not be altered through conversion. This harsh tone weakened under the influence of the Enlightenment, but rabbis of all schools still rejected proselytism. When the lessening social distance between Jews and non-Jews resulted in increasing assimilation and intermarriage, traditionalist rabbis did not seek a solution in conversion; on the contrary, they introduced new restrictions on it in their halakhic rulings. Jews less bound by tradition tended to admire the Enlightenment ideal of religious tolerance, and, desirous of refuting the charge of Jewish parochialism, pointed with pride to the apparent absence of a Jewish proselytizing tradition.[39] While scorning explicit proselytism, they maintained that the embrace of ethical monotheism by Jews was a fulfilment of their divine mission to contribute to civilization's advancement.

Kalischer rejected the contemporary approach to conversion and highlighted textual sources that favoured the missionary impulse. He believed that historical progress consisted of the world's acceptance of Judaism, either as the wholesale adoption of the religion or as a stance of respectful submission to it. He was not the least bit apologetic about proselytism, Judaism's superiority, or Jewish separateness, and he found convincing evidence in Jewish sources that the forces of impurity (*tumah*) within the non-Jewish soul could be purified. Consistent with his stance on miracles, he maintained that true knowledge of God would increasingly spread throughout humanity without miraculous in-

[37] *Sefer haberit*, i. 96 (on Gen. 12: 1); iii. 206 (on Lev. 22: 32). See also *Emunah yesharah*, ii. 103, 121; and *Yetsiat mitsrayim*, 28.   [38] *Yetsiat mitsrayim*, 45.

[39] David Ellenson, 'The Development of Orthodox Attitudes to Conversion in the Modern Period', in his *Tradition in Transition*, 61–70. See also Walter Jacob and Moshe Zemer (eds.), *Conversion to Judaism in Jewish Law: Essays and Responsa* (Pittsburgh, 1994). On Enlightenment attitudes towards proselytism, see Michael A. Meyer, *The Origins of the Modern Jew: Jewish Identity and European Culture in Germany, 1749–1824* (Detroit, 1967), 11–26.

tervention. Jews were to be the active agents: it was their task to propagate the true knowledge of God contained within the Torah. He was already convinced that all of humanity, except for pagans and heretics, recognized 'that the Torah of Moses is true and the foundation of all other religions', so exactly what this activism should involve—explicit proselytizing of non-Jews?—is unclear.[40] In his letter to Rothschild, he described the approach to non-Jews as a request for their help in procuring the Holy Land for the Jews and hastening the advent of redemption. His writings from the 1860s would elaborate further on these points.

Kalischer regarded history's progress as a cumulative, ever-expanding process. It was not determined in all its particulars; what was determined was the eventual achievement of humanity's perfect knowledge of God in the messianic age. Along the way there would be advances and setbacks, and individuals had considerable power to determine in which direction they would go, but the number of right-thinking individuals would ultimately increase. Following Maimonides, he showed that this process sometimes occurred through a divine ruse. Even after the revelation at Mount Sinai, he observed, false religions and philosophies became popular and spread. But even these facilitated the widening acceptance of knowledge of God, because those parts of their beliefs that were identical with the wisdom of the Torah endured. This is how he explained the rise and spread of Christianity and Islam: 'The similarity among these religions was their error. In religious matters they took their foundations from the Torah and Prophets, and thus they paved a road to our God, and the crooked was made straight.'[41] This process would culminate in the messianic age, when all humanity would achieve perfect knowledge of God.

To Kalischer, proper faith included the belief in a divinely governed but naturalistic historical process that culminated in the redemption as outlined in Jewish sacred literature. The historical process he described for the pre-messianic era—advancement as a result of human initiative, divine reaction in the form of hidden miracles, and continuous human and divine interaction—matches the messianic process described in the Rothschild letter. He believed that a truly enlightened Jew would accept the veracity of both.

[40] *Emunah yesharah*, ii. 95. Kalischer's comment continues: 'No one denies this except those without religion, like the nations called heathens (they have no religion or faith, and you cannot think of them as humans), and also heretics (they are like beasts and not humans either, because what differentiates human from beast is . . . a conception of God). . . . But every person who fits this description of human, in that he has some knowledge of God, has no doubt in his heart [in the truth of] the Torah of Moses and the prophetic books. Upon this every race of humanity agrees, "from the sun's rising to its setting" [Ps. 113: 3].' A similar comment is on p. 129.

[41] Ibid. 67, 120. Kalischer's debt here to Maimonides is obvious. See also *Sefer haberit*, iii. 276 (on S. of S. 1: 3–4).

THE MEANING OF THE SACRIFICES

Although a key theme of Kalischer's letter to Rothschild was the importance of sacrificial worship, only in his exegetical writings did he present a full interpretation of the ritual. We can presume that he already espoused these views when he wrote his 1836 letter to Rothschild, for they explain why he felt so strongly about reinstating the sacrifices. His interpretative analysis of the sacrifices fits neatly within his understanding of reason, miracles, and history, for he regarded sacrifice as a ritual laden with hidden miracles that moved humanity to ever higher levels. He enthusiastically explained the logic behind sacrificial worship in order to show that it was, in his words, both the secret (*sod*) and the foundation (*yesod*) of the Torah.

Kalischer seemed well aware that in his own day some people found the sacrifices disturbing, and some of his discussion of the sacrifices is presented in an apologetic form. I have shown in Chapter 3 that Kalischer's assumption in 1836 that most Jews felt positively towards the sacrifices was not too far off the mark. By the 1840s, however, Jews eager for religious reform began publicly to discuss their objection to traditional prayers for the re-establishment of sacrificial worship.[42] In 1841 a second edition of the Hamburg temple prayer book was published, as well as a collection of learned opinions in its defence. Over the next few years, advocates of reform convened three conferences in Germany to discuss liturgical and educational innovations. While a wide range of positions was voiced, there seems to have been general agreement that the liturgical references to the sacrifices were objectionable. The idea of worshipping God and achieving expiation by slaughtering an animal was repugnant to them on aesthetic as well as moral grounds. The Kantian moral philosophy that they had adopted disparaged religious behaviour that resulted from an externally imposed law and the threat of punishment. According to Kant, an act can be considered moral only if it emerges from the individual's internal, autonomous sense of morality and only if full responsibility for it is taken by the individual. The sacrificial system, in which the death of animals was utilized to obtain forgiveness for the individual or to express gratitude, did not meet these moral standards.[43]

---

[42] I shall show below that in 1846 Kalischer felt that the desire for religious reform was a phenomenon that could be suppressed. His conviction remained firm until 1863, when he comprehended the depth of commitment among certain Thorn Jews to modifying synagogue practice; see below, Ch. 7. The exegetical works I shall be analysing here, *Sefer haberit and Yetsiat mitsrayim*, were probably composed during the 1840s and 1850s, though they were published in the 1870s and 1864 respectively.

[43] Meyer, *Response to Modernity*, 114–19. The liturgical reformers did not care to note that pre-modern Jewish critics still anticipated a purified sacrificial system in the future (see e.g. Jer.

Liturgical reformers also sought support for their proposals from negative statements about sacrificial worship from the prophets, the Talmud and Midrash, and especially Maimonides. Embedded within Maimonides' discussion of miracles in *Guide of the Perplexed* (outlined above), was an unfavourable comparison of sacrificial worship with prayer. Maimonides believed that prayer, in contrast to sacrifice, was ideally suited to convey the true conception of God and belief in the Torah. When God gave the commandments, however, people commonly worshipped through prayer and sacrifice. Rather than abruptly prohibit sacrificial worship, God commanded the Jews to offer both prayers and sacrifices, mandating restrictions on the offerings in a manner that would wean the Jews from their false beliefs. The details of specific sacrifices sometimes had this objective—for example, God commanded the sacrifice of animals that the idolaters considered holy—but they were generally arbitrary and without meaning. Nonetheless, Israelite sacrifice could fulfil its purpose of conveying true knowledge of God, though prayer was a more direct approach and superior.[44]

Yet Kalischer's discussion of the sacrifices in *Emunah yesharah, Sefer haberit,* or *Yetsiat mitsrayim* was not constructed as a direct refutation of the reformers' criticism; he mentioned none by name, made no mention of new prayer books, and did not elaborate on contemporary opinion. He was certainly aware of the conference proceedings, for they were reported in the German Jewish press. In 1844 and 1845 he wrote two articles criticizing specific claims made by religious reformers (these are examined in the next section of this chapter). What is most plausible is that he did not want to leave a permanent record of what he regarded as ephemeral irreligious teachings in his books. His pedagogical goals were not well served by explicit polemics. He was addressing the same audience for whom he had written *Emunah yesharah*: men of substantial Jewish education who were seeking enlightenment, curious about secular culture but fearful that it would lead them astray from the path of piety. Kalischer gave more attention to Maimonides' critique of the sacrificial commandments than to the specific statements of his contemporaries. Apparently, he believed that they were not saying anything that had not already been refuted by previous defenders of the faith. Repeating and elaborating on the older polemic would reinforce his argument that contemporary sceptics were simply repeating the mistakes of those who erred in the past. As he wrote in 1841 to

33: 18, and *Guide of the Perplexed*, iii, ch. 34). On the influence of Immanuel Kant on German Jewry, particularly on Orthodox Jews, in liturgical reform and exegesis, see David Ellenson, 'German Orthodoxy, Jewish Law, and the Uses of Kant', and 'Sacrifice and Atonement in the Literature of German-Jewish Orthodoxy: Defense of a Discarded Institution', in *Between Tradition and Culture*, 15–26, 27–40.

[44] *Guide of the Perplexed*, iii, ch. 32.

the man who had compared kabbalah unfavourably with Kant, rabbinic literature was a better resource for resolving problems of faith and reason than the unaided reflections of contemporary men.

The following is one example of this type of argument. Commenting on the conflict between Moses and Pharaoh, Kalischer described it as an ideological battle over inward versus outward expressions of religious devotion. The Egyptians contended that God could be worshipped 'in the heart' and that external rituals such as sacrifices were unnecessary; this is why Pharaoh would not yield to the Jews' request to leave Egypt temporarily to worship their God. God, through Moses, was teaching the indispensability of the performance of acts, specifically sacrifice, signifying love of and obedience to God. Pharaoh eventually capitulated, and the Israelites, too, realized the importance of sacrificial worship.[45] Contemporary hostility towards the sacrificial system, then, was simply a modern version of the false teachings of the Jews' past oppressors.

In the opening passages to his commentary on Leviticus, Kalischer launched into his response to the rationalistic critique of the sacrifices:

Thus the innovators of our generation have based their evil opinions on the great authority Maimonides and say that since there is no longer idolatry, there is no need for sacrifices. 'Why should we retain the Musaf prayers, or mention the sacrifices and the Temple service?' Some of them have been so arrogant as to change the versions of prayer fixed by the Men of the Great Assembly and the prophets among them. They are ignorant and have not sought knowledge of Torah.[46]

Kalischer could not accept Maimonides' approach to the sacrifices, for it denied that there was intrinsic meaning in the rituals. Furthermore, like rabbis then and later he feared that the philosopher's words would be cited by Jews who rejected ritual observance on the basis that it was unnecessary once the intent of the commandment was fulfilled, or who argued that the commandments were merely culturally conditioned practices. This was, in fact, what was occurring in the 1840s. Yet he could not simply condemn Maimonides' approach to the sacrifices, for he had adopted the historical narrative in which it was embedded. His general approach was to reconcile Maimonides with Nahmanides in formulating his own point of view. This posed quite a challenge in the present case, for Nahmanides had described this section of *Guide of the Perplexed* as nonsensical. Nevertheless, previous scholars, for example the fifteenth-century scholar Don Isaac Abrabanel, had attempted to do the same, and Kalischer borrowed and modified their comments for his needs.

---

[45] *Sefer haberit*, iii. 4–5 (on Lev. 1: 2). In *Sefer haberit*, ii. 88–9, 91 (on Exod. 12: 2 and 12: 12) Kalischer makes a similar analogy. On p. 89 he mentions that this point of view was taught by 'hanirgan poh' (the local troublemaker).

[46] Ibid. iii. 4 (on Lev. 1: 2). The Musaf prayer is quoted in Ch. 1.

Kalischer agreed with Maimonides that the sacrifices functioned as a ruse to remove idolatrous beliefs. He believed, however, that the sacrifices were also a ruse to bring the worshipper closer to God. The Jew who began to observe the ritual grudgingly would in the end, through the intimacy with God achieved through the sacrifice, achieve true recognition of God and comply eagerly with his laws. The pedagogical function of the sacrifices as a lesson against idolatry, then, did not interfere with their deep and profound meaning. Furthermore, Kalischer observed that one day that pedagogical function would no longer operate. The ruse would eventually be unnecessary, for 'every time God commands something that will succeed by means of a ruse, he built into it a time when it would no longer be a ruse, but have [only its] intrinsic value and merit'. The ruse would disappear, according to Kalischer, in the messianic age, 'for then there will be no need to prove the falsity of idolatry'.[47]

This notion of the sacrifice as a ruse was at odds with the Kantian notion of ethics that the more acculturated Jews so admired. Kalischer was apparently not bothered by the purity of the individual's motives. He believed that even if the individual had improper motives, perhaps harbouring idolatrous views or negative attitudes towards sacrifice, he would still be transformed by the power inherent in the ritual. Neither did he find problematic the animal's unwitting participation in the ritual or its substitution for the sins of the individual. While it would be ideal if the individual offered sacrifices with the proper intentions, the act was still a moral and sacred one if that did not occur. Here, and in the themes elaborated on below, it becomes clear that Kalischer had arrived at a matter within Judaism that could not be understood by human reason. The sacrificial commandments were part of the category of religion that, as he wrote in *Emunah yesharah*, could not be derived by reason because they were 'above' reason, yet not 'against' it either. This is why he relied on non-philosophic works, primarily rabbinic and kabbalistic teachings, for the substance of his understanding of the sacrifices.

As I have explained previously, even though the ancient rabbis had ruled that prayer, study, and good deeds substituted for the sacrifices, many statements attributed to them testify to the belief that sacrifice was still the highest form of religious expression. In biblical exegesis, for example, this appears in the concept of a heavenly Temple parallel to the earthly one, the idea that at the time of creation the earthly Temple was conceived as an element necessary for the sustainment of the world, and the conviction that the divine pres-

---

[47] Ibid. 6 (on Lev. 1: 2). For this interpretation Kalischer relied primarily on the introduction of Don Isaac Abrabanel (1437–1508) to his commentary on Leviticus. The notion of the disappearance of the ruse was Kalischer's original idea. This argument appears also in *Emunah yesharah*, ii. 110–15.

ence accompanied the performance of the Temple ritual and was absent at its cessation. These conceptions served as a foundation for the kabbalists, who, beginning in twelfth-century Provence, described the powerful effect of the sacrifices on the divine realm.[48] Kalischer relied primarily on these exegetes, Nahmanides among them, for his understanding of the sacrifices.

The kabbalists focused their efforts on explicating the inner workings of God and the consequences that these imposed upon the human realm. According to them, God expresses himself through the ten *sefirot*, each of which encompasses an aspect of his creative power; together they form the dynamic unity of the Godhead. In kabbalistic writings, the savoury smell of the sacrifice is an activating mechanism for the *sefirot*, moving them towards unity. The sacrificial offering not only brings harmony to the divine realm, it brings the sacrificer and the sacrificed object closer to their source there as well.[49] Sacrifice should not be understood as a gift to God, or as a demonstration of one's willingness to deprive oneself of property as proof of love. The essence of sacrifice, Nahmanides explained, is indicated in the word itself: sacrifice, *korban*, is a means of approaching, *kerivah*, and clinging to God, called *devekut*.[50] Sacrifice, then, has a salutary effect on the divine realm, and enables the divine and human realms to function in harmony.

Kalischer elaborated on this theme throughout his exegetical works. The key element of the sacrifice was its aroma, he explained, the pleasing sensation expressed in the Hebrew phrase *rei'ah niho'ah*, savoury smell. The word for smell, *rei'ah*, Kalischer wrote, is related to the word for breath, *ru'ah*. God, who is totally incorporeal, has no connection with his corporeal creation except through *ru'ah elohim*, the divine breath that he blew into Adam in order to implant in humans some of his essence. This created the potential for *devekut*, the intimate encounter of God and his human creations. The aroma of the sacrifice affects both the divine and the human realm. It stirs the *ru'ah* in the sacrificer towards God, and it activates God's compassionate aspect (the *sefirah* known as lovingkindness, *hesed*) and stirs him to consider the needs of humanity. The savoury smell is an intermediary between the divine and human realms. The *rei'ah niho'ah* of Noah's sacrificial offering after the flood restored God's compassion for humanity, and it is indispensable for the reconciliation that will bring redemption.[51]

Kalischer argued that the necessity for sacrifice had been built into the creation of the world. Following the teaching of the sixteenth-century kabbalist Isaac Luria, he divided the corporeal world into four categories: inanimate

---

[48] Yeshayahu Tishby (ed.), *The Teachings of the Zohar*, 2 vols. (Heb.) (Jerusalem, 1971), ii. 184.   [49] Ibid. 194–202.   [50] See the comments of Nahmanides on Lev. 1: 9.
[51] *Sefer haberit*, i. 79–83 (on Gen. 8: 21). Kalischer cites the Zohar for support.

objects, vegetation, living creatures (animals), and speaking creatures (humans).[52] Because human beings have within them a divine element (God's divine breath), they bridge the corporeal and incorporeal worlds. Yet there is a polarity within every person: each has higher and lower aspects, spirituality and beastliness, struggling for mastery. A person who wrestles with his beastliness, or tries to separate entirely from it, he wrote, runs the risk of becoming overcome by it. Human perfection is possible only through a combination of one's spiritual and beastly aspects. This is accomplished through the offering of a sacrifice. Through the animal offerings, the person's bestial aspects are acknowledged and utilized to raise the offerer closer to God, and the power of the bestial aspects is diminished for a while.[53] The two lowest categories of creation—inanimate objects and vegetation—are also elevated to a higher level by being part of the ritual.[54] Self-consciousness is apparently not essential to the ritual's power. The sacrifices possess tangible expiatory powers whether or not one understands how they function. Throughout his commentary on Leviticus he showed how the sacrificial ritual varied in its details and effect according to the stage in the struggle within the offerer's polarized self. Each of the three types of sacrifice—the voluntary offering, the sin offering, and the obligatory offering—had a different effect. During each sacrifice, the offerer was raised up, but during the sin and obligatory offerings God descended to the worshipper, too. Yet the voluntary offering was the best, for through it the worshipper was elevated the most.[55]

It was of paramount importance, Kalischer emphasized repeatedly, to realize that God wants the sacrifices; this is the foundation of the whole Torah.[56] In his elaboration of this theme, he drew on a wide range of exegetical texts, some of them mystical. God's goal for creating the world was to achieve *devekut*, and *devekut*, he wrote, could only occur during a sacrificial offering. The creation of the world was not really completed, then, until the completion of the desert Tabernacle within which the prescribed offering of sacrifices could take place. He explained this with reference to Leviticus 9: 1, which describes the commencement of sacrificial worship by Aaron and his sons on the day after seven days of preparatory offerings. He compared that eighth day to the eighth day after the beginning of creation. God had created nature and human society in seven days, and sacrificial worship enabled its continued existence. Sacrifice sustained the world.[57] Sacrifice was also required for

[52] Ibid. iii. 88 (on Lev. 11: 44). A summary of this theory and its relation to the dietary laws appears also in *Emunah yesharah*, ii. 134–41.

[53] *Sefer haberit*, iii. 4–5, 11 (on Lev. 1: 2) and 123 (on Lev. 14: 14).

[54] Ibid. 11 (on Lev. 1: 2). This explanation appears also in *Emunah yesharah*, ii. 132–4.

[55] *Sefer haberit*, iii. 7 (on Lev. 1: 2) and 39 (on Lev. 6: 2).

[56] Ibid. 7. See also ii. 88–9 (on Exod. 12: 2) and 91 (on Exod. 12: 12).

[57] Ibid. iii. 63 (on Lev. 9: 1).

prophecy, God's intimate communication with humans. Prophecy disappeared when the sacrifices ceased, and with their cessation, false religions proliferated. Prophecy would reappear only when sacrificial worship recommenced.[58] Here is exegetical support for the halakhic claim Kalischer made in his responsum that the prophet Elijah would appear after, not before, the resumption of sacrificial worship.

To Kalischer the post-Temple era presented an onerous spiritual burden. His comments on this matter directly echo those of his teacher, Jacob Lorbeerbaum, in the 1819 controversy on the Hamburg temple prayer book. It is not clear whether Kalischer believed *devekut* could be achieved without the sacrifices. He did maintain, as did Lorbeerbaum, that without sacrificial worship one could no longer be certain of expiation. The instruction in Leviticus 6: 2 to keep the altar fire burning throughout the night means that the Jews must continue to desire to offer the sacrifices and pray for their restoration throughout the night-time of exile. While the renewal of the sacrificial service would bring the messianic age,[59] Jews were required to be patient:

When the Jew has a humbled spirit, for he longs to offer a sacrifice but cannot, because God commanded that one cannot offer sacrifices outside of the holy site [Temple Mount], he will be rewarded for his desire, for abstinence, and for seeking [*derishah*]: abstinence, for he refrains from observing the [sacrificial] commandments because it is God's will, and seeking, for 'he is Zion's seeker' [*doresh tsiyon*] [Jer. 30: 17]. His desire and longing are considered as a sacrifice.[60]

There are two religious ideals here, seeking and abstinence. Seeking means that one must continue to desire sacrificial worship. Abstinence means controlling one's desire to offer sacrifices in a situation in which the proper conditions are not present and the proper procedures cannot be followed. Together, both are equivalent to a sacrifice. Kalischer's comment here illustrates his own situation: faced with the discouragement of rabbis Eger and Sofer, he is resigned to being Zion's seeker in a rather passive mode. Writing years later in *Derishat tsiyon*, he modified this interpretation, de-emphasizing abstinence and urging Jews to seek Zion by building agricultural colonies in Palestine.[61]

The most explicitly messianic interpretation of the sacrifices appeared in Kalischer's commentary on the Haggadah, the anthology of prayers, midrashim, songs, and narrative that is recited at the Passover meal. Since the

---

[58] *Sefer haberit*, iii. 11 (on Lev. 1: 2).

[59] Ibid. 45 (on Lev. 6: 2): 'and thus, in the future, due to the power of the sacrifices, the redemption of the world will arrive'.   [60] Ibid. 42 (on Lev. 6: 2).

[61] *Derishat tsiyon*, 36. The actual phrase from Jeremiah is 'Zion has no seekers'. Kalischer substituted the passive for the negative in order to affirm the talmudic teaching on this passage from BT *RH* 30a (that each Jew should strive to be Zion's seeker).

Haggadah is used at a family ritual, Kalischer's Haggadah, *Yetsiat mitsrayim* (the exodus from Egypt) incorporated family customs and the interpretations that were particularly meaningful to him. He quoted liberally from the Haggadah commentary of his ancestor, Maharal of Prague, and he prefaced the commentary with a summary of the laws of Passover according to his teacher, Jacob Lorbeerbaum. In *Yetsiat mitsrayim*, Kalischer is far more frank than in *Emunah yesharah* and *Sefer haberit* about the desirability of hastening redemption. This is due, first of all, to the genre itself. *Yetsiat mitsrayim* was primarily a kabbalistic work; much of it was written in the highly symbolic language of kabbalah and included many quotations from the Zohar. Kabbalistic exegesis attempts to explicate the inner workings of God, and the way in which sacrifice empowers certain aspects of divinity leading to redemption was quite relevant. Secondly, parts of *Yetsiat mitsrayim* appear to have been written later, when he had decided openly to advocate messianic activism.[62]

To Kalischer, the central element in the ceremonial Passover meal was the teaching about the sacrificial offering. According to Jewish law, three foods had to be explained during the Passover meal in order to meet basic ritual requirements: the matzah, bitter herbs, and the bone signifying the *korban pesah*, the Passover sacrifice. The *pesah* offering was unique among the prescribed sacrificial offerings in several ways. First, it was the only sacrifice that had to be eaten during the night. Second, in the Pentateuch it was the only offering that was slaughtered or eaten in its entirety by non-priests. Third, as it was described in the Torah, none of the *pesah* offering was offered on the altar; it was to be taken away, cooked, and entirely consumed by the designated owners. Finally, there is no reference to a savoury smell, the *rei'ah niho'ah*, in connection with it.[63] The unusual features of the *pesah* offering provided Kalischer with the opportunity to address all the sacrifices and connect them with redemption from Egypt and the future redemption. He found particularly compelling the idea that the Passover meal was the individual's opportunity to take upon himself the role of the High Priest—albeit in a dim imitation of the real event. He explains this while discussing why the adult male conducting the seder wears a white robe:

[62] Kalischer's change of outlook is described below, Ch. 6.

[63] Biblical texts preserve multiple versions of the *pesah* sacrifice, including the sacrifice offered in Egypt and the various accounts of how the *pesah* would be and was offered when the Israelites were in their land. Post-biblical accounts contain other variations. In the Torah, specific references to the *pesah* can be found in Exod. 12: 3–11, 46; Deut. 16: 2, 5, 7. There, and in the case also with the *pesah* sacrifice offered in Egypt, described in Exod. 12: 21–3, there is no reference to the *rei'ah niho'ah*. These accounts leave the slaughtering and consumption in the hands of lay priests. Later sources, for example Mishnah *Pes.* 5: 9–10, stipulate the greater role of the priests and the burning of fat and entrails on the altar.

On this night the common Israelite is considered a priest. . . . Henceforth, [your] souls will be enthused, for it is not often that your clothes are white like those of the High Priest. You will be happy that you merited . . . to worship just as if the altar were built and the burnt offerings [*olot*] rose as a savoury smell to please God. The love in the Israelite's heart is for his Rock and Creator, and when he offers a savoury smelling sacrifice to him, his joy will increase like one who finds a great treasure, and he will give thanks to God with all his heart and soul that he was sustained in life until this night when he donned white clothes like a priest.[64]

Here Kalischer expresses the aspiration—he imagines—of the lay Jew: to serve as a priest. Nineteenth-century western and central European rabbis, when they dwelt upon the sacrificial motif in their Haggadah commentaries, did not make such a claim; they tended to teach that the Passover meal extended priestly holiness into every Jew or Jewish home through the narrative ritual.[65] Perhaps his reference to the burnt offerings signals his longing to go beyond the *pesah* and administer the sacrifices that were more powerful.

In the previous chapter I suggested that the limited power of the *pesah* sacrifice explains why Kalischer was discouraged by Sofer's finding that halakhah permitted Jews to offer only the *pesah* sacrifice and no others. Kalischer never explicitly wrote that the *pesah* was inadequate to bring redemption, but he clearly was interested in a sacrifice that emitted the *rei'ah niho'ah* and was enacted by priests. The less than ideal features of the offering were alluded to in his exegesis. Commenting on Exodus 12: 2, he repeated a midrash about the first *pesah* offering: God made the *pesah* attractive to the reluctant Israelites by attaching to it on that occasion the smell of Paradise.[66] The first *pesah* was a divine ruse, then, a hidden miracle that induced the Israelites to behave in the proper manner.

Nevertheless, it is obvious from *Yetsiat mitsrayim* that the *pesah* sacrifice had an important messianic function. The *pesah*'s lack of *rei'ah niho'ah* as well as its other two features, its night-time offering and its non-priestly character, suggested to the rabbi its status as a preparatory sacrifice. Night-time was a symbol of the exile of the Jewish people and the diminished presence of God. This sacrifice, he wrote, is eaten during a night that is like a day, for it bridges exile and redemption, taking place at the division between slavery and the exodus. It has an inaugurating effect, for with it the Jews became a chosen people

[64] *Yetsiat mitsrayim*, 18. Kalischer credited this interpretation to the Maharal (Judah Loew of Prague).

[65] See e.g. the interpretation of the *pesah* sacrifice in the Haggadah commentary of the German Orthodox rabbi Marcus Lehmann (1831–90), *The Lehmann Haggadah* (Heb. and Eng.) (Jerusalem, 1977), 192–6. This volume is a translation of Lehmann's *Hagadah schel Pessach*, 2nd edn. (Heb. and German) (Frankfurt am Main, 1906).

[66] *Sefer haberit*, ii. 85–6 (on Exod. 12: 2).

who introduced the true faith into the world.[67] He elaborated on this with kabbalistic teachings. The people Israel is identified with the *sefirah* Hesed (lovingkindness), as is the patriarch Abraham. Abraham, wrote Kalischer, 'embraced the aspect of *ḥesed* to make God's name known publicly and to increase the number of royal figures who recognized God'. On this night the Jews must also accept the obligation to spread the covenant to others, especially their children.[68] The three symbols of the seder meal are also identified with *ḥesed*. Each operates to remove impurities from the Israelites and lead them out of Egypt, but the *pesaḥ* is especially efficacious. By eating the sacrifice, the Jew accepts his role as Abraham's descendant to perpetuate the covenant and to restore the Shekhinah, the female element of the divine world, to her place.[69] Thus the *pesaḥ* is the redemptive instrument of the human realm and the means of reconciling the male and female elements of the divine realm. This process of restoration is not completed on Passover, however: Passover marks only the beginning of the process that culminates at the holiday of Sukkot.[70] Whether the *pesaḥ* sacrifice will trigger redemption, or a more complex offering is necessary, remains unclear. For example, here is the precise sequence of messianic events as described in *Yetsiat mitsrayim*:

The *korban* is as its name indicates: it brings Israel close [*mekarev*] to their Father in Heaven. The Shekhinah rests among them as she did at the Tabernacle and at Solomon's Temple. This is the essence of our happiness: God has brought us near to him, and the Shekhinah rests among us. In the future, the complete redemption will arrive when we offer sacrifices to please God; this I have seen in great books. Thus, when the men of the Great Assembly composed the prayers, they first put 'Return the sacrificial worship, etc.' and then 'May our eyes see your return to Zion'. And further, through the *pesaḥ* we realize that God wants our sacrificial worship, as we wrote above, and this is the secret of the entire Torah.[71]

The rest of the passage neatly captures Kalischer's ideology and methodology. Sacrificial worship is vital to human happiness, enabling the unity of heaven and earth. This is a central message of the Torah, and the great authorities of the past knew it. When sacrifices are once again offered, the Jews will be returned to their land and the messianic age will arrive.

Kalischer's treatment of the sacrifices is exemplary of his discussion of miracles and history. It revealed his facility with Jewish philosophical texts, but also the necessity of respecting religious faith over philosophy. The rabbi

---

[67] *Yetsiat mitsrayim*, 21. The same symbol is used in *Derishat tsiyon*, 36–7.

[68] *Yetsiat mitsrayim*, 28.

[69] Ibid. 17, 19, 28–9.   [70] Ibid. 32. See also *Sefer haberit*, ii. 85–6 (on Exod. 12: 2).

[71] *Yetsiat mitsrayim*, 80. This message also appears in *Emunah yesharah*, ii. 156–7. There and in most other references to this message in his exegetical writings, he described the sacrifices as the foundation (*yesod*) of the entire Torah, instead of its secret (*sod*).

was harmonizing the conflicting claims of medieval philosophy and kabbalah, reason and faith, by utilizing appropriate shares of each. To him, finding this balance between tradition and reason was the meaning of true enlightenment. Proper belief, *emunah yesharah*, included realistic messianism. He essentially admitted as much when, decades later, he published his messianic treatise *Derishat tsiyon*, designating it part 3 of *Emunah yesharah*.

RESPONDING TO RELIGIOUS INNOVATION

It is abundantly clear that Kalischer continued to believe that contemporary Jews would be excited at the prospect of once again offering sacrifices. How, then, did he interpret the revived efforts in the 1840s to modify the liturgy, specifically, to omit prayers for the restoration of sacrificial worship? The revival of the movement for synagogue reform, which reached a new height in 1844–6, is the first opportunity we have to see how Kalischer's response to religious innovations differed from that of his teachers. The four articles he wrote for the German Jewish press, like his philosophical and exegetical literature, reveal his distinctive balancing act in relation to modern intellectual challenges to tradition. They also manifest the distinguishing marks of Posen Jewry: its position on the border of the east and of the west. Kalischer knew about the innovators, but he wrote as though their voices were without much influence. Indeed, this seems to have been true for the region in which he lived. His geographic marginality helped sustain the optimism necessary for his messianic ideology and his belief that Judaism could remain intact while absorbing elements of modernity.

One of Kalischer's articles was a review of Rabbi Levi Herzfeld's pamphlet *Zwei Predigten über die Lehre vom Messias*, two sermons on the messianic teaching in Judaism, published in 1844. Herzfeld argued that the Messianic Days should be conceived of as merely an era of world peace and universal monotheism. He found no scriptural basis for the belief in a personal messiah or other human agents of God, and he suggested that biblical passages that seemed to indicate this should be understood allegorically. He asserted that there would be no religious distinctions between people in the messianic era. Consequently, Jews would not be obligated at that time to perform the Torah's commandments. Herzfeld proposed that, as a step towards the messianic age, it was time to begin gradually rescinding the ceremonial commandments. This process had already begun, he claimed, shortly after the destruction of the Temple. At that point, the Sages had nullified the category of law known as *mitsvot ha-teluyot ba'arets*, the commandments that can only be fulfilled in the Land of

Israel. The current generation should emulate the Sages and eliminate more commandments.[72]

Kalischer's response to Herzfeld was a dry and narrow exercise without reference to the wider implications of the proposal. Appearing in the literary supplement to the German Jewish monthly *Der Orient*, it was a six-step refutation of Herzfeld's interpretation of talmudic and biblical statements. Kalischer disagreed with Herzfeld that the messianic phenomena mentioned in the Bible were mere allegories. He insisted that a personal messiah would indeed arrive. He ended the article with a rebuke that was meant to show the hollowness of Herzfeld's universalism: 'What does Herr H. think about the resurrection of the dead, [a doctrine] revealed by the prophets and believed by all religions? Is this, too, merely an allegory? These [Herzberg's] words contain a subtle denial of this universal belief.'[73] Here is the same point made in *Emunah yesharah* and *Sefer haberit*: Christians and Muslims accept the veracity of the biblical prophets in the same manner as Jews. Kalischer's teachers, too, had claimed that non-Jewish kings accepted Jewish messianic beliefs. Then as now it served a polemical function. It was a way to take back the political and moral high ground from the religious reformers, who were modifying the older messianic concepts in the name of universalism. Flagging the universal appeal of traditional messianism was a means of highlighting the patriotism of the conservative camp and the depravity of the innovators.

A more obvious indication of Kalischer's messianic yearning is in the body of the review. His main point was that the Sages did not nullify the commandments dependent on the land, and Jews would still be obligated to observe these in the messianic age. These commandments consisted of agricultural laws, rules of war and peace, procedures for establishing a government, and the sacrificial precepts. Herzfeld was simply ignorant, he wrote, in claiming that the Sages had annulled these laws: they had only suspended them temporarily during the period of the exile. His real worry is evident in his rebuke:

I maintain that Herr H. cannot show that the Talmud ever nullified anything; even the commandments dependent on the land were not nullified, but it was simply impossible to observe them because we did not occupy the land. Contradicting him, the Talmud says 'the first sanctification [of the Temple Mount] sanctified it for that time and eternally'; if we have the permission to act independently in Palestine, we would now be obligated to perform these commandments, such as offering sacrifices, etc.; see Maimonides, *Bet*

---

[72] Levi Herzfeld, *Zwei Predigten über die Lehre vom Messias* (Braunschweig, 1844).

[73] Review of 'Zwei Predigten über die Lehre vom Messias u.s.w. von Dr. Herzfeld', Braunschweig, 1844, in *Literaturblatt des Orients*, 3 (1845), 44–6 at 46. He explained the narrowness of his critique as follows: 'These sermons have, as the author himself says, only a dogmatic and not a homiletical character, and so Herr Herzfeld will not find it strange that attention will be paid only to that aspect' (p. 44).

beḥirah, ch. 6 [*Mishneh torah*, 'Laws of the Temple', 6], and [Joseph Karo's commentary] *Kesef mishneh* there.[74]

The comment about the Temple Mount being eternally fit for sacrificial worship was taken almost verbatim from his letter to Rothschild. Kalischer easily could have drawn attention to commandments other than those dealing with sacrifice. The most relevant to mention would have been the agricultural precepts, for in his day there were Jews in Palestine farming the land. The sacrificial commandments were probably the least persuasive example for the readers; the audience might well have been uncomfortable with them. But to him they had the greatest immediacy and importance. He was concerned to keep alive Jews' eagerness for the messianic age and respond positively when it beckoned. His main worry seems to be that Herzfeld's arguments would convince readers that sacrificial commandments were irrelevant and dispensable.

Kalischer published a second article against religious reform the next year. This addressed a more complex problem, one rooted in Jewish communal politics. A controversy arose in 1844 when a Jewish father in Frankfurt, acting in accordance with the principles of the Frankfurt 'Friends of Reform' association, refused to allow his son to be circumcised, but nevertheless wanted him to be registered as a Jew in the community records. Frankfurt's senior rabbi was incensed by the father's behaviour. He asked the city's Senate to intervene, and he solicited supportive letters from rabbis throughout Germany and Italy. The case raised disturbing questions: would the rabbis be permitted to continue determining Jewish status? Was the father's act the beginning of a wider trend? The father's objections to circumcision received wide sympathy among liberal Jews, but few Reform leaders advocated ending the practice. Rabbi Samuel Holdheim was one of the few rabbis who supported the father in a pamphlet published in that year.[75]

Kalischer reviewed Holdheim's essay soon after it was published. He opened his remarks by acknowledging that there had been widespread opposition to the Frankfurt reformers from all directions, and his remarks might

---

[74] Review of 'Zwei Predigten', 45. On the next page he attacked Herzfeld's suggestion that commandments could be changed if the general consensus of a generation desired it. The accumulated wisdom of a generation, he wrote, was not equivalent to revelation; and it was heresy to imply that the revelation at Sinai was likewise just a matter of human consensus. The distinction between religion and reason was central to *Emunah yesharah*, and is discussed above.

[75] Samuel Holdheim, *Über die Beschneidung in religios-dogmatischer Beziehung* (Schwerin and Berlin, 1844). This incident is thoroughly examined in Robert Liberles, *Religious Conflict in Social Context: The Resurgence of Orthodox Judaism in Frankfurt am Main, 1838–1877* (Westport, Conn., 1985), 43–60. See also Jacob Katz, 'The Changing Position and Outlook of Halakhists in Early Modernity', in Leo Landman (ed.), *Scholars and Scholarship: The Interaction Between Judaism and Other Cultures* (New York, 1990), 93–106 at 96–100.

therefore be considered superfluous, but one of Holdheim's claims still remained to be challenged. Kalischer thus ignored Holdheim's unconventional
evaluation of the many rabbinic rulings on uncircumcised Jews, focusing
instead on his analysis of a text related to sacrifice. Holdheim had claimed that
circumcision was not an eternal commandment, as rabbis had long insisted,
because they had based their ruling on an erroneous reading of Exodus 12: 48,
which prohibited the consumption of the *pesah* sacrifice by an uncircumcised
person. The limitation of the *pesah* sacrifice to circumcised males only applied
to the first offering of the sacrifice; it was not an eternal prohibition. This
incorrect reading invalidated the claim that the commandment to circumcise
was likewise eternal, Holdheim argued. Kalischer could not let this claim pass
unanswered. For him, the gravity of the father's sin was highlighted by the fact
that Jewish law would prohibit an uncircumcised man from eating the *pesah*
sacrifice. Jewish status depended on one's eligibility to participate in the sacrificial ceremonies. Here, as in his review of Herzfeld's sermon, Kalischer was
reminding his readers of the immediate relevance of sacrificial worship to their
lives.[76]

In this article Kalischer introduced a motif that was central to the 1836
Rothschild letter: the alliance between non-Jewish kings and religious authorities in upholding public order. He was disturbed that Frankfurt's rabbi had
not been able to persuade the town Senate to order the father to obey Jewish
law. Until this time, non-Jewish officials consistently regarded traditional Judaism as the sole legitimate form of Judaism. Of course, rabbis had already
lost the ability to enforce Jewish law through physical coercion, and the right
to excommunicate disobedient Jews had been severely curtailed or abolished
entirely. Nonetheless, conservative Jewish leaders had not quite come to terms
with these losses. They expected the state to uphold, at the very least, their
rulings on Jewish status. The refusal of the Frankfurt Senate to uphold the
rabbi's ruling, they warned, would lead to scorn for traditional religious
authority, the growth of sects, the waning of Torah observance, and anarchy in
the political sphere as well. Kalischer surely shared these fears, and more: he
believed that redemption was contingent upon the kings who, acting as God's
agents, would return the Jews to Zion where they would fulfil the commandments of the Torah in purity. If the Frankfurt situation were a taste of things
to come, it did not bode well for either the kings' or the Jews' receptivity to
God's plan.

Kalischer responded to this challenge in much the same way that most of
his colleagues did: he denied that the political situation had changed. He

---

[76] Kalischer, 'Einiges zur Widerlegung der Ansichten des Herrn Dr. Samuel Holdheim, in
seinem Werkchen: "Ueber die Beschneidung"', *Literaturblatt des Orients*, 1 (1846), 1–2.

claimed that the Senate's refusal to intervene was merely a temporary aberration of political life. Ever optimistic and intellectually creative in matters connected with his cause, he suggested a way that the traditionalists of Frankfurt could press their case. Jewish communal leaders merely had to phrase their argument correctly, he implied, and the Frankfurt Senate would support their stance. It is true, he wrote, that the law of the land forbids rabbis to excommunicate wrongdoers or to use any other means of coercion. However, the religious status of an individual *was* the state's legitimate concern, and there were laws that testified to this. One such law stipulated that if parents refused to baptize their child but nevertheless wanted to remain in their church, the child should be removed from their care and turned over to other guardians. The parents, he quoted from the law, 'are regarded as lunatics . . . and the children must not incur disadvantages from their parents' lack of reason'.[77] Kalischer suggested that the Frankfurt traditionalists should cite this law and argue that circumcision was equivalent to baptism, for 'circumcision means to the Jews, if not more, at least as much as baptism means to the Christians'. In other words, refusing to be circumcised was a declaration of rejecting Judaism. Kalischer did not maintain that the consequences of disobedience for Jews should be the same as the law allowed for Christians. Instead, 'when circumcision is not allowed, the newborn may be prevented from entering the Israelite religion'. In this way the community still had some influence over the father's behaviour, and it had the right to keep the boy from its midst until he came of age to accept the rite of circumcision, if that would ever occur.[78]

Kalischer moved from the specific case of Frankfurt to discuss the abstract principle of the state's power of compulsion in matters of religion. He explained why such compulsion was legitimate:

Actually the State is no way empowered to be watchful of the observance of every minute religious law by every individual, but it is nonetheless obligated to protect religion as a whole. If an individual is counted as a member of a religion, he remains free to take the risk of dealing with his obligations with licence; we have power only over his body, not over his spirit. But if he does not already belong to a religious body, the law must compel him to belong, otherwise he will be outside of all religion and thus harm obedient society.[79]

This statement is a distinct echo of what Kalischer's teacher, Jacob Lorbeerbaum, had written during the 1819 Hamburg temple scandal: 'Kings and governments, may their majesty be enhanced, in every land have been zealous in ensuring that every person *is shackled in the chains of his religion, and that there not be factions* within it because everyone does what his heart desires. The

---

[77] Kalischer, 'Einiges zur Widerlegung', 2. He is quoting from a work written by J. C. F. Born cited in Holdheim's pamphlet.   [78] Ibid. 3–4   [79] Ibid. 3.

preservation of the state depends on this unity. . .'.[80] Although Lorbeerbaum's tone is much harsher than his student's, the message is virtually the same—except that Lorbeerbaum acknowledged the possibility of divisions within Judaism, and he insisted that the state had the right to prohibit these as well. Kalischer ignored the matter of sectarianism; it made a stronger case to accuse the dissidents of rejecting religion outright. In such a case, the state had no choice but to compel them to belong to one of the existing religious bodies.

At first glance it may appear that rabbis like Kalischer were simply out of touch with political reality. Perhaps it was too painful to think that the Crown would eliminate the last vestiges of rabbinical power, or that it would allow forms of Judaism that rejected the 'universal beliefs' he imagined the Christians held dear. Yet the actual political situation was complex, and the traditionalists' appeal for the state's reinforcement of their authority was not entirely anachronistic. In fact, the governments of most German states, Britain, and France maintained that religion was very much their legitimate concern, and they mandated that individuals must declare membership of a religious community. The 1840s ushered in a new liberalism, but it was as yet unclear whether governments would abandon their preference for conservative religious leadership.[81] When state officials, for the first time, appointed advocates of reform to key posts on Jewish communal boards in Germany, liberal Jews interpreted it as an endorsement of their agenda. Traditionalists were aware of and lamented these appointments, but they were sensitive to other cues that indicated a continuation of older patterns. This was especially the case in Prussia. There, conservative Christians were openly critical of innovations in Judaism. The recently crowned emperor Frederick William IV was promoting the notion of a Christian state in which Lutheranism formed the moral basis of government. Even political liberals, who recognized reform-minded Jews as among their strongest allies, disapproved of religious liberation and inventiveness.[82] Consequently, despite the opening that government officials began to

[80] *Eleh divrei haberit*, 80 (letter 19). Emphasis is in the original. Lorbeerbaum's outlook is examined in Ch. 1.

[81] Katz, 'The Changing Position and Outlook of Halakhists in Early Modernity', 97, argues that the Frankfurt case was a turning point for western and central European traditional rabbis. They were publicly confronted with the painful truth that they could no longer rely on the state to support their authority.

[82] Liberles, *Religious Conflict in Social Context*, 57, presents testimony of government officials who show their contempt for the religious reformers. He argues that when officials refused to enforce a single standard of religious behaviour for a divided religious community, it was because it did not matter to them if Jewry disintegrated into separate sects. And if the new sect led its members to desert Judaism for Christianity, as its Jewish opponents claimed, that was all the better. From this vantage point, allowing divisions within Judaism might be beneficial as long as the state maintained its control over religion in general.

give to the more liberal elements within Jewry, they continued publicly to voice their intent to uphold established religious authority. When Kalischer concluded that the state had an interest in keeping its subjects under the jurisdiction of religious leaders, he was echoing actual government rulings. His experience as a subject of Prussia formed the basis for his optimism regarding the continuation of halakhic Judaism. It was plausible for him to imagine that the Frankfurt senators were ignorant about the parallels between circumcision and baptism, and once alerted to this, would reverse their decision. The Frankfurt situation was unfortunate, he was saying, but it could provide the traditionalists the opportunity to recoup their strength by articulating their concerns in language close to the hearts of non-Jewish officials.

The most vivid example of Kalischer's tenacious optimism was his essay in the new Jewish German-language monthly, *Der treue Zions-Wächter*, founded in 1845 as a mouthpiece for traditionalist Jews and their conservative leaders. In issue after issue writers lamented the successes that religious reformers had already achieved in their communities, and they broadcast their fears that the innovators would soon dominate western and central European Jewish life. Sandwiched between their anguished accounts in early 1846 was Kalischer's article, 'Das Leben Israels und der Rabbinismus'. In contrast to the name-calling and powerful invectives employed by the conservatives during the Hamburg temple controversy in 1819, and the equally harsh reaction to the current more radical proposals, Kalischer's calm reaction was conspicuous. His writing exudes a sense of confidence. In this piece, he predicts a victory for traditional Judaism in Europe, if only Jewish communities would restructure themselves according to his suggestions.

Kalischer opened his article with a lofty and idealized description of Judaism and the Jewish people. The following is an excerpt from a much longer passage:

Israel's teaching is the life of the heavenly kingdom. While all other peoples languish in the slumber of death, Israel is called to life; while all others wander in darkness, Israel is illumined by the eternal light; while others get drunk on the delusions of poisonous vipers, Jeshurun receives the life source of God's holy balm, and this is sufficient; while Israel is attacked from all sides and in this earthly realm is subjugated and controlled, truthful rulers must confess that its life source is indeed holy. . . . Other peoples convert and leave their beliefs in faithlessness, but Israel remains . . . and through its divine teaching is unified; in all distant lands and isles Israel has one teaching, one law, one Talmud, and proclaims its belief in one God.[83]

---

[83] Kalischer, 'Das Leben Israels und der Rabbinismus', *Der treue Zions-Wächter*, 3 (1846), 57. The article is attributed to 'Rabbinate-Assessor Kalischer zu Thorn'.

But the seamless fabric of world Jewry had recently been torn by people desiring a new fashion, he explained. The rift had begun twenty-five years earlier, when people had tampered with the liturgy that had been introduced by the Men of the Great Assembly and had abolished the universally acknowledged messianic teaching. In the end, the taste for innovation had prevailed, so that the talmudic statutes according to their traditions had been abandoned, and there was opposition to the normative authority of the holy writ.[84] The rabbinate itself had launched these challenges, according to Kalischer. 'What else can one conclude', he wrote, 'when from the pulpit heretical words are preached and the people lend a willing ear to it?' All this had occurred because 'the rabbinate has forced itself to stand under the yoke of fashion'.[85]

Kalischer did not want to discourage his readers. Before explaining how this calamity had come about, he forecast a victorious conclusion:

But Israel's life has not faltered yet. One can see how the true believers among the religious fight against such unholy doings, how they summon all to again fill in the yawning chasm, to restore religion to its people, so then one can rightly say, 'Israel is not widowed' [Jer. 51: 5], 'The remnant of Israel shall do no wrong' [Zeph. 3: 13]. From all sides come the defenders of the holy religion, the holy writ, the Talmud, the old rituals and messianic teaching; thus Israel will remain ever faithful to its life source and priestly function.[86]

His article would arm the true believers among the religious with weapons: a socio-historical understanding of the crisis that would point the way to the solution, and the will to fight.

The key to Jewry's millennia of faithfulness to the law was the structure of Jewish governance, Kalischer explained. According to him, 'since ancient times, for thousands of years, religion has had two spiritual caretakers, a talmudic rabbi and a preacher'. The rabbi was a scholar who was morally and religiously exemplary ('without the slightest blemish') and he served as the community's religious authority, judge, and Talmud instructor. His subordinate, a preacher (often a rabbi as well) used extra-traditional sources to inspire community obedience to the rabbi and love for the Torah. Each functionary required a distinct education. The preacher would study the classical Jewish sources, but also 'external' literature. The latter would enable him to master the contemporary aesthetic and express himself in beautiful language that would arouse the passions of his listeners. The rabbi, however, could delve only minimally into 'external' sources: he must be fluent in the vernacular, and he could learn just enough of the non-Jewish philosophical tradition to understand Jewish philosophical works so that he could 'reconcile his teaching with

[84] Ibid. 58. He is apparently referring to the Hamburg temple contrversy of 1817–19; see above, Ch. 1.   [85] Ibid. 59.   [86] Ibid.

reason'. For example, it would be excessive for a rabbi to try to master Latin and Greek, for it would detract from his main area of study, traditional Jewish legal and exegetical texts. Although the scope of the rabbi's education was more limited than that of the preacher, he was the higher authority.[87]

The current problem within the rabbinate, Kalischer explained, began when the Jewish community demanded that one man must fulfil both functions. The demand for a rabbi who had academic training and who could deliver sermons was entirely unprecedented. With the conjunction of rabbinic and preaching duties in one person, the duties and the perspective of the former were lost. Young men bound for the communal rabbinate learned less Talmud in order to attend universities dominated by Christian clergymen and radical intellectuals. This education, he argued, made them into freethinking rabbis who were less capable of teaching Torah and less desirous of implementing it in its purity. They were the type who advocated reform, because they wanted to reshape Judaism in accordance with the 'fashion' they were mimicking from the Christians.

In order to counteract the influence of these freethinking rabbis, religious Jews would have to do more than fight their proposed innovations, Kalischer warned. They had to restore Jewish spiritual leadership to its older, rightful form:

Even if the defenders of the holy religion achieve a shining victory by fighting the modern rabbinate, the battle still will not end: the enemy will recover and continue to confront the city of religion and attack the believers incessantly until they are worn out from strife. But if we win for the rabbinate its old prerogative, then all is decided. We will also sow the seeds and reap the fruit; we will wrap religion in the mantle of wisdom and illuminate her with the eternal light of reason; then she will thrive to her greatest perfection.[88]

Jewish communal boards had to insist on hiring rabbis and preachers who fitted the older criteria, and who were responsible only for the duties assigned to them in the past. The desire for innovation would be satisfied by the sermons of the preacher, while the reigning religion would be the proper one rooted in the past. Smaller communities should hire either a rabbi or a preacher, and not expect that one man would fulfil both functions.[89]

This proposal captures the various and varied pieces of Kalischer's own life. The picture he paints of the well-functioning Jewish community must have been how he imagined Thorn. The description of the ideal rabbi fits him, of course. He felt he had just enough exposure to non-Jewish culture to understand its limitations, and he had learnt just enough of philosophy to enable him

[87] Kalischer, 'Das Leben Israels und der Rabbinismus', 59.
[88] Ibid. 60.
[89] Ibid. 59.

to 'reconcile his teaching with reason'. His concession to the legitimacy of the impulse for 'the current fashion' expressed itself in Thorn's religious leadership. Other rabbis catered for the need of some members of the community to hear the well-turned phrases of inspiring sermons, while Kalischer's halakhic decisions were respected by the community. He served faithfully without a hint of corruption—he was not even paid. Although he did not explicitly mention Thorn in this article, the overall tone of the article is a bit smug. Signing the article as a rabbi of Thorn was a statement that the city had no religious strife of the kind usually reported in the pages of *Der treue Zions-Wächter*.[90]

The fact that Kalischer was a lone voice amidst the chorus of German Jews writing in *Der treue Zions-Wächter*, and that no one responded to his article in the subsequent issues of the paper, is significant. His situation was somewhat anomalous. He was writing out of his own experience in the stagnant environment of the eastern provinces. Culturally, Jewish life there may have shared more features with east European Jewish communities than with those in the west. In the Polish territories, the movement for liturgical reform was barely discernible, and Kalischer experienced it first-hand only in 1863.[91] Although community leaders were advertising for university-educated rabbis and rejecting candidates educated in the narrow curriculum of east European talmudic academies, this new type of rabbi did not yet prevail. The education campaign of the Prussian government, which promoted Jewish inclusion in public education and German-language instruction in all schools, and the Jews' acquiescence in these goals were already reducing the number of people who could even understand Kalischer's articles.[92] Nevertheless, he does not appear threatened. His essay reveals his uniqueness and confidence among the rabbis: he was deeply immersed in traditional Jewish texts and their values, but unafraid of a self-conscious and selective borrowing from modern culture.

Kalischer's marginality was underscored in an article he wrote for the new journal *Israelitische Annalen*. Its editor, Isaac Marcus Jost, was one of a circle of Jewish scholars attempting to examine Jewish literature according to a

[90] Kalischer noted in his commentary on the Torah that when some people expressed the desire to omit the *meḥitsah*, the architectural barrier dividing men and women, from the new Thorn synagogue under construction in 1846, they were easily silenced by his opposition. See *Sefer haberit*, ii. 77 (on Exod. 10: 11). Only later was there more serious opposition.

[91] This is discussed in Ch. 7.

[92] Lowenstein, 'The 1840s and the Creation of the German-Jewish Religious Reform Movement', in *The Mechanics of Change*, 85–107 at 97 ff., argues that Reform was mainly a west and south German movement in 1844–6. Lowenstein surveyed the first fifteen years of the *Allgemeine Zeitung des Judentums* (1837–51) for information on religious innovations in German Jewish communities. I thank him for sharing with me the rabbinic advertisements in this period. Luncz, 'Tsevi Hirsch Kalischer', 131, claims that vol. i of *Emunah yesharah* was purchased more often in Russia and the Polish territories than in the West.

strictly scientific method. Promoting the cause of religious reform was a subsidiary motive for most of them, despite their claims of objectivity and detachment. These men, pioneers of modern academic Jewish scholarship, were in a different intellectual world from Kalischer's. Yet Kalischer's unique combination of talents brought him to Jost's attention. A more conservative member of Jost's circle, Samuel David Luzzatto, had lately lambasted his colleagues for their excessive admiration of Maimonides. According to Luzzatto, Maimonides had injected foreign concepts into Jewish thought and distorted its pure essence. By implication, Jost and his colleagues were doing the same thing.[93] Jost asked Kalischer to rebut Luzzatto's critique of Maimonides. It was a clever tactic to use a representative of old-style Judaism to scold a conservative colleague for his denigration of the liberals.

Kalischer's essay, 'Maimonides und seine neuern Gegner', was a nearly perfect vehicle for this purpose. It was a paean of praise to Maimonides, repeatedly likening his wisdom to God's omniscience. Kalischer made an elaborate case in defence of the philosopher, quoting from his works and those of his devotees over the generations. The essay was clearly the work of a very learned man. It did not address the underlying issue, whether enlightened Jews' admiration of European culture was threatening the integrity of Jewish life. Perhaps Jost did not ask him to address that, or he did not include his response—for Kalischer did not agree with Luzzatto about Maimonides, but he had more in common with Luzzatto's conservatism than with Jost's liberal attitudes. Jost admitted abridging the essay, however, and he took pains to say that he had translated it into German, preserving the ornate style of the original Hebrew. His editorial comment is most instructive:

This excellent and content-rich Hebrew treatise, from which we here (and that with the permission of the author) can provide only a cramped excerpt, concerns itself also with the dispute having to do with the traditional validity and respective authorization to do away with old sanhedristic legal judgements. This learned discussion, however, is suitable only for Hebrew meetings. With the inclusion of the above exposition we wished not only to demonstrate to our readers our impartiality; we also wished to call attention to the fact that the adherents of the opinions attacked [the contemporary admirers of Maimonides] do not judge from ignorance and the inclination to parrot, but rather also know how to develop their reasons according to their sources.[94]

This comment is packed with carefully crafted ambiguity. Jost's praise of Kalischer is tempered by paternalism and a self-congratulatory attitude of distance

[93] This larger complaint by Luzzatto can be found in the excerpt published in Mendes-Flohr and Reinharz, *The Jew in the Modern World*, 235–7.

[94] Kalischer, 'Maimonides und seine neuern Gegner'. The author is referred to as 'H. K. in Thorn', and the editor takes credit for the translation in a footnote.

from him. He casts Rabbi Kalischer as an anachronism, his expression sophisticated but intelligible only for a type of Jew no longer familiar to most
German Jews.

Kalischer's inhabitation of two worlds meant that he fitted squarely in
neither. It was just such a man who would embrace realistic messianism, that
hybrid of rationalism and religious faith. All his writings would combine elements of the new cultural scene with the religious heritage of old Ashkenazi
Jewry. This admixture was central to his plan to prevent heresy and to promote
messianic enthusiasm. Both contained new and old elements, and both transmitted the same message: progress comes when Jews take the initiative to
re-establish their glorious institutions from the past. No innovation was necessary, no new types of leaders, no deviation from eternal laws. Kalischer refused
to be weighed down by current dilemmas. Whether the problem was religious
deviancy or Jews languishing in the exile, it could be solved by remembering
and heeding old teachings. His role in this was simply to clarify the pure words
of Torah that had always been there, unchanged. Ever optimistic, he was certain that those teachings would prevail in the end, erecting a new–old perfect
world.

SIX

The Return to Activism
1855–1861

THE LATE 1850s were a turning point in Tsevi Hirsch Kalischer's life. God was signalling his readiness to redeem the Jews, he believed, and he stepped forward to lead the way. Gone was his scholastic lifestyle. By the end of the decade, he was directing the local effort to raise funds on behalf of a building project in Jerusalem, he had offered to move to Palestine and serve as rabbinic adviser to Jewish landowners there, and he served as a spokesman for the new Kolonisations-Verein für Palästina (the Society for the Settlement of Palestine), whose headquarters were in Frankfurt. In 1862 that organization published Kalischer's manuscript, an expansion of his 1836 letter to Rothschild that he had entitled *Derishat tsiyon* (Seeking Zion).

What was it that induced the rabbi to adopt an activist stance? This chapter charts the way in which the trials and triumphs of the 1840s and 1850s galvanized Kalischer into action and shaped the writings of the final fifteen years of his life. We can reconstruct his awakening from the correspondence he conducted in the mid- to late 1850s and from the clues found in the text of *Derishat tsiyon*. It appears that, even more than in 1836, he was impressed by the interest of European rulers in establishing a greater Jewish presence in Palestine and the increasing presence of powerful Jews in public life. He interpreted both developments as God's way of enabling Jews to press for their return to Zion. Yet it was the prospect of offering the sacrifices that actually seems to have provoked him into action: in 1855 he discovered new rabbinic support for the restoration of sacrificial worship and reassessed his earlier correspondence with Akiva Eger and Moses Sofer. While returning to this quest, he found a kindred spirit in Elijah Guttmacher (1795–1874), a former classmate. For the next twenty-five years he relied on Guttmacher as an ally and partner in his messianic projects.

Shortly after the initial flurry of attention to the sacrifices, Kalischer redefined his immediate goals. He decided that the logical preliminary step in the messianic scenario was to increase the number of Jews working the land in Palestine. He believed that this goal had already captured the hearts of the

Jewish leaders and philanthropists who, according to his messianic theory, were instrumental to the unfolding of redemption. He reasoned that the observance of the agricultural commandments by Jewish farmers would lead naturally to the bringing of tithes and offerings to a rebuilt altar. His logic also seems to have been strengthened by the reaction of rabbis in Russia and in the Posen district to the terrible impoverishment of the first half of the century: they became more receptive to the proposal that Jews should enter agricultural occupations. It was then not difficult for Kalischer to adapt the pro-agriculture literature of social reformers to the Jews of the Yishuv.

POVERTY AND AGRICULTURAL LABOUR

In the years following Kalischer's overture to Rothschild, the economic condition of the provinces of Posen and West Prussia worsened considerably, becoming even more depressed during the 1840s than it had been earlier. Since the 1820s, the region's once flourishing cloth manufacturers were prohibited from selling their products to Russia but were unable to compete with the west German states on the Prussian market. The newly built railways transported most produce elsewhere to be processed. Local capital was mainly in the hands of estate owners. They had received cash payments from the state with the emancipation of the serfs, and then rental payments from the former serfs who continued to work the land. Except for the provincial capitals, which thrived on the patronage of the military and bureaucracy, the region's cities remained pre-industrial, relying on small-scale artisan production, local trade, and cottage gardening. In these cities, the urban population was quite vulnerable to the agricultural failures and the rise in food prices after 1839; starvation, epidemics, looting of food, and riots were a feature of urban life in the 1840s.[1]

Jews were particularly hard hit by the slump. Urban dwellers and dependent primarily on commerce, they had little opportunity to escape their poverty. Jewish merchants were targeted in the food riots and boycotts of the late 1840s. A study of the Jews in 1849 revealed that more than two-thirds of them were artisans, day labourers, servants, petty merchants, brokers, tavern keepers, and pedlars. The merchant-entrepreneurs among them were so constrained by the trade restrictions that many lost their businesses, resorted to smuggling, or moved outside the region. Emigrating Jews were replaced by illegal immigrants who came from Austrian Galicia or Russian Poland. Fully one-tenth

---

[1] Hagen, *Germans, Poles, and Jews*, 96–7. Bartyś, 'Grand Duchy of Poznań under Prussian Rule', 191–3.

of the Jews in the region lived on alms or begging. The Jewish population was associated with high unemployment, vagrancy, and general misery.[2]

Widespread Jewish impoverishment was a serious problem in Russia and other parts of eastern and central Europe. The internal migration of impoverished Jews from rural areas to towns and cities overtaxed the resources of the larger Jewish communities. *Ostjuden* who migrated west were often an embarrassment to better-off, more acculturated Jews. In the new settings the migrants tended to become lax towards or to cease to observe the laws of the Torah, contributing to tensions in their adopted communities. This miserable situation roused Jewish communal leaders to find solutions beyond the usual request for charity from the few wealthy Jews. It became clear that Jews had to generate new opportunities locally, or find a destination for migrating Jews that was amenable to a religious frame of life.

One widely heard suggestion was to train Jews for agricultural labour. Under the influence of the physiocratic theory that regarded agriculture, unlike commerce, as a productive occupation, social reformers urged that Jews should be prodded into working on the land. Enlightened Jews and Christians maintained that agricultural labour would provide poor Jews with an income and food and end serious Jewish social problems: the Jews' alienation from nature and their physical selves, the over-representation of Jews in commerce, the phenomenon of *luftmenshen* (wandering, impoverished Jews), and the scorn of non-Jews.[3] Prussian officials contemplating the Jews of the eastern territories received these views with some enthusiasm. They hoped that agricultural labour would remove the 'ghetto' from the Polish Jews, make them more useful to the state, and help build the agrarian economy of the region.

Most Jews opposed the suggestion. They were well aware of their inexperience in farming beyond that of the household farm, and the work involved adaptations that few were willing to make. Agriculture was not known as a lucrative and easy way to make a living any time, but it seemed especially unpromising during this period of economic transition. When social reformers criticized Jewish social and economic life and recommended, among other things, that Jews should engage in agricultural occupations, European rabbis were quick to point out that an agricultural lifestyle would prevent the living of a full Jewish life and the transmission of a traditional education to the young.

[2] Hagen, *Germans, Poles, and Jews*, 98–9. Bartyś, 'Grand Duchy of Poznań under Prussian Rule', 193–201.

[3] Mordechai Levin, *Social and Economic Values of the Haskalah* (Heb.) (Jerusalem, 1975), 187–256, collects many primary sources on this topic. One of the most important works promoting agricultural labour among religious Jews was Isaac Baer Levinsohn, *Te'udah beyisra'el* (Vilna, 1828). The book was a manifesto of the east European Haskalah, and the issue of manual labour for Jews was only one element within it.

The unattractive social and personal consequences of rural life were summed up by them in the assertion that agriculture was inherently a non-Jewish occupation. However, in Russia, where the rapid population growth and deteriorating economic conditions led to great suffering, some rabbis had even sanctioned the movement of Jews into small-scale commercial farming.[4]

This precedent, and the dire poverty of the 1840s, prompted Rabbi Shelomoh Eger (Akiva Eger's son and successor) to propose to the Prussian government the establishment of Jewish farm colonies in the Posen region. He suggested a communal structure that would reinforce Jewish religious observance. The colony would remain in the Posen province in order to enhance the likelihood that its residents would preserve their customs. Separate Jewish farm settlements would enable the Jews to live according to their distinctive laws and customs. Residential segregation would also keep the Jews from assimilation, and spare the novice Jewish farmers from the ridicule and hostility of the Polish peasants. While a local colony would certainly benefit the Jews of the Posen region, Eger hoped that it would, as well, be a model for Jews elsewhere.[5]

There are interesting parallels between this effort and one circulating among the local Poles. They formed the overwhelming majority of landowners and agricultural workers, and they were hurt by Prussian economic policies. Historically rather submissive, the gentry was too conservative to revolt or even to form a vocal opposition in regional political forums; indeed, a planned insurrection in 1846 was foiled when a member of the gentry leaked it to the Prussian police. The peasantry was fairly passive and grateful to the regime for its emancipation. The form of resistance favoured most broadly by enlightened Prussian Poles was economic: shore up the economic strength of the Poles and, in the long term, contribute to the nationalist struggle by building Polish solidarity and cultural pride. Polish activists organized cultural centres for the peasants, urban dwellers, and gentry, as well as economic self-help associations to teach landowners to rotate their crops, diversify their farming, and apply other new methods of agricultural production. This effort, later called 'organic work', was begun in the Posen province in the 1840s.[6] It has not yet been established whether the Polish and Jewish efforts were influenced

[4] According to Levin, *Social and Economic Values*, 246–53, the few traditional rabbis who supported Jewish agricultural labour did so only as a solution to Jewish poverty. However, the same rabbis rejected agricultural work for Jews if it was encouraged for ideological reasons or for the social reform of Jews.

[5] Jacob Toury, 'An Early Movement for Agricultural Settlement in Inowrocław (Poznań Province)' (Heb.), *Hatsiyonut*, 2 (1970–4), 37–46 at 38.

[6] Wandycz, *The Lands of Partitioned Poland*, 129–33; Hagen, *Germans, Poles, and Jews*, 76–7.

by each other; but they both represent a collective activism that began with a focus on agriculture.

The attempt to found a Jewish agricultural colony in the Polish territories ultimately failed. There were many poor Jews who signed up to join the colony, but the lack of funds from the government or wealthy Jews to purchase land and the growing scepticism of Jewish community leaders and merchants were serious obstacles. The revolution of 1848, particularly the growing rift between Polish peasants and Jews made manifest in anti-Jewish riots, disrupted any progress, and in the end the proposal was abandoned.[7] Perhaps the most enduring legacy of Shelomoh Eger's agricultural settlement proposal was the precedent that it provided for Kalischer when he turned his attention to the Jewish community of Palestine.

PALESTINE

By the 1850s European interest in Palestine had grown considerably. The Ottoman empire of the Turks had been at its peak in the 1500s, extending from Morocco to south-eastern Europe, from the Black Sea into the Balkans, but its grip on the borderlands loosened considerably over the following centuries. European states worked diligently to wield their influence even within the heart of the empire. France and England had been granted rights and privileges for their subjects resident in the Ottoman empire, and they subsequently claimed also to be the defenders of Roman Catholicism and Protestantism there. Russia made the same claim for its subjects and for Greek Orthodoxy in the Middle East. When Ottoman power began a serious decline in the early 1800s, European powers greedily eyed Turkish territory and found a number of different ways of expanding their bases of power. By the 1820s and 1830s, consuls from at least five European states were present in the Middle East. Representatives of their sovereigns, they claimed authority equal to the regional pashas. The 1853–6 Crimean War between Russia and the allied powers of Turkey, England, France, and Sardinia was essentially a contest over realms of influence in the region. Consular power and activism reached its height during the dozen years after the cessation of the fighting. The growing number of European Jewish immigrants—and even Jews not originally foreign subjects—served to increase the proportion of the population over whom the consuls held authority.[8]

<hr>

[7] Toury, 'Agricultural Settlement', 46, describes the initial support of the Inowrocław merchants and their growing coolness towards the proposal. See also Julian Bartyś, 'The Movement of Jewish Agricultural Settlement in the Kingdom of Poland before the Peasant Liberation' (Heb.), *Zion*, 1–2 (1967), 46–75.   [8] Blumberg, *Zion Before Zionism*, 59–78.

Jews were a valuable tool in European colonialism. Protection of their economic rights and physical security, and the growth of the Jewish community in Palestine, served both imperialistic and religious agendas. Proselytization of the Jews was a major goal of many European Christians resident in the Middle East. Indeed, the establishment of the consuls was heavily promoted by missionary interests, and missionary institutions were supported by consular officers.[9] Jews were, of course, aware of the goals of the missionary institutions. However, they were a vulnerable minority, and they accepted help while resisting proselytism. Ironically, the worst disaster of the nineteenth century was facilitated by the Europeans. The Damascus blood libel of 1840, in which the French consul supported the charges of ritual murder and facilitated mob violence against Jews, was a painful reminder that European prejudices as well as liberties accompanied the colonial intrusion. Prominent Jewish figures such as Sir Moses Montefiore, various members of the Rothschild family, and Adolphe Crémieux stepped forward on behalf of the oppressed Jews. They learned of events and conditions of daily life in Palestine through the reports of Europeans involved in the Crimean War or from the travelogues of European visitors. Wider circles of emancipated west European Jews found a cause in helping their less fortunate co-religionists in the Middle East. The establishment of the Alliance Israélite Universelle in 1860, the first modern international Jewish self-help organization, was an expression of this concern.

Jewish concern for the Jews of Palestine underwent a change during this period. During the Middle Ages the belief had grown that the Torah study and prayer of the Jews in the Holy Land earned merit for the Jews of the Diaspora. A system of financial assistance called the *ḥalukah* had developed, funded by Diaspora Jews, so that the Torah scholars living in Palestine should not have to leave their sacred pursuits in order to toil for their subsistence. With the Yishuv under intensified scrutiny in the nineteenth century, the *ḥalukah* became a matter of controversy. The Ashkenazi Jews in Palestine were divided into groups based on their countries of origin and received money collected by the Jews of their native lands. The money was allotted by the heads of the national communities and was distributed not only to scholars; it was also divided on the basis of a fixed sum per person, with scholars receiving an additional amount in accordance with their status. This system of financial aid was not applied uniformly, and the funds were rarely adequate. The haphazard, inefficient, and decentralized collection of money in the Diaspora partially contributed to the shortage of funds and their inequitable disbursement. A more important destabilizing factor, however, was the increasing number of Ashkenazi immigrants, most of whom needed to draw on these inadequate

[9] Ibid. 37–63.

sums. At this time Palestine was a country with limited opportunities for earning a livelihood, particularly in Jerusalem, where most of the new immigrants were concentrated. Housing and food were expensive there, and occasionally the Jewish community experienced famine. Consequently, there was a great deal of tension between the Ashkenazi residents over the distribution of *halukah* funds, and abuses of the system were not uncommon.[10]

Jews and non-Jews in the Yishuv and in Europe, reluctant openly to criticize the *halukah* lest this diminish the already inadequate funds, became increasingly vocal as they learned of the poverty, hunger, disease, and high death rate of the Jews of Palestine. They blamed the piteous conditions on the *halukah*, since it robbed the Jews of the incentive to support themselves through work, yet did not provide enough to meet their basic needs. The Sephardi Jews of the Yishuv, who came from a variety of Muslim lands or were native to Palestine, were held up as an example to be followed. They were not dependent on the *halukah* to the same extent as the Ashkenazim. A greater number were able to support themselves through trade or labour. Among them, the subdivision into national groups was almost non-existent, and while some of the money was distributed to scholars whose study was their sole occupation, the rest was reserved for general community expenditure. Consequently, they were less racked by dissension and less vulnerable to misfortune.[11] Most of the proposals for the reform and revitalization of the Yishuv, especially those originating in Europe, involved a lessening of dependence on the *halukah* through the creation of jobs that could support a family and benefit the entire community. This marked a shift from a traditional pattern of assistance towards a rational, social-planning approach that focused on imparting skills to the young and able-bodied. Agriculture was most frequently suggested as the best option. The proposals for Jewish occupational transformation that had been generated in Europe for European Jews were applied to the Yishuv. It was a logical choice: Palestine was agriculturally underdeveloped, its past history suggested that the land was fertile, and one of the most serious urban problems was the small and expensive food supply.[12]

Each time that reform-minded Jews and non-Jews attempted to recruit Jerusalem Jews into agricultural work during this period, the Ashkenazi rabbis in the Yishuv obstructed their efforts. Virtually all of them had been educated

---

[10] Mordechai Eliav, *Love of Zion and Men of Hod: German Jewry and the Settlement of Erets Yisrael in the Nineteenth Century* (Heb.) (Tel Aviv, 1970), 13–38.

[11] Ibid. 14–19. Through his memoirs, the English consular representative's harsh words for the *halukah* became known throughout Europe; see James Finn, *Stirring Times*, 2 vols. (London, 1878), i. 81–6.

[12] Jacob Kellner, *For Zion's Sake: World Jewry's Efforts to Relieve Distress in the Yishuv, 1869–1882* (Heb.) (Jerusalem, 1976), 23–41.

in Europe by traditional rabbis, so they echoed the usual objections to Jews entering agricultural work and added several more that were peculiar to their locale. They feared that the existence of self-support schemes would eventually check the flow of Diaspora contributions necessary for those who devoted their lives exclusively to prayer and study. They saw in the implementation of these proposals the eventual creation of or immigration of irreligious Jews, a Diaspora problem that had not yet reached the Holy Land. Some believed that all avocations of life in the Land of Israel should be holy, in conformity with the holiness of the land, and they did not see agricultural work in this light. Finally, they regarded these suggestions as an attack on the honour of scholars who did not work, but devoted themselves to study and prayer on behalf of their benefactors in the Diaspora.[13] The fact of poverty was not as alarming to them as it was for Diaspora onlookers, since Jews who moved to Jerusalem still honoured the ascetic ideal. Despite the firm stance of the Ashkenazi rabbis, however, suggestions for change continued to be aired, and some were even instituted. The Yishuv could simply not escape the rationalizing forces that came with the Europeanization of the region.

Conditions of life for Jews in Palestine, though miserable relative to European standards, improved steadily after 1840. The political and social reforms instituted during the reign of the Egyptian pasha Mehemmed Ali (who occupied Palestine and Syria from 1831 to 1840) were continued after Ottoman rule was resumed. These reforms, known as the Tanzimat, succeeded in centralizing control of the country, checking Bedouin attacks, increasing the general physical security of all subjects, suppressing governmental corruption, and easing the oppressive conditions in the cities. External pressures were a factor in legislation specifically affecting the Jews. In response to the insistence of west European Jewish leaders, and feeling compelled by the pressure from the European consuls, in 1840 the sultan granted the Jews rights equal to all his other subjects. This enabled the Jews to appoint themselves a chief rabbi (hakham bashi) who was to be their legal defender. The following year more rights for the Jewish community of Jerusalem and Palestine were guaranteed, and public worship could now be held everywhere legally. Resident foreign Jews, and even Jews who were not expatriates, benefited considerably from the services and intervention of the consuls. A bank, post offices, newspaper preses, and a medical clinic were established in Jerusalem in the 1840s. These improvements, as well as consular control over the Christian holy places, led to an increase in the number of pilgrims and tourists visiting the land. Their

---

[13] Many of these objections were recorded by James Finn and his wife in the 1850s when they attempted to employ Jerusalem Jews as agricultural labourers during a period of famine; see Finn, *Stirring Times*, ii. 76, 81–6, 333. The Finns were open critics of the rabbinic leadership, but their version of the rabbinic objections is corroborated by other sources.

reports sparked additional concern for and investments in Palestine. By the mid-1850s Jerusalem could boast two hospitals (one funded by the Paris Rothschild family) and a modern school for boys. When the Jews of the Yishuv faced famine and severe distress on account of excessive rain and a poor harvest, European Jews could be counted on for immediate assistance. Moses Montefiore had succeeded in circumventing the laws forbidding land sales to Jews and had purchased land outside the Old City walls for new housing. In 1836 Kalischer's suggestion that Amschel Mayer Rothschild should become patron of Jerusalem was a novel idea. By the 1850s this type of Jewish philanthropy was a well-publicized phenomenon.[14]

THE RISE OF JEWISH NOTABLES AND JEWISH CIVIC EMANCIPATION

As we have seen, the world prominence of a religious Jew in 1836 seemed to Kalischer to be a truly novel phenomenon, explicable only as an act of divine grace. Over the next two decades, he recognized that the rise of Rothschild was not an anomaly. When a number of Jews achieved high political positions in the 1840s and 1850s, he realized that the miracle he had seen in the rise of Rothschild was being multiplied all over Europe. In *Derishat tsiyon*, which was completed by 1860, he unabashedly argued that God had granted these hidden miracles in order for the Jews to steer themselves back to Zion. According to his logic, emancipation was God's way of empowering Jews to take such a course.

One might think that an older rabbi such as Kalischer would take note of the social assimilation that came in the wake of civic emancipation and grow disenchanted with the new freedoms. Or he might recognize that emancipation would root Jews more firmly into the Diaspora, make them less inclined to leave, and cause them to identify more strongly with their non-Jewish hosts. Other rabbis had said as much in the recent past, and a few continued to warn about the seductions of emancipation. Kalischer's optimistic interpretation can be explained largely by his West Prussian environment. His experience of emancipation in the Polish territories of Prussia explains his overwhelmingly positive understanding of emancipation, as well as his conviction that

---

[14] Moshe Ma'oz, 'Changes in the Position of the Jewish Communities of Palestine and Syria in Mid-Nineteenth Century', in id. (ed.), *Studies on Palestine during the Ottoman Period* (Jerusalem, 1975), pp. xvii, 142–63 at 150–9. Abraham Schischa, 'The Letter of Chief Rabbi Nathan Adler and Sir Moses Montefiore to Rabbi Tsevi Hirsch Kalischer' (Heb.), *Cathedra*, 38 (1985), 195–200, chronicles the Yishuv–European Jewish connection in the crisis of 1854. On the involvement of the next generation of Rothschilds in the Yishuv, see Niall Ferguson, *The House of Rothschild: The World's Banker, 1849–1999* (New York, 1999), 278–83.

emancipation was compatible with the Jews establishing a separate, national homeland elsewhere.

Prussia took moves towards emancipation relatively late, during the Napoleonic conquest, and then the process was halting, partial, and at times regressive. In particular, Prussian rulers were reluctant to apply emancipation laws to residents of the territories taken from Poland. Throughout Prussia, candidacy for emancipated status was contingent on the individual's wealth and occupational skills as well as on some index of acculturation: linguistic, educational, dress, adoption of a family name, and so on. Progress towards acculturation was slower in the Polish provinces. However, the province in which Kalischer resided, West Prussia, was changing more rapidly. West Prussia had a larger percentage of Germans, more acquiescent Polish subjects, and a less concentrated Jewish population that was more receptive to Prussian educational goals. Contemporaries began to report that West Prussia's Jews looked like Germans and their Yiddish sounded much closer to German. The number who achieved emancipated status steadily increased. By the middle of the nineteenth century, West Prussian Jews had changed so markedly that one could hear them disparage Posen Jews for their backward and foreign ways.[15]

At the beginning of the 1840s, the political rights of even emancipated Jews in Prussian Poland were still quite limited relative to those of the local Germans and Poles: unlike propertied Germans and Poles, Jews lacked the right to vote or stand for election. Because the towns were largely self-governing, and Jews were such a sizeable proportion of the urban population in Prussian Poland, Jewish enfranchisement would have a significant impact on the make-up of the municipal government. The ruling German and Polish cliques, fearful of new competitors, restricted Jewish participation in the town councils. Sentiment in favour of Jewish inclusion was growing locally, however, and even those who had long opposed it realized that a comprehensive emancipation decree was bound to occur soon. The nearly equal number of Polish and Prussian citizens eligible for elected offices, particularly in the towns, made it essential for the already enfranchised groups to court the soon-to-be-enfranchised Jews. The Germans needed the Jews; even in West Prussia, with the state-sponsored growth in the German population, a Jewish–German coalition would usually be essential for preventing Polish dominance, and the situation was even more urgent in the heavily Polish south. The Poles regarded the Jews as potential allies as well. With such a small number of Jews actively involved in urban government, their position on the Polish question was not known, and the Poles attempted to win their support for the Polish nationalist programme. Poles and Germans began to curry Jewish support by calling for

[15] Aschkewitz, *Zur Geschichte der Juden in Westpreussen*, 100. Prussian emancipation policies are discussed above, Ch. 2.

unconditional Jewish emancipation.[16] Onlookers could very well conclude that enlightened Germans and Poles were embracing the Jews as fellow human beings with equal political rights, and this is indeed how Kalischer perceived it. The more sensitive and cynical observers would also perceive the pragmatic basis of the outreach to Jews and hear, even among the supporters of emancipation, the hope that the Jews, once naturalized, would emigrate.[17]

Calls for a comprehensive Jewish emancipation decree began to be heard at the state level as well. The ascendancy of liberals in Prussian political life in the 1840s increased pressure on the government to hasten Jewish emancipation. The liberal demand to enlarge the franchise and increase the influence of representative institutions in the government gained wider public and bureaucratic support. This goal was linked with the desire to collapse the thirty-nine separate, sovereign German states into a single, unified Germany. The one liberal and constitutional German nation-state would, according to this train of thought, of necessity include Jewish emancipation—the presumption being that the Jews either had no separate national identity or would abandon the national aspects of their Jewishness. While this presumption may have made religious Jews uncomfortable, they appreciated the liberals' tolerance. Furthermore, they were aware that liberals were not intent on erasing Jewish distinctions; they supported the granting of corporate status for Jewish communal bodies (*Gemeinden*), a change long desired by Jewish leaders, particularly the traditionalists.

Conservative views were not entirely negative regarding Jewish status, either. Shortly after Frederick William IV (1840–58) took the throne, he announced his intent to prepare a new, comprehensive Jewry law in accordance with his concept of Prussia as a Christian state. This concept was never implemented as it met with stiff opposition from both the liberals and conservatives in the Prussian ministries, but it was diffused widely in the press. Frederick and his circle of advisers, inspired by a romantic conservatism that idealized the medieval state, conceived of the state as a Christian entity that bonded together unequal, organic corporations in love for and loyalty to God and king. In this Christian state, the Jews would be treated graciously, but with lesser rights than Christians, as a separate, alien nation. But Jews would not be the only distinct group: the state would be composed of freely interacting corporations such as churches, guilds, estates, and so on. The individual corporations would be freed from censorship and government interference. To liberal Jews and Christians this view was not only regressive, but hostile. They

[16] Herbert A. Strauss, 'Liberalism and Conservatism in Prussian Legislation for Jewish Affairs, 1815–1847', in id. (ed.), *Jubilee Volume Dedicated to Curt C. Silberman* (New York, 1969), 114–32: 118.   [17] Hagen, *Germans, Poles, and Jews*, 103–4.

regarded the state as a secular construct and the religion of its citizens as a private matter as long as the religion did not promote a separate, national existence. Frederick William IV's conception of the Christian state appeared to be merely a different, perhaps even more insidious, form of the older conservatism that blocked Jews' entry into the larger society.[18] Yet traditionally religious Jews, who constituted the bulk of the population in West Prussia and the province of Posen, probably had a different perspective. The rabbis among them, at least, would not have regarded the emperor's views as hostile. They were slightly wary of emancipation, and given its tendency to undermine rabbinic authority this is not surprising. The rabbis wanted the benefits of emancipation but were unwilling to pay for them by sacrificing Judaism. Perhaps this tension could be resolved, wrote a correspondent in *Der treue Zions-Wächter* in 1846, by accepting a limited emancipation, one that removed oppressive restrictions but did not confer complete equality and the civic obligations that might compromise Jewish beliefs and practices.[19] We can presume that Kalischer agreed with that. He was certainly not likely to view the conservative position of the emperor, to the extent that he was aware of it, as malevolent; according to his article on the circumcision scandal in Frankfurt, he would have been more comfortable with the notion of the Christian state than with the liberals' secular outlook. What liberals found distasteful about the Jews' role in the theoretical Christian state he probably regarded favourably and interpreted as respectful of the Jewish religion.

The final 1847 law concerning Jews was typical of the Prussian state's gradual approach to Jewish emancipation. It allowed Jews to serve in government and municipal positions, except those connected with judicial, police, or executive authority. They were eligible to teach in schools and universities, though not in all types of schools and not in the humanities and religious studies. Restrictions on other occupations were removed, however, as were restrictions on their movement to other provinces. These new opportunities did not apply to the Jews of the Posen province.[20] They were included, however, in the 1847 law clarifying the parameters of Jewish communal governance, with the decree

[18] Friedrich Julius Stahl, born into a Jewish family and a convert to Protestantism, propagated the concept of a Christian state while teaching at universities and in his *Der christliche Staat und sein Verhaltniss zu Deismus and Judenthum* (Berlin, 1847). Strauss, 'Liberalism and Conservatism', 120–5, elaborates on the liberal disdain for traditional, unreformed Judaism. Liberals believed that it fostered a cohesive, insular Jewish outlook that prevented the economic modernization of lower-class Jews and suppressed the desire to engage in social, political, and intellectual intercourse with Christians. Clark, 'Protestant Missions to the Jews in Prussia', presents an incisive summary of the greatly vacillating attitudes of Protestant liberals and missionaries towards the Jewish Reform movement, and its relation to philosemitism and antisemitism.

[19] Liberles, *Religious Conflict in Social Context*, 80–1.

[20] Rurup, 'The Tortuous and Thorny Path', 26.

that 'Synagogue Congregations' (*Synagogengemeinden*) should be established within each community; their functions were strictly confined to the religious sphere. Throughout the document, Jews were referred to not as Prussian citizens but as Jewish subjects.[21]

Liberal Jews were very disappointed with the law, for it had actually strengthened Jewish political separatism and reinforced occupational restrictions. In contrast, traditionalist rabbis writing in *Der treue Zions-Wächter* overlooked the limitations of the 1847 Jewry law and proclaimed it one of the major victories of the year. They were particularly pleased with the mandated changes in community governance, for these had the effect of strengthening the traditionalist camp. The new law eliminated government-imposed boards (which had included reform-minded Jews) and in their place gave the majority the right to control the religious affairs of the community. The minority had the option of forming its own separate synagogues within the community organization. The new law did not prohibit religious reform, and it did not mandate unity under a traditionalist banner, but because the majority of Jews at this time were in the traditionalist camp, they regained power lost to reform-minded Jews under the previous system. A notion had recently appeared among traditionalist rabbis that the state would grant legal equality as a reward for obedience to religious authority. The new law seemed to affirm this perspective. Traditional rabbis pointed to the community-governance provisions as proof that full emancipation, when it came, would be enacted without harm to traditional Judaism.[22]

The optimism of these rabbis was not put to the test for quite some time. Meanwhile, during the tumultuous years around the revolutions of 1848, virtually all parties in Germany announced their intent to emancipate the Jews or passed constitutions decreeing equality for all regardless of religion. With the collapse of the revolutionary parties, however, the process of emancipation came to a halt. In the aftermath of 1848 Jews lost the political rights they had so recently gained. One exception to this was freedom of movement: after 1848, Jews throughout Prussia were granted permission to move to other

---

[21] Rurup, 'The Tortuous and Thorny Path', 26; Strauss, 'Liberalism and Conservatism', 123.

[22] Liberles, *Religious Conflict in Social Context*, 80–6, with extensive documentation from *Der treue Zions-Wächter*. Jacob Katz, 'Changing Position and Outlook of Halakhists in Early Modernity', 97–8, notes that older and younger rabbis in Frankfurt in the mid-1840s believed in the continuing support of the non-Jewish authorities for the upholding of Jewish law. Furthermore, 'Even stranger is the fact that they wished to use the invocation of the special Jewish oath of *more Judaico*—a practice very much resented by the Jewish public and which indeed was being abolished by state after state under the impact of enlightened public opinion—as a means of coercion.' Yet, the slights that so aggravated the more assimilated Jews clearly did not bother traditional Jews, who regarded themselves as essentially distinct from Christians.

Prussian provinces, and the flow of Jews from the east to central and western Prussia increased markedly.[23]

During the 1850s, despite the lack of progress towards emancipation, traditional rabbis could still find ample evidence for their belief that the state favoured them above all other Jews. During this period of resurgent political conservatism, local and national authorities deferred less to the liberals. It was widely acknowledged that the traditional Jews in the Polish territories had remained loyal to the Prussian state during the revolutionary disturbances. Those in the city of Posen were particularly conspicuous for their loyalty to the Prussian Crown. They were proud of the history of co-operation between their rabbis and Prussian officials during times of crisis.[24] Jews had suffered at the hands of the Poles when it became clear that their allegiance was towards Prussia and not the Polish national cause, and the state seemed to appreciate their sacrifices. Internally, the traditionalists made some headway; in accordance with the new communal regulations of 1847, they made strides towards creating Jewish communities and institutions designed to protect and preserve Jewish traditions. The movement for religious reform seemed to falter; at least, religious reformers operated more quietly and less publicly than they had during the 1840s.[25]

Kalischer testified personally to the persistence of the old religious order. A controversy arose in 1858 when Rabbi Shelomoh Kluger of Brody in Galicia ruled against the new machine-made Passover matzah. In his ruling he castigated the rabbis of Germany for sanctioning the innovation and made a blanket judgement against the rulings of any German rabbi. Kalischer was one of many rabbis upset by this insult, and he sent a letter to the Jewish press protesting the generalization: 'It is true that much of the failing of our many sins comes from those lands, but a remnant of Israel [remains that] has done no sin, and the hearts of these few quake with the fear of God; their piety is all the greater because they have withstood trial.'[26] For the first time Kalischer referred to himself as one of the 'remnant' of Israel. However, neither this comment nor this article is about the mass of Jews in German lands; they were irrelevant to

---

[23] Lowenstein, 'The Rural Community', in *The Mechanics of Change*, 138–44.

[24] According to Heppner, *Aus Vergangenheit und Gegenwart der Juden*, 853, Prussian officials appealed to Shelomoh Eger for help in quelling the disturbances during the Polish rebellions of 1847–8. At their bidding, Rabbi Eger published an announcement during the disturbances requesting that Jewish complaints against Poles be directed to the civil courts and not to the Prussian army, whose excessive punishments provoked more Polish hostilities.

[25] Meyer, *Response to Modernity*, 181–2.

[26] *Hamagid*, 16 (1858). Other sources (including my article 'Zevi Hirsch Kalischer and the Origins of Religious Zionism', in Malino and Sorkin (eds.), *Profiles in Diversity*, 267–94 at 281 n. 29) incorrectly place this comment in the next edition of *Hamagid*.

the controversy, as no aspersion was cast against them—on the contrary, they piously obeyed their rabbis' rulings. And among the rabbis there was a faithful remnant of indeterminate size. Kalischer still maintained what he had written in 1846: the reforming rabbis were responsible for the spread of religious deviancy, and the masses in their innocence merely followed along.[27]

Thus in a region in which emancipation left traditional Judaism dominant, where conservative rabbinic leaders were accorded respect from the non-Jewish authorities, and where Jewish corporate separateness was preserved, Kalischer's belief that the movement towards emancipation was a gift from God as a preparatory step towards redemption makes sense. From his vantage point, it was reasonable to conclude that the same Christian rulers who were clearly well disposed towards Jews as a separate, empowered entity would support the Jews' bid to return to Zion. Of course, his perception was selective. He filtered out messages that he did not want to hear and ignored evidence that contradicted his messianic scenario.

Nevertheless, even a more impartial assessment of Jewish civic emancipation would have done a great deal to reinforce Kalischer's messianic outlook. When he wrote to Rothschild in 1836, he had already rejected the concept of a dominating, overtly controlling deity: 'Do not imagine that God, blessed be his name, will suddenly descend from on high and say to his people "Go forth"', he wrote. 'Redemption will begin through natural causes, through human actions, and through the will of the kings to bring together a few of the scattered of Israel to the Holy Land.'[28] The peaceful grants of emancipation made even less plausible the common messianic belief that there was little human control over history and that Jews could escape their *galut* status only through miracles. In 1836 Kalischer had feared ridicule for declaring that Rothschild's prominence was a sign from God. Since that time, a number of Jews from the first generation of emancipation had risen to positions of power, and many Jews—not simply one wealthy man—could stir the hearts of world rulers towards granting the Jews possession of Jerusalem. The Jewish power base had broadened, and enthusiasm for Jewish settlement in the Holy Land had grown. Clearly, a new era had begun.

[27] David Ellenson, 'The Orthodox Rabbinate and Apostasy', in *Tradition in Transition*, 161–84, shows that there was already a decades-old tradition in responsa literature referring to Reform Jewish leaders—not followers—as apostates. According to Michael K. Silber, 'The Emergence of Ultra-Orthodoxy: The Invention of a Tradition', in Jack Wertheimer (ed.), *The Uses of Tradition: Jewish Continuity in the Modern Era* (New York and Jerusalem, 1992), 23–84 at 74, 'by the 1860s a consensus had emerged among German neo-Orthodox authorities: while they continued to condemn Reform as heresy and the few dozen reform rabbis as rebellious heretics, care was taken to distinguish between the rabbis and the mass of lay reformers who were assumed to be nothing more than misguided innocents, "like infants taken captive by gentiles"'.

[28] *Zionist Writings*, 3.

THE RESTORATION OF SACRIFICIAL WORSHIP

In 1855 Kalischer became free of a project he had been labouring over for decades. He finally completed and published *Moznayim lamishpat* (Scales of Justice).[29] *Moznayim lamishpat* exhibited the range of his talents and personality: his intellectual depth and breadth, ambitious optimism, pragmatism, and humility. The book's topic was quite unlike any of his previous publications. It focused on the civil and criminal laws of the *Shulḥan arukh*, laws that had long been irrelevant to Jewish life. Perhaps he chose the topic in the hope that in a restored Jewish commonwealth these laws would once again be binding. This would certainly fit his messianic scenario, but there is no evidence to establish this theory as anything beyond mere speculation. In his book he mentioned that he was motivated by the desire to achieve consensus within the world of scholarship for this particular area of Jewish law, notable for its contradictory interpretations that had generated volumes of halakhic scholarship.[30]

The publication of *Moznayim lamishpat* marked a new stage of Kalischer's life. The book was very well received by the rabbinic world; it was crafted for the elite, and it cemented his reputation as a first-rate halakhic scholar. It inaugurated him at the higher level of scholarship, perhaps even approaching that of his teachers. On a personal level the publication of his magnum opus freed him to pursue other goals. In fact, completing *Moznayim lamishpat* drew him back to his research on the renewal of sacrificial worship. Travelling

[29] Twelve years earlier, in an effort to attract a publisher, he had published a section of the manuscript fragment under the title *Even boḥan*. When *Moznayim lamishpat* was finally completed and published, it appeared in two separate volumes by two different publishers; this reflected, presumably, the concern of the publishers to minimize their investment in the work, which would have interested only a small number of readers. In the introduction to vol. i, Kalischer expressed some embarrassment over the fact that he had announced his intention to publish the book years earlier. There was a great amount of work involved, he wrote, and only because his wife supported the family through her earnings was he able to finish the project. Actually, he had not even completed it, he disclosed in the introduction to vol. ii. He still intended to produce the third and fourth volumes, 'and may God help me to finish them'.

[30] Jacob Lorbeerbaum had written extensively on these laws in his *Ḥavat da'at*, and Kalischer's interest may have been sparked by his teacher's work. He did not mention Lorbeerbaum in the introduction to the volume, however; he said that his model was Rabbi Abraham Danzig's popular summaries of the *Shulḥan arukh*'s daily ritual and dietary laws, *Ḥayei adam* and *Ḥokhmat adam* (Vilna, 1810 and 1812). He consciously adopted Danzig's methodology, restating older decisions, discussing the conflicting opinions and various options, and presenting a conclusion. In this way he hoped 'to present a compromise between the conflicting opinions through clear arguments and so end disputes in Israel'. Where he could draw no conclusion, he would set out the principles that underlay the different positions and identify the textual sources involved. He explains that the name of the work was a reflection of his method, as well as being equivalent in numerical value to his name.

around the region to collect approbations for his book, he met Rabbi Tsevi Hirsch Chajes, a protégé of Moses Sofer and a great authority on talmudic literature.[31] Visiting Chajes at his home in the town of Kalisch, he learnt that Chajes was familiar with the 1837 correspondence between Sofer and Eger that Kalischer had initiated. Unbeknown to Kalischer, Chajes and Sofer had been in touch with each other when Eger asked Sofer his opinion on the matter of re-establishing sacrificial worship. Shortly before he died, Sofer had sent a copy of his reply to Chajes. Chajes was intrigued by the topic and did further research. In 1842 he published a book on halakhic methodology, *Darkhei hora'ah*, and he included in it Sofer's letter and his own research on the cessation of sacrificial worship during the Roman period. It is clear from the context that he regarded his work on sacrificial worship as a response to the efforts to revise the liturgy. The book appeared in the midst of heated debate between traditionalists and reformers brought on by the 1841 publication of a revised version of the Hamburg temple prayer book and heightened by the first Reform rabbinical conference of 1844. Citing the evidence of the Talmud, he argued that sacrificial worship had continued for about eighty years after the destruction of the Temple. The rabbis who lived immediately afterwards continued to bring offerings as long as they were able, and the evidence showed that they stopped only when the authorities prohibited Jewish worship on the Temple Mount. His essay was a rebuttal of the radicals' claim that post-Temple rabbis had been pleased by the cessation of sacrifice and would approve the present-day omission of prayers for the return of sacrifice. Including Sofer's letter reinforced the message that the renewal of the sacrificial cult was still a real possibility.[32]

Kalischer was energized by his discovery of the aftermath of his query to Eger and the literature it had produced. For the first time, almost twenty years later, he read the unabridged version of Sofer's letter to Eger. It was much

[31] See the introduction to Zvi Hirsch Chajes, *The Student's Guide through the Talmud*, trans. and ed. Jacob Shachter (London, 1952), for full biographical information. Chajes (1805–55) received a traditional Jewish education side by side with an extensive programme of secular studies. Late in his life he was granted the degree of doctor of philosophy from Lemburg University.

[32] On the polemical context of the halakhic literature, see Myers, 'Attitudes toward a Resumption of Sacrificial Worship in the Nineteenth Century', *Modern Judaism*, 7 (1987), 29–49. The continuing conflict over these matters is discussed in Ch. 7. Chajes's *Darkhei hora'ah* confirmed his identity as an opponent of religious reform. Meir Hirschkovitz, *Rabbi Tsevi Hirsch Chajes* (Heb.) (Jerusalem, 1972), 229–32, also cites family testimony for the polemical context of Chajes's stance on the renewal of sacrifice. Chajes positioned Sofer's letter to Eger between denunciations of the Reform movement and a discussion on the limits of innovation in Jewish law. Chajes's essay, entitled 'The Last Pamphlet on the Temple Service', can also be found in his collected responsa, *Kol sifrei maharats ḥajes*, 2 vols. (Jerusalem, 1958), ii. 844–58 (responsum no. 72).

more positive about the restoration of sacrifice than Eger's summary had been.[33] Eger had omitted Sofer's many comments favourable to Kalischer's point of view, including the rulings of earlier authorities who were supportive of Kalischer's position. Sofer had never agreed with Eger that the requirements for priestly clothing were an obstacle; Eger never even addressed the issue. The actual letter opened up many avenues of continued debate, and perhaps even a resolution. Kalischer reassessed his earlier contact with Eger. He could not believe that Eger had deliberately hidden or distorted Sofer's response. He thus concluded that his teacher's ailing condition had hindered him from making an accurate report. Because Eger had stated beforehand that he would accept his son-in-law's ruling, Sofer's more permissive stance now could be attributed to Eger as well. Indeed Kalischer imagined that Eger had deeply desired a resumption of sacrificial worship but had held back his approval out of respect for God's law. One can practically hear Kalischer's exultation at this great victory, as he compared his teacher's dying wish for sacrificial worship to that of King David, about whose unfulfilled plans to build a Temple God said, 'You did well that it was in your heart [1 Kings 8: 18]'.[34] With Chajes's support, Kalischer believed he could press ahead with his messianic proposal.

It appears that Kalischer did not realize the polemical, anti-Reform context of Sofer and Chajes's approving statements. Neither man shared his sincere intention of working towards a resumption of sacrificial worship. Rather, by arguing that sacrificial worship was still necessary, desirable, and halakhically permissible they were saying that present-day Jewish life was attenuated and that the Jewish world was in need of redemption. Asserting the sacrificial essence of Judaism was a way of 'proving' Jewish distinctiveness and the Jewish people's essential link to the Land of Israel. It was one more way to refute the claim that Jewish life could become normal and whole through enlightenment and civic emancipation. The impossibility of rebuilding the altar on the Temple Mount made this a wonderfully safe strategy.

[33] It is not surprising that Kalischer had not read Chajes's book: books were not readily available and were expensive. Readers of Chajes's essay would not have associated Kalischer with Sofer's letter or Chajes's essay, or notified him about them, as Kalischer was not mentioned in either work and did not have a reputation as an advocate of the resumption of sacrificial worship. The most complete version of Sofer's letter was printed in Tsevi Hirsch Chajes, *Darkhei hora'ah* (1842), included in *Kol sifrei maharats hayes*, i. 270. An abridged version can be found in Sofer's collected responsa, *Ḥatam sofer*, 2 vols. (Pressburg, 1860), ii. 98 (responsum no. 236). In the latter volume, the editor omitted Sofer's naive reaction to the mosque on the Temple Mount; see above, at Ch. 4 n. 26.

[34] Kalischer noted this in *Derishat tsiyon*, 92–3, in which he included the correspondence between himself and Eger.

Inspired anew, Kalischer sought to gain wider rabbinic approval of his responsum on sacrifice. Back home in Thorn, he tried to engage Chajes in a correspondence, but he did not respond and died shortly thereafter in 1855. Kalischer may have approached other rabbis for approval, but all that he preserved from this time was the positive response of Rabbi Nathan Marcus Adler, the chief rabbi of London. Adler was persuaded by Kalischer's halakhic arguments, but his reply contained a clear endorsement of the dominant passive messianic approach, and he did not care to pursue the matter any further. As he was prominent among the opponents of religious reform, it appears that he, too, was interested primarily in the subject's polemical value.[35]

It took until 1857 for Kalischer to find a true kindred spirit, Rabbi Elijah Guttmacher of Graditz in the Posen district. Guttmacher had studied with Kalischer in the yeshiva of Akiva Eger and had become adept in kabbalah. He was widely known as a holy man, and many Jews flocked to him to receive his blessing; he even had a following among the hasidic Jews of Jerusalem.[36] Guttmacher shared Kalischer's conviction that an accurate reading of rabbinic literature led directly to active messianism. He contributed kabbalistic as well as halakhic proof texts to Kalischer's arguments.[37] The correspondence shows that the two men were investigating the details of the renewal of sacrifice in order to be prepared for the day when the rulers of Jerusalem would allow Jews to make offerings on the Temple Mount. In their letters the men examined the case for the permissibility of the renewal of the sacrificial worship before the messianic age. They reviewed the letters from Eger and offered further arguments why almost all the community sacrifices could be resumed. Guttmacher

[35] Their correspondence was also included in *Derishat tsiyon*, 95–7. Adler's pastoral letter to British Jews of May 1854, quoted in Nahum Sokolow, *History of Zionism, 1600–1918*, 2 vols. (New York, 1969), 240–3, is an explicit endorsement of passive messianism. On Adler's anti-Reform activism, see M. Friedlander, 'The Late Chief Rabbi, Dr. N. M. Adler', *Jewish Quarterly Review*, 2 (1890), 369–85. See also Eugene C. Black, 'The Anglicanization of Orthodoxy: The Adlers, Father and Son', in Malino and Sorkin (eds.), *Profiles in Diversity*, 295–325.

[36] People flocked to Guttmacher from all over central Europe, despite his public disavowal of possessing any special powers. According to Akiva Eger's great-grandson, the crowds of people visiting Guttmacher were so distracting that he requested the town leaders to prohibit these visitors from entering the town. The leaders refused, since they did not want to lose the income that the visitors brought the town, and they rebuked Guttmacher for his lack of civic concern. See S. Sofer (ed.), *Igerot soferim*, pt. 1, 81–3 nn. In *Hamagid* (1874), no. 12, Guttmacher disclaimed any special powers and asked people to stop coming to him for a blessing. In the same year, Rabbi Simon Berman remarked in a letter to Kalischer that if Guttmacher collected one reichsthaler from each person coming to him, in a few months the amount would equal ten thousand; see *Zionist Writings*, 519. Correspondence between Guttmacher and Kalischer on the proper formulation of a verse in an amulet can be found in the YIVO Archives (New York) and the National and University Library archives (Jerusalem).   [37] This correspondence is in *Derishat tsiyon*, 100–5.

suggested that they strengthen their position by anticipating additional halakhic objections that could be raised by others. Among these were more problems related to the priesthood, ritual impurity, and the practical problem of locating the altar site. On this last problem the men's ignorance of Jerusalem is apparent. They knew that the Foundation Stone was inside the mosque and was therefore unapproachable, so they found a way of discovering the altar site by determining the distance from the western Temple wall and the city gates. Unknown to them, these structures no longer existed. They mistakenly took as fact God's promise, contained in a seventh-century midrashic text, that the walls and gates would never be destroyed. It does not seem to have occurred to them to check this with current residents of Jerusalem.[38]

It seems clear that, at the end of this particular exchange of letters, Kalischer and Guttmacher felt confident that they really had solved all extant halakhic problems connected with the renewal of sacrificial worship. When Kalischer published their letters four years later, he closed with the remark 'As of now, no question or difficulty with our method remains.'[39] This juncture, like the publication of *Moznayim lamishpat*, marked a triumphant moment in his life: he had finally completed the scholarship he had started more than twenty years earlier. Not only that, he even had the stamp of approval from internationally respected rabbis. All that remained was to execute the details on the practical level.

It is unclear how publicly Kalischer and Guttmacher pursued their dream, or whether they did anything at all. However, something about their association caused quite a stir. In 1857 a rumour spread throughout the Posen district that the Jews in Jerusalem wanted to offer sacrifices. This is how it was reported in a March edition of *Hamagid*, a new Jewish periodical published in western Russia:

An honourable correspondent from the newspaper mentioned above [*Allgemeine Zeitung des Judenthums*] has written: 'On the Posen district. Rabbi Elias Guttmacher was appointed a *nasi* from the Land of Israel. Not long ago the rabbis in Jerusalem sent him some halakhic questions, and one question—in the form of *pilpul*—on the laws of sacrifice. Before the rabbi sent them his answer, he wrote to two great rabbis, friends of his, in this district. And who knows how the matter became widely known among the masses and also among non-Jews. Some newspapers heard of it and announced that in Jerusalem people want to offer sacrifices.[40]

---

[38] Ibid. 102–3. Kalischer was later harshly criticized for relying on classical midrashic literature in thinking that the western wall was the Temple wall (when it is actually the western wall of the Temple Mount), and for not using the residents of the city as a resource; see *Halevanon*, 11 (1863), 75.   [39] *Derishat tsiyon*, 105.

[40] *Hamagid*, 16 (1857). The parallel article is in *Allgemeine Zeitung des Judenthums*, 10 (2 Mar. 1857). Guttmacher's appointment as *nasi* indicated that a community of Jews in the Yishuv con-

It is difficult to extract anything definitive from this report. What is clear, however, is that it represents an effort to dispel the rumour and to characterize the rabbinic discussion of sacrifices simply as theoretical scholarship. If there was one lesson Kalischer learnt from this incident, it was that the concept of the return of sacrificial worship provoked considerable passion. Shortly thereafter, he became involved in the efforts on behalf of the Jews of the Yishuv. In 1858 he wrote to Chief Rabbi Adler of London and to Sir Moses Montefiore requesting that he be appointed overseer of Montefiore's newly purchased plantation in Palestine. They politely refused him on the grounds that the position was already filled.[41] In 1859 he served in a local committee supporting a project of the Yishuv support organization of Dutch and German Jews, the building of guest houses in Jerusalem. By 1861 Thorn was one of the collecting posts for donations and a stopover for various emissaries from the Yishuv.[42] In 1860 Kalischer met Rabbi Nathan Friedland, a Lithuanian preacher who was travelling through the region collecting rabbinical recommendations for his manuscript promoting agricultural settlement in Palestine as a means of hastening redemption. Friedland, like Kalischer, set great store by the role of powerful Jews, and he travelled to Paris to deliver his message there.[43] Perhaps in response to Friedland's activism, Kalischer sent a long letter to Albert Cohn, administrator of the extensive charities of the Paris Rothschilds, in 1860, asking to be appointed supervisor of the Rothschild expenditures in the Yishuv. He included the manuscript of his *Derishat tsiyon*, and asked Cohn to consider publishing it.[44] In that same year, Kalischer called a conference in Thorn of rabbis and communal leaders to discuss ways of building support for the agricultural development of the Yishuv.[45] The establishment of the Kolonisations-Verein für Palästina in 1860 intensified his turn towards activism. The organization, which was founded by Dr Hayim Lorje in Frankfurt on the Oder, was dedicated to helping the poor of the Yishuv through the establishment of agricultural colonies there. Kalischer wrote to Lorje, sent him the

sidered him their leader. It may have been merely an honour, or it may have denoted his willingness to collect funds on their behalf.

[41] Israel Klausner, 'Rabbi Zvi Hirsch Kalischer's Derishat Zion', *In the Dispersion*, 5–6 (Spring 1966), 281–9 at 286.

[42] Klausner, Introduction, *Zionist Writings*, 43 (introductory section has its own pagination, separate from the documents). Klausner cites two contemporary reports of Kalischer and Thorn's role in this effort: *Hamagid*, 12 (1859) and 24 (1861).

[43] Klausner, *Zionist Writings*, 39–43 (introductory section); id., 'Rabbi Nathan Friedland of Lithuania', *Ha'umah*, 18 (1966), 227–45.

[44] Kalischer to Albert Cohn (estimated date, 1860), *Zionist Writings*, 180.

[45] Nahum Sokolow, *Ḥibat tsiyon* (Jerusalem, 1934), 20–1. Sokolow heard a report of this conference from Kalischer's son-in-law, M. Gruenberg of Przasnysz, who had been present.

manuscript of *Derishat tsiyon*, and asked him to publish the volume and consider appointing him to supervise the organization's field office in Palestine.[46]

This point marks a new stage in Kalischer's activism. He had been promoting the restoration of sacrificial worship, and now he was turning to the revival of the Yishuv. He had been advocating change from afar, and now he was volunteering to go to Palestine and direct matters personally. He described his proposal, however, as a continuation of the previous quarter-century's work:

It has been about twenty-five years since my heart stirred within me concerning the Yishuv of the land of our ancestors, the place of our Temple. I showed with clear and straightforward proofs the greatness of this commandment and the infinite reward for those who work to create a settled land [*erets noshevet*]. While he was alive I spoke about this with our teacher, the universally respected Akiva Eger, of blessed memory, who agreed with me. After a time I stirred the spirit of the great prince and generous benefactor Sir Moses Montefiore, whose letters I still possess, who responded that his heart also dwells continually on this matter. Also the great scholar Rabbi Nathan Adler, rabbi of London, exchanged letters and halakhic arguments with me on this issue, and he agreed with me. It is all in my possession in writing. In an essay on this particular matter, which I am sending to his honour, I present it all as clear as the sun.[47]

Until the late 1850s, Kalischer had expressed little explicit interest in Jewish agricultural settlement in the Land of Israel; it was barely mentioned in his letter to Rothschild, in his exegetical writings, and in his recent correspondence with Eger and Adler. Yet his testimony to Albert Cohn conflates his scheme to revive sacrificial worship with the strengthening of the Jewish community of Palestine; indeed, the former appears to have dissolved into the latter. In addition, building up the land appears to have achieved the status of a commandment. Kalischer, however, did not admit to any change in his interest or activities. This was probably not a conscious strategy. To him, the renewal of sacrificial worship and the agricultural revitalization of the Land of Israel were inseparable parts of one task. After all, Jewish agriculture was the prerequisite to the production of animals and foodstuffs for the sacrifices, and a healthy economy was necessary for the re-creation of a priestly community there. In the manuscript he was appealing to Cohn to publish, he explained that both agricultural resettlement and sacrificial renewal fell under one commandment called *mitsvat yishuv ha'arets*, the commandment of settling the land.[48]

Since the letter to Cohn was designed to win employment and the publica-

---

[46] Klausner, *Zionist Writings*, 44 (introductory section). Lorje reported Kalischer's overture in *Israelit*, 28 (1860). See also Getzel Kressel, 'The First Palestine Settlement Society' (Heb.), *Zion*, 7 (1941), 197–205.

[47] Kalischer to Albert Cohn (estimated date, 1860), *Zionist Writings*, 178–9.

[48] *Derishat tsiyon*, 48. This argument is analysed at greater length in Ch. 7 below.

tion of his manuscript, its content is an indicator of what Kalischer thought carried appeal at that time. Significantly, he made no mention of his previous work on the renewal of sacrifice or his belief in the messianic impact of sacrificial offerings. This aspect of his messianic theory was missing from the letter. When summarizing his theory to Cohn, he described the evolutionary redemptive process and the indispensable role of powerful Jews like Cohn and Rothschild. He explained that when a community of Jews gathered 'on the holy mountain and increased their prayers', God would hear their plea and bring redemption. The pivotal event here sounds like a mere prayer service, while in the Rothschild letter it is clearly described as a sacrificial offering.[49] Concealing his concern for the sacrifices clearly was a conscious strategy. This is the first obvious manifestation of a tactic that he would increasingly utilize more skilfully. Learning how to cater for public opinion, manifest in the concealment of his long-term objective to restore sacrificial worship, was a necessary prerequisite to the successful achievement of this goal.

By the end of the 1850s, the forces propelling Kalischer out of his study into the public arena were fully assembled. He had completed an ambitious halakhic treatise that established his professional reputation. His enquiry into the renewal of sacrificial worship had ended in a resolution of all outstanding problems. Muslim, Christian, and Jewish 'princes' were working to improve the situation for the Jews in Palestine, and Diaspora Jews were motivated to move there. The relations between Jews and European Christians had never been better. Jews were learning how to operate within their respective political systems, and this could facilitate a friendly transfer of Jewish people and power to the Holy Land.

It is a common belief about Jewish history that messianic enthusiasm increases during bad times, when people are desperate for succour. While that may be so, good times are particularly conducive to the resurgence of the messianic ideology featured here. Realistic messianism is fuelled by feelings of power and entitlement, and encouraged by signs that God is working on behalf of returning the Jews to their land. It becomes less plausible in times of distress. Yet realistic messianism can tolerate some negative developments if they propel the Jews towards Zion. In an era when a few right-minded, fabulously wealthy Jews were present, poverty in the Diaspora was not a serious impediment. The promising developments in the Yishuv could be held out as an alternative.

---

[49] Kalischer to Albert Cohn (estimated date, 1860), *Zionist Writings*, 179; Kalischer to Rothschild (1836), ibid. 4. In each letter the description of the ritual is paraphrased from *Shevilei emunah* by Meir ben Isaac Aldabi (c.1310–c.1360). The source is quoted in full in *Derishat tsiyon*, 62–3.

The historian A. M. Luncz preserved, in 1897, a charming story about Kalischer that is worth retelling here. The incident it describes dramatically illustrates the rabbi's new lease of life at the beginning of the 1860s:

In 1860 the rabbi experienced a narrow escape from death. This is what happened: when he was standing and praying next to a window in the synagogue in the place that he lived, a piece from the wall next to the synagogue fell, and its stones fell through the window and onto his head, breaking his skull. The doctors who rushed to his side worked with great effort to stop the blood loss, and they used their surgical skills to remove a piece of bone from his skull. Despite their success, they abandoned hope because of the fever that often follows such a dangerous operation. But God's kindness was upon him, and he never became feverish, and immediately after the blow and the surgery, while he was still bandaged, he returned to his regimen of constant reflection on Torah, taxing his brain to produce new insights in Jewish law and lore, against his doctors' orders, who warned him not to commence studying until the wound was totally closed. With delightful words he responded to one of the doctors who visited him and wondered at his strength to study in such a condition, and especially to generate with such acuity explanations of the words of our Sages, 'And why should my friend wonder at this idea, *inasmuch as the doctors opened up my brain.*' As soon as he rose from the sickbed, he composed a special prayer and a record of the entire incident, and wrote them into a scroll. He read it every year, for the rest of his life, on the anniversary of the event.[50]

[50] Luncz, 'Zevi Hirsch Kalischer', 132–3.

SEVEN

Seeking Zion, 1862–1874

EAGER to carry its message to a wide audience, and especially to persuade traditional Jews that its goals were legitimate, the Kolonisations-Verein für Palästina published *Derishat tsiyon* in 1862. This brought Kalischer international attention. Serving as a spokesman for the cause of promoting Jewish agricultural settlement in the Yishuv, he dedicated himself to a new form of promotional writing. He wrote extensively for the European Jewish press (which had just recently expanded into monthly and bi-monthly editions and was in need of contributors), solicited rabbis and prominent Jews for support and donations, publicly responded to his critics, and corresponded with anyone who questioned him about his ideas and projects. He added new sections to *Derishat tsiyon* for the German translation and the second Hebrew edition, both published in 1866.[1] This literature is the focus of this chapter.

Achieving his goals in Palestine proved much harder than Kalischer had at first anticipated. When the Kolonisations-Verein für Palästina disbanded in 1864, Kalischer and his friend Elijah Guttmacher started the organization Hevrat Yishuv Erets Yisra'el and ran it from their homes in Thorn and Graditz. The goal of the organization was to buy land in Palestine suitable for agricultural colonies. They raised money themselves, and found agents in distant areas to seek out funds and establish regional offices. Running the organization proved to be an overwhelming task, and in 1866 they convinced the Alliance Israélite Universelle to serve as parent agency. After years of fund-raising there was still not enough to purchase an adequate piece of land upon which to establish an agricultural colony. Nevertheless, in 1873 Kalischer and Guttmacher instructed their agents in Frankfurt and Palestine to begin negotiations, and by the summer of 1874 they had acquired a small plot of land outside Jerusalem. Kalischer joyfully announced it in the papers, requesting donations from readers to pay for the last instalment. He died two months later, leaving his sons to complete the transaction.[2]

[1] Most of this was collected by Israel Klausner in *Zionist Writings*. Among the other publications from this period are *Yetsiat mitsrayim* (Kalischer's commentary on the Haggadah), *Sefer haberit* (his commentary on the Torah), and vol. iii of *Emunah yesharah*. Certain themes in these last three volumes are analysed above, in Ch. 5.

[2] Kalischer's announcement of the purchase is in *Hamagid*, 37 (1874). According to Isaac

The core principles of Kalischer's messianic ideology remained constant over the years. *Derishat tsiyon* was a mature, polished version of his 1836 letter to Rothschild. The many letters, newspaper articles, and pamphlets that followed further elaborated upon, embellished, and refined his earlier ideas.

Although Kalischer's new writing was more accessible, much of it was written for a reader who was highly educated in Jewish literary texts. Some was translated into German, but most of it was in Hebrew and therefore beyond the reach of the vast majority of Jews in western Europe.[3] *Derishat tsiyon* and the book's later addenda were written in a homiletical style. Kalischer connected his major points to an interpretation of a sacred text or a series of texts. While there were sections of the book written 'for the maskil', that is, written from the viewpoint of plain reason, to Kalischer's rabbinic mind the truth of any religious doctrine could not be established by abstract reasoning; rather, he believed that one discovers the clear meaning of revelation by amassing proof texts and reconciling their seemingly discordant messages into a coherent reading. Law was also a source of truth, and so *Derishat tsiyon* contains long passages analysing halakhah (including the opinions with which he disagreed, along with his refutation); of course, this was beyond the understanding of readers lacking a talmudic education. Kalischer's newspaper articles, though generally clear and to the point, were also likely to include some choice quotations, judiciously edited and interpreted to support an activist approach. While his writing was not very straightforward, its very appearance as an assemblage, and its breadth and depth, lent it legitimacy among religious Jews.

What was most notable about the new writing was its rhetoric. Kalischer exhibited an increased sensitivity to the broad range of public opinion and developed unconventional ways to engage his readers: he utilized emotion-laden symbols that manipulated public fears and hopes, he phrased key points as slogans, and he generated narrative and visual metaphors that succinctly conveyed his world view and the imperative of activism. Alongside his messianic reasoning, he promoted the renewal of sacrifices and the agricultural communes with non-religious arguments that emphasized their social, economic, and political benefits. The number and sophistication of these non-religious rationales multiplied over the years. He understood that his audience was a distinctly modern one; that is, it was highly diverse, including rabbinic

---

Arigur, *Tsevi hirsch kalischer* (Heb.) (Jerusalem, 1928), 160, Kalischer's son Judah Leib made the final purchase arrangement. According to the *EJ*, s.v. 'Kalischer, Zevi Hirsch' (written by Getzel Kressel), Kalischer's son Ze'ev Wolf, who was living in Palestine, used the funds from his father's estate to purchase land.

[3] A German translation of *Derishat tsiyon* was published in 1866, and Kalischer occasionally published articles in German-language Jewish newspapers.

scholars of the old school as well as acculturated supporters of proposed reforms of the Yishuv, for whom purely religious values were no longer sufficiently compelling. Kalischer appealed to popular nostalgia for archaic paradigms and, at the same time, advocated progressive reforms; the latter, when they developed along the path he anticipated, would return the Jews to their pristine past.

THE LAND

The basic sequence of events leading to full-fledged redemption remained constant in all Kalischer's writings: first came the partial Jewish return to the Land of Israel, followed by the commencement of sacrificial worship. The sacrificial offerings would trigger the complete ingathering of Jews to the Land of Israel, the apocalyptic wars of Gog and Magog, the appearance of prophets and messiah figures, the new Temple, and all the other miracles mentioned in biblical and rabbinic literature. He expected that hostility between Jews and non-Jews would prevail at the time of the apocalyptic wars, but that it would end with Jewish political hegemony and spiritual leadership of the world. The non-Jews would follow God's laws, flock to the Temple to hear God's teachings, and receive the blessings of the messianic age.[4]

Beginning with *Derishat tsiyon*, Kalischer included proof texts from the Zohar in his clarification of the messianic process. He began to sum up the process with the Aramaic phrase 'the awakening of the lower world will lead to the awakening of the upper world'.[5] Anyone with a basic knowledge of kabbalah would recognize this as the Zohar's succinct statement of the fundamental influence of human (Jewish) behaviour on the divine *sefirot*. Kalischer had long argued that hidden miracles occurring during the present era, if responded to correctly by human initiatives, would yield a response from God, so this change was largely cosmetic. He also borrowed language from the Zohar which, adopting the rabbinic interpretation of the four gradations of light in Song of Songs 6: 10 ('brightening like the dawn, beautiful as the moon, brilliant as the sun, awe-inspiring as an army with banners'), identified four stages

[4] Katz, 'Tzevi Hirsch Kalischer', 218–19, does not accurately convey the order of events. He errs in placing the renewal of sacrifices before the growth of a settled land. He also claims that in 1862 Kalischer began to regard the settled land, not the sacrifices, as the primary condition for the advent of the miraculous messianic events. This was not the case. Kalischer's use of kabbalistic terminology probably contributed to this error. In those passages he referred to *ge'ulat ha'arets* as the prerequisite for the miraculous redemption. Closer examination shows that sacrificial worship was the last phase of *ge'ulat ha'arets*.

[5] For example, see *Derishat tsiyon*, 37, 39, and also in other writings: see *Zionist Writings*, 404, 469, 485.

of an evolving messianic age.[6] Though he tried to superimpose these stages on his own messianic scenario, they fitted awkwardly, and even when he referred to them, he often did not specify at which stage an event would occur. Since the actual order of events remained the same, as did the division between natural and supernatural events, the use of kabbalistic language again did not denote a change in principle. He was validating his theory with sources that would be authoritative to religious Jews; hasidic Jews in particular would have been drawn to the kabbalistic themes. Indeed, it is likely that he added the kabbalistic elements in the 1850s when he started collaborating with Elijah Guttmacher, who had a following among hasidic Jews in eastern Europe and Jerusalem.[7]

The primary change in Kalischer's discourse was his focus on the Jews' agricultural development of the Land of Israel, a goal he summed up in the term *erets noshevet*, settled land. Although *Derishat tsiyon* was published by an organization committed to practical activity, much of the book dealt with theoretical matters, and thus *erets noshevet* was first explained in abstract terms as a fundamental principle of the Torah. Building on the kabbalistic notion of the four redemptions, he asserted that the first redemption was that of the Land of Israel, *ge'ulat ha'arets* (redemption of the land), and this consisted of the *erets noshevet*. This stage fulfilled God's commandment in Leviticus 25: 24, 'you shall grant redemption to the land itself'. The literal meaning of the Leviticus passage meant letting the land lie fallow in the sabbatical year, freeing it from food production. Kalischer, however, interpreted it in the opposite sense, granting the land an end to its abandonment and making it fulfil its potential as a life-giving food source.[8] He also described the land's life-giving power in a less literal, messianic sense. The talmudic declaration that those who live in the Land of Israel are without sin, he explained, teaches that the Land of

[6] For the four redemptions of Israel, Kalischer cited as his source Zohar, 'Pinḥas', 242, and inserted it in *Derishat tsiyon*, 46. The rabbinic interpretation of the Song of Songs is found in *Song of Songs Rabbah* 6: 10. Kalischer cited it frequently, for example in *Derishat tsiyon*, 36–7; *Sefer haberit*, iii. 287 (his commentary on S. of S. 6: 10); *Hamagid*, 25 (1863), 197; *Halevanon*, 8 (1863), 53.

[7] In their correspondence it was always Guttmacher who described the agricultural resettlement of Palestine in kabbalistic terms, and the kabbalistic additions to Kalischer's 1868 pamphlet *Shelom yerushalayim* were written with Guttmacher's assistance. Kalischer had studied kabbalah before the 1850s, as is shown by his 1841 article *Hakabalah vehafilosofiyah*. See above, Ch. 5.

[8] *Derishat tsiyon*, 28. Kalischer explained this in great detail to Rabbi Jehiel Michael Zubludowsky of Białystok in a letter dated 2 Marheshvan 5623 (23 Oct. 1862), repr. in *Zionist Writings*, 187, and to Rabbi Meir Auerbach in an open letter in *Halevanon*, 8 (1863), repr. ibid. 198–202. It was a central element of his messianic argumentation from *Derishat tsiyon* onwards. Jews and Europeans in general regarded Palestine as desolate and agriculturally underdeveloped.

Israel has expiatory powers, especially when those who live there observe the commandments. In particular, if they took care to observe the commandments dependent on the Land of Israel, by which he meant the agricultural and sacrificial commandments, they would be contributing to *ge'ulat ha'arets*. They would be redeeming the land, and they would be redeemed through it.[9]

This theme of the land's power became central to Kalischer's writings on the messianic process. It was already evident in his letter to Albert Cohn in 1860, but it was developed at length in *Derishat tsiyon*. He found a paradigm for his conception of the land's redemptive function in the tale of the Israelite spies in Numbers 13–14. These two chapters describe a monumental lapse of faith among the ancient Israelites. Having left Egypt amidst miracles and wonders, after receiving the Torah at Mount Sinai, the Israelites prepared to conquer the promised land. Moses appointed spies to scout out Canaan and report on its features and inhabitants. It was the time of the grape harvest. The spies returned with a favourable report of the land, but they convinced the Israelites that its current inhabitants would overpower them in battle. After the people complained bitterly of God's callousness and rebelled against Moses, God punished them with a decree of a second 'exile': the faithless Jews, the generation that had been raised in slavery, were consigned to wander through the desert for forty years and die there. Only their children and a few faithful members of the older generation would enter Canaan. According to rabbinic tradition, the date of this sin, 9 Av, was then decreed to be the date of future national tragedies and exiles. To Kalischer, the essence of the Israelites' sin was the rejection of their own land, what he called *elbon ha'arets*, an insult suffered by the Land of Israel. He called the faithless spies 'the opponents' or 'the faction of the first ripe grapes'. He believed that the Jewish people repeated this sin throughout the ages when, given the choice, they chose to live in the Diaspora rather than in the Land of Israel. Each time they rejected their promised land, they were punished with exile and expulsions from their Diaspora resting place. The way to stop this cycle, he argued, was to reverse the sin: desire the promised land, settle in it, and farm it. God would then fulfil his promise to bring redemption.[10] The two concepts, *elbon ha'arets* and *erets noshevet*, form a sort of dyad, the former preventing the latter, or the latter undoing the former.

---

[9] The source in the Talmud is *Ket.* 110–11. Kalischer's comments are in *Shelom yerushalayim* (1868), repr. in *Zionist Writings*, 132.

[10] The insult to the land is generally known by the term used in Num. 13: 32, *dibat ha'arets*, the slander of the land. For a survey of classical rabbinic explanations of this episode, see Louis Ginzburg, *Legends of the Jews*, 7 vols. (Philadelphia, 1937), iii. 276, 281; vi. 96–7. Kalischer outlined this theme in *Derishat tsiyon*, but his first explicit reference to the spies was in his open letter to Meir Auerbach, *Halevanon*, 8 (1863), repr. in *Zionist Writings*, 203.

Much of Kalischer's elaboration of this concept consisted of long excerpts from works by other rabbis, edited and blended into a unified argument. In the first ten pages of *Derishat tsiyon* he quoted and interpreted twenty-one separate passages from the Bible, Talmud, Zohar, prayer book, and other medieval writings supporting the notion that redemption would arrive gradually, and only after human beings had initiated the process.[11] The reader was confronted by an outpouring of testimony through proof texts. Kalischer believed that these texts established the legitimacy of his ideology of realistic messianism, particularly the principle that the Jews had created their own exiled status and would have to take charge of ending it. His new writing was also a popularization. He would excerpt passages from commentaries and specialized literature that were not typically available to most Jews, edit them, and explain them in simple terms. For example, he reinforced his point about the curative power of settling the Land of Israel by quoting the following statement found in the prayer book commentary by the eighteenth-century Rabbi Jacob Emden of Altona:

Every Israelite must resolve in his heart to go and live in the Land of Israel . . . to desire and be worthy to pray in front of the Temple Mount. . . . Our ancestors' sin caused weeping for generations. They rejected the pleasant land. This has followed us throughout our exiles, for in every generation we have been denied quiet and tranquillity. . . . God is just: the concept of exile has left them completely, they intermingle with the gentile and no longer seek Zion . . . thus her children grope in the dark, downcast among gentiles, and find no rest.[12]

Kalischer chose this passage because Emden was a recognized and highly respected scholar whose message here was identical with his own. Emden believed that the ancient rejection of the land led to exile and sorrow, and he felt that the Jews in his own day were currently repeating this sin. Their contentment with life in the Diaspora would be short-lived, he predicted, for they would be turned away from their resting places again and again. He did not articulate what was to Kalischer the logical conclusion of the episode of the spies, that seeking Zion would bring redemption. However, Kalischer explained that Emden, too, supported the notion that the exile could be ended by the rational, human response of simply moving to Palestine.

In the same manner, Kalischer presented selections from *The Kuzari*, the philosophical dialogue penned by Judah Halevi of twelfth-century Spain be-

---

[11] Many of these points are variations of those made in his letter to Rothschild, *Emunah yesharah*, or *Sefer haberit*.

[12] *Derishat tsiyon*, 65–6. Kalischer would refer his readers to this section of *Derishat tsiyon* for an explanation of the land's redemptive power. He took the passage from Emden's prayer book *Sidur amudei shamayim*, 2 vols. (Altona, 1744), i. 30*b*–31*a*.

tween a rabbi and the king of Khazar. According to the rabbi, the Jews insult-
ed God's holy land at the end of the Babylonian exile, when many chose not to
return to Judah when they could. Over the generations they repeated this sin,
although they longed for Zion in their hearts. According to Halevi, this was
not enough:

KING OF THE KHAZARS: If you believe all that you say [concerning his desire to visit
the Land of Israel], God knows your desire, for God knows all secrets.

THE RABBI: This is sufficient if the act is impossible, but one is guilty if he does not try
to enact the deed [if it is possible]. . . . The action and intention must be completed to
claim the reward, etc., and when people take risks and awaken their love for the holy
place, they are graced with the promised great and wonderful reward, as it says, 'You
shall arise and have pity on Zion; it is the time to favour her; the appointed time has
come. For thy servants hold her stones dear, and they have pity on her dust' [Ps. 102:
14–15]. This means that *Jerusalem can only be rebuilt when Israel yearns for her to such an
extent that they embrace her stones and dust.*[13]

According to Halevi, great longing would bring 'the appointed time', the time
when the messianic days could potentially arrive, but only if the longing were
expressed in a concrete activity. Kalischer stressed the final lines to his readers, but he did not mention that the specific expiatory activity proposed by
Halevi was an individual, voluntary exile from one's dwelling place in the
Diaspora with the Holy Land as the ultimate destination, where the Jew
would devote himself solely to prayer. Read in its context, Halevi's message
was consistent with passive messianism: repentance brings the messianic age.
Including the entire passage from Halevi would have been counterproductive,
and thus Kalischer omitted it. Instead, he summed up all the quotations and
exhorted his readers to avoid the sin of *elbon ha'arets*. He urged them to express their piety by banding together to buy land in Palestine and to transform
it into a settled land. In this way the messianic age would begin.[14]

One of the new features of Kalischer's later writings is his development of
slogans and images that succinctly summarize his mission. *Elbon ha'arets* was
such a slogan, and the image of the spies from Numbers 13–14 became a
kind of shorthand reference to defenders of the status quo in the Yishuv. Kalischer turned the story of the spies into the core of a counter-ideology, a mythic
symbol teaching that the campaign to build a settled land was an age-old battle
of historic consequence. He believed that he, like the Israelites in the desert
millennia earlier, was living at a critical juncture in Jewish history. The modern equivalents of the ancient spies were the opponents of Jewish agricultural

---

[13] Judah Halevi, *The Kuzari: An Argument for the Faith of Israel*, trans. and ed. Hartwig
Hirschfeld (New York, 1964), pt. 5, sections 26 and 27, abridged in *Derishat tsiyon*, 66.
Kalischer's emphasis.   [14] *Derishat tsiyon*, 69.

settlement; and the modern heroes were those who loved the Land of Israel so much that they expressed their desire to see it settled and planted.[15] The existence of these groups along with the hidden miracles convinced him that God was testing his people just as he had done then. There was also an element of one-upmanship in his conception of *elbon ha'arets*. Through this paradigm, he was turning his opponents' argument against them. They regarded rebellion against the exile as tantamount to faithlessness, and they equated passivity with obedience. To Kalischer, their inactivity was a rejection of the Land of Israel, a sign of excessive love for the Diaspora, and a lack of faith in God. When they insisted that Jews should repent, and not take more demonstrative action, in order to bring about the coming of the messiah, Kalischer implied that they were manufacturing excuses:

Truly we see that the generations become progressively worse, owing to our many sins, and so how can we hope that all Israel will ever repent fully? The essence of repentance is found in *Tikunei zohar* [a kabbalistic commentary on the first chapters of Genesis], which explains that repentance means return to the Land of Israel with all one's heart, and when we comprise a sizeable group in the land, their repentance will count for all Israel. Thus the principle is to settle the Holy Land. Another reason for this: the reason for our bitter exile was our rejection of the precious land during the generation of the spies. This caused weeping for generations. The equivalent restitution for our ancestors' sin is deeply to yearn for our precious inheritance and *to make an activity out of holy thoughts*. Through this we will merit the coming of redemption, with the help of God, blessed be he.[16]

Jews could never repent sufficiently, Kalischer argued, and so God would not make repentance a condition for redemption. Repentance meant a mass return to the Holy Land followed, he implied, by a conventionally passive repentance. Here he used the tactic of inclusiveness he had originated in the Rothschild letter: he accepted the text at its face value, but he positioned it in a very specific moment in his messianic scenario, and in so doing negated its accepted meaning. He made this explicit in the second edition of *Derishat tsiyon*: repentance in the sense of contrition for sin is necessary during a late stage of redemption, 'but the beginning of redemption does not depend on repentance, but on returning to the land'.[17] The nay-saying Torah scholars, not he, were guilty of obstructing the redemptive process. The story of the spies supplied him with a cast of good and evil characters in his own life's drama.

Unlike the biblical episode, however, the contemporary outcome of events was still in doubt. Kalischer's firm conviction that God allowed human beings

---

[15] See e.g. *Halevanon*, 34 and 45 (1868) and *Hamagid*, 35 (1868), all repr. in *Zionist Writings*, 263, 279, and 266.

[16] Kalischer's open letter to Auerbach, *Halevanon*, 8 (1863), repr. ibid. 202; emphasis is mine.

[17] *Derishat tsiyon*, 54.

free will did not permit the assurance of a positive outcome. History was not predetermined. It is unclear whether the analogy of the spies provided an outlet or a fuel for his anger against his opponents. What is certain is that it added an urgency and a meaning to his task; he believed he was living in a time of great significance and was doing God's work.

Having articulated the theoretical issues at stake, Kalischer turned two-thirds of the way through *Derishat tsiyon* to the pragmatic reason for his focusing on the creation of a settled land:

And if now 'the time to favour her' [Ps. 102: 14] has still not arrived, the time when we request the stratagems by which we may prepare a divine altar in Zion, if the hope is still too distant that the Sultan will grant permission for this, then the following proposal is practical at this particular time, in which, with the help of the blessed Redeemer of Israel, great philanthropists from the Jewish nation have been raised high and seen success, rulers and nobles, honourable princes whose like we have not seen since the time of the destruction [of the Temple]. They hold the rulers' staff, the golden sceptre of those who desire wealth. They are the noble houses of Rothschild, Montefiore, Fould, Albert Cohn, and the like, Jews who are princes of the land, may God prolong their lives. They will seek to establish *a society for a settled land*, and along with them many rich Jews, the leaders of the people, those generous in heart who love God and his holy land, and friends of the dwelling places of Jacob will join with them.[18]

By force of circumstances, preparing for the sacrificial offerings had become a more protracted phase. Whereas he had previously paid little attention to the settled land and assumed that the conditions in the Holy Land would be ripe for the immediate restoration of the sacrificial service, the rabbi now realized that he had been too hasty.

Nevertheless, the agricultural settlement of the Holy Land and the renewal of sacrificial worship were inseparable parts of one task, comprising 'the way of the holy', and subsumed under one commandment of seeking Zion, *derishat tsiyon*.[19] The book *Derishat tsiyon* explained in detail the logic of this commandment and the scriptural support for both aspects of the task. Even though the book also contained Kalischer's reluctant admission that it was time to concentrate on the agricultural development of the Land of Israel, the messianic power of the sacrifices was central to its message. After the book's publication, he learnt that his messianic arguments might often be counterproductive. He seems to have grasped that he was far more acceptable a figure to his contemporaries as a social and economic reformer focusing on the regeneration of the land than he was as a Jew yearning for the sacrifices—a desire that could only

[18] *Derishat tsiyon*, 98–9 (Kalischer's emphasis).

[19] Ibid. 48. 'This great commandment' to seek Zion is equivalent to *mitsvat yishuv ha'arets*, the commandment to settle the Land of Israel. It will be discussed in detail later in this chapter.

be construed in messianic terms.[20] And, if Jews could agree to develop the *erets noshevet*, why bother arguing over what would occur after that? Debates on theory would distract people from taking action or even undermine co-operation on agreed-upon tangible goals. Furthermore, unlike the renewal of sacrifices, there seemed to be no major external obstacle to achieving a settled land. The Jews would do best, he concluded, by reviving the Holy Land and preparing themselves for the day when the Muslims would permit sacrificial worship in Jerusalem.

The actual proposal for agricultural settlement that appeared in *Derishat tsiyon* was a simple one. Many individuals would donate small sums of money to a single organization to purchase land, find settlers, move them to Palestine, and establish them on the land. The settlers would be communally organized in a colony or commune in which a religious culture would be carefully nurtured. Initially the organization would supply the settlers with salaries and advice from agricultural experts. Later the farmers would support themselves by their own produce, and they would donate some of their income to the full-time scholars of the Yishuv. Kalischer did not regard this as a profit-making venture, as he had in 1836. The contributors would receive only intangible benefits: the heavenly reward for giving charity and for helping build the Yishuv, and the vicarious merit of the agricultural labourers who performed the commandments dependent on the Land of Israel.[21] According to the first and second (1866) editions of *Derishat tsiyon*, the organization would hire military guards to protect the settlers and their property from marauding Arabs. Kalischer then became convinced that improvements in security in Palestine made this provision unnecessary, and when the issue of security was raised he denied it was still a problem.[22] In the first edition of *Derishat tsiyon*, he proposed the founding of a school to train potential settlers, with a curriculum of agricultural science, practical economics, and religious studies. He dropped his suggestion for a school from the second edition and began to argue in the

[20] Bernard Dov Weinryb, 'The Foundations of Zionism and its History' (Heb.), *Tarbiz*, 8 (1937), 69–113 at 71–2, makes the unsupportable claim that the motives behind Kalischer's promotion of agricultural work were 'secular'. Kalischer used religious terminology, Weinryb argued, so as not to offend the scruples of his traditional colleagues about reclaiming Palestine before the messianic age. In other words, he was a secularist in disguise.

[21] *Derishat tsiyon*, 99. This was repeated in 1866 by Kalischer and Guttmacher in an announcement published by their organization; see *Zionist Writings*, 243. Kalischer's use of the commandments dependent on the land as a means of gaining support for agricultural development is discussed later in this chapter.

[22] *Derishat tsiyon*, 99. In *Hamagid*, 34 (1863), repr. in *Zionist Writings*, 217–19, Kalischer assured his readers that the European consuls would protect the settlers. In 1868 he announced in the pages of *Der Israelit*, 52 (1868), repr. ibid. 270–3, that residents of the Yishuv no longer feared attacks of Bedouins and Arabs.

mid-1860s that a sizeable number of competent farmers already resided in the Yishuv or were ready to settle there.[23]

The agricultural, as opposed to the urban, development of Palestine was the focus of Kalischer's conception of *erets noshevet*. He was not opposed to the importation of modern technology and urban industries into Palestine, nor the development of residential housing projects in the cities.[24] He felt, however, that these should not be a priority. An industrialized society did not conform to the biblical image of the Land of Israel in the messianic age, and the messianic prophecies were visions of a harmonious and bountiful agricultural life. Whereas he had quoted these prophetic passages in his pre-1862 writings, it was in *Derishat tsiyon* that he began to emphasize their literal meaning instead of simply interpreting them as metaphors for a gradual and organic redemptive process. For example, he writes:

First of all we must plant vineyards for the Jews in the land of their fathers, as it says in *Sanhedrin*: 'for you have no more manifest sign of redemption than this: "But ye, O mountains of Israel, ye shall shoot forth your branches, and yield your fruit to my people Israel, for they are on hand to come" [Ezek. 36: 8]'.[25]

Once that is accomplished, he wrote several pages later, 'then we can wait for the ingathering of the exiles, may it occur speedily in our day, amen'. He felt it was a point in his favour that the plain sense of the biblical prophecies testified to a natural redemption of the land; in contrast, the notion that bountiful food would miraculously and suddenly appear—this was the common understanding—could not be substantiated by Scripture. Furthermore, simple logic was on his side. It was common knowledge that before redemption there would be a movement of great penitence in Jerusalem, but how were the penitents going to be fed, if not by a flourishing and fruitful land? Kalischer pins this point to an excerpt from the fourteenth-century work by Meir Isaac Aldabi, *Shevilei emunah*:

This is what he [Aldabi] says: 'When many pious Jews and Torah scholars voluntarily go to the Land of Israel and settle in Jerusalem—every man according to his ability, with the pure spirit and love of Zion kindled within him, from the four corners of the world,

[23] *Derishat tsiyon*, 99. Klausner suggests (in the footnote on p. 99 of *Derishat tsiyon*) that abandoning the school idea was probably an attempt to appease the Yishuv rabbis who fiercely opposed any non-traditional institution in their midst. However, Kalischer rarely acceded to this type of pressure. He was concerned that such an educational institution would easily fall under the control of non-traditional Jews and was dismayed when the Alliance designed the school for unmarried students. See Kalischer to Guttmacher (fifth day of Selihot [1866]), repr. in *Zionist Writings*, 238–9; Kalischer to the Berlin branch of the Alliance (1873), ibid. 489.

[24] In his open letter to Meir Auerbach, *Halevanon*, 8 (1863), repr. in *Zionist Writings*, 202, Kalischer wrote joyfully of the appearance of rail transportation and the telegraph in Palestine.

[25] *Derishat tsiyon*, 63. The source is BT *San.* 98a. Sometimes only an allegorical interpreta-

'one from a city and two from a family' [Jer. 3: 14] to the holy mountain—and when many settle there and they pray exceedingly on the holy mountain in Jerusalem, the Creator, blessed be he, will hear and hasten redemption'. These are his words. All this is possible [only] by making a settled land, for without it how can they begin to gather there?[26]

Kalischer believed that he was only clarifying the logistical aspects of an event that everyone took for granted. However, many in the Jewish congregation in Jerusalem probably regarded their own situation in Aldabi's terms. They believed that Diaspora Jewish financial support enabled them to devote themselves to holy lives that would persuade God to send the messiah, while Jews who engaged in agricultural labour instead of Torah study were detaining him further.

DEFENDING REALISTIC MESSIANISM

Kalischer's new writings reveal a man extremely sensitive to the fact that his ideas would be regarded as an unorthodox, even subversive, reading of sacred texts. He was certain that he correctly understood the Torah. People who did not see it this way were either ignorant or wrong, and if they merely examined the literary record, they would realize their mistake. He wrote to Elijah Guttmacher that the matter was quite simple, 'the opponents in this generation do not concentrate on the truth; they are seduced by habit'.[27] One of these new arguments is worth examining in some detail. This was his way of dealing with the rabbinic teaching of messianic passivity tied to the oaths in Song of Songs: 'I adjure you, daughters of Jerusalem, by the gazelles and by the hinds of the field, that you awaken not, nor stir up love until it pleases.'[28] Kalischer could not ignore such a fundamental teaching, and he developed two responses to it. One way was to understand the clause 'until it pleases' as an indication that the prohibition was not eternal. According to this understanding, he responded to the prohibition 'Awaken not, nor stir up love until it pleases' by asserting 'but now is the time'.[29] He was not exceeding the limits on human activity; instead, he was merely perceiving God's signs that indicated that the time for awakening had arrived. He proved that 'now is the time' by his definition and identification of the hidden miracles: the rise of Jewish men of renown, the flowering of the Holy Land, the granting of Jewish civic rights,

tion could bring harmony between conflicting messianic prophecies or weaken the plain meaning of biblical and rabbinic passages contrary to his point of view.

[26] *Derishat tsiyon*, 62–3.

[27] Kalischer to Guttmacher (10 Sivan 5628 [31 May 1868]), ibid. 260.

[28] See Ch. 1 n. 9.   [29] *Derishat tsiyon*, 36.

and so on. In short, the prohibitions were authentic, but the time limitation attached to them had to be acknowledged by setting them aside.

Alongside this rather daring response stood a more cautious one in which the oaths were binding and still relevant, but the current interpretation of them was flawed. He argued that the oaths actually only prohibited reclamation of the Holy Land by force; peaceful mass migration, however, was not proscribed. This conclusion rested on his understanding of the language of the first prohibition of going up to the Land of Israel 'in a wall':

> First, the warning 'awaken not, nor stir up' instructs us that we are not to make pilgrimage to the walls of Jerusalem as an armed force, as it explains in the Talmud, 'we should not go up *like* a wall', and Rashi explains that this means in force, and also that we should not rebel against the nations. We should await the grace of God and for him to rest his merciful eyes upon us. Beseeching God is the proper work for our hands. We were sworn only to desist from storming the mountain with force, but to beseech her stones and to build a settled land—how good and how pleasant, and you have no greater commandment than this, as I have explained at length.[30]

Here Kalischer accepted a textual emendation in which the Hebrew word for 'in a wall' (*behomah*) is corrected to a more coherent 'like a wall' (*kehomah*).[31] The former term implies en masse, whereas the revised word implies both en masse and with force. Accepting the revised word as the correct version allows one to regard the oaths as prohibiting violent conquest of the land, thus permitting an en masse return to the land. Only this understanding of the oaths, Kalischer explained, could justify the behaviour of the prophet Nehemiah:

> Is it reasonable to assume that when Nehemiah, may he rest in peace, stood before King Cyrus, sad-faced, and pleaded with him to build the ruins of Jerusalem, he was transgressing the oath, God forbid? No, for he did not go forth with physical might, only with pleading, and so God caused the king to be favourably impressed with Nehemiah, and God desired that he be successful.[32]

Kalischer regarded Nehemiah's behaviour as a very obvious precedent and a reinforcement of his understanding of the oaths as prohibiting only belligerent tactics, such as armed conquest. Clearly, there was no sin in settling Jews on the land with the permission of the Sultan. Kalischer's two approaches to the oaths were mutually exclusive—the first rescinded them, the second accepted them—but he did not seem to notice, and he referred to both over the years.

Why, after rejecting the tradition of messianic passivity, did Kalischer stop

---

[30] *Derishat tsiyon*, 97.

[31] Some editions of the Talmud incorporated this emendation, suggested by Rabbi Jacob Emden.

[32] *Derishat tsiyon*, 97–8; Kalischer repeated this argument, including the references to Nehemiah, in his open letter to Auerbach, *Halevanon*, 8 (1863), repr. in *Zionist Writings*, 202.

short of allowing the armed conquest of the Land of Israel? There was no statement in rabbinic literature urging Jews to conquer the land of Israel. Instead, there were the oaths, and they were so old and central to the messianic tradition that he could not simply admit that they no longer applied. He could limit their application, but not reject them outright. Additionally, he was typical of Jews across the religious spectrum in central and western Europe at this time in avowing respect for political authorities and displaying patriotism. For these Jews, the existence of the oaths was a point of pride, demonstrating Jewish loyalty and obedience to their host countries over the centuries. The rabbi was fundamentally conservative, law-abiding, and respectful of authority; he would not have wanted to encourage violent rebellion. Indeed, the messianic process he outlined required the assistance of non-Jewish rulers. Finally, it was ridiculous to imagine, in the mid-nineteenth century, that Jews would rise up and militarily reclaim Palestine.

Kalischer's stance on the oaths cannot be understood as an objection to the use of violence per se. After all, he had suggested a military defence system for the agricultural colonies. If permission was granted by the local ruler, he wrote elsewhere, the Jews could join the army and fight their enemies in Palestine. Here, too, he appealed to Nehemiah, remarking that Nehemiah had the permission of the king to lead forces against the enemies who interfered with the rebuilding of the Temple and the city walls.[33] The essence of the prohibition was violent rebellion against lawful authority. Kalischer's moderate stance did, in fact, get put to the test. A Hungarian rabbi named Joseph Natonek was trying to initiate negotiations with the Ottoman court in Constantinople to acquire Palestine for the Jews, and he began planning an international Jewish congress that would discuss the formation of a Jewish state.[34] Natonek corresponded with Kalischer, and they worked together collecting money for the purchase of land in Palestine until Kalischer expressed serious reservations about Natonek's ideas. Most of their correspondence has been lost, but the source of the disagreement can be inferred by reference to Natonek's plans and some stray remarks in Kalischer's letters to Guttmacher. After one of his first contacts with Natonek, Kalischer reported that Natonek 'burns with love for the Land of Israel', and added disapprovingly, 'but he is excessive, he asks for too much'.[35] In the next letter he clarified this somewhat: 'I object to his opinion . . . for he wants to remove the government from the Muslims. But this is against his [the Sultan's] religion, and for all his wealth he will not do it. Just this he will do: he will allow his officials to permit us to buy unused land from

---

[33] Kalischer to Auerbach, *Halevanon*, 8 (1863), repr. ibid. 202.

[34] Dov Frankel, *The Beginning of Modern Political Zionism* (Heb.) (Haifa, 1956). See also Gideon Shimoni, *The Zionist Ideology* (Hanover, NH, 1995), 78–81.

[35] Kalischer to Guttmacher (n.d., but probably 1866), repr. in *Zionist Writings*, 237.

its owners.'[36] It seems unlikely that Kalischer's objection was that Natonek was overly enthusiastic; rather, it appears that Natonek was ready to entertain wresting political authority from the Turks. There were certainly statesmen in Europe who suggested as much. Kalischer, however, neither wanted to use those tactics, nor did he regard immediate independence from the Muslims as a goal. Indeed, elsewhere he voiced his disapproval of the hostile attitude he discerned towards the Arabs. It was unfortunate, he wrote, that the notion had spread that no progress could be made while the Muslims lived in Palestine. Convictions such as this had led to the Crusades and to great destruction, and there was no basis to it now. He concluded, 'Every true man, who is not thinking only of his own good, must also honour the Muslim.'[37] The religious tolerance that God had planted in the heart of non-Jews, expressed in their new benevolence towards the Jews, should not be responded to with Jewish intolerance. Messianic activism was limited; the obligation to initiate the messianic age was not a moral or religious absolute.

The corollary to this position, however, was that neither was it permissible to ignore God's hidden miracles: this was tantamount to rejecting God. The same God who bestowed gracious hidden miracles upon his people could also act punitively when spurned. *Derishat tsiyon* was written in a very upbeat tone and hardly depicts the possibility of Jewish apathy or opposition. Yet in private letters and even newspaper articles, particularly after the institutional apparatus for raising funds to buy land was in place, Kalischer did not hesitate to chastise those who had spurned the quest for Zion. He declared that their opposition was an affront to God, and demonstrated 'a lack of faith in aid from Heaven'.[38] To him, the obligation to act was even stronger in the phase immediately prior to redemption, when hidden miracles were being granted in abundance.

Because the responsibility to act was so serious, the rabbi felt it his duty publicly to praise people for their activities or chastise them for their indifference. He rebuked people who did not measure up to the required performance, especially influential rabbis. They were often called 'the opponents' and likened to the spies of Numbers 13–14. He denounced the Ashkenazi rabbis of Jerusalem who opposed his plan to create Jewish agricultural communes in multiple ways: they were selfish and guided by materialistic desires;[39] they might be pious, but the evil impulse had taken hold of them;[40] they denied the truth of prophecy;[41] they were seduced by habit;[42] they were neglecting the

[36] Kalischer to Guttmacher (fifth day of Selihot [1865]), repr. in *Zionist Writings*, 240.

[37] *Der Israelit*, 3 (1869), repr. Ibid. 282.   [38] *Der Israelit*, 27 (1863), repr. ibid. 195.

[39] *Der Israelit*, 37 (1864); *Hamagid*, 23 (1871) and 32 (1871); all repr. ibid. 222, 328, and 330.

[40] Kalischer to Azriel Hildesheimer (Purim 5625 [12 Mar. 1865]), repr. ibid. 230–1.

[41] Kalischer to Guttmacher (10 Sivan 5628 [31 May 1868]), repr. ibid. 260.   [42] Ibid.

opportunity to observe commandments;[43] they prevented others from observing commandments;[44] they were adding to the number of starving Jews in Palestine.[45]

Indeed, Kalischer was convinced that divine wrath was let loose on those who were passive or who obstructed the efforts of others. He perceived warning signs from God that the ancient punishment was about to be repeated in the form of untimely deaths, bad weather and hunger in Jerusalem, and antisemitic outbursts in Europe.[46] On at least eight occasions, he wrote that flooding, famine, drought, and the deaths of certain scholars in Palestine were directly attributable to their opposition to his projects. Here is how he explained it to Guttmacher:

I believe that all the troubles that, due to our many sins, have befallen those in the Holy Land are due to this sin: they oppose the way of the holy. Owing to this sin we have lost the exalted Rabbi Nahum, of blessed memory, for God judges his righteous ones harshly. Also the honourable rabbi from Kutno, and the scholar Schwarz, stricken by the same disease during an eight-day period. They all died, and God followed it with plague and locusts.[47]

These terrible events were signs of divine dissatisfaction. They were hidden miracles, but of a negative kind. They were God's subtle intervention in human events designed to keep history on its proper course. Kalischer inverted all the classic arguments of the passive messianists by claiming that Jewish passivity had provoked God's ire.

Kalischer's colleagues learned that he could be quite persistent in making them fulfil what to him was their obligation. One recipient of his pressure was Rabbi Samson Raphael Hirsch (1808–88), an influential leader of a large congregation in Frankfurt. Kalischer wrote to Hirsch several times in the hope that he would urge the Jews of Frankfurt, especially Wilhelm Carl Rothschild, to support the Kolonisations-Verein für Palästina, as well as to print information about the organization in Hirsch's monthly journal *Jeschurun*.[48] Hirsch

---

[43] *Ivri anokhi*, 3 (1872); Kalischer to Yakkir Gheron (1872); Kalischer to Mordecai Hast; all repr. ibid. 387, 397, and 419.

[44] Kalischer to Rabbi Aryeh Leib in Minsk and Rabbi Baer Bampi (1873), repr. ibid. 455.

[45] *Hamagid*, 35 (1868), repr. ibid. 266.

[46] See e.g. Kalischer to Guttmacher (nineteenth day of the Omer 5626 [19 Apr. 1866]); *Hamagid*, 3 (1871); Kalischer to Mordecai Jaffe (1874); found respectively in *Zionist Writings*, 235, 325, and 522.

[47] Kalischer to Guttmacher (nineteenth day of the Omer 5626 [19 Apr. 1866]), repr. ibid. 235. He was referring to some rabbis who were stricken during an epidemic in Palestine during the summer of 1865.

[48] Kalischer to Rabbi Dov Baer Adler (twenty-fourth day of the Omer, 5626 [9 May 1862]), and Kalischer to Hayim Mordecai of Plock (probably 1862), repr. ibid. 181, 185.

finally responded with an emphatic refusal to co-operate. The letter that sheds the most light on Kalischer's tenacity is one Hirsch wrote to a third party twelve years after Kalischer's death. When asked about his relationship with Kalischer, Hirsch wrote:

I and my colleagues know nothing of him, and you should not wonder at this, because I was absolutely opposed to Rabbi Kalischer, of blessed memory, on this matter. More than three or four times he wrote to me, sent me his writings and essays, and urged me to work on behalf of his plan for the Yishuv. Finally he came to me with rebukes that I was committing evil, as if I were hindering redemption, etc., and I asked him to cease writing to me, since what is to some a great commandment, to me is no small transgression. And thus we would not come to any agreement, and so I wrote to him my reasons and arguments and found rest from him.[49]

Kalischer even pestered and rebuked colleagues who were engaged in assisting the Yishuv. Azriel Hildesheimer (1820–99), a rabbi and educator in Austria-Hungary and then Berlin, was an avid fund-raiser for relief projects in Palestine. However, Hildesheimer refused to support the campaign on behalf of agricultural communes for fear that they would of necessity involve desecration of the sabbath, despite Kalischer's many appeals. In 1873, when Hildesheimer was slandered by Jerusalem zealots who objected to his plans for building an orphanage there, Kalischer wrote to him the following:

Ask yourself well why these contentious men trouble you and God allows it. It is owing to your standing distant from the matter of greater holiness, the settlement of the Land of Israel, planting fields and vineyards in order to fulfil the commandments . . . to bring redemption to the land itself, which is the first stage of the four stages of redemption as explained in the holy Zohar. . . . If I lived in Berlin and had contacts with powerful Jews as you do, God would judge me harshly on this . . . but I live in a small town and can do nothing so the responsibility rests on you.[50]

Kalischer's frustration and helplessness are quite palpable here. It is also likely that he felt he was doing Hildesheimer a favour by warning him.

---

[49] This an excerpt from Hirsch's letter to Jacob Lipschitz (24 Iyar 5646 [29 May 1886]), published in Jacob Lipschitz, *Maḥzikei hadat* (Kovna, 1903), 35–6. Lipschitz's book was a collection of testimonies from rabbis opposed to Zionism. A draft of Hirsch's letter to Kalischer has been preserved in the archives of the Jewish National Library in Jerusalem. A fuller treatment of Kalischer's attempt to correspond with Hirsch is Meir Hildesheimer, 'Rabbi Tsevi Hirsch Kalischer and Rabbi Samson Raphael Hirsch' (Heb.), in *Sefer aviad*, ed. Yitzhak Raphael (Jerusalem, 1986), 195–214. The gap between Hirsch and Kalischer is discussed further below.

[50] Kalischer to Hildesheimer (1873), repr. in *Zionist Writings*, 430. For more on Kalischer's relationship to Hildesheimer, see Klausner, introductory section to *Zionist Writings*, 47, 60–70, 81–2.

THE INTERPRETATIVE KEY AND CONTEMPORARY
HIDDEN MIRACLES

Kalischer's development of the episode of the spies is an example of the way he cultivated phrases, images, and interpretations sanctioning—indeed mandating—Jewish efforts to create a larger Jewish presence in Palestine. He pioneered in this arena, and later activists borrowed and built on his efforts. His interpretative metaphors should not be evaluated on the basis of their originality. What is significant is that his accumulation of supportive texts and his skilful arrangement of them gave meaning to the seemingly unprecedented events arrayed before nineteenth-century European Jews: Jews appointed or elected to government positions, Jewish civic emancipation, the striking improvements in the conditions of life in the Yishuv, and Christian support for the return to Zion. Connected to the familiar world of the Torah, these events became part of God's benevolent plan.

Like the image of the spies and *elbon ha'arets*, Kalischer's rhetorical innovations were embedded in his writings. The most critical ones were those that directed people to specific actions. His theory of history, described above in the analyses of the Rothschild letter and his philosophical writings, taught that God guides history through hidden miracles, events well integrated with the natural order of things. These hidden miracles were God's signals to the Jews to act. He insisted in his commentary on the Torah that 'any clear-minded individual will understand and see the hidden miracles of God and discern them plainly and will not remark "it is only chance"'.[51] Nevertheless, hidden miracles were *not* always obvious, and that reality impelled him to spill much ink and make them visible, and then spell out the specific active response that they demanded. The events he identified as hidden miracles were usually discussed with reference to four biblical metaphors. Each metaphor embodied a progression towards harmony, completion, or perfection—in a word, redemption. The match between the event and the metaphor established the proof that an event was a sign from God, and the metaphor provided a guide for the way to respond to it.

The first metaphor was from Song of Songs, the biblical dialogue of a young woman and her lover who is separated from her. Kalischer accepted the allegorical interpretation of the dialogue as one between God (the male) and Israel (the female). According to this, the people of Israel in exile nostalgically recall her status as God's chosen and hope for the blessings of reunification with God in the messianic age. Kalischer used the book as textual proof that redemption, like the unification of the lovers, would not occur suddenly, but

---

[51] This is how Kalischer expressed it in *Sefer haberit*, iii. 116 (on Num. 13: 13).

in a gradual, sometimes sporadic, process. He found commentaries that described the appearance of redemption from its initial veiled, hidden form until its open manifestation in the fullness of the messianic age. One example of this was the parallel between the four gradations of light in Song of Songs 6: 10 and the four stages of redemption, described above. Phrases in the Song of Songs were also interpreted to point to specific hidden miracles. He explained the phrase 'the blossoms [*nitsanim*] are seen in the land' (S. of S. 2: 12) in the manner taught by *Song of Songs Rabbah* as 'the conquerors [*natsoḥot*] are seen in the land'. In *Song of Songs Rabbah*, the conquerors referred to men who heralded the end of the Egyptian, Babylonian, and present exiles. Kalischer, however, used this passage in reference to the English philanthropist Moses Montefiore, who had recently announced that he would try to persuade Jews to farm the land he had purchased in Palestine.[52] For readers who were familiar with the rabbinic commentary, this was a particularly powerful way of noting the significance of the event and the appropriateness of Montefiore's response. For others unfamiliar with the midrash, Kalischer discussed it in full in *Derishat tsiyon* and explained the connection between the agricultural development of Palestine and redemption.[53]

The second image Kalischer used was that of natural change. As the above passages show, the arrival of redemption was compared to the gradual break of day or the slow, purposeful growth of vegetation. He made this point quite often by quoting Ezekiel 36: 8, 'But ye, O mountains of Israel, ye shall shoot forth your branches, and yield your fruit to my people of Israel, for they are at hand to come.'[54] Sometimes he preferred to treat the naturalistic symbolism of a biblical passage as allegory; for example, he explained 'In the days to come Jacob shall take root, Israel shall blossom and bud' (Isa. 27: 6) to refer to the gradual arrival of the messianic age.[55] Biblical passages that employed the metaphor of flourishing vegetation for the Jews' return from exile could also be read literally as a description of the first messianic phase, the renewed fruitfulness of the Land of Israel. The metaphorical meaning was harmonious with the plain meaning of the text.

The third metaphor was taken from the books of Ezra and Nehemiah. For Kalischer, the sequence of events beginning with King Cyrus's edict enabling the return of the exiled Judahites to Jerusalem and culminating with the rebuilding of the Second Temple served as a model of the beginning phase of the messianic days. He reasoned that when God once again chose to end the exile, he would do so in the same naturalistic manner. And, according to this logic,

---

[52] Kalischer to Shimon Berman (1874), repr. in *Zionist Writings*, 548.

[53] *Derishat tsiyon*, 57. Here Kalischer connected the interpretation with the book of Esther as well; see below.   [54] BT *San.* 98a, cited in *Derishat tsiyon*, 63.   [55] *Derishat tsiyon*, 42.

contemporary Jews were obliged to follow the example set by their ancient forebears: those with political influence should beseech their rulers to assist in the return to Zion, Jewish control over Palestine would be voluntarily granted by the rulers, and the Temple altar could be rebuilt without the appearance of the messiah. We have already seen how Kalischer used Nehemiah's conduct to undermine the strict interpretation of the oaths by insisting that behaviour deemed proper during the Second Temple literature was proper in the present time and should serve as a guide for Jews in a parallel situation. His esteem for the Second Temple period served his messianic goals, but it also dovetailed with literary fashions of Hebrew poets and novelists of the east European Haskalah who glorified the late First Temple and early Second Temple periods as an age of heroism, national freedom, Jewish immersion in pastoral life, and appreciation of aesthetics.[56]

Another image drawn from the biblical narrative was based on the book of Esther: the tale of two Jews who were raised to power in a Persian royal court. Esther is initially reluctant to exercise her influence to preserve the Jews from harm, but Mordecai reminds her of her duties, and together they enable their people to prevail over their enemies. To Kalischer, the story not only teaches about God's unobtrusive guiding of history, it also serves as a model of the messianic process. Before him, he witnessed its unfolding. Six men earned the distinction in his eyes of being evidence of God's hidden miracles: Amschel Mayer Rothschild of Frankfurt, and, after his death, simply 'the house of Rothschild'; Moses Montefiore; Yakkir Gheron, the chief rabbi of Constantinople from 1863 to 1872; Albert Cohn; Adolphe Crémieux, a French politician and leader of the Alliance Israélite Universelle; and Achille Fould, a French statesman and financier.[57] What seems to have impressed him most about these notables was that they had access to royal power, they evinced concern for Jewish causes, and they appealed to non-Jewish governments on behalf of the Yishuv. Even though their rise to power appeared to be a logical outcome of political events, he explained the underlying divine design:

Today the dawn's light shines for the Jews who sit at the king's gate [Esther 2: 19], close to the kingship, and the *maskil* [enlightened, devotee of reason] can understand that

[56] David Patterson, *Abraham Mapu* (London, 1964), 39–52, describes the use of this setting generally and in the works of Mapu.

[57] On Rothschild, *Derishat tsiyon*, 40 and 98; Montefiore is mentioned twice in *Derishat tsiyon*, Kalischer to Eliezer Loewe (1872), Kalischer to Shimon Berman, repr. in *Zionist Writings*, 40, 45, 359, 548; Gheron in Kalischer to Rabbi Nissan Shapiro and Rabbi Samuel Shapiro (5 Adar 5633 [4 Mar. 1873]), repr. in *Zionist Writings*, 424; Cohn in *Derishat tsiyon*, 98; Fould is in the 1st edn of *Derishat tsiyon*, 40 and replaced in the 2nd edn by Crémieux. By then Kalischer probably realized that Fould, unlike his elder brother, was not at all interested in Jewish affairs: he had married a Protestant woman, and was raising his children as Christians; see *EJ* vi. 1445.

when Napoleon I and Holland granted freedom to the Jews there was the first small ray of light, and afterwards freedom came in the rest of the nations. Now they sit close to the kingship, like Montefiore and the like. We have arrived, with the help of God, at a needle's-breadth of light, and we are hoping now for the stage [of redemption] 'fair as the moon' [S. of S. 6: 10] and for the light to grow further until that great day, with the help of God, may he be blessed, speedily in our own day, amen.[58]

Kalischer reminded his fellow Jews of their duties by echoing Mordecai's message to Esther, 'who knows whether you have not come to royal power for such a time as this' (Esther 4: 14). He explained, 'With the golden sceptre of the Jewish notables the ray of salvation for our portion will grow.'[59] He disregarded all other reasons for the change in political policy and insisted that civic emancipation was the direct result of God infusing the hearts of gentiles with love for the Jews: 'God has changed the hearts of kings and princes. . . . He has reversed circumstances and strengthened the hearts of the righteous and honest to walk on the straight and paved road with love for all people, without differentiating between nations, allowing each to live according to its religion.' Consequently, the movement of freedom would expand to new levels: 'From France to Britain he will illuminate the righteous ones with holiness and light, and afterwards from Britain the rays of light will flow and the Germanic lands will follow their lead. The tsar of Russia and the Polish princes will follow them, and their benevolence will not part from them, and they will say, "Let us elevate Jews [to sit] among the heads of the nations".'[60] These men were to exercise their influence on the kings to enable the Jews to establish the *erets noshevet*.

Indeed, Kalischer became convinced by the end of his life that just such an eventuality was before him. In the mid-1860s he made guarded statements about the problems of banditry and violence in the Holy Land, noting that the present rulers were attempting to control the problem and that security was better adjacent to cities than in the countryside, where settlements might be isolated.[61] By 1868 he grew more confident that a new era of security had begun, and by 1872 he joyously noted this as a positive sign from heaven.[62] In the same year he referred to the Jews' new right openly to purchase land in Palestine as a sign that 'God is calling to us, and he has given the heart of

[58] *Derishat tsiyon*, 40.

[59] The echo of Mordecai's rebuke and the reference to the growth of redemption appear, among other places, in *Derishat tsiyon*, 36–7 and 129.

[60] Both excerpts are from *Hamagid*, 25 (1863), repr. in *Zionist Writings*, 191.

[61] *Statut des Kolonisations-Vereins für Palästina* (1867), 3; *Hamagid*, 19 (1866); 34 (1863); repr. ibid. 233, 218.

[62] *Der Israelit*, 52 (1868), repr. ibid. 268. *Ḥavatselet*, 19 (1872); Kalischer to Henry Moses (1874); repr. ibid. 342, 542.

the ruler to say, "Come, and inherit the portion of your father Jacob."' The fruitfulness of the land was returning as well.[63] When the chief rabbi of Constantinople, Rabbi Yakkir Gheron, decided to move to Jerusalem, Kalischer declared this, too, as a sign from God. He was convinced that with Gheron's tremendous prestige and connections to the rulers in Constantinople, the first Jewish agricultural colony could soon be established.[64]

Kalischer's references to contemporary prominent Jews are a rich weave of the messianic anticipation of the Song of Songs, the images of natural change, and Esther. 'The sound of the turtledove [*tor*] is heard in our land' (S. of S. 2: 12), understood as the hint of imminent redemption, is connected to 'Esther's turn [*tor*] arrived' (Esther 2: 15), and both signify readiness for redemption.[65] A similar combination is in a passage from rabbinic exegesis that Kalischer quoted at length:

'Who is she that looketh forth as the dawn' [S. of S. 6: 10]. It is related that Rabbi Hiyah and Rabbi Simeon ben Halafta were once walking in the valley of Arbel in the early morning, and as they saw the dawn coming up, R. Hiyah Rabbah said to R. Simeon b. Halafta: 'Even so shall the deliverance of Israel break forth, as it is written, "Though I sit in darkness, the Lord is a light unto me" [Mic. 7: 8]. At first it comes on little by little, then it begins to sparkle, then it gathers strength, and then it spreads over the sky. So at first, "In those days, while Mordecai sat at the king's gate" [Esther 2: 21]; then, "Mordecai went forth from the presence of the king in royal apparel" [Esther 8: 15]; and finally, "the Jews had light and gladness"' [Esther 8: 16].[66]

Building upon the above motifs, he repeatedly evoked the image of 'the extension of the golden sceptre' in explaining the probable success of the efforts to build a settled land.[67]

Because God engineered Jewish civic emancipation for the purpose of hastening the messianic redemption, the proper response was to buy land in Palestine, farm it, and build up a settled land:

When will 'the spirit of God begin to stir' [Judges 13: 25]? When 'you have loosed my bonds' [Ps. 116: 16]. For he has given me freedom among the nations, not as in past years, when Jacob was very wretched and did not raise his head. . . . God has made us

[63] Kalisher to Zevulun Leib Barit, *Halevanon*, 3 (1872), repr. ibid. 374.

[64] Kalischer to Rabbi Nissan Shapiro and Rabbi Samuel Shapiro (5 Adar 5633 [4 Mar. 1873]) and Kalischer to Rabbi Menahem Heilprin (1872), repr. ibid. 424 and 384. Gheron promised to arrange the purchase of land for Hevrat Yishuv Erets Yisra'el.   [65] *Derishat tsiyon*, 57.

[66] Ibid. 40. The translation of *Song of Songs Rabbah* 6: 10 is from *Midrash Rabbah* (London, 1951), ix. 268.

[67] Kalischer seems utterly unable to comment on the rise of Jews to power without using phrases from Esther such as this one from Esther 5: 2. See the following: *Derishat tsiyon*, 37, 40, 53, 57; *Hamagid*, 25 (1863), repr. in *Zionist Writings*, 29; *Der Israelit*, 27, repr. ibid. 195–6.

free in most countries, and we can also possess fields and vineyards in the Holy Land, just like the great Sir Moses Montefiore has done.[68]

To those who ridiculed the notion that this era of good fortune was distinctive from others in the past, Kalischer pointed out the unprecedented breadth of emancipation. Furthermore, he argued, powerful Jews could even profess their love for Zion and not suffer expulsion or loss of their property.[69] He believed that European governments, whose consuls in Palestine had already come to the aid of the Jews of the Yishuv, would support the growth of the Jewish community there. Kalischer never deviated from his belief that the rulers of the world supported traditional Judaism. One notable expression of this was in his letter to the Russian Jewish philanthropist Kalonymus Ze'ev Wissotzky, to petition the tsar to end the confiscation of publications by Hevrat Yishuv Erets Yisra'el and the intimidation of the organization's agents. Kalischer did not believe that the officials in Moscow knew of the injurious behaviour of the local censors. Once they were made aware that Hevrat Yishuv Erets Yisra'el was promoting the performance of the commandments, he wrote, the organization would be left in peace, because the officials 'desire the fulfilment of the Torah'.[70]

The heaven-sent hidden miracle that Kalischer discerned behind the rise of Jewish notables was also evident in non-Jews' more open expression of enthusiasm for Jewish messianic hopes. Here again, his conviction rested on assumptions that were not altogether correct. He assumed that all God-fearing gentiles who regarded the Hebrew Bible as a sacred work understood it in the same manner as Jews. This is how he expressed himself in *Emunah yesharah*, part 2:

Every man knows and every human understands that the Torah of Moses is true and the foundation of all other religions. No one denies this except those without religion, like the nations called heathens (they have no religion or faith, and you cannot think of them as humans), and also heretics (they are like beasts and not humans either, because what differentiates human from beast is . . . a conception of God) . . . but every person who fits this description of human, in that he has some knowledge of God, has no doubt in his heart [in the truth of] the Torah of Moses and the prophetic books. Upon this every race of humanity agrees, 'from the sun's rising to its setting' [Ps. 113: 3].[71]

Even though they had added to the Torah and Prophets, he continued, other religions (Christianity and Islam) maintained that these books were true. He

[68] *Derishat tsiyon*, 45; see also p. 69.

[69] Kalischer to Auerbach, *Halevanon*, 8 (1863), repr. in *Zionist Writings*, 200; Kalischer to David Gordon, *Hamagid*, 14 (1863), repr. ibid. 191.

[70] Kalischer to Kalonymus Ze'ev Wissotzky (1873), repr. ibid. 426.

[71] *Emunah yesharah*, ii. 95–6; similarly, p. 129. Pt. 2 was written by 1842 and re-edited for publication in 1870.

remained convinced of this in the 1860s, writing of the non-Jews that they would not harbour in their midst religious leaders who did not respect the Bible, but 'if a priest of the Christians or Muslims denied one word of the Torah and Prophets, they would unanimously remove him from his post'.[72]

By 1863 it seemed to Kalischer that there were many Christians who had rejected the conventional messianic theory and had accepted one like his. The editor of the Hebrew newspaper *Hamagid* took special joy in publicizing the statements and sermons of Christians declaring that the messianic age would arrive gradually through natural means and that the beginning of the redemptive process was evident in current events. The editor speculated that these men must have read Kalischer's *Derishat tsiyon*.[73] Kalischer noted this non-Jewish support in his retort to Auerbach's derisive comments about *Derishat tsiyon*: 'How is it that you do not fear to publish these criticisms, preventing the holy people from worthy and great thoughts that are pure in deed? Without a doubt, the righteous gentiles of the world, whom the Holy Spirit has inspired to act on behalf of the holy, will stand by us at the end of days to bring redemption near.'[74] He had anticipated non-Jewish support of his messianic programme. In the section of *Derishat tsiyon* addressed to the maskil, the worldly Jew who would be more sensitive to remarks offensive to non-Jews, he made sure to emphasize the universalistic results of the messianic age. He would be arguing from logic alone here, he wrote, to show that his theory could be derived from it, and then he added parenthetically, 'and so the wise among the gentiles will pay attention to it'.[75] Woven into this section was the theme of Jewish dependence on the non-Jews and the blessings non-Jews would receive during the messianic age. He did not discuss the chastening of the gentiles during the war of Gog and Magog in *Derishat tsiyon* and his articles for the press. He buried those comments in his commentary on the Haggadah, a work designed for an audience capable of reading the Zohar and the Talmud. There he discussed the wars between the Jews and gentiles, making clear that only those nations that submitted totally to 'God and his messiah and his people' would be saved.[76] In *Derishat tsiyon* he stressed that non-Jews would benefit from redemption, and he pointed out that because they believed in the prophets, they had a responsibility to hasten redemption as well: 'All the peoples of faith believe in the words of the prophets, and thus it is appropriate

---

[72] *Halevanon*, 34 (1868), repr. in *Zionist Writings*, 264; similarly, *Hamagid*, 35 (1865), repr. ibid. 267.   [73] See *Hamagid*, 13 (1862) and 15–17 (1863).

[74] Kalischer to Auerbach, *Halevanon*, 8 (1863), repr. in *Zionist Writings*, 200. In *Hamagid*, 25 (1863), repr. ibid. 190, Kalischer expressed his delight in hearing of the support of Christian clergymen.

[75] *Derishat tsiyon*, 46, 47, 101. The section in *Derishat tsiyon* 'to the maskil' can be found on pp. 59–63, and the comment is found on p. 59.   [76] *Yetsiat mitsrayim*, 17.

also that every person of religion from the officers of religion among the Christians and Muslims should help us to make a settled land.'[77] It was, of course, characteristic of Europeans to regard their colonial enterprises as a gift to the peoples they would be dominating. Kalischer's thinking fitted easily into that framework, although he was probably unusual in believing that the indigenous people could enjoy redemption without changing their religion.

There is some evidence, however, that Kalischer anticipated a wave of conversion to Judaism in the messianic era. In *Derishat tsiyon* he cited biblical passages that described an influx of proselytes at the end of days, positioned after the rebuilding of the Temple.[78] It may be that this conviction influenced his halakhic judgement on an issue that engaged the European rabbinate in the 1860s, the propriety of ritually circumcising baby boys who were not halakhically Jewish. The issue arose when a rabbi living in the United States heard of a Jewish man and his Christian wife who did not want to convert their newborn son, but wanted him to be ritually circumcised. The rabbi ordered the local *mohel* (ritual circumciser) not to circumcise their son, and when the *mohel* disregarded the rabbi's ruling, the rabbi declared him unfit to serve. After this decision was met with protest, the rabbi wrote to his colleagues in Europe in order to elicit their opinion on the matter. Kalischer was the only rabbinic authority among those who publicly reacted to the case who felt that the rabbi had been wrong on all counts. He believed that the Jewish community should not discourage potential converts. It was not only meritorious, he argued, but a religious obligation to circumcise a gentile who desired it, even if he had no intention to convert. He based his opinion on Jewish legal sources and the following considerations:

The source of all the religions of the nations is our holy Torah. . . . God wanted to grant it to all his creations, but they did not prove worthy, but without a doubt he left open a hope for them in that anyone who desires to convert and join God's inheritance will merit the light of the Godhead . . . and thus, when an idolater wants to be circumcised, we allow him his free choice, and when he decides sincerely and truthfully to join the congregation of Israel, he can then easily accept the ritual immersion and the commandments.[79]

Kalischer was well aware of acculturated Jews' ambivalence towards ritual circumcision, and so his stance cannot be regarded solely as a result of his naivety.[80] He refused to see the Jewish people as a closed ethnic or religious

---

[77] *Derishat tsiyon*, 61.   [78] Ibid. 59.

[79] Kalischer to Azriel Hildesheimer (Purim 5625 [12 Mar. 1865]), printed in Moritz Stern (ed.), *Festschrift zum vierzigjährigen Amtsjubiläum des Herrn Rabbiners Dr. Salomon Carlebach in Lübeck* (Berlin, 1910), 272. This is the complete version of the letter cited in n. 40.

[80] This is suggested by David Ellenson, 'A Jewish Legal Decision by Rabbi Bernard Illowy of

entity. In his description of Jewish origins, he proudly stressed the growth of the nation through the proselytizing efforts of the patriarchs and prophets. In his comments on the assimilationist Jews of his own time, he insinuated that some should withdraw from the community entirely rather than destroy traditional practice from within.[81] When he composed his legal opinion on conversion, he believed that God had planted love for Jews in the gentiles. Thus, while he tended to be strict towards irreligious Jews, he was inclined to be generous towards sympathetic non-Jews. It would not be proper for the Jewish community to react to God's hidden miracle by discouraging potential converts.

Kalischer was embarrassed and disappointed at Jews' relative disinterest in Palestine, and he used the behaviour of the Christians to shame the Jews into action. All his statements about European nationalism, often quoted by historians to show its influence on him, must be regarded as a rhetorical flourish designed to prod the Jews into action out of shame and guilt. The only reference to European nationalism in the first edition of *Derishat tsiyon* appears in the introduction: 'Why do people of Italy and of the other countries sacrifice their lives for the land of their fathers? How much more so should we [sacrifice] for this land, which all peoples of the world call holy. But we stand like a man without strength and courage.'[82] The second edition (1866) repeats the same sentiment in a new afterword with the added mention of Polish and Hungarian national movements, but with the same emphasis on Jewish shortcomings.[83] In only one other source, an article in *Der Israelit* in 1863, did he raise the issue of nationalism. There too he contrasted the willingness of Europeans to sacrifice for their homelands with Jewish apathy.[84] His other comments about European national movements compared them unfavourably with the Jewish messianic dream. He felt that the Jewish cause went far beyond these national movements in both method and scope. In the second edition of *Derishat tsiyon*, immediately following his reference to European nationalism, he wrote, 'All other nations have striven only for their own honour. But we strive for more than our ancestors' honour, but for the honour of God, blessed be he, who chose Zion. . . . We will claim that land we seek "not by might, nor by power" [Zech. 4: 16], but with the golden sceptre that is extended to the

New Orleans and its Discussion in Nineteenth-Century Europe', *American Jewish History*, 69 (Dec. 1979), 174–95 at 194–5.

[81] Kalischer's narrative of Jewish history is discussed in Ch. 5, and his admiration of the proselytizing efforts of the patriarchs can be found in his exegetical works such as *Sefer haberit*, i. 96 (on Gen. 12: 1), iii. 206 (on Lev. 22: 32); iv. 129 (on Num. 14: 9); *Emunah yesharah*, ii. 103, 121; *Yetsiat mitsrayim*, 28. See Kalischer's harsh comments against assimilating Jews in *Hamagid*, 16 (1869), repr. in *Zionist Writings*, 286–7.   [82] *Derishat tsiyon*, 29.

[83] Ibid. 129.   [84] *Der Israelit*, 27 (1863), repr. in *Zionist Writings*, 194.

notables of Israel.'[85] Here he explained the distinction in methods: Jews did
not need to depend on military might for the reclamation of their land, because they had the help of God's hidden miracles. In addition, the Jewish return to Zion had a broader scope and would be recognized by the other nations
as superior:

> We do not wait for our own [redemption], but for all the people of the world. They will
> be illuminated by our light, as it is written, 'all the nations will flow unto us' [Isa. 2: 21],
> and 'in those days ten men from the nations of every tongue shall take hold of the robe of
> a Jew, saying, "Let us go with you"' [Zech. 8: 23], etc. Thus, everyone will profit and be
> illuminated by divine light when we are redeemed.[86]

This language differentiates Kalischer not only from nationalists, but also from
his own teachers, Eger and Lorbeerbaum, who had been so careful during the
Hamburg temple controversy to demonstrate that the Jews had no nationalistic
designs of their own. Kalischer's dissociation from nationalism is of a different
kind. He exploits the admiration of nationalism, yet at the same time boasts
that the Torah surpasses it.

Kalischer had initially greeted Christian support for the Jews' return to
Zion with joy, but by the late 1860s he began to fear that the Jews' love for the
Land of Israel was no match for the Christians' love for the Holy Land. He
anxiously followed the reports in *Hamagid* of American Christian settlers who
founded an agricultural colony near Jaffa. The leader of the group informed an
interviewer that anyone could join the group, but Jews were especially wel-
come and would not be asked to leave their faith.[87] This venture failed and
was replaced by another group of Christians from Germany. Kalischer began
to realize that while he was struggling to persuade Jewish leaders to support
agricultural settlement in Palestine, Christian groups were buying land and
winning concessions from the local rulers. 'God forbid', he wrote, 'that the
foreigners awaken but we stand distant.'[88]

It was just this fear that provoked Kalischer's new, harsh attacks on Reform
leaders. Two years after the publication of *Derishat tsiyon*, he wrote an open
letter to the readers of *Hamagid* about a new era in Thorn. The letter testifies
to his amazement at the power of Reform. Though coloured by an idealized

---

[85] *Derishat tsiyon*, 129.

[86] *Halevanon*, 34 (1868), repr. in *Zionist Writings*, 265; similarly *Hamagid*, 35 (1868), repr.
ibid. 267.

[87] Shelomoh Edelberg, 'The American Colony in Jaffa' (Heb.), *Hado'ar*, 36, 28 (1957), 224–9.
Edelberg explains that the leader believed that the messianic age was near and that it was best to
emigrate to Palestine since the price of land would rise once the Jews started to return.

[88] Kalischer to Rabbi Abraham Ashkenazi (7 Elul 5634 [20 Aug. 1874]), repr. in *Zionist Writings*, 539. See also *Hamagid*, 3 (1871), repr. ibid. 325.

memory of the past, his words are nevertheless powerful testimony to Thorn's earlier respect for its paternalistic rabbi:

Until now, this city in which I have lived for some forty years was a faithful city. Crooked ways were stopped by choosing the straight path, and the footsteps of the sheep made a path to our God through zealous guarding of our holy ancestors' ways. But now *new faces* have come here. And though their hands have not found much room in which to make reforms and to root out everything, God forbid, nevertheless, little by little they begin to make a breach in the wall of the house of Israel. From the depth of my broken heart I see that this is just their beginning. Who knows what more they will add, they and their children after them.[89]

The new faces, it appears, were recent arrivals whose ideas had taken root and could not be eradicated. The pious Jews of Thorn, heretofore passive and obedient, had been won over. That this had occurred in his town, where the religious authorities were stalwart and the structure of the Jewish community was identical to what he believed was the age-old model, shocked Kalischer deeply. The extension of the Prussian railway to Thorn in 1857 had stimulated the local economy, facilitated contacts with other cities and regions, and led to the town's growth.[90] These changes were accompanied by behaviour and beliefs that he could only characterize as a denial of Torah. It seemed irrelevant that, relative to the demands of Reform Jews elsewhere in Germany, the changes sought by the locals were quite minor: a more orderly synagogue decorum, a *bimah* (reader's desk) in front of the pews rather than in the middle of the synagogue, and deletions of liturgical passages calling for divine vengeance on recalcitrant gentiles and slanderous Jews. What mattered was the change in attitude. After this point, Kalischer would never again minimize the seriousness of the new religious challenges. He denounced the leaders of Reform Judaism in the most severe terms in the pages of the Hebrew press throughout the 1860s and 1870s. Gone were the moderate and studied pronouncements that characterized his articles from the 1840s. Instead, he echoed the condemnations his teachers had uttered, sounding like any other outraged conservative.

One might imagine that the appearance of Reform Judaism would alter Kalischer's perception that redemption was at hand. After all, how could he continue to maintain that the freedoms granted to Jews were a gift from God, when they so quickly led to irreligiousness? Yet he did not appear to revise his optimistic outlook. This may be owing to a number of factors. When he first

---

[89] *Hamagid*, 25 (1863); emphasis is in the original.

[90] The opening of the Thorn connection on the Prussian railway was announced in *Hamagid*, 17 (1857). See Lowenstein, 'The Pace of Modernization of German Jewry', in his *Mechanics of Change*.

articulated his messianic interpretation of current history, he had barely seen evidence of these unfortunate phenomena; by the time he realized they were serious problems, he was already committed to his point of view. After 1863 there are few references to Jewish civic emancipation in his writing. The other phenomena signifying God's hidden miracles—the rise of powerful Jews, improvement in physical security in the Yishuv, amelioration of Turkish prohibitions against Jewish land purchases, and so on—remained; indeed, he found evidence of more as the years passed. The negative events were so few that he was able to integrate them into his ideology; for example, poverty in Europe was construed as an inducement for emigration to Palestine, isolated tragedies were seen as signs of God's anger at opponents of agricultural colonization, and—as we shall see below—the religious licence in Europe made the repressive regime of the Turks seem more attractive.

Thus Kalischer's new comments about the Reform movement differed from his 1844 and 1845 remarks only in the harshness of their tone; the arguments are much the same. For example, responding to the account of Rabbi Abraham Geiger's sermon declaring that it was time for Jews to embrace Europe as their Jerusalem, he wrote the following:

This 'soothsayer' spreads his voice of heresy on God's Torah and shows his arrogance to God's messiah; may this heretic be blown away like dust. And his [Geiger's] curses do not fall only on the congregation of Jeshurun, but upon all inhabitants of the earth, for the foundations of their faith rest on Israel's divine Torah and the prophets of the tribes of Jacob. If he says 'Destroy it utterly, even unto its foundations' [Ps. 137: 7], then a siege would be mounted against all belief, truth would be the casualty, people of faith would be lost, and the pillars of the world would be weakened, for every man will do what seems right in his own eyes, and God's promise would never be established on the face of the earth.[91]

In this passage Kalischer still maintains that the messianic prophecies are universally recognized, the basis of all religious belief, and indispensable to law and order. He further points out that non-Jewish rulers and common people would never allow heretical words like these to be uttered by their priests. They knew, he wrote, that God 'had built a lofty edifice for Israel his treasure, and for the salvation of the nations to whom her light appears'. They recognized that their own salvation rested upon Israel's messianic redemption, and their support for it remained firm.[92]

It must have been bitter indeed for Kalischer to witness Jews rejecting so explicitly and publicly the hope to return to Zion and rebuild the Temple. According to the reasoning he displayed in *Emunah yesharah*, such people were heretics, lower than the rest of humanity. To this new type of Jew, Kalischer's

---

[91] *Hamagid*, 8 (1870), repr. in *Zionist Writings*, 299.   [92] Ibid.

clever interpretations of biblical symbols, his decoding of the phenomenal events of the nineteenth century, were nonsensical.

THE SECONDARY RATIONALES

Kalischer's activism was driven by messianic motives, but he crafted arguments on behalf of the agricultural communes that emphasized their contribution to Jewish social, economic, and religious life. These non-messianic arguments focused attention away from his messianism and towards the pragmatic benefits of his proposal. To have influence in the Yishuv, one had to appeal to the more acculturated Jewish leaders in western Europe who were raising funds and devising plans to improve the Jewish situation in Palestine. They were not concerned with theology, exegesis, or Jewish legal precedents for restoring sacrificial worship. The rabbis and pious Jews in Jerusalem, whose approval for Yishuv reforms was also necessary, did care about these matters, and it would have been evident to them that *Derishat tsiyon* was a messianic tract. Some of them were excited by the book's defence of realistic messianism, but the Ashkenazi Jerusalem rabbinate, the group most influential with west and central European Jews, were alarmed. One of the most powerful, Rabbi Meir Auerbach (1815–78) of Jerusalem, took him to task for claiming that redemption had begun. In response, Kalischer explicitly articulated his new, more moderate approach: 'Why should we continue [to argue] whether a hope for redemption will grow from this? . . . How beautiful and pleasant our lot will be if we busy ourselves with these serious ideas and tasks. In either case, if we act, certainly good will result. And if, God forbid, we do not succeed, our good intention will be considered.'[93] It was more sensible to focus on concrete tasks that improved life in the Yishuv, he remarked pragmatically. They should ignore the issue of messianism and co-operate for the good of all.

Consequently, Kalischer took more care to elaborate on the economic and social advantages of the agricultural colonies in comparison with other philanthropic projects. He also addressed the religious needs that would be met by Jewish agricultural colonies in Palestine: they would provide a stable religious environment, they would allow Jews to live according to the religious ideal of combining Torah study with a worldly occupation, and they would enable the

---

[93] Auerbach had denounced Kalischer's messianic theory in an open letter in the pages of *Halevanon* (4 and 8, 1863), but he also conceded that he admired Kalischer's desire to improve the conditions of life in the Yishuv. Kalischer responded in *Halevanon*, 8 (1863), repr. in *Zionist Writings*, 200 (more than ten years later, in 1874, he repeated himself in a private letter: repr. ibid. 528). Following Auerbach's letter, Kalischer toned down his messianic rhetoric, saying that the beginning of the first phase was near.

fulfilment of the many commandments dependent on the Land of Israel. Read alone, these non-messianic rationales make him sound like a Religious Zionist of the 1890s or a leader of the Mizrahi Zionist movement of the early twentieth century. Strategy, however, was not substance. None of the social, economic, and religious issues he raised was ever purely that; each contained a bit of extraneous messianic symbolism or interpretation of proof texts that betrayed his primary motivation. Sharp-sighted colleagues comprehended this. Yehiel Brill, the publisher of many of Kalischer's articles in *Halevanon*, noted in an editorial that he typically offered non-messianic rationales only after his messianic arguments had failed to convince.[94]

One of Kalischer's first modifications was his discussion of the religious value of labour. The Jerusalem Ashkenazi rabbinate was known to insist that residence in the Holy Land imposed extra religious requirements and a higher degree of piety; spending one's time in agricultural labour and living in a rural setting away from the urban enclaves of study and prayer fell short of the ideal. In *Derishat tsiyon* he dealt rather cursorily with these religious concerns. One was a simple statement, 'all work there is essentially [the fulfilment of] a great commandment'.[95] This comment is ambiguous. If it referred to his belief that seeking Zion (which throughout *Derishat tsiyon* meant messianic activism) was in itself a commandment, it would draw objections from those who believed that such activism was a great sin. His statement could also be interpreted broadly, marking a revolutionary break with the traditional attitude towards Torah study and its superiority over all worldly occupations. Yet, he did not believe this, as he himself had spurned a worldly occupation in order to study Torah. His second mode of defending agricultural labour was clearer, and it made Torah study central to the entire venture: he asserted that engaging in such labour would protect the Torah from debasement. He felt very strongly that the Jews who were being supported by charity so that they could spend their days entirely devoted to Torah study were making the Torah 'a spade for digging'. He did not deny outright the value of a *ḥalukah* mode of support, but he certainly implied it. He wrote wistfully of the type of life exemplified by certain rabbis of the Mishnah and Talmud who were able to participate in both Torah study and a worldly occupation. Their priority was Torah, he explained, and because they worked only as much as they needed to support themselves, they were successful in both areas. Participation in both spheres of life created understanding between them and the working population. They recognized that Torah and labour were both important productive activities; after all, as they pointed out, 'without flour there is no Torah'. Adopting the language of the maskilim, he called this integrated life 'a unity of

---

[94] *Halevanon*, 21 (1872).   [95] *Derishat tsiyon*, 28.

Torah and worldly matters [*torah im derekh erets*]'.[96] Nevertheless, in *Derishat tsiyon* he did not explain how agricultural labourers would manage to engage in Torah study.

Kalischer remedied this in later writings by including daily Torah study in the lives of potential settlers. In some articles and letters, he proposed that the daily schedule of the agricultural communes would include a regular time of Torah study for all.[97] In others, he suggested that the farm labourers would fulfil their duty to study through agents; that is, in return for their contribution of food to the Yishuv Torah scholars, the labourers would receive part of the scholars' merit.[98] But Kalischer believed strongly that a life of true piety included actual Torah study, and so more often he declared his desire to see within the labourers' workday a regular time of study for all, even those who came without prior learning experience.[99]

In the contemporary debate over agricultural labour in Palestine, then, Kalischer's position was somewhere between the rational social planners and the *halukah*'s loyal supporters. He did not hide his contempt for the current distribution of funds and the deleterious effects it had on the Yishuv. Yet he was a strong supporter of Torah study. He defended the Yishuv scholars from charges of laziness, but he insisted that under the conditions in the Yishuv, their lives inevitably led to sin.[100] According to the sages, he wrote, one should unite the study of Torah with a worldly occupation, 'for the toil in both of them drives away sin'. There are two sins here, he explained: one sin occurs when one works so much that one does not schedule regular times for study. The other sin is 'enjoying the fruits of others and the sin that inevitably follows poverty'.[101] The poverty of the Ashkenazi Jews of the Yishuv and their dependence upon community funds, he asserted, put Torah study in disrepute. They were constrained to quarrel and cheat in order to provide for their basic needs. The consequences were visible in the Yishuv, where contentious-

---

[96] This argument appeared in *Derishat tsiyon*, 28 and 30. The sources are BT *Ber.* 30*b*, 17*a*, and Mishnah *Avot* 3: 21.

[97] Kalischer to Azriel Hildesheimer (4 Kislev 5623 [7 Nov. 1862]), repr. in *Zionist Writings*, 188.

[98] In *Halevanon*, 45 (1868), repr. in *Zionist Writings*, 280, Kalischer suggested a graded system: Jews who labour and do not study Torah will give one-tenth of their produce to full-time scholars; Jews who labour and study Torah are self-sufficient; Jews who only study Torah receive the tenth. He repeated this in *Hamagid*, 3 (1871), and *Havatselet*, 10 (1871), repr. ibid. 327, along with a chastisement of Jews who prevent others from working the ground.

[99] Kalischer to the administrators of Kolel Holland and Germany (the Fast of Gedaliah, 5635 [14 Sept. 1874]), repr. ibid. 547.

[100] Kalischer to Zevulun Leib Barit in *Halevanon*, 3 (1872), repr. ibid. 372.

[101] Kalischer to Azriel Hildesheimer (14 Sivan 5623 [20 June 1872]), repr. ibid. 355. For a similar message, see *Halevanon*, 44 (1872), repr. ibid. 357. The mishnaic source is *Avot* 2: 2.

ness and corruption among *ḥalukah* recipients were common.[102] These comments did not endear Kalischer to the Jerusalem Ashkenazim; in fact, his own impeccable reputation as a Torah scholar put them on the defensive. The realistic components and religious values of Kalischer's arguments gave him the image of a progressive conservative. His encouragement of a different religious lifestyle exemplifies this fusion.

Kalischer struck a similar balance in his description of the potential agricultural labourers. In these writings, however, he was more careful to aim his words at specific audiences. When he explained his plans to west European readers, for whom the return to Zion was a politically unattractive idea, he described the potential settlers as 'those who live now in the Holy Land in hardship and distress'.[103] However, when he wrote for others, he openly advocated the emigration of pious Jews eager to live in the Land of Israel. In this case, he indicated that the potential settlers' Jewish knowledge was not as critical as their willingness to obey Jewish law and participate in the religious life of the community.[104] He assumed, correctly for his time, that any Jew who would choose to move to Palestine was ipso facto religious. When many Jews began leaving Romania in the early 1870s, defenders of the status quo in the Yishuv expressed the fear that irreligious Jews would find their way to Palestine through Kalischer's project. He responded as follows: 'To those who say that the Romanian Jews do not desire the holy: the remnant of the people have a fear of God like "an awesome crystal hung over their head" [Ezek. 1: 22]. *They* will go to the Land of Israel in joy and happiness. And he who has no holy spirit in him will go to America.'[105] Because Kalischer regarded the Jews who had chosen to make their lives in America as a lost cause, he never suggested that they should emigrate to Palestine; towards west European Jews he was also reticent. He regarded Jews from eastern and south-eastern Europe, North Africa, and Palestine as the optimal candidates. He considered that they were poor enough to need to labour, hardy and accustomed to manual labour, and sufficiently sheltered from modern culture that their traditional simplicity and piety were still intact.

Despite his confidence that the emigrants would be observant Jews, Kalischer was anxious to prove that the agricultural communes would not nurture irreligiousness in the Holy Land. The assimilation that was appearing in European Jewish communities had not touched Palestine, but many thought it was

---

[102] Kalischer to Azriel Hildesheimer (14 Sivan 5623 [20 June 1872]), repr. in *Zionist Writings*, 355. See also the unused part of an article for *Hamagid*, 34 (1863) that Klausner published in *Sinai* (Iyar 5699 [Apr.–May 1939]), 613–14.

[103] *Der Israelit*, 7 (1870), repr. in *Zionist Writings*, 298.

[104] Kalischer to Rabbi Katringer [Krantinger] (1863), repr. ibid. 216.

[105] *Ivri anokhi*, 25 (1873), repr. ibid. 434.

merely a matter of time until it did. He certainly did not want to be the one who compromised the piety of the Yishuv. Consequently, he envisaged the agricultural colonies as communities of labourers fulfilling both their work and religious duties under paternalistic control. Each colony would be assigned a rabbi whose duties would include supervising the observance of the agricultural precepts in the fields, overseeing the contribution of produce for the Torah scholars, teaching all the workers on a regular basis, and making sure that Jewish law was obeyed. Kalischer himself longed to serve in that capacity. 'Though I have no knowledge of farming', he admitted, 'I will find trained and learned men whom I can guard from laziness and supervise in the observance of the commandments.'[106] In a regulated, non-individualistic setting, religious deviancy would be avoided. If it did appear, it would be dealt with quickly and firmly. His model for this type of control was taken from a Jewish agricultural colony in Poland and from an example from the Second Temple period. This is one way he described it:

> We will have guards and policemen (just as Nehemiah, may he rest in peace, did) so that we have, Heaven forbid, no desecration of the sabbath by the labourers and farmers of the holy ground. But all will be obliged to gather in the nearby villages from Friday night until Saturday night to pray there and learn together . . . and anyone who violates these things, Heaven forbid, will be driven off his land, denied work, excommunicated, and shunned.[107]

Whereas in *Derishat tsiyon* Kalischer mentioned a Jewish police force that would protect the settlers from Arab brigands, here its function is to police Jews who might be tempted to break religious laws. Indeed, in regard to the observance of the commandments, he considered Arabs less of a threat than non-observant Jews. In 1874 a case was brought to his attention of a rabbi who bought land in Palestine and hired Arab labourers to work the land and perform the agricultural precepts. It was permissible to do so, he wrote, but the precepts would not be observed correctly unless their performance were supervised by a Jew.[108] He assumed that the Arab labourers, if instructed properly, would comply.

[106] *Halevanon*, 3 (1872), repr. ibid. 373. On many occasions Kalischer expressed his desire to serve as supervising rabbi in the future agricultural colony; see e.g. *Zionist Writings*, 238, 255, 262, 288, 352–3.

[107] Kalischer to Azriel Hildesheimer (4 Kislev 5623 [7 Nov. 1862]), repr. ibid. 188. The reference to the Polish colony can be found in *Hamagid*, 3 (1871) and *Ḥavatselet*, 10 (1871), repr. ibid. 327.

[108] Kalischer to Meir Auerbach, Mordechai Jaffe, and Fischel Lapin (7 Elul 5634 [20 Aug. 1874]), repr. ibid. 538. In *Derishat tsiyon*, 51, Kalischer explained that a non-Jew who was not bound by the Torah could perform the work for the Jewish landowner, but the ideal was that each Jew should perform the commandments dependent on the land rather than hire non-Jewish labourers to do it for him.

The state would also take a role in monitoring religious behaviour. Kalischer was reassured by the Ottoman government's religious conservatism: 'for it was not like our country where there is religious freedom with no restrictions on what the people set their hearts to do. . . . This is not the way in the lands of the East, where the authority stands over us with bans and punishments for the violation of religious law.'[109] It is not clear just how he imagined Turkish enforcement of religious law, but the dominance of religious orthodoxy in the Yishuv was attractive to him. The lack of religious freedom in Palestine meant to him that the decisions of rabbinic authorities would be enforced by the state. In essence, what he hoped to see for the religious leadership of the agricultural communes was a theocracy. While he regarded religious tolerance in Europe as a beneficent divine portent, he was reassured by the Ottoman government's contrary stance. What had been lost in Europe—in rabbinic memory, the idealized rabbinic control over the economic, social, and religious spheres of Jewish life—would be resurrected in Palestine.

When Kalischer turned to the economic and social benefits of the agricultural colonies, his comments seem more modern. He described his project as the solution to the Yishuv's hunger problem, specifically a means to lower the high cost and end the shortage of food. Increasing the amount of financial aid to individuals would not solve the problem, he explained, for the problem was not simply one of poverty:

We will do much by sending collections from all our countries to support our Jewish brethren in the Holy Land. But this is merely like rain falling on a mountain, for the dry mountain absorbs very little while the valley fills up with the blessing of rain. All that we send goes to the farm labourers who are Arabs and foreigners. They fill their purses with the gold and silver of the donation, for they sell a small amount of bread for much money.[110]

As long as food production was controlled by non-Jews, money from abroad would be inadequate to support the community; the producers could simply keep raising the price of food. The only long-term solution was for Jews to purchase and farm the land themselves, he thought. Still, he was very modest about the effect of this venture: he admitted that even with the aid of a Jewish agricultural industry, the halukah would be necessary to support the full-time

---

[109] Kalischer to Azriel Hildesheimer (4 Kislev 5623 [7 Nov. 1862]), repr. in Zionist Writings, 188. 'Religious freedom' in Europe was harmful to Jewish life, even though the emancipation accompanying it would ultimately lead to a return of the Jews to Zion. As we have seen in Ch. 5, Kalischer understood emancipation as not including religious licence or a diminution of communal religious authority.

[110] Announcement by Guttmacher and Kalischer (1866), repr. in Zionist Writings, 243.

scholars. The difference was that both systems together would adequately meet the scholars' needs.[111]

Within this sober analysis of the Yishuv's hunger problem, Kalischer introduced a religious assumption: the present lack of Jewish economic control in Palestine actually hampered the fertility of the land. He believed that the soil would respond better to Jewish ownership and labour because, after all, the land had been designated for them: '[Many people now want] to sow righteousness and mercy in the land of life [to aid the poor through the land's produce], the land that God's eyes behold from the beginning to the end of the year. But how can God above exact [produce] from her, if she brings forth fruit only through the labour of foreigners?'[112] Many pious Jews agreed that Palestine's infertility was a consequence of non-Jewish rule, but Kalischer thought he could do something about it. The notion that the land would not be fertile for its foreign possessors was bound up in his mind with *elbon ha'arets*, the insult to the land, and it would be reversed by seeking Zion. When Jews began to work the land, the land would respond. The land would no longer be abandoned and would, once again, give abundantly.[113]

Another rationale for the creation of a settled land was that the establishment of agricultural colonies was the most efficient and inclusive of charity projects for the Yishuv. West European Jews had recently launched the building of houses, a hospital, and an orphanage in Jerusalem, but Kalischer found these rather limited; they would assist isolated individuals and would not address the problems of hunger and unemployment. The development of an agricultural industry, however, was more extensive in its scope: the unemployed would be put to work, the work would produce food for labourers and Torah scholars, and a foundation would be established for the growth of the Yishuv.[114]

When Kalischer explained himself at greater length, however, the other motives behind his reasoning became apparent. He was pleased to hear about the Jerusalem building project, he wrote to one of his colleagues, 'but it has not been heard that they will specifically work for making the land fruitful, "for you have no more manifest sign of redemption than this: 'But ye, O mountains of Israel, ye shall shoot forth your branches, and yield your fruit to my people

---

[111] *Derishat tsiyon*, 28.

[112] *Hamagid*, 38 (1864), repr. in *Zionist Writings*, 224. Yehiel Brill put this another way: 'The land is in mourning for its people and will not be fertile for its foreign owners'; see *Halevanon*, 5 (1863).   [113] *Hamagid*, 38 (1864), repr. in *Zionist Writings*, 226.

[114] Kalischer to Azriel Hildesheimer, in *Zionist Writings*, 304. See also Kalischer to Hildesheimer (on the twenty-eighth day of the Omer, 5828 [5 May 1868]), and *Der Israelit*, 52 (1868), repr. ibid. 254 and 270.

Israel, for they are on hand to come'" [Ezek. 36: 8].'[115] Ending unemployment, helping support the scholars, and lowering food costs were not his primary goals. He wanted to build a settled land; he was only interested in social welfare projects that would hasten redemption. Jews engaged in agricultural work in Palestine served this end, but similar work in the Diaspora hindered redemption. He was contemptuous of certain Jewish social reformers who advocated farm colonies in Europe: '[You] do not know the nature of the evil in the people from this state. They say, "What is Palestine to me? . . .Why do we need that desolate land, destroyed for thousands of years?" This is what they say, these evil people who do not believe the prophets, and in this way they prevent many philanthropists from giving to the poor of the Land of Israel.'[116] He did not want the Jews to root themselves more firmly in the Diaspora, and investing in a European Jewish agricultural project would do just that. Yet in the same article he referred warmly to Rabbi Shelomoh Eger's proposal to establish a Jewish agricultural colony in the Posen district. Eger designed his plan, Kalischer wrote, 'so that every man will sit under his vine [Mic. 4: 4] and not wander about studying the sciences, for irreligiousness has increased as a result, due to our many sins'.[117] In other words, Eger made his proposal to deal with the problem of *luftmenshen*, the Yiddish term for unemployed men who, Kalischer felt, had such a destabilizing effect on Jewish society. Kalischer, however, would establish agricultural colonies in the Land of Israel, fill them with pious Jews, and allow the *luftmenshen* to observe from a safe distance: 'When they [the *luftmenshen*] see that the Land of Israel is built up as a blessing and praise, then all her abusers will be ashamed and mortified and see that there is a hope in her at the end of days, with the help of God, speedily in our day, amen.'[118] In short, the vision of vigorous Jewish farmers transforming the Land of Israel into a thriving and fertile land would silence the criticism of these sceptical Jewish men and restore their faith in God's messianic promises.

One of the earliest, but least successful, of Kalischer's religious rationales was his claim that the building of agricultural settlements was a fulfilment of *mitsvat yishuv ha'arets*, the commandment to settle the Land of Israel. This is the commandment that some rabbis derived from Numbers 33: 53, 'And you shall take possession of the land and settle in it, for I have assigned the land to

---

[115] Kalischer to Azriel Hildesheimer (on the twenty-eighth day of the Omer, 5828 [5 May 1868]), repr. in *Zionist Writings*, 304. The proof text is quoted in BT *San.* 98a.

[116] *Halevanon*, 45 (1868), repr. in *Zionist Writings*, 280. When the Alliance opened its agricultural school outside Jaffa, Kalischer was dismayed that the student body was composed of children, not heads of families, from the Diaspora. In his letter to the Berlin branch of the Alliance (1873), repr. ibid. 489, he pointed out that the students could leave Palestine with their skills upon graduation, 'and thus we would totally fail to achieve our goal'.

[117] *Halevanon*, 45 (1868), repr. ibid. 280.　　　　　　　　　　　　　　　[118] Ibid.

you to possess.' 'Seeking Zion' or 'this great mitsvah' is how Kalischer referred to his decades-old quest to build the Jewish community in Palestine and restart the sacrificial service. It was summed up in Numbers 33: 53.[119] In the opening chapter of *Derishat tsiyon*, he promised to expound on the commandment's meaning: 'We shall elaborate, with the help of God, in the second chapter of this essay, the great merit of one who lives in the Holy Land. Our great rabbi, Ramban [Nahmanides], of blessed memory, counted as one of the positive commandments settling in the Land of Israel in order not to leave it barren; see there.'[120] Despite this promise, he did not elaborate on this point in the first edition of *Derishat tsiyon*.[121]

The consideration of whether Numbers 33: 53 is an eternal commandment or refers only to the initial conquest of the Land of Israel is really a question of the normative place of the Jews in history. This question was answered differently in different eras and is part of the larger debate on realistic and passive messianism. Certainly in the biblical period before the dispersion to Babylonia, the Israelites understood their destiny as irretrievably bound up with residence in the Land of Israel. The Torah text assumes this connection, and in narratives in which the Israelites are outside their land, it mandates certain behaviours for conquest and upon returning home. When the Jews became largely a Diaspora people near the end of the biblical period, the Torah's laws of conquest and return to the land were subjected to interpretation. When the conditions of life in Palestine worsened considerably under the Romans and the centre of Jewish life moved to Persia, the rabbinic opinions about these commandments were absorbed into the evolving perspective of passive messianism. The Jewish dispersion was eventually understood as *galut*, or exile, willed by God as punishment, and it was considered sinful—a violation of the oaths—

[119] Kalischer to Albert Cohn (estimated date, 1860), repr. ibid. 178–9: 'It has been about twenty-five years since my heart stirred within me concerning the Yishuv of the land of our ancestors, the place of our Temple. I showed with clear and straightforward proofs the greatness of this commandment and the infinite reward for those who work to create *erets noshevet*. While he was alive I spoke about this with our teacher, the universally respected Akiva Eger, of blessed memory, who agreed with me.' Kalischer's contact with Cohn is discussed in greater detail in Ch. 6.   [120] *Derishat tsiyon*, 27.

[121] In the first edition of *Derishat tsiyon* (p. 67), Kalischer wrote the following: 'We find that the talmudic rabbis permitted purchase on the sabbath that would lead to the settlement of the Land of Israel, and as it says in [BT] *Gitin* 5 and *Shulḥan arukh*, 'Oraḥ ḥayim', 206: 11 this is because it is a great commandment to increase the [size of] the Yishuv in the Land of Israel. Even for one house and one field they remove the rabbinic prohibition. How much more so for the sake of the land as a whole, such as planting vineyards and olive orchards, building the ruins, and returning many Jews there—you have no greater commandment than this.' This is not the same as *mitsvat yishuv ha'arets*, which is a mandatory positive obligation. The law described in the Talmud and *Shulḥan arukh* is a voluntary meritorious act, and no punishment is incurred for not doing it.

to attempt to conquer the Land of Israel before the messianic age. The minority position represented by advocates of realistic messianism would articulate
the eternity of the Torah's directives and condense them into one law, *mitsvat
yishuv ha'arets*, based on Numbers 33: 53. The debate on this commandment
started with Nahmanides, who castigated Maimonides for omitting it in his
enumeration of the 613 precepts of the Torah. Nahmanides, in contrast, un-
equivocally stated that the Jews were commanded in the Torah to take possession of and strengthen the land. His statement identified Numbers 33: 53 as
a positive mandatory commandment, meaning that it was an obligation that
must be discharged in order not to incur a penalty. Later followers of Nahmanides attempted to prove that Maimonides' omission was a mere oversight; they
claimed that his other legal judgements on related issues, as well as the allu-
sions to realistic messianism sprinkled through his writings, indicated that he
regarded emigration to the Land of Israel as a binding obligation.[122]

Kalischer joined the chorus of defenders of *mitsvat yishuv ha'arets* in the
second edition of *Derishat tsiyon*. 'There are those who contrive to destroy the
holy way when they say that presently it is not a commandment to ascend to
Mount Zion, to the Holy Land, since the law [Num. 33: 53] applied only at the
time the Temple stood', he wrote. 'I shall make clear that this position is a result of the [evil] impulse.'[123] He brought forth a number of legal texts in an
attempt to prove that the obligation to settle in the Land of Israel was biblically
mandated. He admitted that it was not an absolute obligation, but that the conditions under which it could be suspended were not applicable at present. He
insisted that Maimonides, too, regarded Numbers 33: 53 as binding.[124] Then,
by the sheer weight of his conviction, he insisted that *mitsvat yishuv ha'arets*
included the obligation to renew the sacrifices: 'For why should I emigrate and
settle in it? It is true and certain that the intention of . . . Ramban
[Nahmanides] in this passage was the reference to sacrifice, that we travel there
from the Diaspora in order to anticipate the allotments of the sacrifices if it so
happens that permission is granted by him [the sovereign power], may he be
blessed.'[125] Kalischer was incapable of understanding a return of the Jews to
the Land of Israel that did not include a renewal of the sacrificial cult.

[122] With the rise of Religious Zionism and new forms of active messianism in Israel in the
1970s, many popular and scholarly publications appeared that weighed in on the activist side of
this debate. One example of this can be found in J. David Bleich, *Contemporary Halakhic Problems*
(New York, 1977), 3–9.   [123] *Derishat tsiyon*, 32.

[124] He wrote very briefly in *Derishat tsiyon*, 33: 'Rambam [Maimonides] ruled that it is [a
mitsvah] in his practical decisions.' Kalischer gave as his source *Mishneh torah*, 'Laws of Kings',
5: 9. It was not accurate to quote Maimonides' statement that it was absolutely forbidden to emigrate from the Land of Israel, and summarize it, in Maimonides' name, as 'it is a great mitsvah to
immigrate to the Land of Israel'. These are two separate matters.

[125] *Derishat tsiyon*, 48; see also pp. 52–3.

Asserting the existence of *mitsvat yishuv ha'arets*, then, was problematic on two accounts: it was not plausible that one could find much rabbinic support for the view that all Jews living in the Diaspora were violating the law; and it was tantamount to announcing one's support for active messianism. As in most debates about messianism, this one was conducted in code, focusing on obscure institutions and utilizing legal terminology. The rationale did not have the intended effect of distracting the audience from Kalischer's messianic motives. Indeed, it did just the opposite, exposing the gap between Kalischer's ideology and the prevailing exilic forms of Judaism. It alerted the guardians of messianic passivity, which included staunchly conservative Jews as well as acculturated Jews intent on adapting Judaism to the new demands of the modern, national state, that messianic fervour had surfaced and must be suppressed. Kalischer's promotion of *mitsvat yishuv ha'arets*, like his championing of the renewal of sacrifice, pitted him against these two types of Jews. As he could not afford to alienate them, he referred to it far less often, or linked it with other, less controversial, religious laws: the category of commandments called *mitsvot hateluyot ba'arets*, the commandments dependent on the Land of Israel.[126]

These commandments include agricultural precepts, rules of war and peace, procedures for establishing a government, and the laws of sacrifice—all of which were understood as binding and applicable only in the Land of Israel. After the destruction of the Temple, all but the agricultural laws were of academic significance only. According to the rabbinic consensus, a Diaspora Jew would not be judged culpable for not performing these commandments and was not required to move to the Land of Israel in order to fulfil them; at the most, he would gain merit for helping others in the Holy Land discharge their obligation. Kalischer, however, took an aggressive stance, arguing that Jews should buy land in Palestine in order to be able to fulfil this category of Jewish law. Apart from its usefulness to his fund-raising campaign, this rationale was a response to the religious opponents of Jewish agricultural labour. They claimed that the ignorance of contemporary rabbis—not to mention the labourers—in this realm of law and the reduction in agricultural produce that

---

[126] Whereas Kalischer refers emphatically to *mitsvat yishuv ha'arets* in his 1864 article (*Hamagid*, 38, repr. in *Zionist Writings*, 224), in his 1866 addendum to *Derishat tsiyon*, called *Rishon letsiyon*, he makes clear that he has already moved towards replacing this theme with the reference to the commandments dependent on the Land of Israel. While he sometimes warned that the Jews were culpable and would be punished for each of the commandments dependent on the land that were not performed, he ceased making the same claim about *mitsvat yishuv ha'arets*. Perhaps these fine distinctions indicate little, for he often warned opponents (those who did not support the development of 'the settled land') that they were committing a grave sin and would suffer divine punishment.

would result from the performance of the precepts (observing the sabbatical year, for example) would prevent the laws from being properly performed. Some feared that the profanation of the sabbath was necessary to sustain the livestock and crops. One critic pointed out that contemporary Jews were neglecting those commandments they were already required to fulfil, and it did not make sense to add more.

Kalischer, however, used the unfulfilled commandments dependent on the land as a religious symbol that would draw pious Jews to his cause. Beginning in the opening chapter of *Derishat tsiyon*, he counted them among the many benefits that would accrue from the establishment of agricultural communes. After explaining the social and economic benefits, he wrote the following: 'There is another great advantage: we will be able to observe the commandments dependent on the land. The labourers will perform them under supervision, and anyone who aids in the agricultural labour is considered as if he observed the commandments dependent on the land himself.'[127] Working in the agricultural settlements, or even merely contributing funds on their behalf, constituted the fulfilment of the agricultural precepts. This was not a matter to be taken lightly, he wrote, for 'Moses longed to go there for the sake of performing these laws, and we, who already have merited the opportunity, how can we not fulfil them?'[128] In *Derishat tsiyon* and subsequent letters and articles, he reassured his readers that there were no insurmountable obstacles to farming the land in accordance with the Torah. He confessed that he himself hoped to move to Palestine and supervise the observance of the commandments there. When his reassurances were met with scorn, he grew suspicious. He was particularly incensed by opponents who were Jerusalem residents or closely tied to the *ḥalukah*. He called them 'the faction of the first ripe grapes' and claimed that their concern for the law was merely a veneer for their selfishness. He thought it especially sinful that these negative comments were being made at a time when it was becoming easier for Jews to purchase land in Palestine.[129]

Kalischer's references to the commandments dependent on the land began to increase in the mid-1860s. By then he had concluded that the improvement in security and public order in Palestine was a sign from God that it was time to build a settled land. He wrote expansively about the commandments in his pamphlet *Shelom yerushalayim*, a defence of *Derishat tsiyon* and the agricultural colonies:

These three are tied together: Israel, the Holy Land, and the Torah. Even though each has its separate parts, they are all one body: the members of Israel are bound to one

---

[127] *Derishat tsiyon*, 28.　　　　　　　　　　　　　　　　[128] Ibid. 51.

[129] *Hamagid*, 23 (1871), repr. in *Zionist Writings*, 328; *Ivri anokhi*, 3 (1872), repr. ibid. 387.

another, the 613 commandments necessitate each other, the Holy Land includes Jerusalem and Jerusalem contains the Temple and the Holy of Holies. . . . And now, each one of the Israelites, pay attention to what occurs when one law of the Torah, which is like one body, is missing. It is as if several threads woven into one garment were missing— because of this the entire garment is torn apart. And if you lack water, God forbid, you will die of thirst. How much more so if you lack the many commandments dependent on the land—your wound is as great as the sea, as if your heart were broken within you. And where will the heavenly blessing go? There is no vessel to hold it unless there is peace, a wholeness without any part lacking. But it will not occur with the absence of much of the Torah and the absence of peace—for quarrels are proliferating in the Holy Land now, and causeless hatred of the type that destroyed the Temple.[130]

This hyperbole is just one example of the heights Kalischer reached in his praise of the commandments. They would restore wholeness to the Torah, end national strife through the increased food supply from the agricultural colonies, contribute to the revitalization of the Yishuv, and heal and strengthen all of Jewish life. Although there is no explicit mention of redemption, this theme very graphically illustrates his deep conviction that exilic Judaism was sorely inadequate.

When restrictions on Jewish landownership were loosened in the 1870s, the tone of urgency in his writings grew. The commandments dependent on the land became a staple of his letters and articles. The following statement from 1870 is typical of his many pronouncements on the subject:

These many commandments—about which we can no longer say: 'We are shackled, we cannot perform them', because, thank God, now the Sultan has given permission to buy land and has provided refuge and protection from the marauders, as we all know—can be fulfilled by any man who does not lack money. He can observe every commandment through an agent, and Heaven forbid, his sin will increase if he does not do God's commandment when he is able.[131]

Eventually Kalischer began to point out their necessity to the health of the individual. He reminded his readers that the talmudic rabbis had established a connection between the 248 positive commandments and (according to their reckoning) the 248 organs of the human body as a way of teaching 'that every organ says to man, "do a mitsvah with me"'.[132] He echoed this well-known teaching in reference to the commandments dependent on the land. The following is a typical example of his use of this argument:

Every God-fearing man who truly loves God must long with all his heart to fulfil what is

---

[130] *Shelom yerushalayim vekontras shivat tsiyon* (Thorn, 1868), repr. ibid. 132–3.

[131] Announcement in Nathan Friedland's *Kol abirei haro'im* (Leslau, 1870), repr. ibid. 309.

[132] This can be found in Mishnah *Ohol.* 1: 49, BT *Mak.* 23*b*; and in Maimonides' introduction to *Sefer hamitsvot*; see *Sefer hamitsvot leharambam im hasagot haramban* [Maimonides' Book of the Commandments with Glosses by Nahmanides], ed. Chaim Dov Chavel (Jerusalem, 1981).

denied to him in the Diaspora, many of the 248 positive commandments, for our bodies are not whole without them. Every man with the fire of Torah burning within him to fulfil all that he can should take the 248 in his hand. If he cannot go there [to the Holy Land] himself, he can perform them through an agent.[133]

If the vision of an incomplete body was not enough to goad people into taking these commandments seriously, Kalischer elaborated on the punishment negligent Jews would receive after death:

It is a source of amazement to me that those who live in the Holy Land, the righteous leaders of German and French Jewry, and all Jews do not realize that every moment and hour they transgress many positive commandments dependent on the land. Where there is any possibility to attempt their observance, [if one makes no attempt] it is as if he violates them continuously. The author of *Shenei luḥot haberit* wrote in his commentary . . . that souls such as these will have to be reincarnated, God forbid, many times, for anyone who missed the opportunity of performing any commandment, even if it was not directly in front of him, has to be reincarnated until he does it.[134]

By late 1871, the commandments dependent on the land ceased being one of Kalischer's secondary rationales; they became explicitly messianic. For years he resisted making this claim, but he finally began to integrate the commandments into his discussion of *ge'ulat ha'arets*, the full-scale redemption of the Land of Israel.[135] The following linear interpretation of Psalm 112 illustrates this synthesis:

The wise-hearted person will regard these commandments with great joy, more than he regards all his gain and time-bound treasures. About these the poet, may he rest in

---

[133] Kalischer to Hevrat Dorshei Tsiyon Veyerushalayim, repr. in *Zionist Writings*, 379.

[134] *Hamagid*, 47 (1872), repr. ibid. 394. He repeated this argument at least six times in 1872.

[135] According to Bromberg, *Rabbi Tsevi Hirsch Kalischer*, 72, Guttmacher had been the first to assert that the commandments dependent on the land would hasten redemption, and he quotes Guttmacher (without reference to source or date) as follows: 'Due to our many sins, many are mistaken in thinking . . . that suddenly the gates of mercy will open and signs will appear in the sky and earth and all the testimonies of the prophets will be fulfilled, and everybody will be called forth from their dwelling place. But this is not so. . . . I say that it will occur with the community in the Land of Israel, when a beginning is made to awaken the earth from its sleep in the hands of the Arabs, and when the commandments possible for us to fulfil now are fulfilled in order that land give its fruit to the nation of Israel.' In *Shelom yerushalayim* (*Zionist Writings*, 128), Guttmacher prescribed the observance of the commandments dependent on the land in order to reverse the ancient insult to the Land of Israel and hasten the messianic age. In the same pamphlet, Kalischer was careful to separate the commandments from the redemption. Chapter 5 deals with the benefits of the agricultural communes and the commandments dependent on the land for the Yishuv. Chapter 6 begins: 'Apart from the fulfilment of commandments and sustenance of hungry and thirsty people, there is in this a hope for opening the gates of redemption.' This is followed by a discussion of the four stages of the redemption. In 1870 an announcement signed by the two men contains a remark about the messianic import of the commandments, but

peace, said, 'Happy is he who fears the Lord, who greatly delights in his commandments; his descendants will be mighty in the land.' 'Mighty in the land'—this means the land itself will see its might. 'His descendants [lit.: his seed]'—when he sows the land. 'The generation of the righteous will be blessed'—every righteous generation will bless those who sowed for charitable purposes. Then 'wealth and riches are in his house, and his righteousness endures for ever'—because he 'makes light shine in the darkness'— while the world is still dark he provides light for the upright. . . . And if we 'establish his vault on the land' [Amos 9: 6], then 'righteousness will shine down from Heaven' [Ps. 85: 12] and God will be pleased by our deeds. He will shine light on all his nation and bring redemption, may it come speedily in our day, amen.[136]

The performance of the commandments was equivalent to the other human efforts that could initiate the redemptive process and stir the heavenly forces into action. As he often did in his interpretations of texts, Kalischer exploited the images of light and darkness, vegetative growth, and the reflexive movements of the earthly and divine realms.

Kalischer's concern culminated in a special article he wrote on the subject for a Jewish periodical in 1872 in which he called for an international meeting of Jews to deal with the commandments dependent on the land. He concentrated in it all the different arguments he had previously used: the necessity of observing the commandments, the connection with the organs of the body, the opportunities presented by new political conditions in Palestine, fulfilling the precepts through an agent, the punishment meted out to the negligent soul, and the imperative of settling the land in order to hasten redemption. The commandments dependent on the land, he pointed out, 'are truly new to us' and merit extraordinary attention:

Therefore, let the voices ring out from every Jewish community and from all the other journalists who call for justice in Israel, in order that all the holy Jews unite in one association [*agudah*] with the intent to appoint a man, whom none will suspect of acting in his own self-interest, and he will supervise the whole matter and see it to the finish. Then we will have sufficient funds for this holy task, and through this we will earn some money. And if we 'establish his vault [*agudato*] on the land' [Amos 9: 6] then 'righteousness will shine down from Heaven' [Ps. 85: 12] and God will be pleased with our deeds. God willing, he will be placated by our labour, shine light on his nation, and hasten redemption, speedily in our day, amen.[137]

Here Kalischer's impatience for progress is evident. There were signs that the idea of the agricultural development of the Yishuv was becoming widely

Kalischer took pains to dissociate himself from it in a separate statement of his own in which he attributed the comment about the commandments to Guttmacher and added his usual exhortation that every God-fearing person should try to observe these precepts. See Nathan Friedland, *Kol abirei haro'im*, in *Zionist Writings*, 307–8. Kalischer's dissociating remark is on p. 309.

[136] *Ivri anokhi*, 3 (1872), repr. ibid. 388.   [137] *Hamagid*, 47 (1872), repr. ibid. 394–5.

accepted. The Alliance had agreed in 1868 to promote agricultural education in Palestine, and to this end it opened the Mikveh Israel agricultural school in 1870. More Jews in the Yishuv were publicly expressing their desire to support themselves through agricultural work, and potential immigrants from eastern Europe contacted Kalischer and expressed an interest in living in an agricultural commune. Organizations similar to the original Kolonisations-Verein were founded in 1871 in Jerusalem and Tiberias. Kalischer regarded all these as hidden miracles and Heaven's vindication of his cause. In 1873 his writing vacillated between elation at seeing success close at hand, and agitation over the lack of concrete gains. He seemed to stop censoring himself. For example, here is his response to the 1873 pogroms in Romania:

Be angry, but do not sin [Ps. 4: 5], because all that we have lost, due to our many sins, and which has caused many tears to flow from my eyes, is all due to our standing back from fulfilling this great commandment upon which the existence of the [other] commandments depend. We lacked this for thousands of years, but now we can easily fulfil it. For [neglecting] the commandments, God forbid, we are punished in a time of distress, as it says in the Talmud.[138]

'This great commandment' was Kalischer's term for *mitsvat yishuv ha'arets*. As he grew bolder about his messianic intent, he no longer bothered to pair it with the commandments dependent on the land.

In his last year, Kalischer wrote unabashedly about the messianic function of the agricultural revival of the Yishuv. He and Guttmacher were delighted to have the assistance of Rabbi Yakkir Gheron, a resident of Jerusalem and the former chief rabbi of Constantinople. Gheron began the purchase of a plot of land near Jerusalem, but he died before the arrangements were completed. Kalischer eulogized him as 'almost the only hope' of Hevrat Yishuv Erets Yisra'el and of the world as well, since, he wrote, 'from this [the settled land] redemption will gradually flourish, as I have explained at length in my books'.[139] Yet he found others to take Gheron's place, and several weeks later he was able to publish an open letter in *Hamagid* that Hevrat Yishuv Erets Yisra'el had begun the cumbersome acquisition process. He called for readers to send donations to cover the balance of the cost, and closed his letter as follows:

I hope that the Lord on high will bestow success upon us. The judge of all the earth will prepare his throne in the land and reveal himself in the land by turning its desert into a lush garden. May all contributors be decreed a long and pleasant life. Signed [these are the words of] him who hopes for eternal redemption, the servant of God's servants, the insignificant Tsevi Hirsch Kalischer.[140]

---

[138] Kalischer to Seligmann Baer Bamberger (1873), repr. in *Zionist Writings*, 436–7.
[139] *Hamagid*, 12 (1874), repr. ibid. 502.   [140] *Hamagid*, 37 (1874), repr. ibid. 546.

Meanwhile Kalischer was overjoyed to hear that the Alliance had agreed that its agricultural school would soon begin observing the sabbatical year, one of the commandments dependent on the Land of Israel. These accomplishments represented the first real progress towards the creation of a settled land.

THE SACRIFICES

The debates about sacrificial worship that ensued at the appearance of *Derishat tsiyon* were part of the continuing dispute over religious modernization. Although the contenders focused on obscure, theoretical points and subtle turns of phrase, they understood the real stakes of the battle. The objections raised against Kalischer's proposal were not different in substance from those raised before 1862. A crucial difference, however, was that they emanated from the Orthodox rabbinate in no uncertain terms.

Derishat tsiyon was published by the Kolonisations-Verein für Palästina in order to promote the cause of Jewish agricultural settlement in the Yishuv, but only a small segment of the book dealt with the subject. Kalischer wrote the book to provide a religious rationale and textual support for his messianic beliefs in order to generate public support for activities that would lead to the sacrificial worship that would trigger redemption. The section of the book dealing with sacrifice was longer than all the previous chapters combined. Any reader, whether or not he or she could understand the halakhic arguments, would come away with the impression that great and renowned rabbis had agreed that the resumption of sacrificial worship was permissible and desirable. Despite Kalischer's declaration that the present task was to focus on creating a settled land, the structure of the book brought the focus back to the renewal of the sacrificial offerings. The creation of a settled land was never an end in itself; it was the first step to the restoration of the sacrificial service.

The controversy generated by *Derishat tsiyon* was due to its message about sacrificial worship, not to its promotion of agricultural communes. Hebrew newspapers from 1862 and 1863 record the tremendous enthusiasm and alarm the book provoked. One Russian critic explained in late 1862 that he was motivated to send his objections to the Jerusalem-based paper *Halevanon* that the Jerusalem rabbis supported the renewal of sacrifices. 'Last month', he wrote, 'I heard from someone who had just returned from the Holy Land that the rabbis living there in holiness already agreed to rebuild the destroyed altar of God and to offer the *pesaḥ* sacrifice.'[141] The paper's editor, Yehiel Brill, clarified the source of this rumour in his comments accompanying a disapproving article.

---

[141] *Halevanon*, 6 (1863), 37. The writer was Rabbi David Friedmann (1828–1917), who was later to write a separate pamphlet vigorously objecting to the renewal of sacrifices.

In his capacity as editor of *Halevanon*, Brill was the spokesman for the Ashkenazi non-hasidic rabbinic leaders of Jerusalem. His comments reflect the hostility these men felt towards the prospect of the efforts to re-establish sacrificial worship:

Whoever told his honour the rabbi this story lied when he said that the Jerusalemites are considering making 'gaily patched altars' [Ezek. 16: 6] in order to sacrifice *zevaḥim* and *olot* [sacrifices and burnt offerings] without a divine altar as God's law teaches. When the book *Derishat tsiyon* by Rabbi Tsevi Hirsch Kalischer, may God protect and preserve him, arrived here, the masses heard and concluded wrongly that the law had been decided according to him and that the *pesaḥ* sacrifice had been permitted here in our state of impurity, but God forbid that anyone should think this.[142]

Brill's derision of the Jewish masses and their enthusiasm for the renewal of sacrifices is obvious in his comparison of a new altar with the 'gaily patched altars'—these were the many illegitimate altars built by errant Jews in ancient times. Brill carefully differentiated between Kalischer and the rumour, and in a continuation of the editorial note, he explained that this differentiation was why the rabbis had not made any public statements about all the speculation:

The rabbis and the great rabbinical court here in the holy city, may it be speedily rebuilt, have not hurried to respond to the above-mentioned book. Its author is a great man, a rabbi brilliant in Torah, piety, and wisdom. They have concluded that he only wrote his words to fulfil the saying, 'We offer the bullocks of our lips' [Hos. 14: 3]—his piety and love are 'flashes of fire from a divine flame' [S. of S. 8: 6] that burn in him to ten levels of holiness—pursue Torah and reap a reward.[143]

According to Brill, the rabbis believed that Kalischer never intended to suggest the actual restoration of the cult; he studied the possibility only as an act of piety, and he argued the legal issues for their own sake and not for their practical application. In fact, the rabbis knew that the author was quite serious about the practical application of his halakhic study. Brill's statement was a gracious attempt to allow Kalischer to retract his proposal and save face.

This dismissal of Kalischer's intent was also an attempt to dispel the public enthusiasm. Guttmacher had loyal followers in the city among the hasidim, and they certainly recognized that his words were not merely pious sentiments. The 1862 uproar was connected with the earlier, 1857 rumour that grew out of Kalischer and Guttmacher's collaboration. Since that time, support for the re-establishment of the sacrificial cult had grown. Indeed, the chief rabbi of the Sephardi community in Palestine, Rabbi Hayim David Hazan, endorsed in early 1863 the message of *Derishat tsiyon*, including the renewal of sacrifices.

---

[142] *Halevanon*, 6 (1863), 37.

[143] Ibid. This interpretation of Hosea 14: 3, taken from BT *Yoma* 86*b* (see also Rashi's comment), is discussed above in Ch. 2.

Hamagid, a Europe-based newspaper whose editors welcomed Kalischer's book, promptly published Hazan's letter at Kalischer's initiative, while the Jerusalem-based *Halevanon* never mentioned it at all.[144] The gap between the Ashkenazi non-hasidic rabbis and the Jewish masses is also apparent in the comments of Rabbi Meir Auerbach, the leader of the former group, who wrote an open letter to Guttmacher in *Halevanon* later that year:

> We felt no obligation then to explain to our brothers in the Diaspora to what extent we agree or disagree [with Kalischer]. Through the force of his love for Zion and Jerusalem and his trembling before the holy, this rabbi's honourable reputation has become exaggerated in the hearts of our brothers Israel who say, 'the coming of redemption is dependent upon him'. Scripture says, 'there is a time to be silent' [Eccles. 3: 7], and we do not argue with that.[145]

The rabbis were wary of Kalischer because of his book's powerful impact on the public. Had his reputation been weaker, the rabbis might have responded earlier and more aggressively. However, Kalischer was one of them, and they did not want to denounce him as a charlatan. Many of the Jerusalem Ashkenazi rabbis were recent immigrants—Auerbach had emigrated in 1860 from a town just south-east of Thorn—and they might have known first-hand that, unlike Guttmacher, who swayed under pressure, Kalischer would not budge. The rabbis recognized *Derishat tsiyon* for exactly what it purported to be: an effort to convince pious Jews that true piety and love of Torah involved messianic activism along realistic lines. Had Kalischer's halakhic arguments for the renewal of sacrifices appeared in another context, the rabbis might have commended him for defending the faith. However, the author had left no doubt in the book about his objectives, and the rabbis regarded these as inflammatory.

The publication of *Derishat tsiyon* generated a shift in Ashkenazi rabbinic discourse. Earlier in the century, anti-Reform polemics included the insistence that sacrificial worship was still a fundamental, central, and meaningful aspect of Judaism, and that the sacrifices could be reinstated if Palestine's rulers gave permission. When Kalischer publicly advocated the restoration of sacrificial worship, and the revival of the sacrificial cult seemed more likely as Jews gained presence in Palestine, the inherently revolutionary consequences of such a move made Ashkenazi rabbis reconsider their earlier rhetoric. They publicly reversed their previous consensus and began to insist that Jewish law

---

[144] Hazan's letter was dated 3 Shevat 5623 (23 Jan. 1863) and was published in *Hamagid*, 11 (1863), the edition appearing on 21 Adar 5623 (12 Mar. 1863). On Sephardi support of Kalischer, see also *Hamagid*, 23 (1865).

[145] *Halevanon*, 4 (1863). This appeared about one month after Hazan's letter was published. Apparently Kalischer had written to them a few months earlier, and when he received no response, he asked Guttmacher to write.

would not permit the resumption of sacrificial worship before the messianic age.[146] They realized that discussions of the issue, in an era of increased interest among religious Jews in a return to Zion, indicated support for realistic messianism and were no longer theoretical. Opponents of the renewal of sacrifices after this date voiced many different reservations: some found the messianic ferment a threat to community stability and smooth relations with the Muslims, some felt discomfort with sacrificial worship, some felt unworthy to replicate the ancient rituals, and so on. These were a later version of the issues raised in the 1782 conflict between Naphtali Herz Wessely and Ezekiel Landau, and between the reformers and conservatives in 1819 and in the 1840s: fear that Jews would be suspected of political disloyalty, questions regarding reason and faith, contestations of religious authority, and disputes about modernity. Just as in earlier cases, this objection to modernity was coded in halakhic or exegetical arguments.

Kalischer's first inkling of a new attitude among traditional rabbis came during his correspondence with Meir Auerbach. Auerbach regarded the notion that redemption was imminent as ridiculous and dangerous, and he rejected realistic messianism. Perhaps all the halakhic problems connected with the sacrifices could be solved and widely approved, Auerbach wrote, but they were meant to be resumed only in the messianic age, and no rabbi would agree to pursue their restoration. He regarded the correspondence published by Kali-

---

[146] Sephardi rabbis were not so inclined. See my 'Attitudes toward a Resumption of Sacrificial Worship in the Nineteenth Century'. The following critiques appeared in Kalischer's lifetime: David Friedmann, 'Derishat tsiyon veyerushalayim', in *Halevanon*, nos. 6, 7, 9 (1863), also found in Friedmann's book of responsa, *She'elat david* (Peterkov, 1913), pt. 1, pp. 14–17; Jacob Ettlinger, *Binyan tsiyon*, 2 vols. (Altona, 1868), i. 1; Jacob Sapir, an essay called 'Hilkhita lemeshiḥa' that was serialized in *Halevanon*, 40–6 (1869–70). These three are lengthy and serious examinations of the issue. Levinger, *From Routine to Renewal*, 121, described Friedmann's responsa as one of the most complete and respected in response to Kalischer. However, it appears to me as if he merely glanced at Kalischer's responsa. He agreed with Kalischer on a major point of discussion (Jews are not commanded to build a Temple) but seemed unaware of the agreement; one of his main contentions was refuted by Moses Sofer—and this was no small matter in the rabbinic world—but he did not explain this; and in general he did not take Kalischer's treatment of the issues into consideration. Others wrote criticisms of Kalischer's sacrifice renewal responsa during his lifetime, and Kalischer referred to these in his additions to *Derishat tsiyon*. A rebuttal of Chajes's responsa on the renewal of sacrifices was published in 1872 by Rabbi Hayim Nathan-zohn, *Avodah tamah* (Altona, 1872). Because of this opposition, during the 1860s and 1870s the renewal of sacrifices became so discredited as a halakhic possibility that even rabbinic leaders sympathetic to active messianism later in the 19th and 20th cc. disavowed any interest in it. In addition, owing both to the waning of kabbalistic study and the increasing acceptance of modern ideas by traditional Jews, very few people felt enough ardour for the sacrifices to take on the opposition and try to restore them. The periodic appearance of halakhic essays against the renewal of the sacrifices, however, unmistakably indicates the persistence of sympathy for this move by isolated groups of Jews.

scher in *Derishat tsiyon* as proof that Eger and Sofer, at least, became involved in the matter as a purely theoretical exercise undertaken for the sake of Torah study; Sofer regarded his own responsum as such, Auerbach claimed, and Eger's letters reveal that he did not even wish to consider the matter. Auerbach pointed out that the pre-messianic renewal of sacrifices was impossible as well: the Jews could not, through natural means like those Kalischer described, win the Muslims' consent to rebuild the altar.[147] Then Auerbach's attack took an unusual turn. He confessed that the unfortunate state of affairs—Muslim possession of the Temple Mount—was one for which rabbis should be grateful. The Jews were disunited and self-control was on the wane, he wrote, and if they were permitted access to the Temple Mount they would not properly observe the commandments. Since they were ignoring many commandments that could already be fulfilled, he saw no reason to add more that would go unheeded. Besides, he argued, the prophets had not admired sacrificial worship much.[148]

These were serious objections. Kalischer's integrity as a faithful transmitter of his teacher's teachings was belittled and his idealism was portrayed as silly enthusiasm. There was not much that he could have replied to these charges, as they could not be rebutted by tangible evidence. However, Auerbach's lack of enthusiasm for sacrificial worship left him wide open to criticism. Auerbach described the fulfilment of the sacrificial commandments as a privilege that the Jews did not deserve at the moment; yet, from a halakhic perspective, one's personal virtue does not determine whether or not a commandment is binding. Auerbach's interpretation of the prophets contradicted an exegetical principle that was central to Jewish apologetics, that these prophetic passages were protests against rituals unaccompanied by the proper moral and religious behaviour. Virtually every advocate of prayer book reform in the nineteenth century cited prophetic support for their denigration of the temple ritual. Their conservative opponents invariably accused them of ignoring the true meaning of the prophecy.[149]

Kalischer did not criticize Auerbach for holding errant opinions. This correspondence was taking place on the pages of *Halevanon*, the highly influential voice of the Ashkenazi Yishuv. His two letters to Auerbach were exceedingly respectful, even obsequious; he closed his first with 'these are the words of a doormat in the dust of scholars' feet, [signed], the insignificant Hirsch Kalischer'.[150] Owing to Auerbach's authority and influence over Yishuv affairs, his approval was necessary for the success of Kalischer's plans and for the survival of the fledgling Kolonisations-Verein für Palästina. Auerbach also had consid-

---

[147] *Halevanon*, 8 (1863).   [148] Ibid. The prophetic texts cited are Jer. 7: 22 and Mal. 1: 10.
[149] See above, Ch. 1.   [150] *Halevanon*, 8 (1863), repr. in *Zionist Writings*, 203.

erable influence with Guttmacher. Twice in the next five years Guttmacher was persuaded by Auerbach not to lend his name or assistance to Kalischer's cause. Thus, Kalischer's response to Auerbach may not be an accurate reflection of his feelings. He stressed their geographic and kinship ties and their similar hopes for improved living conditions in the Yishuv, and promised to be more moderate in raising the hopes of the masses. Then, with characteristic obstinacy, he ended the letter with a recapitulation of his entire messianic theory.[151]

A more vulnerable critic of Kalischer's messianic theory was Rabbi Jacob Ettlinger, and to him Kalischer spoke his mind. Ettlinger (1798–1891) was a prominent German rabbi who, along with his students Samson Raphael Hirsch and Azriel Hildesheimer, was laying the foundations of German neo-Orthodoxy. His influence and prominence increased after the conference of Reform rabbis in 1844, when he rallied and presided over a protest meeting of almost 200 rabbis. Soon thereafter he established the first official newspaper of Orthodox Judaism, *Der treue Zions-Wächter*.[152] Following the publication of *Derishat tsiyon* in 1862, Ettlinger sent his criticisms to Kalischer privately in a letter, and Kalischer responded. Several years later Ettlinger published a revised version of the letter in his newspaper and as the first entry in his collected responsa, without referring to Kalischer's rebuttal. This omission alone was offensive, and there was another issue: Ettlinger had recently become a leader of a residential building project in Jerusalem and became a vocal supporter of the Jerusalem Ashkenazim.[153] Kalischer's agricultural settlement plan did not fit his conception of the Yishuv, and it competed with his housing project for funds and community support. Objecting to Kalischer's halakhic opinion was an oblique attack on the legitimacy of his project.

Kalischer and Ettlinger's written exchange, however, focused primarily on the latter's novel interpretation of a biblical text. Ettlinger's main point was that after the destruction of the Second Temple in 70 CE, Jews were enjoined not to offer sacrifices until the messianic age, even if they had permission from the ruling authorities and could solve all the halakhic problems. He based this opinion on the divine warning in Leviticus 26: 31 against building illegitimate altars, 'and I will make your sanctuaries desolate, and I will not smell your savoury odours'. Ettlinger explained that the passage should actually be read 'once I make your Temple desolate, I will not smell your savoury odours'. He pointed out that Leviticus 26: 31 applied only when the Temple Mount was

[151] *Halevanon*, 10 (1863), repr. in *Zionist Writings*, 204. It is unclear exactly how Auerbach and Kalischer were related; Bromberg, *Rabbi Tsevi Hirsch Kalischer*, 98, vaguely refers to this link, but I have not found this claim elsewhere.

[152] Eliav, *Love of Zion and Men of Hod*, 63.   [153] Ibid. 61–3.

made truly desolate, and this did not occur until the Romans destroyed the Second Temple. Then the Sages realized that the prophecy of Leviticus had been fulfilled, and it would have been pointless, and disobedient, to offer sacrifices.[154] The thrust of his message was that Judaism was, from its beginning, meant to evolve from sacrificial worship to prayer.

Ettlinger's opinion evinced a disturbing similarity to Reform writings on the sacrifices. Both demonstrated a lack of enthusiasm for the return of sacrificial worship. Both regarded sacrifice as a form of worship suitable only for the early stages of Israel's religious development. Both tried to legitimize this opinion by rooting it in the Bible: for Ettlinger, the priestly code foretold its own demise, while Reform spokesmen regarded the prophets as the agents of spiritual maturation. Both depicted the early Sages recognizing and accepting the start of the new era. While Reform theorists regarded the cessation of sacrifice as absolute, Ettlinger anticipated the restoration of the Temple in the messianic age. However, this was not enough of a difference to hide another significant similarity between Ettlinger and the reformers: his decision-making method here was decidedly unconventional. His opinion was not based on a legal precedent, but, like those of many who justified liturgical innovation, on a principle derived from his own exegesis.[155] This distinguished Ettlinger from almost all Kalischer's other critics among the rabbinate; even those whose objections were primarily based on their objection to active messianism found a halakhic difficulty on which to hang their opinion. The only other critic to refer to non-halakhic considerations was Auerbach. And Auerbach, like Ettlinger and the liturgical reformers, had indicated his gratitude that the sacrifices disdained by the prophets could no longer be offered.

Whereas Kalischer had not objected to Auerbach's opinion, he did not hold back his contempt for Ettlinger's viewpoint. Over the course of the 1860s his remarks about Ettlinger grew shriller and sounded increasingly like his condemnation of Reform leaders:

from the examination of an insignificant point [in the Babylonian Talmud] in *Megilah* based on his own interpretation, he is building a battering ram to destroy a strong and

---

[154] My reconstruction of Ettlinger's initial argument (1862) is based on Kalischer's 1866 comments, the 1868 version, and Ettlinger's article in the Hebrew supplement to *Der treue Zions-Wächter* called *Shomer tsiyon hane'eman*, 16 (1847), where he first presented his interpretation of Lev. 26: 31. He based his reading of Leviticus on BT *Meg.* 28a. The discussion there centres on the continued sanctity of the Temple site, and therefore, Ettlinger argued, the proof text from Lev. 26: 31 must also refer to the Temple site.

[155] Examples of this type of exegesis among Reform leaders are numerous. Yonah Emanuel, 'Rabbi Jacob Ettlinger's Stance against the Present-Day Renewal of Sacrifices' (Heb.), *Hama'ayan* (Nisan 5732 [Mar.–Apr. 1972]), 53, points out the uniqueness of Ettlinger's type of response in the Orthodox camp.

holy building that was a precious cornerstone of all the great authorities I have cited and the Jerusalem Talmud, in order to mount a siege against the lofty, exalted, and holy, by introducing *an innovation in our holy Torah*. Not even a prophet is permitted to add or subtract from the 613 commandments, saying 'a change in time requires a change in the law'.[156]

The reformers misunderstood the intent of the prophets who criticized sacrificial worship, Kalischer continued, and Ettlinger's interpretation of the passage in Leviticus repeated their error. How could Ettlinger not realize what he was doing? 'God forbid that he lend a hand to the sinners who at present say that God does not desire sacrificial worship . . . for his words will give them, God forbid, a pretext, for the way of the evil ones is to fabricate a long testimony to their liking from a single point.'[157] He was concerned that Ettlinger's prominence would strengthen the 'destroyers of law'. He also knew that the religious outlook distancing the sacrifices was the same outlook blocking the agricultural development of the Yishuv. He implied as much by raising the Yishuv issue in the same essay:

And this is also a source of wonder about Rabbi Ettlinger: why doesn't he gird his loins and stop the gap by working actively for the settlement of the Holy Land through the purchase of fields and vineyards for the sake of the fulfilment of the commandments dependent on the land? It is known that he is a great scholar of influence and many will heed his voice. Through him others will receive merit and will sanctify the holy.[158]

Kalischer scolded Ettlinger in virtually the same language he used against 'the faction of the first ripe grapes', the Jerusalem recipients of *ḥalukah* funds.

Kalischer did not seem to realize the difficulties his proposals raised for west European Jews such as Ettlinger, Samson Raphael Hirsch, and Azriel Hildesheimer. These men were concerned with encouraging a form of belief and practice suitable for modern and worldly Jews. They upheld the authority of halakhah and the traditional principles of Jewish faith, but they also tried to minimize the practical effect of practices and beliefs that might reflect negatively on the emancipated Jewish community.[159] Passivity in regard to the messianic hope was just as essential to their needs as it was for Reform Jews.

---

[156] *Shivat tsiyon* (1868), repr. in *Zionist Writings*, 151. The emphasis is Kalischer's.

[157] Ibid.   [158] Ibid. 148.

[159] Of the three men, Hirsch was the most determined to create a modernized orthodoxy. The analysis of the contacts between the two men by Meir Hildesheimer, 'Rabbi Tsevi Hirsch Kalischer and Rabbi Samson Raphael Hirsch', 196–9, shows Hirsch's attempt to avoid any association with Kalischer. Unlike Hildesheimer and Ettlinger, Hirsch refused to recognize the work of the Alliance Israélite Universelle (on the grounds that the leaders were irreligious) and did not participate in activities on behalf of the Yishuv, except to co-operate in raising money for the victims of the periodic crises suffered there. For Hirsch's treatment of the sacrifices, see above, Ch. 3 n. 36.

Ironically, the Jerusalem Ashkenazi rabbis were also indebted to passive messianism. When Meir Auerbach confessed that the Jews of his day were too impious and impure to be worthy of the sacrificial offerings, he was ensuring the continuation of the constant devotion to prayer and study, the patronage of the Diaspora, and the persistence of exilic rabbinic forms of Judaism. On these issues, the separatist Ashkenazi rabbis living in Palestine had more in common with European Reform and neo-Orthodox Jews than with Kalischer.

The lines were drawn in this contest. Each side recognized the stratagems of the other, the obfuscation, and the excuses. Neither would budge. Writing several months before his death, Kalischer told his story to Moses Sofer's son, Rabbi Simon Sofer, in the hope of winning the support of the next generation:

I received a letter from Rabbi S. Berman that he spoke to you of Hevrat Yishuv Erets Yisra'el and you received the matter favourably owing to your great love for the Holy Land, as did your father, author of *Ḥatam sofer*, in which is recorded his response to our great Rabbi Akiva Eger, who discussed the matter and in the end agreed [with me] and consulted the holy Hatam Sofer. The two agreed on the matter, but the Sultan prevented [the implementation of the decision], but now the situation has changed in its favour. . . . But people said that this [Hevrat Yishuv Erets Yisra'el] would reduce contributions to [the Torah scholars]. . . . This great sin surely caused the [excessive] rain and snow that has never occurred before in the Holy Land. It is a sign of the sin, and God is indicating this clearly, saying, 'Go up to the land, for the ruler has permitted the purchase of fields and vineyards'. . . . One thing I ask of you: please do not pay heed to the words of the deceivers, but follow the lead of your father who strengthened the holy. For when many study the holy words and observe the commandments, God will then send his spirit and we will inherit the altar place for a savoury offering before him, and gradually redemption light will illuminate us, may it come speedily in our day, amen.[160]

[160] Kalischer to Rabbi Simon Sofer of Kraków (1874), repr. in *Zionist Writings*, 518.

Conclusion

IN 1836 Kalischer could not have imagined that it would take almost forty years to buy a small plot of land in Palestine and achieve just a fraction of the goal he had outlined to Amschel Mayer Rothschild. How much easier it would have been had the messiah appeared without warning from heaven to blow the great shofar and gather the scattered of Israel! It was just this magical thinking, however, that he regarded as a distortion of God's teachings. According to him, the prophets, sages, Torah scholars, and philosophers knew better and presented a far more rational view of the progress of history. Jews were required to take responsibility for their past failings and for their future by taking the first steps towards the restoration of the land, the economy, the system of worship, and the kingdom that they were meant to have. The task was made easier because God had indicated his readiness to facilitate the process.

Kalischer came to his vision because of a convergence of factors. Immersed in rabbinic culture and imbued with the conviction that reason and faith could be reconciled, he articulated a religious ideology that legitimated activism, granted people a large measure of control over their fate, and favoured pragmatic tactics. It was both modern and pious, rooted in medieval Jewish philosophy and amenable to the optimism of the nineteenth century, and responsive to the needs of the moment. His facility with the Hebrew language enabled him to blend disparate and contradictory fragments of sacred literature into a rich and meaningful vision of present, past, and future. Living in the Posen region and West Prussia during a peaceful era under conservative rule, he could reasonably conclude that the persistence of religious social norms, Jewish civic emancipation, the rise of Jews to positions of power, and the burgeoning interest of European rulers in establishing an outpost in the Middle East were all evidence of God's unseen hand in advancing the Jews towards a better age.

The distinctly non-rational and non-modern belief in the power of sacrificial worship, however, held a intense allure for Kalischer. At the centre of his rationalistic, modern ideology was a markedly old-fashioned ritual that was a throwback to primitive religiosity. His teachers, men who dreamt of engaging in unceasing Torah study that was likened to 'offering the bullocks of our lips' and who defended that mode of worship against contemporary detractors, brought the issue to the fore. But Kalischer's interest in the sacrifices was independent of them. Something in his imagination was riveted by the thought of bringing one's produce to the priest, watching the smoke waft up from the altar, and feeling free of sin as one clung in devotion to God. The irony is that the ideal that was nurtured in him by his teachers was the same that eventually estranged him from conservative as well as liberal Jewish religious leaders.

At various times during his life, Kalischer adopted the tactic of hiding his messianic goals or of revealing them only to select audiences. In the decades following his death, his ideas seemed to gain more appeal. In 1891 a collection of rabbinic testimonies supportive of the Hibat Tsiyon movement was published, and there were a significant number who sketched out a messianic scenario identical with or very similar to Kalischer's.[1] These men did not have wide influence, and, unlike Kalischer, they did not produce a sizeable amount of writing on the subject, and so it is hard to know whether they represented a larger group. What is clear, however, is that religious Jews who gained prominence in Hibat Tsiyon and the Zionist movement, men like Shmuel Mohilever (1824–98) and Isaac Jacob Reines (1839–1915), took pains publicly to dissociate their activism from the messianic idea.[2] It may be that their silence was, like Kalischer's occasional silences, a tactic designed to avoid provoking opposition and denunciation. Rabbinic support for the agricultural settlement of the Yishuv was sizeable during the 1890s, but as secular Jews took the leadership of the movement and rumours of the settlers' violation of halakhah spread, this support dissipated. By 1901, the majority of east European rabbis denounced

[1] In the first forty pages of *Shivat tsiyon*, ed. Avraham Yitzhak Slutzki (Warsaw, 1891), virtually all letters are by men who espouse messianic interpretations of current events and regard the agricultural development of the Yishuv as preliminary to the messianic age: Naftali Tsevi Judah Berlin (pp. 17–18), three rabbis from Kovna (pp. 19–23), Jonathan Eliasberg (pp. 25–32) Mordecai Eliasberg (pp. 33–5), Pinhas Rozovski (pp. 36–8). Shimoni, *The Zionist Ideology*, 139, reads the editor's introductory essay as an effort to minimize the messianic content of the rabbinic testimonies in the volume, but I do not see this.

[2] Shimoni, *The Zionist Ideology*, 143–4 (and footnotes) adduces intriguing evidence that Reines, in his private correspondence, accepted Kalischer's distinction between miraculous redemption and 'the beginning of the redemption by natural means'. Religious Jews sympathetic to Zionism tend to ignore these distinctions, regarding their forebears as maintaining convictions similar to theirs. For example, Shmuel Hacohen Weingarten, 'The Beginning of Redemption', in Yitzhak Raphael and Shlomo Z. Shragai (eds.), *The Book of Religious Zionism* (Heb.), 2 vols. (Jerusalem, 1977), i. 112, a religious historian of the movement, has explained that 'among the [early religious Zionists] were those who omitted mentioning their primary objective—bringing redemption; they were content to mention in their writings only the objective of working for the settlement of the land'.

Zionism on many grounds, and among these was the accusation that Zionism was an illegitimate attempt to 'hasten the end'.[3]

This functional explanation for the marginalization of messianism does not entirely account for the unpopularity of messianic ideologies at the end of the nineteenth and beginning of the twentieth century. There is also the plausibility factor. Realistic messianism appeared during the first two-thirds of the nineteenth century because events occurred then that could be interpreted as positive, divine signals of the redemption. The events of the last third of the century did not lend themselves as well to an optimistic interpretation. By the 1870s and 1880s religious Jews increasingly perceived themselves as living in a time of crisis: they saw widespread disregard of *mitsvot*, a serious curtailment of institutions devoted to Torah study, and the growth of antisemitism. In Kalischer's day, the creation of a lush *erets noshevet* peopled by religious Jews performing the commandments seemed within the realm of the possible; by the end of the century, it did not—and this was, ironically, owing in part to the growing numbers of secular Jews devoted to Zionist ideals. Yet the dire political developments posed a greater challenge. It simply became more challenging to find unblemished 'hidden miracles' to substantiate an enthusiastic outlook. There is plenty of evidence that individual Jews accepted the theoretical tenets of realistic messianism—the notion that redemption would occur gradually and naturally—but it is harder to prove that they were confident that they were living at the start of a redemptive process that would culminate in their lifetime.[4] And even those who believed in a gradual redemption did not subscribe to the sequence of events presented by Kalischer; significantly, not until well into the twentieth century did any figure publicly call for the restoration of sacrificial worship.

Those who regarded themselves as the next link in the chain of leadership begun by Kalischer and Guttmacher were, for the most part, motivated by the concern to solve problems and ameliorate suffering. Indeed, an abiding sense of fear animates the writings of Mohilever and Reines. They repeatedly refer to the widespread poverty and anti-Jewish violence in Russia, the dislocation and distress resulting from mass migration, and widespread antisemitism. Mohilever defended the activities of Hibat Tsiyon as *pikuaḥ nefesh* (necessary to prevent the endangerment of life), describing the Jewish people as trapped in a house on fire. In such a case, he argued, one has an overriding duty to dis-

---

[3] Shimoni, *The Zionist Ideology*, 139–44. Yosef Salmon, 'Zionism and Anti-Zionism in Eastern Europe', in Shmuel Almog, Jehuda Reinharz, and Anita Shapira (eds.), *Zionism and Religion* (Hanover, NH, 1998), 25–43 at 31.

[4] Shimoni, *The Zionist Ideology*, 140, quotes at length from a Hebrew booklet published in Warsaw in 1899 by a layman, Eliezer Eliyahu Friedman, that is virtually identical with Kalischer's. One gets the impression that this view was not uncommon among religious maskilim.

pense with theological niceties and such principles as non-association with freethinkers.[5] Reines, too, wrote with great feeling about the pervasiveness of Jew-hatred and the urgent necessity to relieve Jewish distress. Kalischer's writings could not be drawn upon to explain antisemitism (it was not part of his experience), but his non-messianic religious rationales were borrowed and refined. Mohilever and Reines could not, as Kalischer did, claim that Palestine was pristine and the regime would not tolerate religious deviancy, but they did agree that mass emigration still offered an opportunity to build a rejuvenated, Torah-centred Jewry. They ignored Kalischer's messianic interpretations or relegated them to prayerful closing words; in essence, their messianic stance was that God would eventually send the messiah and create a perfect world, but 'in the meantime' it was time to improve the Jewish situation. This decidedly non-messianic religious activism constituted the Religious Zionist philosophy of Mizrahi, a branch of the Zionist movement started in 1902 under the leadership of Reines. The ideology of late nineteenth- and early twentieth-century Religious Zionism does not fit neatly into the framework of either secular Zionism or Jewish tradition. Passive messianism was respected as a theological doctrine—God is the ultimate power responsible for the exile, and human efforts to hasten redemption are improper—and retained, of course, in the prayers and rituals that religious Jews did not dare to modify. In the realm of practical politics, however, this outlook of powerlessness was abandoned. There, Mizrahi urged its followers to take responsibility for their national fate, to adopt pragmatic means for the return to Zion, and to work for a mass ingathering of Jews to the land of Israel and a restoration of political autonomy there. They regarded the establishment of a Jewish commonwealth as a solution to the immediate religious, social, and economic problems. This hybridized stance of Religious Zionism prevailed until shortly after the 1967 Six-Day War.[6]

In the interim, there were a few individuals who wrote more extensively about realistic messianism and in whose writings Kalischer's imprint is visible. Rabbi Abraham Isaac Kook (1865–1935) borrowed from Kalischer's messianic

[5] See his message to the First Zionist Congress (1897), as quoted in Hertzberg, *The Zionist Idea*, 402.

[6] There are numerous studies and anthologies of Religious Zionism in addition to the ones cited throughout this work, among them Abraham Bick (ed.), *Exponents and Philosophy of Religious Zionism* (Brooklyn, 1942); Mordechai Eliav and Yitzhak Raphael (eds.), *Sefer shragai* [Essays on the History of Religious Zionism and Aliyah to the Land of Israel] (Heb.) (Jerusalem, 1981); Yehuda Leib Hacohen Maimon [Fishman] (ed.), *The Evolution of Religious Zionism*, 2 vols. (Heb.) (Jerusalem, 1937–8), repr. as *Israel, Torah, Zion* (Heb.) (Jerusalem, 1989); Abraham Rubinstein (ed.), *In the Paths of Renewal: Studies in Religious Zionism* (Heb.) (Jerusalem, 1983); Yosef Tirosh (ed.), *Religious Zionism: An Anthology* (Jerusalem, 1975).

arguments, his interpretative key, and his manner of demonstrating that the conventional understanding of the messianic process was in error.[7] Through the use of kabbalistic principles he found solace in the unfortunate—from a religious point of view—situation in Palestine: secular Zionists, Kook taught, are part of a larger cosmic schema and imbued with a divine spirit that they do not recognize but which has drawn them to the Holy Land. The inherent holiness of the land would ultimately filter out the impurities of exile attached to them, and they would return to Judaism. Ultimately, he wrote, 'an awakening from below will cause an awakening above'.[8] He also accounted for the evil around him by expounding upon the mishnaic prediction that redemption would be preceded by a generation known for its brazenness and would be a time of great destruction. Kalischer had felt no need to refer to the 'birth pangs of the messiah'; for him, tragedy was a divine punishment, a sign of impatience with opponents of the land's redemption. For Kook, however, destruction and rupture with the past were inherent in the messianic process.[9] He required this dialectical dynamic in order to understand God's purpose in the deep irreligiousness as well as the intense idealism of secular Zionists in Palestine.

That this dialectical element became an indelible aspect of twentieth-century realistic messianism is most poignantly evident in the writings of Rabbi Yisakhar Shelomoh Teichthal (1885–1943).[10] While in hiding from the Nazis in Budapest, he recanted the extreme anti-Zionist teachings central to his Hungarian hasidic community. Kalischer's *Derishat tsiyon*, he declared, was the model for his new discovery of proper belief that he recorded as *Em habanim semehah* (The Happy Mother of Children). Out of blindness and selfishness, he wrote in his book, Jewish leaders had rooted themselves in the Diaspora, rejected all initiatives for self-redemption, and erroneously regarded Zionist efforts to reclaim the Holy Land as a violation of the Torah. Like Kook, he regarded the non-observant Zionist settlers as a catalyst of redemption. Teichthal believed that God had decreed the exiles and hardships of the past to

---

[7] The examples are too numerous to mention here. Unfortunately, Kook did not credit his predecessors.

[8] Zvi Yaron, *The Philosophy of Rabbi Kook* (Jerusalem, 1991); Ravitzky, *Messianism, Zionism, and Jewish Religious Radicalism*, 86–109. Ravitzky (p. 103) regards Kook's optimism as an indication that he was 'a typical figure of the nineteenth century, when the prospects for the human spirit, human achievement, and human freedom were thought to be constantly improving'.

[9] Ravitzky, *Messianism, Zionism, and Jewish Religious Radicalism*, 107–9.

[10] Yisakhar Shelomoh Teichthal, *The Happy Mother of Children* (Heb.) (Warsaw, 1943). An English translation is available as Yisakhar Shelomoh Teichthal, *Em Habanim Semeha: Restoration of Zion as a Response during the Holocaust*, trans. and ed. Pesach Schindler (Hoboken, NJ, 1999). For a comparison with two of Teichthal's contemporaries, see Gershon C. Bacon, 'Birth Pangs of the Messiah: The Reflections of Two Polish Rabbis on their Era', *Studies in Contemporary Jewry*, 7 (1991), 86–99.

induce the Jews to return to Zion, and he was convinced that the present hor-
rors were designed to show the rabbinic leadership that they had erred griev-
ously in promoting passive messianism. He set great store by the concept 'birth
pangs of the messiah', hoping that Nazi persecution was his generation's pur-
gation immediately before the End of Days. It is unlikely that he was familiar
with Kook's writings, but the men were contemporaries, versed in the same
rabbinic texts, struggling to understand the divine element in the evil and the
good facing them.[11]

The Holocaust prevented Teichthal's book from finding an audience or
political expression for quite some time. Realistic messianism induces political
activism when there is a relatively strong or potentially improved Jewish political position in relation to the Land of Israel. This explains why it emerged as
such a significant force following the Israeli victory in the 1967 war. A generation of leaders, guided in part by the teachings of Rabbi Tsevi Yehudah Kook
(son of Abraham Isaac Kook), rejected classical Religious Zionism in favour of
an explicitly messianic ideology. Calling themselves Gush Emunim (the bloc
of the faithful), they regarded the 1917 Balfour Declaration, the victory in the
1948 war of independence, and the capture of Jerusalem and the ancient
lands of Samaria and Judah in the 1967 war as hidden miracles presaging 'the
first flowering of redemption'. Their political activism was designed to promote Jewish settlement in the new territories as a step towards the complete
conquest of the Holy Land and ingathering of the Jews. They regarded the
exchange of the land for peace, or making other concessions to Palestinian residents, as regressive and sinful.[12] On the heels of each new war, policy change,
and ruling political coalition, dozens of other groups have formed with similar
agendas. They teach that advances are evidence of God's guiding hand and
setbacks are tests of the faithful or birth pangs of the messiah, and they support
their claims with collections of proof texts from Torah, Talmud, and Midrash.
Kalischer's plan to restore sacrificial worship on the Temple Mount once again
provokes enthusiasm among circles of Jews in Jerusalem and elsewhere.[13]

Today's dedicated adherents of realistic messianism live in a situation quite

[11] Pesach Schindler, the editor and translator of Teichthal's volume, leaves the question open
to discussion; see Editor's Introduction, p. xv n. 6. Kook's writings were not widely disseminat-
ed until decades after his death. Teichthal did not refer to Kook at all, and he was very careful
to credit his sources.

[12] Gideon Aran, 'From Religious Zionism to Zionist Religion: The Roots of Gush Emunim',
Studies in Contemporary Jewry, 2 (1986), 116–43; Tsevi Ra'anan, *Gush Emunim* (Heb.) (Tel Aviv,
1980).

[13] There has been an interesting meeting of the minds between Jewish messianists and secular,
right-wing Zionists who, since the beginning of the Mandate period, agitated for Jewish hegemony in the lands on the east and west bank of the Jordan. Christian millenarians, who see the

unlike that in Kalischer's own day. Their experiences and activism occur in a far more violent and divisive context. The destruction of European Jewry discredited the ideology of passive messianism, and bloody battles between Palestinian Arabs and Jews have introduced new challenges to older concepts of the Holy Land. But even before the Holocaust and the first concerted attacks against Jewish residents of Palestine, many Jews stopped believing that their political condition was determined by God on the basis of Jews' obedience or disobedience to the commandments. Secular ideas undermined the religious conviction that God controls history; and most religious Jews, unlike Teichthal, had difficulty believing that the Holocaust was God's punishment for Jewish wrongdoing. Even Jews who saw the hand of God in history ceased to believe that working for Jewish sovereignty over Palestine was sinful. Jews today are nearly unanimous in the belief in the legitimacy of Jewish statehood. Currently only a tiny minority of Jews—perhaps only 10,000 in Israel today and several times that number in the United States—comprise the sum total of the staunchly religious anti-Zionists who preach passive messianism. This viewpoint has been so marginalized that most people cannot imagine a time when it held sway.

Within the world of traditional Jewry, Kalischer was a pioneer and an innovator. 'Do not imagine that God, blessed be his name, will suddenly descend from on high and say to his people "Go forth"', he wrote to Amschel Mayer Rothschild in 1836. Years later he declared to a sceptical public, 'The redemption will begin by awakening support among the philanthropists and by gaining the consent of the nations to the gathering of some of the scattered of Israel into the Holy Land.' With reason, faith, and scholarship, he built what he thought was a holy path that would lead humanity to eternal joy.

erection of the Third Temple as a necessary precondition for the Second Coming, are very eager to support the efforts to restore sacrificial worship and rebuild the Temple. See Ehud Sprinzak, *The Ascendance of Israel's Radical Right* (New York, 1991).

Bibliography

ALMOG, SHMUEL, JEHUDA REINHARZ, and ANITA SHAPIRA (eds.), *Zionism and Religion* (Hanover, NH, 1998).

ALON, GEDALIA, 'The Attitude of the Pharisees to Roman Rule and the House of Herod', in *Jews, Judaism, and the Classical World*, trans. Israel Abrahams (Jerusalem, 1977), 18–47.

—— *Studies in Jewish History in the Times of the Second Temple, the Mishnah, and the Talmud* (Meḥkarim betoledot yisra'el bimei bayit hasheni uvitekufat hamishnah vehatalmud), 2 vols. (Tel Aviv, 1957–8).

ARAN, GIDEON, 'From Religious Zionism to Zionist Religion: The Roots of Gush Emunim', *Studies in Contemporary Jewry*, 2 (1986), 116–43.

ARIGUR, ISAAC [ISAAC GUR-ARYEH], 'Rabbi Tsevi Hirsch Kalischer' (Heb.), *Hator*, 7/35, 37, 38, 40, 42, 45, 47 and 8/2–5 (1928). This also appeared in book form as *Tsevi hirsch kalisher* (Heb.) (Jerusalem, 1928).

ASCHKEWITZ, MAX, *Zur Geschichte der Juden in Westpreussen* (Marburg an der Lahn, 1967).

ASSAF, SIMCHA, *Sources for the History of Jewish Education* [Mekorot letoledot haḥinukh beyisra'el], 4 vols. (Tel Aviv, 1925–42).

AVI-YONAH, M., *The Jews of Palestine: A Political History from the Bar Kokhba War to the Arab Conquest* (New York, 1976).

Babylonian Talmud, trans. and ed. I. Epstein, 30 vols. (London, 1936–52).

BACKHAUS, FRITZ, 'The Last of the Court Jews: Mayer Amschel Rothschild and his Sons', in Vivian B. Mann, Richard I. Cohen, and Fritz Backhaus (eds.), *From Court Jews to the Rothschilds* (Munich, 1996), 79–95.

BACON, GERSHON C., 'Birth Pangs of the Messiah: The Reflections of Two Polish Rabbis on their Era', *Studies in Contemporary Jewry*, 7 (1991), 86–99.

BARAS, TSEVI (ed.), *Messianism and Eschatology* [Meshiḥiyut ve'eskatologiyah] (Jerusalem, 1984).

BARON, SALO, 'From the History of the Jewish Yishuv in Jerusalem' [Mitoledot hayishuv hayehudi birushalayim], in *Sefer klausner* (Tel Aviv, 1939), 302–12.

BARTYŚ, JULIAN, 'Grand Duchy of Poznań under Prussian Rule: Changes in the Economic Position of the Jewish Population, 1815–1848', *Leo Baeck Institute Yearbook*, 17 (1972), 191–204.

—— 'The Movement of Jewish Agricultural Settlement in the Kingdom of Poland before the Peasant Liberation' (Heb.), *Zion*, 1–2 (1967), 46–75.

BEN-SASSON, HAIM HILLEL (ed.), *A History of the Jewish People* (Cambridge, Mass., 1976).

BERGER, DAVID, 'Miracles and the Natural Order in Nahmanides', in Isadore Twersky (ed.), *Rabbi Moses Nahmanides (RAMBAN): Explorations in his Religious and Literary Virtuosity* (Cambridge, 1983), 107–28.

BICK, ABRAHAM (ed.), *Exponents and Philosophy of Religious Zionism* (Brooklyn, 1942).

BIRNBAUM, PIERRE, and IRA KATZNELSON (eds.), *Paths of Emancipation: Jews, States, and Citizenship* (Princeton, 1995).

BLACK, EUGENE C., 'The Anglicanization of Orthodoxy: The Adlers, Father and Son', in Frances Malino and David Sorkin (eds.), *Profiles in Diversity: Jews in a Changing Europe, 1750–1870* (Detroit, 1997), 295–325.

BLEICH, J. DAVID, *Contemporary Halakhic Problems* (New York, 1977).

——'A Review of Halakhic Literature Pertaining to the Reinstitution of the Sacrificial Order', *Tradition*, 9 (Fall 1967), 103–24.

BLUMBERG, ARNOLD, *Zion Before Zionism, 1838–1880* (Syracuse, NY, 1985).

BRENNER, MICHAEL, STEFI HERSCH-WENZEL, and MICHAEL A. MEYER (eds.), *German-Jewish History in Modern Times*, ii: *Emancipation and Acculturation, 1780–1871* (New York, 1997).

BREUER, MORDECHAI, 'The Debate on the Three Oaths in Recent Generations' [Hadiyun bishelosh hashevuot bedorot ha'aharonim], in *Redemption and State* (Jerusalem, 1979), 49–57.

—— 'Emancipation and the Rabbis' (Eng.), *Niv hamidrashiyah*, 13 (1978–9), 26–51.

—— *Modernity within Tradition: The Social History of Orthodox Jewry in Imperial Germany*, trans. Elizabeth Petuchowski (New York, 1992).

BROMBERG, ABRAHAM ISAAC, *Rabbi Elijah Guttmacher* (Heb.) (Jerusalem, 1969).

—— *Rabbi Jacob Lorbeerbaum* (Heb.) (Jerusalem, 1957).

—— *Rabbi Tsevi Hirsch Kalischer* (Heb.) (Jerusalem, 1960).

CHAJES, TSEVI HIRSCH, *Kol sifrei maharats hayes* [Complete Works of Tsevi Hirsch Chajes], 2 vols. (Jerusalem, 1958).

—— *The Student's Guide through the Talmud*, trans. and ed. Jacob Shachter (London, 1952).

CLARK, CHRISTOPHER, 'Protestant Missions to the Jews in Prussia', *Leo Baeck Institute Yearbook*, 38 (1993), 33–50.

CORTI, EGON CAESAR, *The Reign of the House of Rothschild, 1830–1871* (London, 1928).

Daily Prayer Book: Ha-Siddur Ha-Shalem, trans. and annotated with an introduction by Philip Birnbaum (New York, 1977).

DANZIG, ABRAHAM, *Ḥayei adam* [Human Life] (Vilna, 1810).

—— *Hokhmat adam* [Human Wisdom] (Vilna, 1812).

DAVIES, NORMAN, *God's Playground: A History of Poland*, 2 vols. (New York, 1982).

EDELBERG, SHLOMO, 'The American Colony in Jaffa, 1866–1868' [Hamoshav ha'amerika'it beyafo, 1866–1868], *Hado'ar*, 36/28 (1957), 224–9.

EGER, AKIVA, *Eleh divrei haberit* [These are the Words of the Covenant] (Altona, 1819).

EISENBACH, ARTUR, *The Emancipation of the Jews in Poland, 1780–1870*, trans. Janina Dorosz, ed. Antony Polonsky (Oxford, 1991).

ELIAV, MORDECHAI, *Jewish Education in Germany during the Haskalah and Emancipation* [Haḥinukh hayehudi begermaniyah bimei hahaskalah veha'mantsipatsiyah] (Jerusalem, 1961).

—— *Love of Zion and Men of Hod: German Jewry and the Settlement of Erets Yisrael in the Nineteenth Century* [Ahavat tsiyon ve'anshei hod: yehudei germaniyah vishuv erets-yisra'el bimei hayod-tet] (Tel Aviv, 1970).

—— and YITZHAK RAPHAEL (eds.), *Sefer shragai* [Essays on the History of Religious Zionism and Aliyah to the Land of Israel] (Jerusalem, 1981).

ELLENSON, DAVID, *Between Tradition and Culture: The Dialectics of Modern Religion and Identity* (Atlanta, 1994).

—— 'A Disputed Precedent: The Prague Organ in Nineteenth-Century Central European Legal Literature and Polemics', *Leo Baeck Institute Yearbook*, 40 (1995), 251–64.

—— 'A Jewish Legal Decision by Rabbi Bernard Illowy of New Orleans and its Discussion in Nineteenth-Century Europe', *American Jewish History*, 69 (Dec. 1979), 174–95.

—— *Tradition in Transition: Orthodoxy, Halakhah, and the Boundaries of Modern Jewish Identity* (Lanham, Md., 1989).

EMANUEL, YONAH, 'Rabbi Jacob Ettlinger's Stance against the Present-Day Renewal of Sacrifices' [Al ta'anat 'velo ariaḥ' shel harav ya'akov etlinger neged ḥidush hakorbanot bazeman hazeh], *Hama'ayan* (Nisan 5732 [Mar.–Apr. 1972]), 49–69.

EMDEN, JACOB, *She'elat yavets* [Responsa], 2 vols. (1739–69; repr. Lemburg, 1883).

—— *Sidur amudei shamayim*, 2 vols. (Altona, 1744).

ESTORI (ISAAC BEN MOSES) HAPARHI, *Sefer kaftor vaferaḥ* [Book of the Bud and Flower] (Venice, 1549); *Kaftor vaferaḥ*, ed. A. M. Luncz (Jerusalem, 1897).

ETTLINGER, JACOB, *Binyan tsiyon* [The Building of Zion], 2 vols. (Altona, 1868).

FERGUSON, NIALL, *The House of Rothschild: The World's Banker, 1849–1999* (New York, 1999).

FINN, JAMES, *Stirring Times*, 2 vols. (London, 1878).

FRANKEL, DOV, *The Beginning of Modern Political Zionism* [Reshit hatsiyonut hamedinit hamodernit] (Haifa, 1956).

FRANKEL, JONATHAN, *The Damascus Affair: 'Ritual Murder', Politics, and the Jews in 1840* (Cambridge, 1997).

FRIEDLAND, NATAN, *Kol abirei haro'im* [The Call of Courageous Shepherds] (Leslau, 1870).

FRIEDLANDER, M., 'The Late Chief Rabbi, Dr. N. M. Adler', *Jewish Quarterly Review*, 2 (1890), 369–85.

FRIEDMANN, DAVID, *She'elat david* [Responsa] (Petergov, 1913).

FUNKENSTEIN, AMOS, *Perceptions of Jewish History* (Berkeley and Los Angeles, 1993).

GIEYSZTOR, ALEXANDER, STEFAN KIENIEWICZ, EMANUEL ROSTWOROWSKI, JANUSZ TAZBIR, and HENRYK WERESZYCKI (eds.), *History of Poland* (Warsaw, 1979).

GINZBURG, LOUIS, *Legends of the Jews*, 7 vols. (Philadelphia, 1937).

GOLDENBERG, ROBERT, 'Talmud', in Barry Holtz (ed.), *Back to the Sources: Reading the Classic Jewish Texts* (New York, 1984), 129–75.

GRAETZ, HEINRICH, *History of the Jews*, 6 vols. (Philadelphia, 1898).

—— *Tagebuch und Briefe*, ed. Reuven Michael (Tübingen, 1977).

GRAFF, GIL, *Separation of Church and State: Dina de-Malkhuta Dina in Jewish Law, 1750–1848* (University, Ala., 1985).

GUTTMAN, ALEXANDER, 'The End of the Jewish Sacrificial Cult', *Hebrew Union College Annual*, 38 (1967), 137–48.

HABERMAN, JOSHUA O., *Philosopher of Revelation: The Life and Thought of S. L. Steinheim* (Philadelphia, 1990).

HAGEN, WILLIAM W., *Germans, Poles, and Jews: The Nationality Conflict in the Prussian East 1772–1914* (Chicago, 1980).

HALEVI, JUDAH, *Sefer hakuzari*, trans. and ed. Yehuda Even Shemuel (Tel Aviv, 1972); in English, *The Kuzari: An Argument for the Faith of Israel*, trans. and ed. Hartwig Hirschfeld (New York, 1964).

HEPPNER, A., and J. HERZBERG, *Aus Vergangenheit und Gegenwart der Juden und der jüdischen Gemeinden in den Posener Ländern*, 2 vols. (Koschmin, 1909).

HERTZBERG, ARTHUR, *The Zionist Idea: A Historical Analysis and Reader* (New York, 1960).

HERZFELD, LEVI, *Zwei Predigten über die Lehre vom Messias* (Braunschweig, 1844).

HESS, MOSES, *Rome and Jerusalem: A Study in Jewish Nationalism*, trans. Meyer Waxman (New York, 1943).

HILDESHEIMER, MEIR, 'Rabbi Tsevi Hirsch Kalischer and Rabbi Samson Raphael Hirsch' [Harav tsevi hirsh kalisher veharav shimshon rafa'el hirsh], in *Sefer aviad*, ed. Yitzhak Raphael (Jersualem, 1986), 195–214.

HIRSCH, SAMSON RAPHAEL, *Choreb, oder Versuche ueber Jissroels Pflichten in der Zerstreuung* (Altona, 1837); in English, *Horeb: A Philosophy of Jewish Laws and Observances*, trans. I. Grunfeld, 2 vols. (London, 1962).

—— *Neunzehn Briefe über Judenthum* (Altona, 1836).

HIRSCHKOVITZ, MEIR, *Rabbi Tsevi Hirsch Chajes* (Heb.) (Jerusalem, 1972).

HOLDHEIM, SAMUEL, *Das Ceremonialgesetz im Messiasreich* (Schwerin, 1845).

—— *Über die Beschneidung in religios-dogmatischer Beziehung* (Schwerin and Berlin, 1844).

HUNDERT, GERSHON, 'The Implications of Jewish Economic Activities for Christian–Jewish Relations in the Polish Commonwealth', in Chimen Abramsky, Maciej Jachimczyk, and Antony Polonsky (eds.), *The Jews in Poland* (Oxford, 1986), 55–63.

—— 'Some Basic Characteristics of the Jewish Experience in Poland', *Polin*, 1 (1980), 28–34.

HYMAN, PAULA E., *The Emancipation of the Jews of Alsace: Acculturation and Tradition in the Nineteenth Century* (New Haven and London, 1991).

JACOB, WALTER, and MOSHE ZEMER (eds.), *Conversion to Judaism in Jewish Law: Essays and Responsa* (Pittsburgh, 1994).

KALISCHER, JUDAH LEIB, *Hayad haḥazakah* [The Strong Hand] (Breslau, 1820).

KALISCHER, TSEVI HIRSCH, 'Einiges zur Widerlegung der Ansichten des Herrn Dr. Samuel Holdheim in seinem Werkchen: "Ueber die Beschneidung"', *Literaturblatt des Orients*, 1 (1846), 1–4.

—— *Emunah yesharah* [Proper Belief], i (Krotoszyn, 1843); ii (Lyck, 1871); iii: *Derishat tsiyon veḥevrat erets noshevet* [Seeking Zion, and the Society for a Settled Land] (Lyck, 1862). Citations of *Derishat tsiyon* are from the edition in *Zionist Writings*.

—— *Even boḥan* [A Sturdy Stone] (Krotoszyn, 1842).

—— 'Hakabalah vehafilosofiyah' [Kabbalah and Philosophy], *Tsiyon* (Av/Elul 1841).

—— 'Das Leben Israels und der Rabbinismus', *Der treue Zions-Wächter*, 3 (1846), 58–60.

—— 'Maimonides und sein neuern Gegner', *Israelitische Annalen*, 1 (1840), 5–7.

KALISCHER, TSEVI HIRSCH, *Moznayim lamishpat* [Scales of Justice], 2 vols. (Krotoszyn and Königsberg, 1855).

—— *Seder hagadah shel pesaḥ im biur yakar yetsiat mitsrayim* [The Exodus from Egypt, a Commentary on the Passover Haggadah] (Warsaw, 1864).

—— *Sefer haberit al hatorah* [The Book of the Covenant, a Commentary on the Torah], 5 vols. (Warsaw, 1873–6).

—— *Shelom yerushalayim vekontras shivat tsiyon* [The Peace of Jerusalem, and the pamphlet *The Return to Zion*] (Thorn, 1868).

—— *The Zionist Writings of Rabbi Tsevi Kalischer* [Haketavim hatsiyoni'im shel harav tsevi kalisher: bitosefet mavo, he'arot ubiurim], ed. Israel Klausner (Heb.) (Jerusalem, 1947).

—— 'Zwei Predigten über die Lehre vom Messias u.s.w. von Dr. Herzfeld', Braunschweig, 1844 (book review), in *Literaturblatt des Orients*, 3 (1845), 44–6.

—— and ELIJAH GUTTMACHER, *Statut des Kolonisations-Verein für Palästina* (1867).

KAPLAN, MARION A., *The Making of the Jewish Middle Class: Women, Family, and Identity in Imperial Germany* (New York and Oxford, 1991).

KARO, JOSEPH, *Shulḥan arukh* [The Set Table], 10 vols. (Venice, 1565; repr. New York, 1975, 1984).

KATZ, DAVID S., *Philo-Semitism and the Readmission of the Jews to England, 1603–1655* (Oxford, 1982).

KATZ, JACOB, 'The Changing Position and Outlook of Halakhists in Early Modernity', in Leo Landman (ed.), *Scholars and Scholarship: The Interaction between Judaism and Other Cultures* (New York, 1990), 93–106.

—— 'The Forerunners of Zionism' [Levirur hamusag mevasrei hatsiyonut], in *Shivat tsiyon*, 3 vols. (Jerusalem, 1950–3), i. 91–105; English translation in *Jewish Quarterly Review*, 7 (1978), 10–21.

—— 'The Historical Image of Rabbi Tsevi Hirsch Kalischer' [Demuto hahistorit shel harav tsevi hirsh kalisher], in *Shivat tsiyon*, 3 vols. (Jerusalem, 1950–3), iii. 26–41; English translation, 'Tsevi Hirsch Kalischer', in Leo Jung (ed.), *Guardians of our Heritage* (New York, 1958), 209–27.

—— 'Israel and the Messiah', *Commentary*, 73 (Jan. 1982), 34–41.

—— 'The Ordination Controversy between Rabbi Jacob Berab and Rabbi Levi ibn Habib' [Maḥloket hasemikhah bein rabi ya'akov beirab veharalbaḥ], *Zion*, 17 (1959), 28–45; repr. in *Binah*, 1 (1989), 119–41.

—— 'Orthodoxy in Historical Perspective', *Studies in Contemporary Jewry*, 2 (1986), 3–17.

—— 'Towards a Biography of the Hatam Sofer', in Frances Malino and David

Sorkin (eds.), *Profiles in Diversity: Jews in a Changing Europe, 1750–1870* (Detroit, 1997), 223–66.

—— *Tradition and Crisis: Jewish Society at the End of the Middle Ages*, 2nd edn., trans. B. D. Cooperman (New York, 1993).

KATZ, ROBERT L., 'David Caro's Analysis of the Rabbi's Role', *CCAR Journal*, 13/2 (1966), 41–6.

KELLNER, JACOB, *For Zion's Sake: World Jewry's Efforts to Relieve Distress in the Yishuv, 1869–1882* [Lema'an tsiyon: hitarevut hakelal-yehudit bemetsukat hayishuv 5630–5642/1869–1882] (Jerusalem, 1976).

KLAUSNER, ISRAEL, 'Rabbi Nathan Friedland of Lithuania' [Rabi natan fridland milita], *Ha'umah*, 18 (1966), 227–45.

—— 'Rabbi Zvi Kalisher's *Derishat Zion*', *In the Dispersion*, 5/6 (Spring 1966), 281–9.

KLAUSNER, JOSEPH, *The Messianic Idea in Israel* (New York, 1955).

KRESSEL, GETZEL, 'The First Palestine Settlement Society' [Haḥevrah harishonah leyishuv erets yisra'el], *Zion*, 7 (1941), 197–205.

LAQUEUR, WALTER, *A History of Zionism* (New York, 1976).

LEDERHENDLER, ELI, 'Interpreting Messianic Rhetoric in the Russian Haskalah and Early Zionism', *Studies in Contemporary Jewry*, 7 (1991), 14–33.

—— *The Road to Modern Jewish Politics: Political Tradition and Political Reconstruction in the Jewish Community of Tsarist Russia* (New York, 1989).

LEHMANN, MARCUS, *The Lehmann Haggadah* (Heb. and Eng.) (Jerusalem, 1977). Translation of *Hagadah schel Pessach*, 2nd edn. (Heb. and German) (Frankfurt am Main, 1906).

LEIBOWITZ, YESHAYAHU, *Discussions on* Pirkei avot *and Maimonides* [Siḥot al pirkei avot ve'al harambam] (Tel Aviv, 1979).

LEVENSON, ALAN, 'The Posen Factor', *Shofar*, 17 (Fall 1998), 72–80.

LEVIN, MORDECHAI, *Social and Economic Values of the Haskalah* [Arkhei ḥevrah vekalkalah be'idiologiyah shel tekufat hahaskalah] (Jerusalem, 1975).

LEVINGER, JACOB, *From Routine to Renewal: Pointers in Contemporary Jewish Thought* [Bein shigrah leḥidush: kavim lemaḥshevet hayehudit bizemaneinu] (Jerusalem, 1973).

LEVINSOHN, ISAAC BAER, *Te'udah beyisra'el* [A Testimony in Israel] (Vilna, 1828).

LEWIN, ISAAC, *The Jewish Community in Poland: Historical Essays* (New York, 1985).

—— 'On Rabbi Jacob Lorbeerbaum of Lissa' [Letoledot hagaon ba'al ḥavat da'at], in Menahem M. Kasher, Norman Lamm, and Leonard Rosenfeld (eds.), *The Leo Jung Jubilee Volume* (New York, 1962), 167–86.

LEWIN, LOUIS, *Geschichte der Juden in Lissa* (Pinne, 1907).

LIBERLES, ROBERT, *Religious Conflict in Social Context: The Resurgence of Orthodox Judaism in Frankfurt am Main, 1838–1877* (Westport, Conn., 1985).

LIEBERMANN, ELIEZER, *Nogah hatsedek* [The Splendour of Righteousness] (Dessau, 1818).

—— *Or nogah* [Light of Splendour] (Dessau, 1818).

LIEBMAN, CHARLES S., 'Extremism as a Religious Norm', *Journal for the Scientific Study of Religion*, 20 (1983), 75–86.

LIPSCHITZ, JACOB (ed.), *Maḥzikei hadat* [Upholders of Religion] (Kovna, 1903).

LOEWE, L. (ed.), *Diaries of Sir Moses and Lady Montefiore*, 2 vols. (Chicago, 1890).

LORBEERBAUM, JACOB, *Ḥavat da'at* [Opinion] (Polna, 1805).

—— *Naḥalat ya'akov* [The Inheritance of Jacob] (Breslau, 1849).

LOWENSTEIN, STEVEN M., *The Berlin Jewish Community: Enlightenment, Family and Crisis, 1770–1830* (New York and Oxford, 1994).

—— *The Mechanics of Change: Essays in the Social History of German Jewry* (Atlanta, 1992).

LUNCZ, A. M., 'The Biography of the Great Rabbi, Seeker of Zion, Tsevi Hirsch Kalischer' [Toledot harav hagaon doresh tsiyon tsevi hirsh kalisher], *Luaḥ erets yisra'el* (1897), 126–46.

LUZ, EHUD, *Parallels Meet: Religion and Nationalism in the Early Zionist Movement, 1882–1904*, trans. L. J. Schramm (Philadelphia, 1988).

MAIMON, SOLOMON, *Solomon Maimon: An Autobiography*, trans. Moses Hadas (New York, 1967).

MAIMON, YEHUDA LEIB HACOHEN [FISHMAN] (ed.), *The Evolution of Religious Zionism* [Hatsiyonut hadatit behitpatḥutah] (Jerusalem, 1937); repr. as *Israel, Torah, Zion* (Heb.) (Jerusalem, 1989).

MAIMONIDES, MOSES, *Crisis and Leadership: Epistles of Maimonides*, trans. Abraham Halkin (Philadelphia, 1985).

—— *Guide of the Perplexed*, trans. Shlomo Pines and Leo Strauss (Chicago, 1969).

—— *Mishneh torah*, 8 vols. (Jerusalem, 1953).

—— *Perush hamishnah* [Commentary on the Mishnah], 2 vols., ed. M. D. Ravinovits (Tel Aviv, 1948–9).

—— *Sefer hamitsvot leharambam im hasagot haramban* [Maimonides' Book of the Commandments with Glosses by Nahmanides], ed. Chaim Dov Chavel (Jerusalem, 1981).

—— *Treatise on the Resurrection of the Dead*, in *Epistles of Maimonides*, ed. Abraham Halkin and David Hartman (Philadelphia, 1985), 209–33.

MALINO, FRANCES, and DAVID SORKIN (eds.), *Profiles in Diversity: Jews in a Changing Europe, 1750–1870* (Detroit, 1997).

MA'OZ, MOSHE (ed.), *Studies on Palestine during the Ottoman Period* (Jerusalem, 1975).

MENDELSSOHN, MOSES, *Jerusalem, or, On Religious Power and Judaism*, trans. Alan Arkush (Hanover, NH, 1983).

MENDES-FLOHR, PAUL, and JEHUDA REINHARZ (eds.), *The Jew in the Modern World: A Documentary History*, 2nd edn. (New York and Oxford, 1995).

MEVORACH, BARUCH, 'Messianism as a Factor in the First Reform Controversies (1810–1820)' [Ha'emunah bemashiah bepolmosei hareformah harishonim], *Zion*, 34 (1969), 189–219.

MEYER, MICHAEL A., *The Origins of the Modern Jew: Jewish Identity and European Culture in Germany, 1749–1824* (Detroit, 1967).

—— *Response to Modernity: A History of the Reform Movement in Judaism* (Oxford and New York, 1988).

Midrash Rabbah, trans. H. Freedman and Maurice Simon, 3rd edn., 10 vols. (London and New York, 1983).

MINTZ, ALAN, *Banished from their Father's Table: Loss of Faith and Hebrew Autobiography* (Bloomington, Ind., 1989).

MYERS, JODY, 'Attitudes toward a Resumption of Sacrificial Worship in the Nineteenth Century', *Modern Judaism*, 7 (1987), 29–49.

—— 'The Messianic Idea and Jewish Ideologies', *Studies in Contemporary Jewry*, 7 (1991), 3–13.

—— 'Zevi Hirsch Kalischer and the Origins of Religious Zionism', in Frances Malino and David Sorkin (eds.), *Profiles in Diversity: Jews in a Changing Europe, 1750–1870* (Detroit, 1997), 267–94.

NAHMANIDES, MOSES, *Kol kitvei haramban* [Complete Works], ed. Chaim Dov Chavel (Jerusalem, 1963).

NATHANZOHN, HAYIM, *Avodah tamah* [Pure Worship] (Altona, 1872).

NOWAK, ZENON HUBERT, 'Zur Geschichte der Thorner Juden in der ersten Hälfte des 19. Jahrhunderts', *Leo Baeck Institute Bulletin*, 87 (1990), 19–28.

OPALSKI, MAGDALENA, and ISRAEL BARTAL, *Poles and Jews: A Failed Brotherhood* (Hanover, NH, and London, 1992).

OPPENHEIMER, AHARON, 'The Messianism of Bar Kokhba' [Meshihiyuto shel bar kokhba], in Tsevi Baras (ed.), *Messianism and Eschatology* (Jerusalem, 1983), 153–6.

PATAI, RAPHAEL, *The Messiah Texts* (Detroit, 1979).

PATTERSON, DAVID, *Abraham Mapu* (London, 1964).

PELLI, MOSHE, *The Age of Haskalah: Studies in Hebrew Literature of the Enlightenment in Germany* (Leiden, 1979).

PETUCHOWSKI, JAKOB J., *Prayerbook Reform in Europe: The Liturgy of European Liberal and Reform Judaism* (New York, 1968).

PLAUT, W. GUNTHER, *The Rise of Reform Judaism: A Sourcebook of its European Origins* (New York, 1963).

RA'ANAN, TSEVI, *Gush emunim* (Heb.) (Tel Aviv, 1980).

RAPHAEL, YITZHAK, and SHLOMO Z. SHRAGAI (eds.), *The Book of Religious Zionism* [Sefer hatsiyonut hadatit], 2 vols. (Jerusalem, 1977).

RAVITZKY, AVIEZER, *Messianism, Zionism, and Jewish Religious Radicalism*, trans. Michael Swirsky and Jonathan Chipman (Chicago and London, 1996).

REGGIO, ISAAC, *Hatorah vehafilosofiyah* [The Torah and Philosophy] (Vienna, 1827).

RICHARZ, MONIKA (ed.), *Jüdisches Leben in Deutschland*, 2 vols. (Stuttgart, 1976); abridged English version: *Jewish Life in Germany: Memoirs from Three Centuries*, trans. Stella P. Rosenfeld and Sidney Rosenfeld (Bloomington, Ind., 1991).

RUBINSTEIN, AVRAHAM, and MORDECHAI ELIAV (eds.), *In the Paths of Renewal: Studies in Religious Zionism* [Bishevilei hatehiyah: mehkarim batsiyonut hadatit] (Jerusalem, 1983).

RUDERMAN, DAVID B., *Jewish Thought and Scientific Discovery in Early Modern Europe* (New Haven and London, 1995).

RÜRUP, REINHARD, 'The Tortuous and Thorny Path to Legal Equality: "Jew Laws" and Emancipatory Legislation in Germany from the Late Eighteenth Century', *Leo Baeck Institute Yearbook*, 31 (1986), 3–33.

SA'ADIAH BEN JOSEPH, *Sefer ha'emunot vehade'ot* [The Book of Beliefs and Opinions] (Jerusalem, 1991). Translation of selected passages in Hans Lewy (ed.), *Three Jewish Philosophers* (New York, 1960).

SACHAR, HOWARD M., *The Course of Modern Jewish History*, 2nd edn. (New York, 1990).

SALMON, YOSEF, *Religion and Zionism: First Encounters* [Dat vetsiyonut: imotim rishonim] (Jerusalem, 1990).

—— 'The Rise of Jewish Nationalism on the Border of Eastern and Western Europe: Rabbi Z. H. Kalischer, David Gordon, Peretz Smolenskin', in Isadore Twersky (ed.), *Danzig, between East and West: Aspects of Modern Jewish History* (Cambridge, 1985), 121–37.

—— 'Tradition and Modernity in Early Religious-Zionist Thought' [Mesoret umoderniyut bemaḥshavah datit bereshitah], *Tradition*, 18/1 (Summer 1979), 79–98.

—— 'Zionism and Anti-Zionism in Eastern Europe', in Shmuel Almog, Jehuda Reinharz, and Anita Shapira (eds.), *Zionism and Religion* (Hanover, NH, 1998), 25–43.

SAPERSTEIN, MARC, *Jewish Preaching, 1200–1800: An Anthology* (New Haven, 1989).

SAPIR, JACOB, 'Hilkhita lemeshiḥa', *Halevanon*, 40–6 (1869–70).

SCHISCHA, ABRAHAM, 'The Letter of Chief Rabbi Nathan Adler and Sir Moses Montefiore to Rabbi Tsevi Hirsch Kalischer' [Hamikhtav shel harav harashi natan adler vemosheh montefiori leharav tsevi hirsh kalisher], *Cathedra*, 38 (1985), 195–200.

SCHOLEM, GERSHOM, *The Messianic Idea in Judaism and Other Essays on Jewish Spirituality* (New York, 1971).

SCHORSCH, ISMAR, 'Emancipation and the Crisis of Religious Authority: The Emergence of the Modern Rabbinate', in Werner E. Mosse, Arnold Paucker, and Reinhard Rürup (eds.), *Revolution and Evolution: 1848 in Jewish History* (Tübingen, 1981), 205–47.

SEPTIMUS, BERNARD, '"Open Rebuke and Concealed Love": Nahmanides and the Andalusian Tradition', in Isadore Twersky (ed.), *Rabbi Moses Nahmanides (RAMBAN): Explorations in his Religious and Literary Virtuosity* (Cambridge, 1983), 11–34.

SHIMONI, GIDEON, *The Zionist Ideology* (Hanover, NH, 1995).

Shivat tsiyon [The Return to Zion], ed. Avraham Yitzhak Slutzki (Warsaw, 1891).

SILBER, MICHAEL K., 'The Emergence of Ultra-Orthodoxy: The Invention of a Tradition', in Jack Wertheimer (ed.), *The Uses of Tradition: Jewish Continuity in the Modern Era* (New York and Jerusalem, 1992), 23–84.

SILVER, ABBA HILLEL, *A History of Messianic Speculation in Israel* (New York, 1927).

SOFER, MOSES, *Ḥatam sofer* [Responsa], 2 vols. (Pressburg, 1860).

SOFER, SHLOMO (ed.), *Igerot soferim* [Correspondence of the Sofer Family] (Vienna, 1929).

SOKOLOW, NAHUM, *Ḥibat tsiyon* [Love of Zion] (Jerusalem, 1934).

—— *History of Zionism, 1600–1918*, 2 vols. (New York, 1969).

—— 'Rabbi Tsevi Hirsch Kalischer' (Heb.), *Ha'olam*, 51 (1924), 1030–1.

SOLOVEITCHIK, JOSEPH B., *Halakhic Man*, trans. Lawrence Kaplan (Philadelphia, 1983).

SORKIN, DAVID, *Moses Mendelssohn and the Religious Enlightenment* (Berkeley and Los Angeles, 1996).

SPRINZAK, EHUD, *The Ascendance of Israel's Radical Right* (New York, 1991).

STAHL, FRIEDRICH JULIUS, *Der christliche Staat und sein Verhaltniss zu Deismus and Judenthum* (Berlin, 1847).

STEINHEIM, SALOMON LUDWIG, *Die Offenbarung nach dem Lehrbegriff der Synagoge*, i (Frankfurt, 1835).

STERN, MORITZ (ed.), *Festschrift zum vierzigjahrigen Amtsjubiläum des Herrn Rabbiners Dr. Salomon Carlebach in Lübeck* (Berlin, 1910).

STRAUSS, HERBERT A., 'Liberalism and Conservatism in Prussian Legislation for Jewish Affairs, 1815–1847', in id. (ed.), *Jubilee Volume Dedicated to Curt C. Silberman* (New York, 1969), 114–32.

—— 'Pre-Emancipation Prussian Policies towards the Jews 1815–1847', *Leo Baeck Institute Yearbook*, 11 (1966), 107–36.

TALMON, YONINA, 'The Pursuit of the Millennium: The Relation between Religious and Social Change', *Archives européennes de sociologie*, 3/1 (1962), 125–48.

TEICHTHAL, YISAKHAR SHELOMOH, *The Happy Mother of Children* [Em habanim semeḥah] (Warsaw, 1943). In English, Yisakhar Shlomo Teichthal, *Em Habanim Semeha: Restoration of Zion as a Response during the Holocaust*, trans. and ed. Pesach Schindler (Hoboken, NJ, 1999).

TICKER, JAY, 'The Centrality of Sacrifice as an Answer to Reform in the Thought of Zvi Hirsch Kalischer', *Working Papers in Yiddish and East European Jewish Studies*, 15 (Max Weinreich Center, New York, 1975), 1–26.

TIROSH, YOSEF (ed.), *Religious Zionism: An Anthology* (Jerusalem, 1975).

TISHBY, YESHAYAHU (ed.), *The Teachings of the Zohar* [Mishnat hazohar], 2 vols. (Jerusalem, 1971); published in English as *The Wisdom of the Zohar: An Anthology of Texts*, trans. David Goldstein, 3 vols. (London, 1989).

TOURY, JACOB, 'An Early Movement for Agricultural Settlement in Inowracław (Poznań Province)' [Hatenuah lehityashvut ḥakla'it bekehilat leslo (poznah) bishnat 1846], *Hatsiyonut*, 2 (1971), 37–46.

TWERSKY, ISADORE, *Introduction to the Code of Maimonides (Mishneh Torah)* (New Haven and London, 1980).

—— (ed.), *Rabbi Moses Nahmanides (RAMBAN): Explorations in his Religious and Literary Virtuosity* (Cambridge, 1983).

URBACH, EPHRAIM E., *The Sages: Their Concepts and Beliefs* (Cambridge, Mass., 1987).

VERETE, MAYIR, 'The Restoration of the Jews in English Protestant Thought, 1790–1840', *Middle Eastern Studies*, 8 (1972), 3–50.

WANDYCZ, PIOTR S., *The Lands of Partitioned Poland, 1795–1918* (Seattle and London, 1974).

WEINRYB, BERNARD D. (DOV), 'The Foundations of Zionism and its History' [Yesodot hatsiyonut betoledoteihah], *Tarbiz*, 8 (1937), 69–113.

—— *The Jews of Poland: A Social and Economic History of the Jewish Community in Poland from 1100–1800* (Philadelphia, 1972).

WERBLOWSKY, R. J. Z., 'Messianism in Jewish History', in H. H. Ben Sasson and S. Ettinger (eds.), *Jewish Society through the Ages* (New York, 1969), 30–45.

WESSELY, NAPHTALI HERZ, *Divrei shalom ve'emet* [Words of Peace and Truth], 4 vols. (Berlin, 1782–5).

YARON, ZVI, *The Philosophy of Rabbi Kook* (Jerusalem, 1991).

Index of Biblical and Rabbinic References

General Index

A

Abrabanel, Don Isaac 9, 122, 123 n. 47
Abraham ben David, *see* Rabad
absolutism 9–10, 15, 36–7, 85
acculturation:
  and circumcision 190
  and emancipation 151
  and liturgical reform 21, 23
  and messianism 18, 32, 195, 205
activism, messianic v, vii, 25–6, 204 n. 122
  and Eger 102
  of Kalischer 142–65, 177–80, 195–6, 220
  and Kalischer's letter to Rothschild 62–8,
    83–4, 89
  oaths against 7, 18 n. 30, 30, 177–9
  and passive messianism 6–7, 90–1, 205, 226
  rabbinic condemnation of 87, 91–2, 213
  and realistic messianism 4–5, 30, 62–8,
    83–4, 90, 93, 105, 182
  and re-establishment of sacrificial worship
    89–93, 98–101
  seen as rebellion 92
  see also realistic messianism
activism, non-messianic 221–3, 225
Adam, Jacob 16 n. 27
Adler, Nathan Marcus 160, 162–3
agency, human 60–6, 68–9
agriculture, *see* colonies, agricultural;
    commandments: concerning agriculture;
    labour, agricultural; poverty, Jewish: and
    agricultural labour
Akiva, R. 6 n. 6
Aldabi, Meir Isaac, *Shevilei emunah* 176–7
Alliance Israélite Universelle 147, 166, 176 n.
    23, 185, 202 n. 116, 210–11, 218 n. 159
altar (Jerusalem):
  Foundation Stone 161
  location 94, 98, 161
  rebuilding 96, 159, 174, 185, 211–12, 215
  sanctity of site 90, 92–3
Amidah prayer 7, 122
antisemitism, in Europe 181, 222–3
Aramaic, and liturgical reform 22
Aschkewitz, Max 81 n. 51
Ashkenazi Jews:
  in Europe 45, 141

in Palestine 147–9, 180, 195–8, 212–13,
  215–16, 218–19
assimilationism:
  18th-century 39–40
  19th-century 17, 29, 81–2, 103, 118, 145,
    150, 191, 198–9
Auerbach, Meir:
  and Kalischer's messianism 195, 213,
    214–16, 217, 219
  Kalischer's open letter to 169 n. 8, 170 n.
    10, 173 n. 16, 176 n. 24, 189
Austria:
  and absolutism 9–10, 15
  and partitions of Poland 36, 38
  and religious freedom 10, 17, 77 n. 39
autonomy, Jewish:
  18th- and 19th-century 9–10, 17, 32–4,
    36–7, 38–9, 48, 82
  medieval 9
Avi-Yonah, M. 92–3 n. 9

B

Balfour Declaration (1917) 225
Bar Kokhba revolt 6, 92 n. 8
battle, metaphors 13–14, 16, 24
Berlin:
  and educational reform 51
  and liturgical reform 20–1, 24
  and Torah scholarship 14
  and Wessely 13–14, 16
Berlin, Naftali Tsevi Judah 221
Berlin, Nahman of Lissa 75 n. 35
Berman, Simon 160 n. 36, 219
Breuer, Mordecai 83 n. 54
Brill, Yehiel 196, 201 n. 112
Britain:
  and Jewish emancipation 17, 185
  religion and the state 135
Bromberg, Abraham Isaac 20 n. 135, 43 n. 27,
    48 n. 38, 53–4 n. 49, 55 n. 51, 57 n. 57
'bullocks of our lips', *see* sacrifice: and Torah
    study

C

Caro, David 51, 75 n. 35, 76, 77
Chajes, Tsevi Hirsch, and sacrificial worship
    158–60, 214 n. 146

Printed and bound by CPI Group (UK) Ltd, Croydon, CR0 4YY

13/04/2025

14656579-0003